Classical Sub

RHETORIC Alive!

BOOK 1:
PRINCIPLES OF PERSUASION

PERSUASIVE SPEECH AND WRITING
IN THE TRADITION OF ARISTOTLE

ALYSSAN BARNES, PHD

Dedication:

To Annie, June, and Zoe

Rhetoric Alive! Book 1: Principles of Persuasion

Version 1.1

ISBN: 978-1-60051-300-8

Classical Academic Press
515 S. 32nd St.
Camp Hill, PA 17011

www.ClassicalAcademicPress.com

Content editors: Christopher Perrin, PhD; Joelle Hodge; and Stephen Barnes

Editor: Sharon Berger

Illustrator: David Gustafson

Book designer: Robert Baddorf

VP.03.23

TABLE OF CONTENTS

List of Figures, Tables, and Chart

Figures

Tables

Chart

FOREWORD

The art of rhetoric has had a number of classical defenders, but the choice comes down to two mighty figures when one wants to learn this art: Aristotle or Cicero. For a very long time in the history of the West, educators chose Cicero; in the European cultures of the medieval, Renaissance, and Enlightenment periods, to study rhetoric was to study Cicero. The Latinate oratory of Roman culture assumed but displaced the Greek rhetoric of Athenian culture—at the least into the nineteenth century, and possibly even into the twentieth and twenty-first centuries. And, even though Aristotle's *Rhetoric* has had a renaissance recently, teachers of the practical language arts still usually follow Cicero. Yet here Alyssan Barnes has chosen Aristotle. How might one defend that choice, and how does the Aristotelian conception of the art of rhetoric provide clues to what one can expect from this book?

Aristotle's *Rhetoric* is a part of his entire canon, a large and varied body of works that explore a rather startling number of subjects of human knowledge. We might not want to agree with John Henry Newman in *The Idea of a University* that Aristotle is "the oracle of nature and of truth,"[1] but he did, more or less, invent what we know about many of the most important subjects of our understanding. One should not end with Aristotle, but one should always start with him. He wrote about the natural sciences, psychology, the language arts (including logic), poetry, rhetoric, ethics, politics, and metaphysics—all the while defining terms and classifying their parts in such a way as to determine their study for millennia. And he did so in a clear, inventive, and even humorous Greek prose, which is a philosophical and literary marvel. To study Aristotle's *Rhetoric* is to study the thought of someone who relates this art of persuasion to the rest of human concerns, the result being that the art is not divorced from other arts and sciences, but enriches and is enriched by them.

By itself, the treatise is simply the best rhetoric that exists. In his *In Defense of Rhetoric*, Brian Vickers makes a remarkable claim: "[Aristotle's *Rhetoric*] remains the most penetrating analysis of speech in its full individual and social dimension."[2] Vickers is right: Aristotle's treatment is the deepest—that is, the most philosophical—discussion of the art of rhetoric, an art he relates to a large number of other fields in order to fashion a comprehensive, detailed explanation of the fundamental human activity of speech, understood in its most capacious sense as the *logos* that distinguishes us from the other animals and allows us to choose the good, determine the just, and marvel at the noble. Aristotle opens the *Politics* (in Rackham's Loeb translation) with a vision of the human being as essentially the animal dignified by speech:

1. John Henry Newman, *The Idea of a University* (Notre Dame, IN: University of Notre Dame Press, 1982), V.5.
2. Brian Vickers, *In Defense of Rhetoric* (Oxford: Clarendon Press, 1988), 26.

> And why man is a political animal in a greater measure than any bee or any gregarious animal is clear. For nature, as we declare, does nothing without purpose; and man alone of the animals possesses speech. . . . [S]peech is designed to indicate the advantageous and the harmful, and therefore also the right and the wrong; for it is the special property of man in distinction from the other animals that he alone has perception of good and bad and right and wrong and the other moral qualities, and it is partnership in these things that makes a household and a city state.[3]

It is clear from this passage that, when Aristotle thinks of speech or *logos*, one of the forms he has in mind is that of the art of rhetoric. Whether in writing or speaking, Aristotle imagines rhetoric as a social art.

One characteristic of Aristotle's thought that does not receive enough notice is this: He is often only suggestive without being conclusive—and often about the most important questions at hand! That is, much of his thought—and this is especially true of his *Rhetoric*—requires an active interpretation, a reader willing to do a great deal of invention herself to discern what Aristotle did and to supplement that with new thought.

He has found such an interpreter in Alyssan Barnes. *Rhetoric Alive! Book 1* is a highly knowledgeable, comprehensive, and clear Aristotelian treatment of the art of rhetoric, one that is willing to supplement where necessary to see what Aristotle saw about the persuasive in human speech. The virtues of *Rhetoric Alive!* are many, but two are especially prominent: its patient pedagogy, and its detailed and interesting exercises. Barnes is a master teacher, so she knows how to put a sequence of explanations together for a student who does not yet know what she does. As well, Barnes understands that knowing requires doing; to learn an art—what Aristotle calls in several works "the reasoned capacity to make"—one must practice the smaller arts that make up an art. Aristotle says at one point in his *Rhetoric* that the appeal to character (*ethos*) is almost the whole of persuasiveness. Barnes's credibility as interpreter, practitioner, and teacher of the art of rhetoric is trustworthy and admirable. This is a living rhetoric bound to animate the spoken and written suasions of any teacher or student who submits to its instruction. It makes rhetoric *alive*!

—Scott F. Crider, PhD,
Author of *The Office of Assertion: An Art of Rhetoric for the Academic Essay*

3. Aristotle, *Politics*, Rackham's Loeb translation, 1.1.10–11.

Acknowledgments

Many thanks to those who served as readers, offering insights and suggestions; the comments of content editors Joelle Hodge and Christopher Perrin, in particular, helped improve this text. I also greatly appreciate Sharon Berger's care and skill in editing, and I am thankful to Lauraine Gustafson for overseeing the project, Rob Baddorf for designing the book, and David Gustafson for creating the illustrations. My deepest debt of gratitude is owed to my husband, Stephen, for his generosity and sacrifice in meticulously revising each chapter. His keen understanding of rhetoric has sharpened my own.

Those who have enriched the text most are my students, especially those at Live Oak Classical School, for they continually teach me about rhetoric, through both my failures and my successes in the classroom. Their insights are peppered throughout the work, and they are the audience I've kept in mind while writing it.

I'm grateful for support from Alison Moffatt and Carolyn Still, who not only have offered me freedom to explore these ideas in the classroom but also have served as model rhetors for the entire school community. Their winsome speech and manifest virtue are genuinely persuasive.

Thanks are due to a few others who may not know the degree to which they have inspired this work: Pat Gordon, Leo Paul de Alvarez, Raymond DiLorenzo, Monica Ashour, Dayspring Brock, and DeAnn Stuart. Likewise, without my mother's support, I never could have completed it.

I first read Aristotle's *Rhetoric* in a graduate course taught by Scott F. Crider at the University of Dallas. Whatever is worthwhile in the pages that follow must be credited largely to Professor Crider, whose insights into rhetoric in general and Aristotle's texts in particular have illuminated this project from its beginning.

Finally, I offer a special and continuing thanks to my three daughters—Annie, June, and Zoe—to whom this book is dedicated.

NOTE TO STUDENT

You may be apprehensive about studying rhetoric from the view of Aristotle. After all, who is he? But be sure of this: Thinking along with Aristotle will offer an understanding of the art of persuasive language *unlike* a typical public speaking or written composition class. You may have imagined a course where you turn off your brain and turn on your charm, learn to gesture and count the times you say "um," and wrap up by going for the jugular, so to speak, during arguments. But that, my friend, would be sophistry.[1] So whatever is in store for you in this text, it sure beats studying mind-numbing communication charts and humdrum Venn diagrams. Instead, you will encounter firsthand some of the most fundamental and insightful ideas ever uttered about language and communication. It's no wonder the history of Western philosophy can be seen as one long footnote to the Ancients![2] So enjoy the mental exercise—after all, it's a chiefly human enterprise.

1. The term *sophistry* has always had connotations of unethical speech—smooth talk with little substance or concern for truth. As we will learn, the term has a history that can shed light on its contemporary usage.
2. This is a variation of Alfred North Whitehead's famous claim, "The safest general characterization of the European philosophical tradition is that it consists of a series of footnotes to Plato." See Whitehead's *Process and Reality*, ed. David Ray Griffin and Donald W. Sherburne, corrected ed. (New York: The Free Press, 1979), 39.

Overview of Chapters

Rhetoric's past is a checkered one. The study of it began in Ancient Greece with the wily sophists, foreigners who taught rhetoric as an art of sorts—an art of persuasion with little regard for truth. Their misuse of rhetoric gave the art a bad reputation: To be a rhetor was to be a linguistic trickster, one who used language not to reveal truth but to manipulate and deceive. Such was the near-fatal attack on the sophists by Socrates in the works of Plato. But even in Plato's day, some thinkers—those who recognized the absolute necessity of persuasive speech—refused to cast rhetoric aside where it would be used and abused by charlatans alone. And so, with the help of Aristotle and other like-minded defenders of the art, rhetoric became a central study for many centuries, only gaining in esteem as it passed to the Romans and became the crowning study for the citizen.

The story is, of course, much messier, much more tumultuous and complicated, than any brief introduction could tell. One result of rhetoric's tortuous history is that the art at times appears to have been robbed of its philosophic soul. What remains of rhetoric today is a shell of techniques and figures of speech along with a few sophistic parlor tricks—an area of study pretty much deserving of Socrates's castigation so many centuries ago, that rhetoric is a just a branch of flattery. "Rhetoric" is once again a dirty word.

This text, then, has two purposes. First, it hopes to be a breath of fresh air to the discipline itself, one that would reinvigorate the soul of rhetoric. By reconnecting rhetoric to its philosophic roots, we hope to save rhetoric from ignominy and beckon it back into the sunlight of truth. Second, it offers instruction in the practice of rhetoric. Conscious practice not only helps one grow in the skills of persuasion but also teaches that same person how to more nimbly dodge cheap rhetorical shots by others.

If this project of rhetoric's revival is a daunting one, consider this: Rhetoric is actually nothing new; it's something you use every day. And just as a fish is unaware of water, so are we generally unaware of the world of words and ideas in which we swim. Better to study the art of persuasion, making its practice and distortions less fearsome, not more so. Rhetoric, then, is nothing to be scared of. And the ever-so-common *glossophobia*—anxiety of speaking before a crowd—will also be rendered manageable once under the bridle of reason.

Section 1: A Brief Introduction

Chapter 1—Rhetoric and the Song of the City

Aristotle, the first true organizer of rhetoric, believed that the ability to speak is what makes humanity unique. And although Aristotle is a philosopher, he is willing to admit that man cannot live by contemplative dialectic alone. Rhetoric is its *antistrophe*, its necessary complement, its harmonic counterpart. Rhetoric is, as he defines it, "*the faculty of observing in any given case the available means of persuasion.*"[1]

Section 2: The Three Rhetorical Appeals[2]

Chapter 2—*Ethos*: Revealing the Speaker's Credibility

Does the speaker's character really matter, so long as the message makes sense and feels right? For Aristotle, the answer is a resounding yes. *Ethos* is paramount; it legitimizes not only the *pathos* being evoked but also the *logos* being appealed to. This chapter focuses on what makes up a speaker's *ethos*—common sense, moral virtue, and goodwill. One must appear to know what is right, do what is right, and want what is right for one's audience.

Chapter 3—*Pathos*: Guiding the Audience's Emotion

Aristotle begins his *Rhetoric* with a castigation of contemporary rhetoric: It is, for one thing, too emotional. But when he goes on to discuss the three rhetorical appeals, he not only dives into the emotions, but also seems to enjoy the dip. The key to his surprising attention to *pathos* is its unique function within rhetoric: It is emotion that propels one to judgment. His charge for the rhetor is to stir emotions appropriate to the situation, thus allowing for persuasion, full and proper.

Chapter 4—*Logos* in the Enthymeme: Abbreviating the Syllogism

Whereas *ethos* resides in the speaker and *pathos* in the audience, *logos* is shared between them. Chapter 4, then, addresses the logical appeal. And it's in exploring the deductive reasoning of the enthymeme, a verbal syllogism with a missing premise, that we find a fundamental link between philosophy and rhetoric.

Chapter 5—More on *Logos*: Top-Down Versus Bottom-Up Reasoning

Inductive and deductive reasoning are tools of philosophy, but they have counterparts in rhetoric, too. In fact, a wise rhetor is content to utilize a looser form of logic than the philosopher may be. Maxims, examples, comparisons, fables—rhetors ought not shy away from arguments that delight as well as instruct.

Section 3: The Five Canons of Rhetoric

Chapter 6—Canon One, Invention: Finding Something to Say

Figuring out *what* to say—invention—need not remain the mystery it's reputed to be. Aristotle offers us the commonplaces, metaphorical locales one can visit in order to find arguments.

1. See Aristotle, *Rhetoric* 1355b. (See note in chapter 1 regarding the Bekker numbering citation system.)
2. In order to give proper attention to the three rhetorical appeals and to introduce them in a clear fashion, these appeals are the sole focus of section 2. They are, of course, constituents of *invention*, which is the first of the five canons of rhetoric (discussed in section 3).

Chapter 7—Canon Two, Organization: Ordering the Content

A text's division should be, according to Aristotle, short and sweet: State the point and then demonstrate it. He goes on to say that adding an introduction and conclusion is a nice touch. This simple but compelling approach would later evolve into a six-part system of classical organization, handy for almost any rhetorical occasion. Chapter 7 teaches how to compose and divide a speech to achieve the greatest effect, so that the audience isn't lost en route to the persuasive end.

Chapter 8—Canon Three, Style: Choosing the Language

Style is not just icing on the rhetorical cake. It turns out it's really more than that: It is thought put into words. Perhaps more than all the canons of rhetoric, style injects personality into an argument, bringing it to a new level of persuasion. This chapter introduces various aspects of style and explores several figures of speech, considering them as more than mere ornamentation.

Chapter 9—Canon Four, Memory: Storing What's Valuable

It is true that Aristotle doesn't mention memory, but Augustine of Hippo would later devote an entire chapter of his *Confessions* to its exploration. For Augustine, memory means much more than downloading data. Memory is a matter of the soul. On the practical side, rhetors can construct imaginative locales—memory palaces—in which their ideas can be "stored."

Chapter 10—Canon Five, Delivery: Presenting the Whole

Delivery, Aristotle holds, is a "vulgar matter"—a condescension that must be made because the human is not influenced only by the proofs of *ethos*, *pathos*, and *logos*. But, in another sense, delivery is a natural companion to *ethos*: One should be audible, clear, and pleasant to listen to, or else the entire project of speaking becomes senseless. And while histrionic delivery should be anathema to us in the same way it was to Aristotle, there is yet much to learn in the way of tailoring technique to the message. This chapter focuses on how to use the voice, eye contact, and gestures, as Aristotle says, "neither to offend nor to entertain."

Section 4: The Three Kinds of Rhetoric

Chapter 11—Deliberative Rhetoric: Considering Goods

Time: *future* Action: *urge to do/urge not to do* End: *advantage*

Chapter 11 considers human happiness as defined by Aristotle, and it turns out that his definition is a comprehensive one. In fact, before cataloguing the sundry ways people define happiness, he suggests that happiness might be the guiding principle for every decision a person or a community ever makes. Perhaps this is why Aristotle starts off with deliberative rhetoric, speech that targets the public good.

Chapter 12—Epideictic Rhetoric: Praising the Beautiful

Time: *present* Action: *praise/censure* End: *honor*

Virtue and vice trigger praise and blame. And because different groups play favorites with different virtues, Aristotle, with an eye to the political, shows how epideictic rhetoric can serve a deliberative end. What virtue do you want to see more of? Honor it. The political place of praise and blame is far from trivial; honoring virtues, rather, is another key ingredient of a flourishing community.

Chapter 13—Judicial Rhetoric: Judging the True

TIME: *past* ACTION: *defend/attack* END: *justice*

One of Aristotle's most startling claims is that people act willingly for two reasons and two reasons only: because they want a good or because they want to be pleased. If he's right, that means that rhetors are called to be more than mere prosecutors or defendants; they are to be students of the good and of the pleasurable. Aristotle goes on to discuss wrongdoing, dividing law into two types: the specific and the universal. Specific law is distinct to a people, and universal law, also known as "natural law," is common to all. Students of the *Rhetoric* are urged, then, to consider justice itself—not in just a limited, personal way, but in that far-reaching sense of what is fundamentally right and wrong. In other words, sophistry is no option; a rhetor must be moral.

Section 5: Rhetoric Gone Wrong

Chapter 14—Fallacies and Sophistry: Spotting Bad Arguments

Consider this chapter a crash course in logic with a spotlight on the most common fallacies. After a quick look at the three kinds of syllogisms (categorical, hypothetical, and disjunctive), we analyze their most frequent imposters. The accompanying class exercise lets you practice spotting those verbal missteps. Common informal fallacies are also introduced.

Section 6: A Brief Conclusion

Chapter 15—Conclusion: The Good Student Speaking Well

After studying all the nitty-gritty of rhetoric and after fleshing out the concepts using workshops and presentations, you'll now have the chance to consider your role as a rhetor, one who uses the ever-so-powerful gift of language. Indeed, to wield the power of the word is a grave yet inescapable responsibility, one for which you should seek to practice wise and virtuous stewardship. This final chapter, we hope, will find you well on the way toward wise and virtuous stewardship.

Aristotle's *Rhetoric* is an ambitious and sweeping project, for he seeks to raise rhetorical discourse to newfangled heights. By shining the gleam of reason onto rhetorical discourse, he hopes to enlighten the entire civic project of speaking, from the rhetors—that is, those who practice the art of rhetoric—to the audience members who hear them. Hence, a rhetor would seek the common good rather than a private one, speech would animate the fullness of the audience members rather than only their passions, and both parties would grow more astute and judicious. The sum effect? A burgeoning civic discourse based upon an ever-increasing alignment with truth.

Rhetoric Map

In the mind map of rhetoric on the following page, you see the various definitions rhetoric has earned over the years: optimistic ones such as "the study of misunderstanding and its remedies" and not-so-friendly ones such as Plato's famous comparison of rhetoric to makeup, the quick cosmetic fix that passes off an ugly person as beautiful.

You'll also find the five so-called canons of rhetoric. Four of those are lifted from Aristotle's *Rhetoric*, but by the time of Cicero, the rhetorical tradition had added a fifth: memory. You can think of the canons as stages in the development of an argument. First generate material—*invention*, or what to say. Then, after developing your speech's content, comes *organization*, in which you arrange that invention in a coherent and sensible way. *Style* is third, casting the invented and organized material into just the right words. If it's a speech that you're working on, then the next step would be to commit it to *memory*. Lastly, the speech or paper must be carefully presented, so *delivery*, whether orally for the former or written for the latter, is the fifth and final canon.

You'll also notice the three rhetorical appeals of *ethos*, *pathos*, and *logos* are technically part of invention. This connection means that appeals to the character of the speaker (*ethos*), the emotional predisposition of the audience (*pathos*), and the reasoned argumentation in words (*logos*) must be drawn from the speech itself. In other words, your character must be established *in the speech*, the audience's emotion must be guided *by the speech*, and the logic of the arguments must be communicated *through the speech*.

The map also includes the three species of rhetoric: judicial, epideictic, and deliberative. Because they concern the past, present, and future, respectively—and may even line up with the transcendentals of the True, the Beautiful, and the Good—these three species are exhaustive of persuasive discourse.

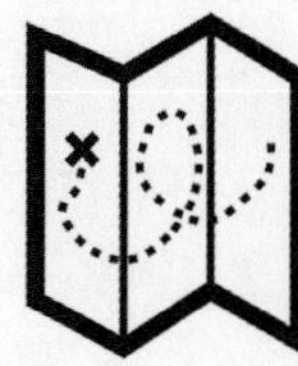

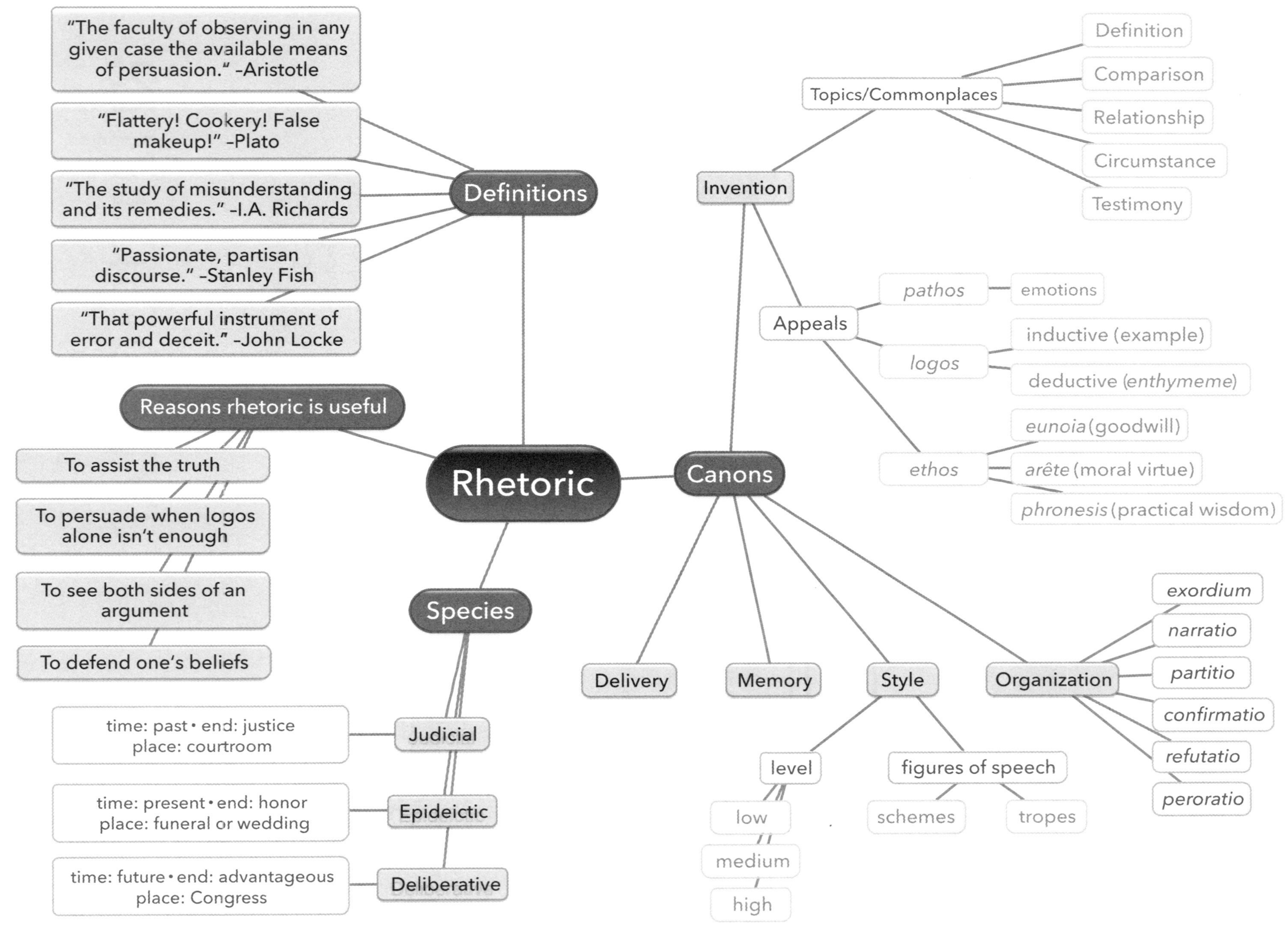
"The faculty of observing in any given case the available means of persuasion." -Aristotle
"Flattery! Cookery! False makeup!" -Plato
"The study of misunderstanding and its remedies." -I.A. Richards
"Passionate, partisan discourse." -Stanley Fish
"That powerful instrument of error and deceit." -John Locke
Definitions
Reasons rhetoric is useful
To assist the truth
To persuade when logos alone isn't enough
To see both sides of an argument
To defend one's beliefs
Rhetoric
Species
Judicial
time: past • end: justice
place: courtroom
Epideictic
time: present • end: honor
place: funeral or wedding
Deliberative
time: future • end: advantageous
place: Congress
Canons
Invention
Topics/Commonplaces
Definition
Comparison
Relationship
Circumstance
Testimony
Appeals
pathos
emotions
logos
inductive (example)
deductive (enthymeme)
ethos
eunoia(goodwill)
arête (moral virtue)
phronesis (practical wisdom)
Delivery
Memory
Style
level
low
medium
high
figures of speech
schemes
tropes
Organization
exordium
narratio
partitio
confirmatio
refutatio
peroratio

Notes

Notes

Section 1
A Brief Introduction

What is it that makes humanity distinct? Is it our intelligence, our power to dominate rationally? Is it the large temporal cortex or the opposable thumbs? Why are we different from, arguably higher than, other animals?

Aristotle has an answer for this: Humanity has speech.[1] Language and its ability to give voice to certain characteristics—for example, right and wrong, the noble and the shameful, or the harmful and the helpful—give birth to culture. With language, then, culture can be built and continually rebuilt, ever evolving and being shaped by the words spoken within it. *Words do things*, and it is this great power that makes them worthy of our study.

Aristotle wrote the first book on **rhetoric**, but of course he was not the first to *practice* rhetoric. Rhetoric is ubiquitous! Where there is language, there is rhetoric; thus, rhetoric had been around long before Aristotle came along to write about it. As far as we know, however, he was the first in the West to create a scientific, comprehensive study of it as an art.

One could also say that Aristotle wrote the *last* book on rhetoric. This is an even grander claim, for surely Cicero, Quintilian,[2] and great thinkers all the way up to our own day are not to be passed over. Surely, rhetoric continued to develop, and surely, the Greeks didn't figure it *all* out way back in the fourth century BC, right? These are all good points to consider. And yet, there is a sense in which Aristotle's approach to rhetoric, while often challenged, has never once dropped out of sight. All the theorists following Aristotle must wrestle with his ideas. The language he uses and the concepts he introduces are peppered throughout rhetoric's long history. And so one might justly, if hyperbolically, claim that Aristotle—although he has not had the last word on rhetoric—has had the first and the most influential word on the art. His is the word to be reckoned with.

1. For more on this idea, see also Aristotle's *Politics* 1253a.
2. This references Marcus Tullius Cicero, Roman orator, and Marcus Fabius Quintilianus, Roman rhetorician.

Chapter 1

Rhetoric and the Song of the City

Each chapter in this text will begin with an excerpt from Aristotle's *Rhetoric*, an ancient text with plenty of relevance to our day. A student of Plato, **Aristotle** (384–322 BC) was a Greek philosopher whose influence on Western thought—in such areas as ethics, politics, psychology, science, logic, and, of course, rhetoric—is immense. His *Rhetoric* is not an easy read; it is, after all, a collection of his lecture notes that can feel a bit dry and dusty at times. However, this work is largely responsible for our understanding of the field today, and it's important to be radical (from the Latin *radix*, meaning "root") in our approach to persuasion, going all the way back to rhetoric's roots. You should begin each chapter by reading Aristotle's own words on the topics at hand and then explore those concepts and how they've developed.

[1] (1354a)[2] Rhetoric is the counterpart of Dialectic. Both alike are concerned with such things as come, more or less, within the general ken of all men and belong to no definite science. Accordingly all men make use, more or less, of both; for to a certain extent all men attempt to discuss statements and to maintain them, to defend themselves and to attack others. Ordinary people do this either at random or through practice and from acquired habit. Both ways being possible, the subject can plainly be handled systematically, for it is possible to inquire the reason why some speakers succeed through practice and others spontaneously; and everyone will at once agree that such an inquiry is the function of an art.

. . .

(1355a) Rhetoric is useful (1) because things that are true and things that are just have a natural tendency to prevail over their opposites, so that if the decisions of judges are not what they ought to be, the defeat must be due to the speakers themselves, and they must be blamed accordingly. Moreover, (2) before some audiences not even the

1. Aristotle, *Rhetoric*, trans. W. Rhys Roberts, hypertextual resource compiled by Lee Honeycutt (online), http://homepage.cs.uri.edu/courses/fall2007/csc305/Schedule/rhetoric/ (no longer online). Unless otherwise specified, the translations of *Rhetoric* throughout this book were referenced via this online resource, based on the 1954 translation of W. Rhys Roberts, which was obtained in ASCII text format from Virginia Tech's gopher site of online literary works in the public domain. For other links to Aristotle's text, see http://capress.link/ra10101 (hosted by the Internet Classics Archive) or http://capress.link/ra10102 (from the Perseus Digital Library of Tufts University).
2. There is no need to have a particular translation of Aristotle's *Rhetoric*. The standard way of referencing Aristotle's works uses the Bekker numbering system, which enables readers to locate passages in different editions. Bekker numbers take the form of up to four numbers to indicate page number, followed by a letter to indicate column (e.g., a, b), and sometimes followed by a line number as well. You will notice these numbers in parentheses in the body text when Aristotle's works are cited.

possession of the exactest knowledge will make it easy for what we say to produce conviction. For argument based on knowledge implies instruction, and there are people whom one cannot instruct. Here, then, we must use, as our modes of persuasion and argument, notions possessed by everybody, as we observed in the *Topics* when dealing with the way to handle a popular audience. Further, (3) we must be able to employ persuasion, just as strict reasoning can be employed, on opposite sides of a question, not in order that we may in practice employ it in both ways (for we must not make people believe what is wrong), but in order that we may see clearly what the facts are, and that, if another man argues unfairly, we on our part may be able to confute him. No other of the arts draws opposite conclusions: dialectic and rhetoric alone do this. Both these arts draw opposite conclusions impartially. Nevertheless, the underlying facts do not lend themselves equally well to the contrary views. No; things that are true and things that are better are, by their nature, practically always easier to prove and easier to believe in. (1355b) Again, (4) it is absurd to hold that a man ought to be ashamed of being unable to defend himself with his limbs, but not of being unable to defend himself with speech and reason, when the use of rational speech is more distinctive of a human being than the use of his limbs. And if it be objected that one who uses such power of speech unjustly might do great harm, *that* is a charge which may be made in common against all good things except virtue, and above all against the things that are most useful, as strength, health, wealth, generalship. A man can confer the greatest of benefits by a right use of these, and inflict the greatest of injuries by using them wrongly.

. . .

(1355b) Rhetoric may be defined as the faculty of observing in any given case the available means of persuasion. This is not a function of any other art. Every other art can instruct or persuade about its own particular subject-matter; for instance, medicine about what is healthy and unhealthy, geometry about the properties of magnitudes, arithmetic about numbers, and the same is true of the other arts and sciences. But rhetoric we look upon as the power of observing the means of persuasion on almost any subject presented to us.

Rhetoric Versus Dialectic

In ancient Greek chorals, a *strophe*, or stanza, is echoed and altered in its *antistrophe*, or response—much like a song being sung in harmonic parts. This makes Aristotle's opening definition of rhetoric nothing short of poetic: "Rhetoric is the counterpart [Greek, *antistrophos*] of dialectic." The image we have here, then, is that of dance partners, each working in accord with the other. Or perhaps a better image to carry with us is that of a choir, with the speech of the city—**dialectic** and rhetoric—together producing the song.

What are these two concepts, rhetoric and dialectic, and who sings them? Aristotle says that dialectic aims to test and maintain arguments; it is philosophy's primary tool. In dialectic, one privileges ***logos***—that is, reasoned argumentation—in order to hone in on ideas. You can think of it as the mode of an intense philosophical conversation. In theory, the goal of dialectic is not to win the argument, but rather to bring both parties to the truth of things. The word itself, from the Greek *dia* ("across") and *legein* ("to speak"), suggests the nature of the activity: It is a back-and-forth discussion trying to get to the heart of the matter.

Rhetoric, however, is the art not of philosophy but of persuasion. In this case, we have a different image in mind: not that of the contemplative philosopher, but instead (as just one example) that of the politician. *Influence* is the key word here—rhetoric is aimed at directing people's decisions. It can exist in less-than-noble forms, such as a slick car salesman convincing a customer to buy a lemon. But it also comes in admirable variations, such as defending those wrongly accused or passing laws that protect people's rights.

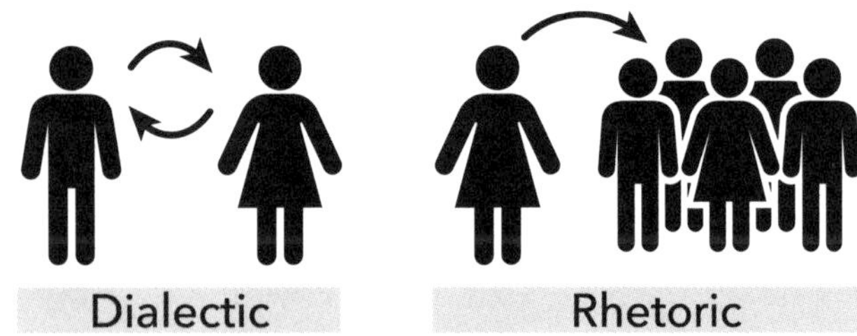

Figure 1. Communication in dialectic and rhetoric.

While they have distinct goals, Aristotle shows that rhetoric and dialectic are not vastly different—not in their beginnings, at least. Both use *endoxa*, or common opinion, as their starting points, and neither has a field of study particular to it. In other words, rhetoric and dialectic can take up any issue under the sun. And everyone, says Aristotle, does a little of both.

But Aristotle is actually not so interested in how dialectic and rhetoric are similar to or different from each other. He's interested in how they are *counterparts*, or complements. They complement each other—that is, they go well together—because of the way the mind works. According to Aristotle, there is only one power of the intellect, but it can be used in two ways: theoretically and practically.

First is the theoretical intellect, which simply seeks *to know*. The theoretical intellect is abstract and principled. It is the theoretical intellect, then, that rejoices in the knowledge that two plus two equals four, or longs to figure out questions such as "What is justice?" It acts as a no-nonsense umpire who calls strikes and balls, totally unmoved by the cheering and jeering fans in the seats, or by the batter at the plate and the pitcher on the mound.

Take a common example: baking a cake. The theoretical intellect may seek to know the nature of cakes, contemplating what might playfully be called *cakeness*. To explore the nature of cake, one may ask the following questions: *What is the difference between cake and bread? Must cake be sweet? Does bread become cake if it is decorated with icing? Can the term* cake *be used for any celebratory birthday treat? Is a large cookie served at a birthday a "cookie cake," or does it remain a large cookie? Is ice cream, when shaped and served at a party, an "ice-cream cake," or is it still just ice cream?* All of these questions—serious questions about a not-so-serious subject—could be answered by the theoretical intellect. But if your task

Table 1. Contrast between dialectic and rhetoric.

	Starting Point	Appeals	Privileged Means	Participants	Objectives	*Telos* (purpose)
Dialectic	common opinion (*endoxa*)	*logos*	syllogism	one speaking *with* one	the True the Beautiful the Good	certain knowledge
Rhetoric		*ethos* *pathos* *logos*	enthymeme	one speaking *to* many	the just the honorable the advantageous	right judgment

is to bake a cake for a friend, then your attempts to answer such questions will be pointless, leaving your real work undone.

So how does one actually bake a cake? Interestingly, for Aristotle, it is also the work of the intellect that helps here, for *knowing* is not the intellect's only function; it also helps one to *do*. The intellect, then, can also be practical. It can come alongside and actively help in the work: It calculates, measures, and plans, all in order to get that cake to the table.

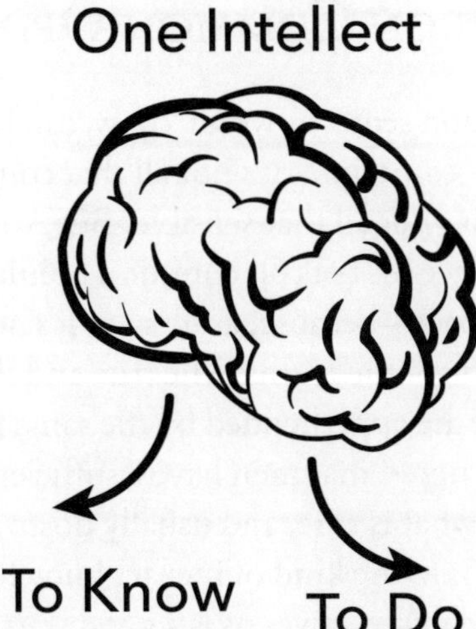

Figure 2. Theoretical and practical powers of the intellect.

Now, you might notice that the theoretical intellect and the practical intellect are rarely exercised simultaneously, which is why people tend to wind up strong in one and weak in the other. Think, for example, of the absentminded professor who is brilliant at quantum physics but cannot match his socks. Considering this, Aristotle does something truly ingenious in calling rhetoric the counterpart of dialectic. He is making the claim that rhetoric is not an exercise of the theoretical intellect; it's actually the exercise of the *practical* intellect. Don't be mistaken! That's no knock against it, not at all. After all, the practical intellect is vital for life on earth. The chair you're sitting on was made by the practical intellect, as were the clothes you are wearing. But what's the point in sitting in chairs and wearing clothes if you can't contemplate higher things, such as love and beauty and truth? If both the theoretical and the practical intellects are necessary for a flourishing human community—and they are—then so are dialectic and rhetoric.

Because dialectic and rhetoric are parts "sung" by all citizens, we often end up with civic speech akin to bad karaoke. It's also true that some speakers are naturally gifted and a few are just plain lucky. So what about the rest of us, those for whom public speaking is often awkward and almost always nerve-wracking? Aristotle offers us hope: We can learn by watching. In other words, we can see what works and what doesn't work for other speakers. We can turn what might be otherwise random or intuitive behavior into principles to be known and used. Rhetoric can become something more than just plain luck: It can become an **art**, a reasoned practice. A scientific analysis of persuasive speech means that the entire project of persuading others—the suspect business of potential **sophistry**, or verbal trickery—is brought into the light of reason. In doing so, we will grow not only in skill as speakers but also in shrewdness as listeners.

Why Bother with Rhetoric?

By 350 BC, rhetoric had already earned itself a bad name. The **sophists**, foreigners who taught young Greek men how to persuade and manipulate, had split rhetoric from ethics, using speech as a clever means to any profitable end. And Plato, calling rhetoric mere "flattery," had divorced it from philosophy. But Aristotle brushes off both the glitz and the grunge from rhetoric and re-establishes it as a necessary, even worthy, topic of study. He analyzes the art of rhetoric and attempts to bring it under the rule of reason.

Reread the excerpt at the beginning of this chapter. You'll notice that Aristotle makes the claim that rhetoric is actually a potential good, and for a number of reasons. His first argument is made in terms of use and abuse. In the philosophic dialogue *Gorgias*, Socrates accuses rhetoric of making the weak argument appear the stronger. Aristotle turns this attack on its head: Rhetoric can just as easily come to the aid of truth, assisting the truly stronger argument when it appears to be weak!

Aristotle's second argument is that, because one cannot always teach—our poor brains sometimes need a break—rhetoric is necessary, even good. Like dialectic, rhetoric uses ***logos*** (reason), but it also draws upon the speaker's ***ethos*** (credibility) and the audience's ***pathos*** (emotion) in order to persuade. That is, rhetoric recognizes that people make decisions based on factors other than pure reason.

Next, rhetoric can help a speaker understand the issue at hand more fully. In other words, preparation for an argument should involve arguing *both sides* of a case, not in order to choose one's side willy-nilly or for personal gain but rather to better understand all of the ins and outs of the argument.

Finally, Aristotle says that just as someone should be able to defend his body from attack, so too should he be able to defend his beliefs. In fact, the ability to defend yourself only against physical attacks is less than human, for even the beasts do this. For Aristotle, because our distinction is our ability to speak, defending ourselves with words is the higher and nobler art. And our verbal defense is the art of rhetoric.

Table 2. Reasons why rhetoric is useful.

1. To assist the truth
2. To persuade when *logos* alone isn't enough
3. To see both sides of an argument
4. To defend one's beliefs

Another way of saying it is this: Doesn't the truth deserve to be protected? If, in the dealings of the city, a counterfeit wins over the truth, someone is to blame for allowing the truth to go undefended. Aristotle's audience, we should remember, is the aspiring idealist who claims to care about the fate of truth and justice. Aristotle is calling this philosopher to defend truth within the city; Aristotle is calling the good man to become what Quintilian would call the "good man speaking well."

Relying on Common Opinion

Common sense, as we all know, can be quite a misnomer—sometimes it's not all that common, and sometimes it's not all that sensible. But Aristotle is willing to place his bets on common opinion—what he calls ***endoxa***—because, as he says, it's not usually very far off from the truth: "The true and the approximately true are apprehended by the same faculty; it may also be noted that men have a sufficient natural instinct for what is true, and usually do arrive at the truth" (1355a). The kind of inexact knowledge "the approximately true" gives us is a good starting point for personal understanding, and it is also a great basis for speaking with an audience. After all, audiences aren't often comprised of logicians and philosophers; they're usually full of ordinary people with conventional beliefs. These conventional beliefs are, by definition, *endoxa*, which can serve as a springboard for making new judgments. By knowing what the audience holds to be true, the **rhetor** can reveal his or her position as the logical deduction of what the audience already believes.

But Aristotle isn't a Pollyanna about common opinion; he knows very well that the thoughts on the street can be contradictory, or even flat-out wrong. The fact that *endoxa* falls short of perfect reliability means that the judicious rhetor must be choosy in opting for one belief over the other. As such, Aristotle's reliance on *endoxa* presupposes a rhetor who seeks real truth outside of its many imperfect and jumbled renderings. Because wisdom is the final goal, the best rhetor is an aspiring philosopher.

Defining Rhetoric

Aristotle begins by calling rhetoric the *antistrophos* of dialectic, but he then goes on to define rhetoric more specifically. He defines rhetoric as the "faculty of observing in any given case the available means of persuasion." Let's carefully examine that definition, starting from its end goal and its final term, *persuasion*. Notice that Aristotle does not see rhetoric as a type of force, as if the audience is strong-armed into agreement based on sheer logic or mere emotional pull. Instead, the goal is convincing, something closer to counsel than force.

Moving back to the beginning of Aristotle's definition, we find what might be a surprise. The art of rhetoric, for Aristotle, begins with observation. Aristotle emphasizes that one achieves the end goal of persuasion by first observing, by *seeing*. The rhetor, then, is not a *maker* as much as a *seer*; in this way, the rhetor is akin to the philosopher, who wants to see the truth—in this case, the truth of which means are available. Rhetoric is, in a way, the discerning of wisdom; it is the power of seeing what ought to be practiced in the moment.

Rhetoric makes the truth convincing; sophistry makes the speaker convincing.[3]

The next key term in Aristotle's definition of rhetoric is *available*. Sometimes, the rhetor will see that she can use certain arguments to persuade a given audience at a particular time, but those same arguments and proofs may not be available in a different context, in a different rhetorical situation. This is one reason why you might use different arguments with your mother than you would with your father to convince each parent to grant you permission to do something: No one makes decisions in exactly the same way and for exactly the same reasons. Plus, reality—as well as the soul of the audience—is not entirely under your control. That is to say, people aren't the only limiting factor; the circumstances at hand can alter, and the rhetorical possibilities will change, too. In the case of trying to convince your mother, say, to allow you to borrow the car, it will matter very much whether you have recently had an accident. Ask her one week, and she may give you an easy yes, but if you get involved in a fender bender, the circumstances will change; you'll have to work much harder for an affirmative.

Aristotle's definition tells us that rhetors should look different from sophists, who at best focus on the here and now, amounting to a shortsighted convincing; at worst, sophists make the weaker argument appear as the stronger one, resulting in manipulation. Rather, the true aim of a good rhetor is to see the rhetorical situation blossom forth in its fullness, with all of its radical contingencies accounted for by the speaker, who helps the audience flourish within the realm of language. In short, rhetoric can help reveal the best goods, and that's a good thing!

The three rhetorical appeals that Aristotle discusses, which will be examined in this book, are *ethos*, *pathos*, and *logos*. Aristotle believes *ethos*—the

3. This is a paraphrase of Charles Sears Baldwin, *Ancient Rhetoric and Poetic, Interpreted from Representative Works* (New York: Macmillan, 1924), 5, 247.

speaker's character—is so important that he calls it, according to one translation, "almost, so to speak, the controlling factor in persuasion" (1356a).[4] One must appear to know what is right, do what is right, and want what is right for one's audience. *Pathos*, the second appeal, concerns the **emotions**, and it can be a real trouble spot for rhetoric because of the potential for manipulation and abuse. By showing that emotions are obedient to reason, Aristotle ties *pathos* to *logos*, healing both the Platonic and Sophistic splits that did such damage to rhetoric proper. Finally, *logos* will be discussed in this text, with special attention given to the enthymeme.

Rhetoric and the Transcendentals

Before explaining his project, Aristotle offers some comments on the state of rhetoric.[5] From his rebukes, we can bet that rhetoric looked a lot back then like it does now: overdoses of the emotional appeal, disregard of wisdom, and plenty of suspect speakers. And his audience seems no better off than today's masses, either. Aristotle says that judgments tend to be made based more on "feelings of friendship or hatred or self-interest" (1354b) than on clear-sighted prudence. What we have here, then, is an ancient but surprisingly relevant book. And the fact that it was composed by the man single-handedly responsible for so much of Western philosophy means we can expect an insightful inquiry into civic speech.

Rhetoric is inescapable—it is the speech of the city—and it is also the most available vehicle we have for encountering truth. Hence, rhetorical arguments are often necessary. This is the case especially in matters where certainty escapes us, which, we must admit, is probably most of life. So we must take the art seriously if we are to attempt it at all. Aristotle's task, then, is a noble one: to offer to the city and the household a way of better understanding their speech. He seeks to bring rhetoric into the domain of reason as much as possible, isolating and distinguishing the three types of civic rhetoric: deliberative (concerning the advantageous), epideictic (/ˌepiˈdīktik/; concerning the honorable), and judicial (concerning the just).[6] This articulation divides rhetoric into judgments about things that are good, beautiful, and true, respectively. That is, whereas dialectic seeks to understand *the Good, the Beautiful, and the True* in their absolute senses, rhetoric tracks them in their real-world manifestations: those things that are advantageous, honorable, and just. If all rhetorical discourse falls within one or more of these three categories, as Aristotle argues, then this division suggests something about humanity itself: Our desire is for what our tradition calls the **transcendentals**—goodness, beauty, and truth.

4. Translation from George A. Kennedy, *On Rhetoric: A Theory of Civic Discourse* (New York: Oxford University Press, 1991), 38.
5. See Aristotle, *Rhetoric* 1354b.

6. See chapter 11 in this book for alternate names for the three species. This text uses George A. Kennedy's translation of *symbouleutikon* (deliberative), *dikanikon* (judicial), and *epideiktikon* (epideictic), as used in *On Rhetoric*.

Discussion Text:
Plato: The Republic *(360 BC)*[7]

Focus:
Rhetoric and Philosophy

1

This passage contains what may be the most famous allegory for philosophic education in the Western world. Speaking with his friend Glaucon, Socrates likens human reality to a cave in which people look at only the shadows of reality, not reality itself. Escaping the "cave" is the business of philosophy.

Book VII

Socrates – Glaucon

Socrates. And now let me show in a figure how far our nature is enlightened or unenlightened: Behold! Human beings living in an underground den, which has a mouth open towards the light and reaching all along the den; here they have been from their childhood, and have their legs and necks chained so that they cannot move, and can only see before them, being prevented by the chains from turning round their heads. Above and behind them a fire is blazing at a distance, and between the fire and the prisoners there is a raised way; and you will see, if you look, a low wall built along the way, like the screen which marionette players have in front of them, over which they show the puppets.

Glaucon. I see.

Socrates. And do you see men passing along the wall carrying all sorts of vessels, and statues and figures of animals made of wood and stone and various materials, which appear over the wall? Some of them are talking, others silent.

Glaucon. You have shown me a strange image, and they are strange prisoners.

Socrates. Like ourselves; and they see only their own shadows, or the shadows of one another, which the fire throws on the opposite wall of the cave?

Glaucon. True; how could they see anything but the shadows if they were never allowed to move their heads?

Socrates. And of the objects which are being carried in like manner they would only see the shadows?

Glaucon. Yes.

Socrates. And if they were able to converse with one another, would they not suppose that they were naming what was actually before them?

7. Plato, *Republic*, trans. Benjamin Jowett, provided by The Internet Classics Archive, http://classics.mit.edu/Plato/republic.html. Accessed June 26, 2016.

GLAUCON. Very true.

SOCRATES. And suppose further that the prison had an echo which came from the other side; would they not be sure to fancy when one of the passers-by spoke that the voice which they heard came from the passing shadow?

GLAUCON. No question.

SOCRATES. To them the truth would be literally nothing but the shadows of the images.

GLAUCON. That is certain.

SOCRATES. And now look again, and see what will naturally follow [if] the prisoners are released and disabused of their error. At first, when any of them is liberated and compelled suddenly to stand up and turn his neck round and walk and look towards the light, he will suffer sharp pains; the glare will distress him, and he will be unable to see the realities of which in his former state he had seen the shadows; and then conceive someone saying to him, that what he saw before was an illusion, but that now, when he is approaching nearer to being and his eye is turned towards more real existence, he has a clearer vision—what will be his reply? And you may further imagine that his instructor is pointing to the objects as they pass and requiring him to name them—will he not be perplexed? Will he not fancy that the shadows which he formerly saw are truer than the objects which are now shown to him?

GLAUCON. Far truer.

SOCRATES. And if he is compelled to look straight at the light, will he not have a pain in his eyes which will make him turn away and take in the objects of vision which he can see, and which he will conceive to be in reality clearer than the things which are now being shown to him?

GLAUCON. True.

SOCRATES. And suppose once more, that he is reluctantly dragged up a steep and rugged ascent, and held fast until he's forced into the presence of the sun himself, is he not likely to be pained and irritated? When he approaches the light, his eyes will be dazzled, and he will not be able to see anything at all of what are now called realities.

GLAUCON. Not all in a moment.

SOCRATES. He will require to grow accustomed to the sight of the upper world. And first he will see the shadows best, next the reflections of men and other objects in the water, and then the objects themselves; then he will gaze upon the light of the moon and the stars and the spangled heaven; and he will see the sky and the stars by night better than the sun or the light of the sun by day?

GLAUCON. Certainly.

SOCRATES. Last of [all] he will be able to see the sun, and not mere reflections of him in the water, but he will see him in his own proper place, and not in another; and he will contemplate him as he is.

GLAUCON. Certainly.

SOCRATES. He will then proceed to argue that this is he who gives the season and the years, and is the guardian of all that is in the visible world, and in a certain way the cause of all things which he and his fellows have been accustomed to behold?

GLAUCON. Clearly, he would first see the sun and then reason about him.

SOCRATES. And when he remembered his old habitation, and the wisdom of the den and his fellow-prisoners, do you not suppose that he would felicitate himself on the change, and pity them?

GLAUCON. Certainly, he would.

SOCRATES. And if they were in the habit of conferring honours among themselves on those who were quickest to observe the passing shadows and to remark which of them went before, and which followed after, and which were together; and who were therefore best able to draw conclusions as to the future, do you think that he would care for such honours and glories, or envy the possessors of them? Would he not say with Homer,

> Better to be the poor servant of a poor master, and to endure anything, rather than think as they do and live after their manner?

GLAUCON. Yes, I think that he would rather suffer anything than entertain these false notions and live in this miserable manner.

SOCRATES. Imagine once more . . . , such a one coming suddenly out of the sun to be replaced in his old situation; would he not be certain to have his eyes full of darkness?

GLAUCON. To be sure.

SOCRATES. And if there were a contest, and he had to compete in measuring the shadows with the prisoners who had never moved out of the den, while his sight was still weak, and before his eyes had become steady (and the time which would be needed to acquire this new habit of sight might be very considerable), would he not be ridiculous? Men would say of him that up he went and down he came without his eyes; and that it was better not even to think of ascending; and if anyone tried to loose another and lead him up to the light, let them only catch the offender, and they would put him to death.

GLAUCON. No question.

SOCRATES. This entire allegory you may now append, dear Glaucon, to the previous argument; the prison-house is the world of sight, the light of the fire is the sun, and you will not misapprehend me if you interpret the journey upwards to be the ascent of the soul into the intellectual world according to my poor belief, which, at your desire, I have expressed whether rightly or wrongly God knows. But, whether true or false, my opinion is that in the world of knowledge the idea of good appears last of all, and is seen only with an effort; and, when seen, is also inferred to be the universal author of all things beautiful and right, parent of light and of the lord of light in this visible world, and the immediate source of reason and truth in the intellectual; and that this is the power upon which he who would act rationally, either in public or private life, must have his eye fixed.

GLAUCON. I agree, as far as I am able to understand you.

SOCRATES. Moreover, you must not wonder that those who attain to this beatific vision are unwilling to descend to human affairs; for their souls are ever hastening into the upper world where they desire to dwell; which desire of theirs is very natural, if our allegory may be trusted.

GLAUCON. Yes, very natural.

SOCRATES. And is there anything surprising in one who passes from divine contemplations to the evil state of man, misbehaving himself in a ridiculous manner; if, while his eyes are blinking and before he has become accustomed to the surrounding darkness, he is compelled to fight in courts of law, or in other places, about the images or the shadows of images of justice, and is endeavouring to meet the conceptions of those who have never yet seen absolute justice?

GLAUCON. Anything but surprising.

SOCRATES. Anyone who has common sense will remember that the bewilderments of the eyes are of two kinds, and arise from two causes, either from coming out of the light or from going into the light, which is true of the mind's eye, quite as much as of the bodily eye; and he who remembers this when he sees anyone whose vision is perplexed and weak, will not be too ready to laugh; he will first ask whether that soul of man has come out of the brighter light, and is unable to see because unaccustomed to the dark, or having turned from darkness to the day is dazzled by excess of light. And he will count the one happy in his condition and state of being, and he will pity the other; or, if he have a mind to laugh at the soul which comes from below into the light, there will be more reason in this than in the laugh which greets him who returns from above out of the light into the den.

GLAUCON. That is a very just distinction.

SOCRATES. But then, if I am right, certain professors of education must be wrong when they say that they can put a knowledge into the soul which was not there before, like sight into blind eyes.

GLAUCON. They undoubtedly say this.

SOCRATES. Whereas, our argument shows that the power and capacity of learning exists in the soul already; and that just as the eye was unable to turn from darkness to light without the whole body, so too the instrument of knowledge can only by the movement of the whole soul be turned from the world of becoming into that of being, and learn by degrees to endure the sight of being, and of the brightest and best of being, or in other words, of the good.

GLAUCON. Very true.

SOCRATES. And must there not be some art which will effect conversion in the easiest and quickest manner; not implanting the faculty of sight, for that exists already, but has been turned in the wrong direction, and is looking away from the truth?

GLAUCON. Yes, such an art may be presumed.

SOCRATES. And whereas the other so-called virtues of the soul seem to be akin to bodily qualities, for even when they are not originally innate they can be implanted later by habit and exercise, the [virtue] of wisdom more than anything else contains a divine element which always remains, and by this conversion is rendered useful and profitable; or, on the other hand, hurtful and useless. Did you never observe the narrow intelligence flashing from the keen eye of a clever rogue—how eager he is, how clearly his paltry soul sees the way to his end; he is the reverse of blind, but his keen eyesight is forced into the service of evil, and he is mischievous in proportion to his cleverness.

GLAUCON. Very true.

SOCRATES. But what if there had been a circumcision of such natures in the days of their youth; and they had been severed from those sensual pleasures, such as eating and drinking, which, like leaden weights, were attached to them at their birth, and which drag them down and turn the vision of their souls upon the things that are below—if, I say, they had been released from these impediments and turned in the opposite direction, the very same faculty in them would have seen the truth as keenly as they see what their eyes are turned to now.

Glaucon. Very likely.

Socrates. Yes; and there is another thing which is likely, or rather a necessary inference from what has preceded, that neither the uneducated and uninformed of the truth, nor yet those who never make an end of their education, will be able ministers of State; not the former, because they have no single aim of duty which is the rule of all their actions, private as well as public; nor the latter, because they will not act at all except upon compulsion, fancying that they are already dwelling apart in the islands of the blest.

Glaucon. Very true.

Socrates. Then, I said, the business of us who are the founders of the State will be to compel the best minds to attain that knowledge which we have already shown to be the greatest of all—they must continue to ascend until they arrive at the good; but when they have ascended and seen enough we must not allow them to do as they do now.

Glaucon. What do you mean?

Socrates. I mean that they remain in the upper world: but this must not be allowed; they must be made to descend again among the prisoners in the den, and partake of their labours and honours, whether they are worth having or not.

Glaucon. But is not this unjust? Ought we to give them a worse life, when they might have a better?

Socrates. You have again forgotten, my friend, the intention of the legislator, who did not aim at making any one class in the State happy above the rest; the happiness was to be in the whole State, and he held the citizens together by persuasion and necessity, making them benefactors of the State, and therefore benefactors of one another; to this end he created them, not to please themselves, but to be his instruments in binding up the State.

Glaucon. True, I had forgotten.

Socrates. Observe, Glaucon, that there will be no injustice in compelling our philosophers to have a care and providence of others; we shall explain to them that in other States, men of their class are not obliged to share in the toils of politics: and this is reasonable, for they grow up at their own sweet will, and the government would rather not have them. Being self-taught, they cannot be expected to show any gratitude for a culture which they have never received. But we have brought you into the world to be rulers of the hive, kings of yourselves and of the other citizens, and have educated you far better and more perfectly than they have been educated, and you are better able to share in the double duty. Wherefore each of you, when his turn comes, must go down to the general underground abode, and get the habit of seeing in the dark. When you have acquired the habit, you will see ten thousand times better than the inhabitants of the den, and you will know what the several images are, and what they represent, because you have seen the beautiful and just and good in their truth.

Discussion Questions

The Republic

1. Socrates says the prisoners are "like ourselves." How so?

2. At which points are the prisoner's eyes dazzled and rendered blind? What could be the meaning of this? (Later, when he returns to the cave, he is blinded again. Are the two moments of blindness equally undesirable?)

3. Is it true that truth is sometimes painful? Is it always better to know than not to know?

4. Identify what could be considered "shadows" in the world today.

5. Which is better, the upper world or lower world? (Remember, the chained prisoners never have to experience the pains of ascent!)

6. What is the relationship between the fire and sun?

7. Should the freed prisoner be allowed to remain in the upper world? Is it unjust to force him back into the cave to serve the good of others?

8. Given Socrates's depiction of the cave, what does he seem to think about rhetoric? Where do you see possible analogs for rhetors and rhetoric? For philosophers and philosophy?

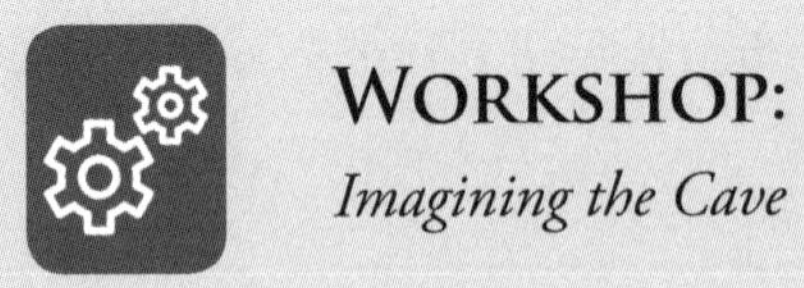

Workshop: *Imagining the Cave* 1

Draw the cave. Be sure to account for all of the factors—the shadows, the figures, the chains, the fire, the cave opening, the light, and the figures and objects in the upper world. Where would you locate the philosopher? The rhetor? The average citizen?

Then, write the following words within your drawing based upon where you think they belong: rhetoric, dialectic, the just, the advantageous, the honorable, *ethos*, *pathos*, *logos*, syllogism, enthymeme. Where would the transcendentals of Truth, Goodness, and Beauty be located? Write them in, too.

Finally, draw yourself in the scene. Where do you think you are?

WORKSHOP: *Rhetorical Analysis of an Ad* 2

Bring in a magazine ad you especially like (or don't like) for rhetorical analysis. How is this ad attempting to persuade the viewer? Is it successful or unsuccessful? Fill out the graphic and questions below to help you dissect and analyze the ad. You will then present the ad to the class and offer an analysis, using the ideas you've generated to explain the rhetorical power of the ad.

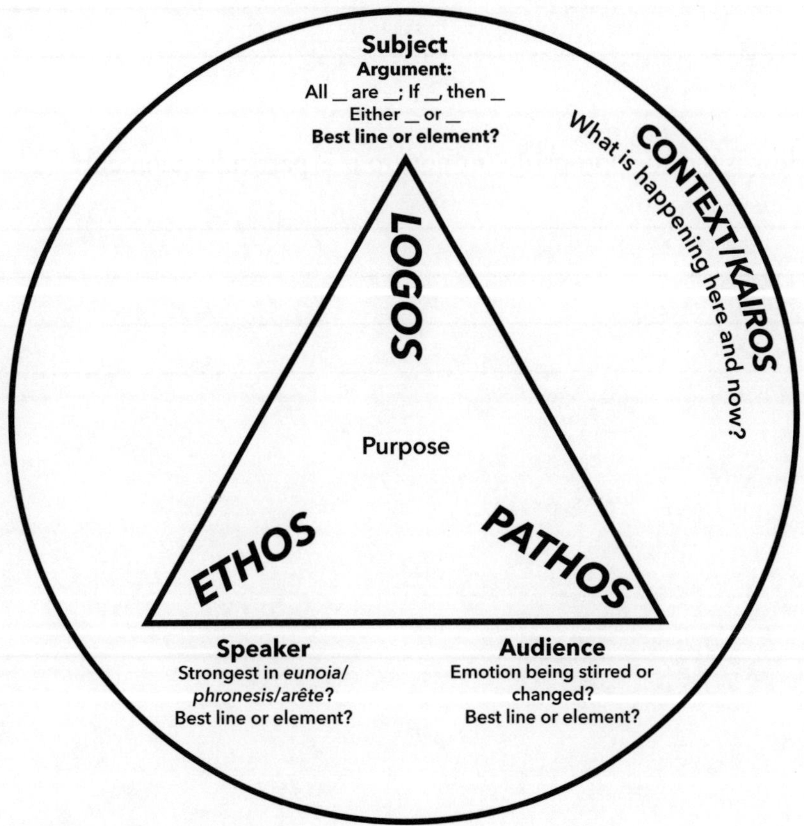

Figure 3. Rhetorical analysis diagram.

Rhetor/*Ethos*: How does the ad establish goodwill, moral virtue, or practical wisdom?

____

____

____

____

Audience/*Pathos*: What emotions is the ad playing on? What desires is it commodifying?

___

___

___

___

Text/*Logos*: How is reason used to support the persuasion?

___

___

___

___

Context/*Kairos*[8]: How is the ad appropriate (or not) to this particular moment?

___

___

___

___

8. *Kairos* means time, but in a special sense. Whereas *chronos* means a specific time, such as a clock might keep record of, *kairos* means the opportune or crucial moment, a time not tied to a particular hour of the day. (Think about jokes, for example. "Comic timing" is all about *kairos*. Falling in love is also more about *kairos* than *chronos*.) Rhetoric is terribly concerned with *kairos* because it is dependent on all of the factors of influence lining up at a crucial moment for full persuasion.

Discussion Questions

1. What does this ad reveal about our society's values?

2. What unstated messages are within the ad?

3. What does the ad want the audience to do?

Figure 4. Sample ad. Picture used with permission, courtesy of Habitat for Humanity.

PRESENTATION:
Great Speech Excerpt

SPOTLIGHT
Voice

Choose one of the following excerpts to deliver to the class. Practice it ten times. Pay attention to what *isn't* said in the speech, the common opinions—*endoxa*—that aren't specifically mentioned but are clearly assumed. List those at the bottom of your paper so that you can share them with the class at the end of your speech.

The focus for this speech is on your voice. In fact, those in the audience should close their eyes as you deliver the speech from the front of the room.

Here are three rules to remember as you give the speech:

1. Speak loudly.
2. Speak clearly. To enunciate, you will have to open your mouth wider than you're accustomed to doing, even slightly exaggerating your facial movements.
3. Speak slowly. (Most speakers speed up when they're nervous.) Include at least two dramatic pauses, and mark them in your text at points that deserve emphasis.

QUESTIONS:

1. What lines in the speech can you identify as relating to *logos*? To *ethos*? To *pathos*?

____

____

____

____

2. Note any *endoxa* appealed to or assumed.

____

____

____

____

3. Is this speech concerned with justice in a situation, the honor of people/deeds, or the advantageousness of an action? We will discuss the three types of rhetoric later (judicial, epideictic, and deliberative, respectively), but you can probably still identify what is most at stake in this speech. That is, is this speech concerned with passing judgment (judicial), praising and blaming (epideictic), or influencing a future decision (deliberative)?

____

____

____

____

Alternate Activity

Record yourself reading your speech, observing the same rules that were provided at the beginning of this presentation exercise. The recording will be played for an audience.

Roman Empress Theodora: "Royal Purple Is the Noblest Shroud" (January 18, AD 532)

Run, or stay and fight? When riots broke out and a new emperor was named by his enemies, the Roman emperor Justinian planned to do the former, but his wife Theodora's speech persuaded him otherwise. Her courage, in fact, would mean the saving of his empire—they stayed, and the rebels were roundly defeated.

My lords, the present occasion is too serious to allow me to follow the convention that a woman should not speak in a man's council. Those whose interests are threatened by extreme danger should think only of the wisest course of action, not of conventions.

In my opinion, flight is not the right course, even if it should bring us to safety. It is impossible for a person, having been born into this world, not to die; but for one who has reigned it is intolerable to be a fugitive. May I never be deprived of this purple robe, and may I never see the day when those who meet me do not call me empress.

If you wish to save yourself, my lord, there is no difficulty. We are rich; over there is the sea, and yonder are the ships. Yet reflect for a moment whether, when you have once escaped to a place of security, you would not gladly exchange such safety for death. As for me, I agree with the adage that the royal purple is the noblest shroud.[9]

Louis Pasteur: "The Spirit of Criticism" (November 14, 1888)

. . . [10] Worship the spirit of criticism. If reduced to itself, it is not an awakener of ideas or a stimulant to great things, but, without it, everything is fallible; it always has the last word. What I am now asking you, and you will ask of your pupils later on, is what is most difficult to an inventor.

It is indeed a hard task, when you believe you have found an important scientific fact and are feverishly anxious to publish it, to constrain yourself for days, weeks, years sometimes, to fight with yourself, to try and ruin your own experiments and only to proclaim your discovery after having exhausted all contrary hypotheses.

9. Quoted in William Safire, *Lend Me Your Ears: Great Speeches in History* (New York: W.W. Norton & Co., 1997), 37.
10. Many speeches throughout this book are not the original speeches in full; they have been shortened to take into consideration length for memorization, oration, and context.

But when, after so many efforts, you have at last arrived at a certainty, your joy is one of the greatest which can be felt by a human soul, and the thought that you will have contributed to the honour of your country renders that joy still deeper.[11]

Jonathan Winthrop: "A Model of Christian Charity" (1630)

. . . Now the only way to avoid this shipwreck, and to provide for our posterity, is to follow the counsel of Micah, to do justly, to love mercy, to walk humbly with our God. For this end, we must be knit together, in this work, as one man. We must entertain each other in brotherly affection. We must be willing to abridge ourselves of our superfluities, for the supply of others' necessities. We must uphold a familiar commerce together in all meekness, gentleness, patience and liberality. We must delight in each other; make others' conditions our own; rejoice together, mourn together, labor and suffer together, always having before our eyes our commission and community in the work, as members of the same body. So shall we keep the unity of the spirit in the bond of peace. The Lord will be our God, and delight to dwell among us, as His own people, and will command a blessing upon us in all our ways, so that we shall see much more of His wisdom, power, goodness and truth, than formerly we have been acquainted with. We shall find that the God of Israel is among us, when ten of us shall be able to resist a thousand of our enemies; when He shall make us a praise and glory that men shall say of succeeding plantations, "may the Lord make it like that of New England." *For we must consider that we shall be as a city upon a hill. The eyes of all people are upon us. . . .*[12]

Ben Franklin: "So Near to Perfection" (September 17, 1787)

Mr. President: —I confess that there are several parts of this Constitution which I do not at present approve, but I am not sure I shall never approve them. For, having lived long, I have experienced many instances of being obliged, by better information or fuller consideration, to change opinions, even on important subjects, which I once thought right, but found to be otherwise. It is therefore that the older I grow, the more apt I am to doubt my own judgment, and to pay more respect to the judgment of others.

. . . I doubt, too, whether any other Convention we can obtain may be able to make a better Constitution. For, when you assemble a number of men to have the advantage of their joint wisdom, you inevitably assemble with those men, all their prejudices, their passions, their errors of opinion, their local interests, and their selfish views. From such an assembly can a perfect production be expected? It therefore astonishes me, sir, to find this system approaching so near to perfection as it does; and I think it will astonish our enemies, who are waiting with confidence to hear that our councils are confounded, like those of the builders

11. René Vallery-Radot, *The Life of Pasteur*, trans. R. L. Devonshire (New York: McClure, Phillips, 1923), provided by the Internet Archive, http://www.archive.org/details/lifepasteur00unkngoog.
12. John Winthrop, "A Model of Christian Charity," 1630, *The Winthrop Society: Praeservare Et Transmittere*, provided by The Winthrop Society, http://winthropsociety.com/doc_charity.php.

of Babel; and that our states are on the point of separation, only to meet hereafter for the purpose of cutting one another's throats. Thus I consent, sir, to this Constitution, because I expect no better, and because I am not sure, that it is not the best.

. . . On the whole, sir, I cannot help expressing a wish that every member of the Convention, who may still have objections to it, would with me, on this occasion, doubt a little of his own infallibility, and to make manifest our unanimity, put his name to this instrument.[13]

Lucy Stone: "A Disappointed Woman" (1855)

From the first years to which my memory stretches, I have been a disappointed woman. When, with my brothers, I reached forth after the sources of knowledge, I was reproved with "It isn't fit for you; it doesn't belong to women." Then there was but one college in the world where women were admitted, and that was in Brazil. I would have found my way there, but by the time I was prepared to go, one was opened in the young State of Ohio—the first in the United States where women and Negroes could enjoy opportunities with white men. I was disappointed when I came to seek a profession worthy an immortal being—every employment was closed to me, except those of the teacher, the seamstress, and the housekeeper. In education, in marriage, in religion, in everything, disappointment is the lot of woman. It shall be the business of my life to deepen this disappointment in every woman's heart until she bows down to it no longer. I wish that women, instead of being walking showcases, instead of begging of their fathers and brothers the latest and gayest new bonnet, would ask of them their rights.[14]

Sojourner Truth: "Ain't I a Woman?" (May 29, 1851)

This speech was delivered at the Women's Convention in Akron, Ohio.

Well, children, where there is so much racket there must be something out of kilter. I think that 'twixt the negroes of the South and the women at the North, all talking about rights, the white men will be in a fix pretty soon. But what's all this here talking about?

That man over there says that women need to be helped into carriages, and lifted over ditches, and to have the best place everywhere. Nobody ever helps me into carriages, or over mud-puddles, or gives me any best place! And ain't I a woman? Look at me! Look at my arm! I have ploughed and planted, and gathered into barns, and no man could head me! And ain't I a woman? I could work as much and eat as much as a man—when I could get it—and bear the lash as well! And ain't I a woman? I have borne thirteen children, and seen most all sold

13. *The Debates on the Adoption of the Federal Constitution in the Convention held at Philadelphia in 1787*, with a Diary of the Debates of the Congress of the Confederation as reported by James Madison, revised and newly arranged by Jonathan Elliot, vol. 5, supplement to *Elliot's Debates* (Philadelphia, 1836), http://oll.libertyfund.org/titles/1909#Elliot_1314-05_5612.

14. Elizabeth Cady Stanton, Susan Brownell Anthony, and Matilda Joslyn Gage, eds., *History of Woman Suffrage*, vol. 1 (Rochester, NY: Fowler and Wells, 1889), 165.

off to slavery, and when I cried out with my mother's grief, none but Jesus heard me! And ain't I a woman?

Then they talk about this thing in the head; what's this they call it? [member of audience whispers, "intellect"] That's it, honey. What's that got to do with women's rights or negroes' rights? If my cup won't hold but a pint, and yours holds a quart, wouldn't you be mean not to let me have my little half measure full?

Then that little man in black there, he says women can't have as much rights as men, 'cause Christ wasn't a woman! Where did your Christ come from? Where did your Christ come from? From God and a woman! Man had nothing to do with Him.

If the first woman God ever made was strong enough to turn the world upside down all alone, these women together ought to be able to turn it back, and get it right side up again! And now they is asking to do it, the men better let them.

Obliged to you for hearing me, and now old Sojourner ain't got nothing more to say.[15]

George Bernard Shaw: "To the Greatest of Our Contemporaries, Einstein" (October 28, 1930)

Napoleon and other great men were makers of empires, but these eight men whom I am about to mention were makers of universes and their hands were not stained with the blood of their fellow men. I go back 2,500 years and how many can I count in that period? I can count them on the fingers of my two hands.

Pythagoras, Ptolemy, Kepler, Copernicus, Aristotle, Galileo, Newton and Einstein—and I still have two fingers left vacant.

Even among those eight men I must make a distinction. I have called them makers of the universe, but some of them were only repairers. Newton made a universe which lasted for 300 years. Einstein has made a universe, which I suppose you want me to say will never stop, but I don't know how long it will last.

. . .

What have all of those great men been doing? Each in turn claimed the other was wrong, and now you are expecting me to say that Einstein proved that Newton was wrong. But you forget that when science reached Newton, science came up against that extraordinary Englishman. That had never happened to it before.

. . .

15. Ibid.

For 300 years we believed in that Newtonian universe as I suppose no system has been believed in before. I know I was educated in it and was brought up to believe in it firmly. Then a young professor came along. He said a lot of things and we called him a blasphemer. He claimed Newton's theory of the apple was wrong.

He said, "Newton did not know what happened to the apple, and I can prove this when the next eclipse comes."

We said: "The next thing you will be doing is questioning the law of gravitation."

The young professor said: "No, I mean no harm to the law of gravitation, but for my part, I can go without it."

"What do you mean, go without it?"

He said: "I can tell you about that afterward."

The world is not a rectilinear world: It is a curvilinear world. The heavenly bodies go in curves because that is the natural way for them to go, and so the whole Newtonian universe crumpled up and was succeeded by the Einstein universe. Here in England, he is a wonderful man.

This man is not challenging the fact of science; he is challenging the action of science. Not only is he challenging the action of science, but the action of science has surrendered to his challenge.

Now ladies and gentlemen, are you ready for the toast? I drink to the greatest of our contemporaries, Einstein.[16]

Queen Elizabeth: "I Have the Heart of a King" (1588)

My loving people, we have been persuaded by some, that are careful of our safety, to take heed how we commit ourselves to armed multitudes, for fear of treachery; but [I] assure you, I do not desire to live to distrust my faithful and loving people. Let tyrants fear; I have always so behaved myself that, under God, I have placed my chiefest strength and safeguard in the loyal hearts and good-will of my subjects. And therefore I am come amongst you at this time, not as for my recreation or sport, but being resolved, in the midst and heat of the battle, to live or die amongst you all; to lay down, for my God, and for my kingdom, and for my people, my honour and my blood, even in the dust. I know I have but the body of a weak and feeble woman, but I have the heart of a king, and of a king of England, too; and think foul scorn that Parma or Spain, or any prince of Europe, should dare to invade the borders of my realms: to which, rather than any dishonour should grow by me, I myself will take

16. Michael Holroyd, "Albert Einstein, Universe Maker," *New York Times*, March 13, 1991, http://www.nytimes.com/1991/03/14/opinion/albert-einstein-universe-maker.html.

up arms: I myself will be your general, judge, and rewarder of every one of your virtues in the field. I know already, by your forwardness, that you have deserved rewards and crowns; and we do assure you, on the word of a prince, they shall be duly paid you. In the mean time my lieutenant general shall be in my stead, than whom never prince commanded a more noble and worthy subject; not doubting by your obedience to my general, by your concord in the camp, and your valour in the field, we shall shortly have a famous victory over those enemies of my God, of my kingdom, and of my people.[17]

Pope Urban II: "Enter upon the Road to the Holy Sepulcher" (November 1095)

The First Crusade Speech

O race of Franks, race from across the mountains, race beloved and chosen by God[!] . . .

From the confines of Jerusalem and from the city of Constantinople a grievous report has gone forth and has repeatedly been brought to our ears; namely, that a race from the kingdom of the Persians . . . has violently invaded the lands of those Christians, and has depopulated them by pillage and fire. . . . The kingdom of the Greeks is now dismembered by them, and has been deprived of a territory so vast in extent that it could not be traversed in two months' time.

On whom, therefore, is the labor of avenging these wrongs and of recovering this territory incumbent, if not upon you—you, upon whom, above all others, God has conferred remarkable glory in arms, great courage, bodily activity, and strength to humble the heads of those who resist you? Let the deeds of your ancestors encourage you and incite your minds to manly achievements:—the glory and greatness of King Charlemagne, and of his son Louis, and of your other monarchs. . . . Let the holy sepulcher of our Lord and Saviour . . . especially arouse you. . . . Let none of your possessions retain you, nor solicitude for your family affairs. For this land which you now inhabit, shut in on all sides by the seas and surrounded by the mountain peaks, is too narrow for your large population; nor does it abound in wealth; and it furnishes scarcely enough food enough for its cultivators. Hence it is that you murder and devour one another, that you wage war, and that very many among you perish in [civil] strife.

Let hatred therefore depart from among you, let your quarrels end, let wars cease and controversies slumber. Enter upon the road to the Holy Sepulcher. . . . Jerusalem is the center of the earth; the land is fruitful above all others, like another paradise of delights. . . . She seeks, therefore, and desires to be liberated and ceases not to implore you to come to her aid. . . . Accordingly, undertake this journey eagerly for the remission of your sins, with the assurance of the reward of imperishable glory in the kingdom of Heaven. . . .

17. David Hume, *The History of England, from the Invasion of Julius Caesar to the Revolution in 1688*, vol. 6 (London: A. Wilson, 1819), 374–375.

When an armed attack is made upon the enemy, let this one cry be raised by all the soldiers of God: "It is the will of God! It is the will of God!" [*Deus vult! Deus vult!*] . . .[18]

Mahatma Gandhi: "I Do Not Ask for Mercy" (March 1922)

. . . I wanted to avoid violence. Non-violence is the first article of my faith. It is also the last article of my creed. But I had to make my choice. I had either to submit to a system which I considered had done an irreparable harm to my country, or incur the risk of the mad fury of my people bursting forth when they understood the truth from my lips. I know that my people have sometimes gone mad. I am deeply sorry for it and I am, therefore, here to submit not to a light penalty but to the highest penalty. I do not ask for mercy. I do not plead any extenuating act. I am here, therefore, to invite and cheerfully submit to the highest penalty that can be inflicted upon me for what in law is a deliberate crime, and what appears to me to be the highest duty of a citizen. The only course open to you, the Judge, is, as I am going to say in my statement, either to resign your post, or inflict on me the severest penalty if you believe that the system and law you are assisting to administer are good for the people. I do not expect that kind of conversion. But by the time I have finished with my statement you will have a glimpse of what is raging within my breast to run this maddest risk which a sane man can run.

(He then read out the written statement:) I owe it perhaps to the Indian public and to the public in England, to placate which this prosecution is mainly taken up, that I should explain why from a staunch loyalist and co-operator, I have become an uncompromising disaffectionist and non-co-operator. To the court too I should say why I plead guilty to the charge of promoting disaffection towards the Government established by law in India.[19]

Winston Churchill: "Iron Curtain" Speech (March 5, 1946)

I have a strong admiration and regard for the valiant Russian people and for my wartime comrade, Marshal Stalin. There is deep sympathy and goodwill in Britain—and I doubt not here also—towards the peoples of all the Russias and a resolve to persevere through many differences and rebuffs in establishing lasting friendships. We understand the Russian need to be secure on her western frontiers by the removal of all possibility of German aggression. We welcome Russia to her rightful place among the leading nations of the world. We welcome her flag upon the seas. Above all, we welcome constant, frequent and growing contacts between the Russian people and our own people on both sides of the Atlantic. It is my duty however, for I am sure you would wish me to state the facts as I see them to you, to place before you certain facts about the present position in Europe.

18. James Harvey Robinson, *Readings in European History: From the Breaking of the Roman Empire to the Protestant Revolt*, vol. 1 (Boston: Ginn, 1904), 313–15.

19. M. K. Gandhi, *The Voice of Truth*, ed. Shriman Narayan (Ahmedabad, India: Navajivan Pub. House, 1969), 14–15, provided by Gandhian Institutions – Bombay Sarvodaya Mandal & Gandhi Research Foundation, http://www.mkgandhi.org/ebks/voice_of_truth.pdf.

From Stettin in the Baltic to Trieste in the Adriatic, an iron curtain has descended across the Continent. Behind that line lie all the capitals of the ancient states of Central and Eastern Europe. Warsaw, Berlin, Prague, Vienna, Budapest, Belgrade, Bucharest and Sofia, all these famous cities and the populations around them lie in what I must call the Soviet sphere, and all are subject in one form or another, not only to Soviet influence but to a very high and, in many cases, increasing measure of control from Moscow. . . .

Whatever conclusions may be drawn from these facts—and facts they are—this is certainly not the Liberated Europe we fought to build up. Nor is it one which contains the essentials of permanent peace.[20]

Jonathan Edwards: "Sinners in the Hands of an Angry God" (1741)

O sinner! [C]onsider the fearful danger you are in: it is a great furnace of wrath, a wide and bottomless pit, full of the fire of wrath, that you are held over in the hand of that God, whose wrath is provoked and incensed as much against you, as against many of the damned in hell. You hang by a slender thread, with the flames of divine wrath flashing about it, and ready every moment to singe it, and burn it asunder; and you have no interest in any Mediator, and nothing to lay hold of to save yourself, nothing to keep off the flames of wrath, nothing of your own, nothing that you ever have done, nothing that you can do, to induce God to spare you one moment. . . .

Oh that you would consider it, whether you be young or old! There is reason to think, that there are many in this congregation now hearing this discourse, that will actually be the subjects of this very misery to all eternity. We know not who they are, or in what seats they sit, or what thoughts they now have. It may be they are now at ease, and hear all these things without much disturbance, and are now flattering themselves that they are not the persons, promising themselves that they shall escape. If we knew that there was one person, and but one, in the whole congregation, that was to be the subject of this misery, what an awful thing would it be to think of! If we knew who it was, what an awful sight would it be to see such a person! . . .

And now you have an extraordinary opportunity, a day wherein Christ has thrown the door of mercy wide open, and stands in calling and crying with a loud voice to poor sinners; a day wherein many are flocking to him, and pressing into the kingdom of God. Many are daily coming from the east, west, north and south; many that were very lately in the same miserable condition that you are in, are now in a happy state, with their hearts filled with

20. Winston Churchill, "The Sinews of Peace," delivered at Westminster College, Fulton, MO, March 5, 1946, provided by The Churchill Centre, http://www.winstonchurchill.org/resources/speeches/1946-1963-elder-statesman/the-sinews-of-peace.

love to him who has loved them, and washed them from their sins in his own blood, and rejoicing in hope of the glory of God. How awful is it to be left behind at such a day! . . .[21]

Frederick Douglass: "That Which Is Inhuman Cannot Be Divine" (July 4, 1852)

Would you have me argue that man is entitled to liberty? That he is the rightful owner of his own body? You have already declared it. Must I argue the wrongfulness of slavery? Is that a question for Republicans? Is it to be settled by the rules of logic and argumentation, as a matter beset with great difficulty, involving a doubtful application of the principle of justice, hard to be understood? How should I look today, in the presence of Americans, dividing and subdividing a discourse, to show that men have a natural right to freedom, speaking of it relatively and positively, negatively and affirmatively? To do so would be to make myself ridiculous, and to offer an insult to your understanding. There is not a man beneath the canopy of heaven who does not know that slavery is wrong for him.

What, am I to argue that it is wrong to make men brutes, to rob them of their liberty, to work them without wages, to keep them ignorant of their relations to their fellow men, to beat them with sticks, to flay their flesh with the lash, to load their limbs with irons, to hunt them with dogs, to sell them at auction, to sunder their families, to knock out their teeth, to burn their flesh, to starve them into obedience and submission to their masters? Must I argue that a system thus marked with blood, and stained with pollution is wrong? No! I will not. I have better employment for my time and strength than such arguments would imply.

What, then, remains to be argued? Is it that slavery is not divine; that God did not establish it; that our doctors of divinity are mistaken? There is blasphemy in the thought. That which is inhuman cannot be divine! Who can reason on such a proposition? They that can, may; I cannot. The time for such argument is past.[22]

21. Jonathan Edwards, Henry Rogers, and Sereno Edwards Dwight, *The Works of Jonathan Edwards, A.M.*, ed. Edward Hickman, vol. 2 (London: Ball, Arnold, 1840), 10–11.

22. Molefi Kete Asante and Abu Shardow Abarry, eds., *African Intellectual Heritage: A Book of Sources* (Philadelphia: Temple University Press, 1996), 639.

SECTION

The Three Rhetorical Appeals

(1356a) Of the modes of persuasion furnished by the spoken word there are three kinds. The first kind depends on the personal character of the speaker; the second on putting the audience into a certain frame of mind; the third on the proof, or apparent proof, provided by the words of the speech itself. Persuasion is achieved by the speaker's personal character when the speech is so spoken as to make us think him credible. We believe good men more fully and more readily than others: this is true generally whatever the question is, and absolutely true where exact certainty is impossible and opinions are divided. This kind of persuasion, like the others, should be achieved by what the speaker says, not by what people think of his character before he begins to speak. It is not true, as some writers assume in their treatises on rhetoric, that the personal goodness revealed by the speaker contributes nothing to his power of persuasion; on the contrary, his character may almost be called the most effective means of persuasion he possesses. Secondly, persuasion may come through the hearers, when the speech stirs their emotions. Our judgments when we are pleased and friendly are not the same as when we are pained and hostile. It is towards producing these effects, as we maintain, that present-day writers on rhetoric direct the whole of their efforts. This subject shall be treated in detail when we come to speak of the emotions. Thirdly, persuasion is effected through the speech itself when we have proved a truth or an apparent truth by means of the persuasive arguments suitable to the case in question. There are, then, these three means of effecting persuasion.

The Rhetorical Triangle

In a rhetorical situation, there are three elements: the rhetor, the audience, and the speech. That means there are also three ways to persuade: by making the rhetor convincing (*ethos*), by stirring the audience (*pathos*), or by highlighting the reasoning of the speech itself (*logos*). In other words, you can imagine that each factor houses a different element: *Ethos* resides in the speaker, *pathos* in the audience, and *logos* in the speech. Now, that's painting with a broad brush, but it's a handy way to picture it, nonetheless.

Figure 5. The rhetorical triangle.

Section 2—The Three Rhetorical Appeals

Now, a true story: A mother wanted her three daughters to eat broccoli for dinner, but all three despised the vegetable. The middle daughter proved to be the easiest case; she trusted, even idolized, her mother, and therefore responded to the request without hesitation or argument. The youngest, a spirited girl, required something different; the trick in her case was to promise a scoop of ice cream to chase the vegetable, and down it went. For the eldest, it was a matter of reasoning—listing the vitamins and health benefits was all it took to convince her to gulp down the nutrient-rich food. These three sisters epitomize the three appeals, the three reasons people would ever change their minds about anything: They trust the speaker (*ethos*), their desires are influenced (*pathos*), or the argument makes sense (*logos*).

As we learned in the last chapter, dialectic attempts to use only one of those three appeals: *logos*. *Ethos* and *pathos*, in fact, have no place in philosophical reasoning toward absolute truths. After all, truth doesn't play favorites based on prestige, nor does truth change based on the audience's feelings about it. But the wise rhetor knows that people are more than mere brains. People make decisions based on things other than pure logic. In fact, if we are being frank about these matters, we must acknowledge that *ethos* and *pathos* are often more influential for the average person than the *logos* of a sound argument. The shrewd speaker, then, knows how to appeal to all three—*ethos*, *pathos*, and *logos*.

2

Chapter 2

Ethos: Revealing the Speaker's Credibility

(1377b) . . . [T]he orator must not only try to make the argument of his speech demonstrative and worthy of belief; he must also make his own character look right and put his hearers, who are to decide, into the right frame of mind. Particularly in political oratory, but also in lawsuits, it adds much to an orator's influence that his own character should look right and that he should be thought to entertain the right feelings towards his hearers; and also that his hearers themselves should be in just the right frame of mind. That the orator's own character should look right is particularly important in political speaking: that the audience should be in the right frame of mind, in lawsuits. . . .

(1378a) There are three things which inspire confidence in the orator's own character—the three, namely, that induce us to believe a thing apart from any proof of it: good sense, good moral character, and goodwill. False statements and bad advice are due to one or more of the following three causes. Men either form a false opinion through want of good sense; or they form a true opinion, but because of their moral badness do not say what they really think; or finally, they are both sensible and upright, but not well disposed to their hearers, and may fail in consequence to recommend what they know to be the best course. These are the only possible cases. It follows that any one who is thought to have all three of these good qualities will inspire trust in his audience.

Practical Wisdom, Moral Virtue, and Goodwill

Although we might wish that valid logic and sound arguments were the only factors in persuasion, the truth is that the audience is made up of humans, and at some point those humans can get lazy or confused, or they simply may be unable to make the intellectual leap we're steering them toward; because of this, *ethos* becomes crucial. If they trust the speaker, they can be persuaded. And we all unwittingly side with *ethos* all the time, such as when we believe in the power of the atom or trust a person's court testimony or adopt a new fashionable hairdo—it's a blind leap made because we trust the one who says to jump.

If anyone wanted to persuade based on pure logic, it would be the philosopher Aristotle. And yet Aristotle's remarks are extraordinary. *Ethos*, he says, is almost the whole of persuasion. And he narrows *ethos* down to exactly three things: the speaker's ***phronesis*** (practical wisdom), ***arête*** (moral virtue), and ***eunoia*** (goodwill). Aristotle insists that any rhetor who wants to be trusted must be seen to possess these three attributes, and with these three, the speaker cannot help but be persuasive.

You may be asking whether there are other characteristics that a speaker could exhibit in order to be seen as trustworthy. And if so, you are asking the right question. At first glance, the recipe does seem rather arbitrary, doesn't it? What is so important about these three—and only three—ingredients?

Imagine that a classmate, Dan, has asked to borrow your car. A friend since kindergarten, he has always been kind and generous to you, so goodwill is no issue. He's a morally upright person, too, so you can be sure that he would not use the car to do anything fishy. But his nickname is Daydreamer Dan: He's distractible and klutzy. Why, then, are you nervous to loan him your car? He lacks common sense, or practical wisdom (*phronesis*), and you'd prefer to have your car back in one piece.

Now imagine another classmate, Mike. He is perfectly well equipped with practical wisdom, and, again, you have no reason to believe that he would ever intentionally bring you harm. The trouble in this case is that you heard Mike was caught shoplifting last semester, and you have the sneaking suspicion that he might get into trouble using your car. The missing component this time is moral virtue, *arête*.

Finally, think of a third classmate, Chip. He is coordinated and levelheaded, full of practical wisdom. He's also virtuous, the type who always does the right thing. There's nothing at all wrong with Chip—nothing except that he's never been especially friendly to you. You don't feel compelled to loan him your car. Why not? Lack of goodwill (*eunoia*)—you don't sense that he's on your side.

All three elements of *ethos* are necessary; when one is missing, persuasion is stunted. What is interesting is that Aristotle spends most of his time discussing goodwill, and for good reason. After all, when friends get together, the conversation flies fast—no one stops to define words or backs up to substantiate a point. But consider something of an opposite experience: facing a lawyer who is prosecuting you. You would suddenly become careful about the words you choose, stopping to define exactly what you mean, scrutinizing what the prosecutor says. You may even become hesitant to speak, lest your words be held against you. The difference in those two scenarios is an important factor in *ethos*: We believe our friends have goodwill toward us, even if they fail in other ways. No tricks up the sleeve, no smoke, and no mirrors—the feeling of goodwill enables us to let down our guards. The lack of it, such as in a case of confronting a prosecutor, results in our guard going up and staying up.

That is, we trust those who are friendly to us. As speakers, then, we must keep in mind these two realities: first, that *ethos* is almost the whole of persuasion; second, that goodwill (*eunoia*) does the heavy lifting when it comes to the establishment of *ethos*. We need to be sure that our care for the audience members—the fact that we want what is best for them—is completely unquestioned.

Saying What Needs to Be Said

Rhetors often make the mistake of assuming their credibility before an audience. Bad idea. Aristotle goes so far as to say that one's *ethos*, rather than existing within the person, is established by the speech itself: "This kind of persuasion, like the others, should be achieved by what the speaker says, not by what people think of his character before he begins to speak."[1] In other words, you may have

1. Aristotle, *Rhetoric* 1356a8–10.

a good reputation, but if you don't draw upon it verbally, it just sits by uselessly.

You can easily imagine scenarios Aristotle might have in mind should he be with us today: a star athlete who delivers an award acceptance speech but fails to thank others who have contributed to his success (lack of moral virtue), a US president who rarely mentions concern for the American people (lack of goodwill), an employee who makes a business pitch to his boss without having included a budget (lack of practical wisdom). The opposite is also true. Even the person who, on paper, looks to be a failure in life can turn the rhetorical tables simply by revealing good *ethos* in the speech itself. For example, a convicted felon may seem like a poor choice for talking to young people about avoiding a life of crime. But if he reveals himself as one who has learned from his mistakes and has turned his life around (moral virtue), and he assures them that he speaks to them for their own betterment (goodwill), he'll gain an audience. If his message is also one of clear and useful advice (practical wisdom), then he has all three ingredients and is virtually bound to be persuasive.

Now, drawing upon one's *ethos* is not the same as tooting one's own horn, which ends up—ironically, to be sure—destroying *ethos*, not establishing it. But it does mean that if the speaker has good character, he should reveal that good character. Of course, we would think it unethical for a person of *bad* character to pretend otherwise. Just as bad character deserves to be brought out into the light and seen for what it is, the same is true for good character. That is, one could argue that a speaker who hides her good character is also wrong, for she is withholding from the listeners an important factor in their decision-making. After all, audiences ought to take into account what a virtuous, friendly, and prudent person advises.

In a way, Aristotle's general discussion of *ethos* could seem a little troubling—isn't he just talking about *appearing* to have moral virtue, goodwill, and practical wisdom? That is, can't the speaker merely present himself as a virtuous person without actually being virtuous? Fair enough. But Aristotle's discussion of *ethos* must be read in light of his entire critique of the sophists. Early on, Aristotle distinguishes the rhetor from the sophist not by ability but by moral choice.[2] And although Aristotle is quite willing to admit there are corrupt audiences, he is also just as willing to point the finger at the rhetor who refuses to reveal his or her *ethos*, thus failing to persuade others of the truest or most just decision. One must make the effort to appear wise, good, and friendly because—although imposters will feign these qualities—the ideal orator should have them in truth. That is, they are the essential qualities of a credible person. And if orators are unpersuasive because they have not made their good character apparent, then the fault is their own.

Again, we have found ourselves in the messy business of real life. There's no way to know for certain where appearances end and reality begins. But the virtuous rhetor does have an advantage over the sophist: Whereas the moral rhetor needs only to reveal good character he already possesses, the sophist has to hide bad character—and that's much harder to do. Aristotle is reminding us that, because *ethos* is such a powerful persuader, a rhetor needs to be ready to draw upon that cache of rhetorical reserve. In other words, Quintilian's "good man speaking well" is actually responsible for putting his goodness on display.

2. Ibid., 1355b.

Discussion Text:

George Washington: "A Faithful Friend to the Army" (1783)[3]

Focus:

Ethos

1

An anonymous letter had been circulating within the Revolutionary Army, calling for the military to revolt against a Congress that was not paying their wages. In Newburgh, New York, General Washington himself surprised an assembly of officers and personally addressed the conspiracy. The address is said to have ended with a dramatic moment: Washington took from his pocket a letter. Squinting, he then took out a pair of glasses and said this: "Gentlemen, you must pardon me, for I have not only grown gray but almost blind in service to my country." The Newburgh Conspiracy was ended.

Cantonment, 15 March, 1783[4]

Gentlemen, by an anonymous summons, an attempt has been made to convene you together. How inconsistent with the rules of propriety, how unmilitary and how subversive of all order and discipline, let the good sense of the army decide.

In the moment of this summons, another anonymous production was sent into circulation, addressed more to the feelings and passions than to the reason and judgment of the army. The author of the piece is entitled to much credit for, the goodness of his pen; and I could wish he had as much credit for the rectitude of his heart; for, as men see through different optics, and are induced by the reflecting faculties of the mind, to use different means to attain the same end, the author of the address should have had more charity than to mark for suspicion the man who should recommend moderation and longer forbearance, or, in other words, who should not think as he thinks, and act as he advises. But he had another plan in view, in which candor and liberality of sentiment, regard to justice and love of country, have no part; and he was right to insinuate the darkest suspicion to effect the blackest design. That the address is drawn with great art, and is designed to answer the most insidious purposes; that it is calculated to impress the mind with an idea of premeditated injustice in the sovereign power of the United States, and rouse all those resentments which must unavoidably flow from such a belief; that the secret mover of this scheme, whoever he may be, intended to

3. Michael Hattem, "Newburgh Conspiracy," in George Washington Digital Encyclopedia, edited by Joseph F. Stoltz III, Mount Vernon Estate, 2012–, http://www.mountvernon.org/digital-encyclopedia/article/newburgh-conspiracy/.
4. George Washington, "Newburgh Address: Cantonment, 15 March, 1783," from Library of Congress, *Journals of the Continental Congress, 1774–1789* [pp. 307–310], http://www.loc.gov/teachers/classroommaterials/presentationsandactivities/presentations/timeline/amrev/peace/newburgh.html.

take advantage of the passions, while they were warmed by the recollection of past distresses, without giving time for cool deliberative thinking, and that composure of mind which is so necessary to give dignity and stability to measures, is rendered too obvious, by the mode of conducting the business, to need other proof than a reference to the proceeding.

Thus much, gentlemen, I have thought it incumbent on me to observe to you, to shew upon what principles I opposed the irregular and hasty meeting which was proposed to have been held on Tuesday last, and not because I wanted a disposition to give you every opportunity, consistent with your own honor, and the dignity of the army, to make known your grievances. If my conduct heretofore has not evinced to you that I have been a faithful friend to the army, my declaration of it at this time would be equally unavailing and improper. But as I was among the first who embarked in the cause of our common country; as I have never left your side one moment, but when called from you on public duty; as I have been the constant companion and witness of your distresses, and not among the last to feel and acknowledge your merits; as I have ever considered my own military reputation as inseparably connected with that of the army; as my heart has ever expanded with joy, when I have heard its praises, and my indignation has arisen when the mouth of detraction has been opened against it, it can scarcely be supposed, at this late stage of the war, that I am indifferent to its interests. But how are they to be promoted? The way is plain, says the anonymous addresser. "If war continues, remove into the unsettled country; there establish yourselves and leave an ungrateful country to defend itself."—But who are they to defend? Our wives, our children, our farms and other property which we leave behind us? or, in this state of hostile separation, are we to take the two first (the latter cannot be removed) to perish in a wilderness with hunger, cold and nakedness? "If peace takes place, never sheath your swords," says he "until you have obtained full and ample justice." This dreadful alternative of either deserting our country in the extremest hour of her distress, or turning our arms against it, which is the apparent object, unless Congress can be compelled into instant compliance, has something so shocking in it, that humanity revolts at the idea. My God! what can this writer have in view, by recommending such measures? Can he be a friend to the army? Can he be a friend to this country? Rather is he not an insidious foe? Some designing emissary, perhaps, from New York, plotting the ruin of both, by sowing the seeds of discord and separation between the civil and military powers of the continent? and what a compliment does he pay to our understandings, when he recommends measures, in either alternative impracticable in their nature? But, here, gentlemen, I will drop the curtain, because it would be as imprudent in me to assign my reasons for this opinion, as it would be insulting to your conception to suppose

you stood in need of them. A moment's reflection will convince every dispassionate mind of the physical impossibility of carrying either proposal into execution. There might, gentlemen, be an impropriety in my taking notice, in this address to you, of an anonymous production; but the manner in which that performance has been introduced to the army, the effect it was intended to have, together with some other circumstances, will amply justify my observations on the tendency of that writing.

With respect to the advice given by the author, to suspect the man who shall recommend moderate measures and longer forbearance, I spurn it, as every man who regards that liberty and reveres that justice for which we contend, undoubtedly must; for, if men are to be precluded from offering their sentiments on a matter which may involve the most serious and alarming consequences that can invite the consideration of mankind, reason is of no use to us. The freedom of speech may be taken away, and, dumb and silent, we may be led, like sheep, to the slaughter. I cannot, in justice to my own belief, and what I have great reason to conceive is the intention of Congress, conclude this address, without giving it as my decided opinion, that that honorable body entertain exalted sentiments of the services of the army, and from a full conviction of its merits and sufferings, will do it compleat [*sic*] justice: that their endeavours to discover and establish funds for this purpose have been unwearied, and will not cease till they have succeeded, I have not a doubt.

But, like all other large bodies, where there is a variety of different interests to reconcile, their determinations are slow. Why then should we distrust them, and, in consequence of that distrust, adopt measures which may cast a shade over that glory which has been so justly acquired, and tarnish the reputation of an army which is celebrated through all Europe for its fortitude and patriotism? And for what is this done? To bring the object we seek nearer? No, most certainly, in my opinion it will cast it at a greater distance. For myself, and I take no merit in giving the assurance, being induced to it from principles of gratitude, veracity and justice, a grateful sense of the confidence you have ever placed in me, a recollection of the cheerful assistance and prompt obedience I have experienced from you, under every vicissitude of fortune, and the sincere affection I feel for an army I have so long had the honor to command, will oblige me to declare, in this public and solemn manner, that in the attainment of compleat [*sic*] justice for all your toils and dangers, and in the gratification of every wish, so far as may be done consistently with the great duty I owe my country, and those powers we are bound to respect, you may freely command my services to the utmost extent of my abilities.

While I give you these assurances, and pledge myself in the most unequivocal manner, to exert whatever ability I am possessed of in your favour, let me entreat you, gentlemen, on your part, not to take any measures, which, viewed in the calm light of reason, will lessen the dignity, and sully the glory you have hitherto maintained. Let me request you to rely on the plighted faith of your country, and place a full confidence in the purity of the intentions of Congress; that, previous to your dissolution as an army, they will cause all your accounts to be fairly liquidated, as directed in their resolutions which were published to you two days ago; and that they will adopt the most effectual measures in their power to render ample justice to you for your faithful and meritorious services. And let me conjure you, in the name of our common country, as you value your own sacred honor, as you respect the rights of humanity, and as you regard the military and national character of America, to express your utmost horror and detestation of the man, who wishes, under any specious pretences [*sic*], to overturn the liberties of our country; and who wickedly attempts to open the flood-gates of civil discord, and deluge our rising empire in blood.

By thus determining, and thus acting, you will pursue the plain and direct road to the attainment of your wishes; you will defeat the insidious designs of our enemies, who are compelled to resort from open force to secret artifice. You will give one more distinguished proof of unexampled patriotism and patient virtue, rising superior to the pressure of the most complicated sufferings: and you will, by the dignity of your conduct, afford occasion for posterity to say, when speaking of the glorious example you have exhibited to mankind—"had this day been wanting, the world had never seen the last stage of perfection to which human nature is capable of attaining."

Discussion Questions

"A Faithful Friend to the Army"

Use the following visual aid to analyze Washington's speech and to discuss it with the class. Notice that answers may be found to be implicit as well as explicit; for example, you could assume that Washington was speaking not only to the men before him but also, indirectly, to his anonymous "enemy." Which appeal—*ethos*, *pathos*, or *logos*—predominates?

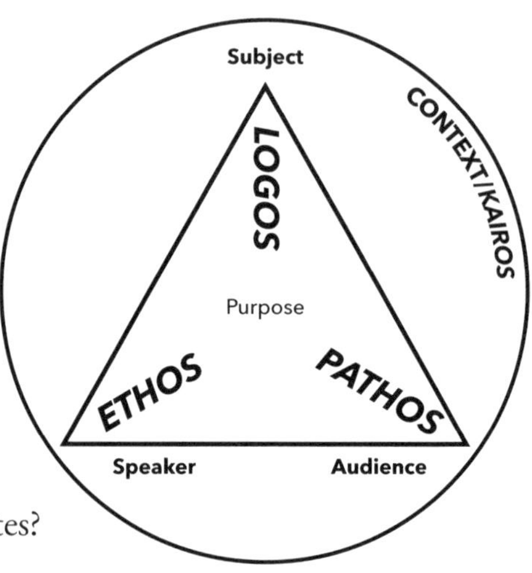

Figure 6. Rhetorical analysis diagram (see also pg. 17).

1. Find any allusions to *ethos* and *pathos* in the second paragraph of Washington's speech. Which appeal does Washington accuse the anonymous letter of using, and which does he say it ignores?

2. In what sentence in the second paragraph does Washington point out that the writer of the letter has remained anonymous? How does anonymity immediately render *ethos* questionable?

3. Mark any references in the third paragraph to goodwill. That is, how does Washington demonstrate his friendliness to the men to whom he speaks? How does he make them feel as if he is on their side?

4. In which lines in the third and fourth paragraphs does Washington establish his moral virtue?

5. Washington says this: "Can he be a friend to the army? Can he be a friend to this country? Rather is he not an insidious foe?" Which aspect of *ethos* is he attacking in the writer of the letter?

6. Washington also considers the measures proposed as being "impracticable." Which aspect of *ethos* is at stake in this charge?

7. Reread the introduction to this speech. Why is it that this comment, "Gentlemen, you must pardon me, for I have not only grown gray but almost blind in service to my country," would have caused some officers to weep as it did? What bearing does Washington's comment regarding his spectacles have on his *ethos*?

Workshop:

Just Trust Me!

1

Imagine you have found yourself in one of the following situations. Choose one of the listed scenarios and draft five or more sentences that establish your *ethos* (credibility). You will deliver your response in front of the class.

Remember that *ethos* comprises *phronesis* (practical wisdom), *arête* (moral virtue), and *eunoia* (goodwill). Your situation may call for stressing one of the factors more than the others. Underline phrases that concern *phronesis*, double underline those that concern *arête*, and circle those that concern *eunoia*.

Please note that the focus in this exercise is not on the reasons but, rather, on the establishing of your character. That is, if you were attempting to persuade your parents to buy you a motorcycle, you should not list the reasons why motorcycles are beneficial, such as good gas mileage and lower upkeep costs. You should instead make clear your wisdom, virtue, and goodwill as one who is deserving of such a gift.

Scenario 1: Convince your grandmother to loan you $100. (It is for a good reason, but you can't explain why you need the money.)

Scenario 2: You have run out of gas on the highway and are hitchhiking to the nearest gas station. You have flagged down a soccer mom driving a minivan full of kids. Introduce yourself to her and try to get a ride.

Scenario 3: You want an extra day off work. Start a conversation with your boss and ask for the extra day. (You are not allowed to explain why you need the day off.)

Scenario 4: You are late for curfew because a friend needed help. It is a private or embarrassing matter, so you cannot tell your parents the specific reason. Your parents meet you at the door, and they are upset. Convince them that their trust in you should not be rattled.

Scenario 5: You're at a job interview to be a summer camp counselor at an outdoor sports camp. Introduce yourself to the interviewers.

WORKSHOP:

College Application Essay

2

When you apply for college, you'll likely be required to write essays for your application for admission. Because schools are interested not only in the academic potential of their students but also in their personal qualities, these essay prompts often ask about *ethos*—what kind of character the applicant has. For this assignment, go online to find an essay prompt from a college or university to which you intend to apply.[5] Respond to one of the prompts in an essay of no more than 650 words. Identify sentences that establish *arête*, *phronesis*, and *eunoia* within your essay.

5. The Common Application is an undergraduate college admission application accepted by over 500 colleges and universities. It includes essay prompts that work very well for this assignment. Search online for the current year's list of Common Application essay prompts.

WORKSHOP: *The Rhetoric of E-Mail* 3

When you miss class, you may be tempted to send your teacher an e-mail such as the following:

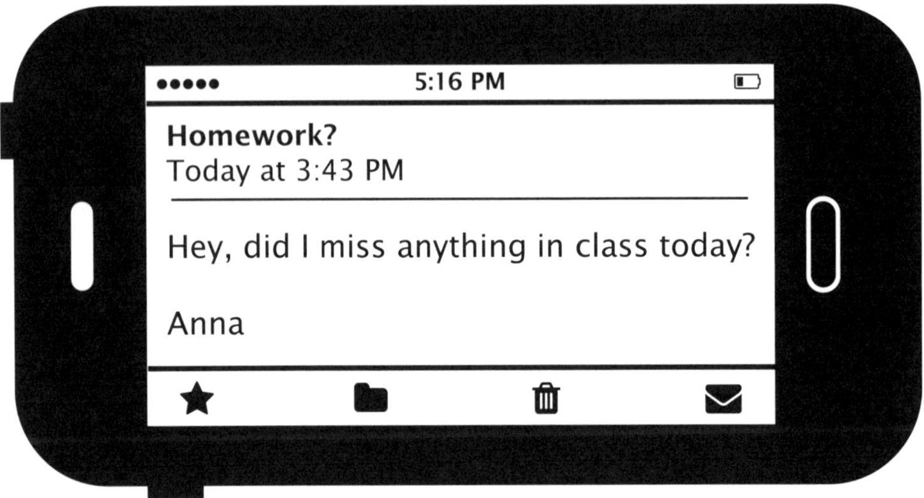

This would be fine as a message sent from one friend to another, but it doesn't exhibit much *ethos* when delivered from a student to her teacher.

To practice e-mail etiquette, compose and send an e-mail to your teacher that accomplishes one of the following:

- politely asks for an extension on a major essay,
- apologetically explains why you have been late to class three times this week, or
- politely informs your teacher that you will be absent on Friday and kindly requests the make-up work in advance.

Remember, e-mail is not the same as texting! The tone should be semiformal (not casual). Make sure you identify who you are as well as to whom you're writing. And do not include any acronyms or emoticons! Pay attention to your punctuation.

Ethos is key: You must establish goodwill, moral virtue, and practical wisdom. Indicate which lines address each factor by noting them in parentheses after the particular sentence that demonstrates the factor.

Presentation:
Great Speech Excerpt

Spotlight
Voice

Choose a different speech to deliver from the list of great speech excerpts found in the class presentation exercise of chapter 1. Practice it ten times. Like the last presentation, pay close attention to your vocal quality, as the class will be focusing on your voice.

Here are three rules to remember as you give the speech:

1. Speak loudly.
2. Speak clearly. To enunciate, you will have to open your mouth wider than you're accustomed to doing, even slightly exaggerating your facial movements.
3. Speak slowly. (Most speakers speed up when they're nervous.) Include at least two dramatic pauses, and mark them in your text at points that deserve emphasis.

Questions:

1. How does the speech build (or not build) the speaker's *ethos*?

____

____

____

____

____

____

2. If possible, identify particular lines for each of the aspects you detect—*eunoia* (goodwill), *phronesis* (practical wisdom), and *arête* (moral virtue).

____

____

____

____

____

____

3. Which aspect is most emphasized, and why?

4. Which aspect, if any, seems to be missing?

Alternate Activity

Record yourself reading your speech, observing the same rules that were provided at the beginning of this presentation exercise. Play back your recording and try to give a fair evaluation of your own vocal presentation.

Chapter 3

Pathos: Guiding the Audience's Emotions

When people are feeling friendly and placable, they think one sort of thing; when they are feeling angry or hostile, (1378a) they think either something totally different or the same thing with a different intensity: when they feel friendly to the man who comes before them for judgement, they regard him as having done little wrong, if any; when they feel hostile, they take the opposite view. Again, if they are eager for, and have good hopes of, a thing that will be pleasant if it happens, they think that it certainly will happen and be good for them: whereas if they are indifferent or annoyed, they do not think so. . . .

The Emotions are all those feelings that so change men as to affect their judgements, and that are also attended by pain or pleasure. Such are anger, pity, fear and the like, with their opposites. We must arrange what we have to say about each of them under three heads. Take, for instance, the emotion of anger: here we must discover (1) what the state of mind of angry people is, (2) who the people are with whom they usually get angry, and (3) on what grounds they get angry with them. It is not enough to know one or even two of these points; unless we know all three, we shall be unable to arouse anger in any one. The same is true of the other emotions.

The Legitimacy of the Emotional Appeal

Playing on an audience's **emotions** has earned a bad rap, and it's no wonder why. No one likes to feel emotionally manipulated. The sophists of Aristotle's day were notorious for such manipulation, and Aristotle faulted them for it, as should we. But that's not to say that emotions should be ignored altogether. Doing so is not simply impractical; it is also unethical.

Imagine for a moment that your dearest friend died. Sorrow would be quickly at your door, and rightly so. But what if you felt no sorrow? What if you felt nothing at all? A lack of sorrow in the situation would be an inappropriate response; in other words, *your emotions would be wrong*. And recognizing this wrong response illustrates how rhetors can appeal to an audience's emotions in a way that moves them toward what we might call the *truth* of a given experience. So by appealing to emotions that are actually suited to the occasion, rhetors aren't stooping too low; they're helping the audience to thrive. They're seeking to align the emotions with reason, to get them in sync. One without the other would split man in half, treating him as either mere intellect or mere emotions. Real virtue, then, is not just a matter of reason trumping emotions—it's a harmony between the two, and fostering that kind of harmony is the job of the rhetor.

Not only should emotion (*pathos*) be in line with reason (*logos*), but Aristotle hints that both are tied up with what Aristotle called "the most effective means of persuasion" (1356a)[1]—the speaker's credibility (*ethos*). In fact, this section in the text jumps back and forth between the speaker and the audience, suggesting that the way you, as a rhetor, handle your audience's passions says a lot about your character. Do you fire them up at every turn and fan the flames willy-nilly? Do you speak dispassionately about grave evils, such that the reality of wrongdoing is denied? Both are approaches of the sophist. But if you handle their passions appropriately, if you allay the misguided ones and invoke the apt ones, you are a rhetor in the best sense, a friend to both the audience and the city.

1. Kennedy, *On Rhetoric*, 38. Kennedy translates this line as "almost, so to speak, the controlling factor in persuasion."

Pain and Pleasure

We might imagine that the ideal rhetorical situation would involve intellect alone, that dealing with emotions is really beneath the dignity of the best kind of speech. But Aristotle recognizes that such a project would be impossible. *Ethos* and *logos*, the other two appeals, may be more venerable, but the pleasure and pain tied to the emotions make *pathos* downright fundamental.

Aristotle's definition for emotions is this: "all those feelings that so change men as to affect their judgements [*sic*], and that are also attended by pain or pleasure." This definition, however elaborate it may seem at first glance, is striking in its insight. It points out that the emotions (Greek pl., *pathē*) are experienced as psychological pain or pleasure and that, as emotions change, they influence our decisions. If a voter is fearful of a tax hike, for example, he votes one way. As his emotions change—he grows confident that taxes will not go up, for example—his judgment alters, and he votes differently. Or just think of your own experience: If you want to ask your parents for a special privilege, such as going to the movies with friends, do you ask them at just any random time, or do you wait until they're in a good mood? No doubt you pay careful attention to their current state of mind because you know that your chances of getting permission depend on it, at least in part. In the same manner, rousing or calming an audience's emotion is one way for a rhetor to change the minds and thus affect the decisions of his or her audience.

Although they are not mere bodily sensation nor pure contemplation, the emotions do have a foot in both camps. They are tied to pain and pleasure, but they are tied to those feelings based upon a mental connection. For example, anger is a pain that is based upon a judgment, such as *That man wronged me!* To the extent that the emotions are rash responses, they can be unreasonable. But to the extent that they are logical responses, they can be rational.

Rational Passions?

We all know that our passions can influence our judgments, which is why maxims such as "Never go grocery shopping hungry" are wise advice. In the case of the famished grocery shoppers, the cart ends up full of items that might otherwise never have tempted them; their judgment, that is, has been altered by their passionate craving. But what Aristotle wants to emphasize is that it works the other way around, too: Our minds can influence our emotions. Emotions respond to arguments, and thus one can change the emotions by changing the mind.

Yes, a speaker must recognize not only the emotions of his audience members but also how those emotions can affect their judgment. More importantly, however, the speaker should realize that emotions reside on a *two-way* street. Emotions arise from judgment about *ideas*, and so the speaker who can influence the ideas of his audience can also influence the emotions of that audience. No one wants to face an angry mob, but that anger might be redirected or calmed by a judicious rhetor.

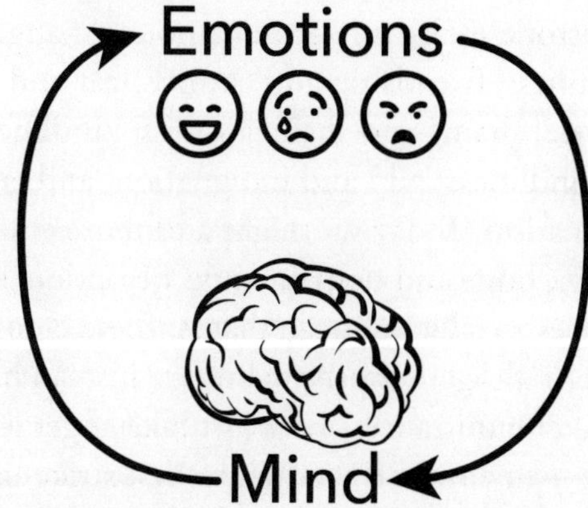

Figure 7. The reciprocal relationship between emotions and mind.

Aristotle points out that the problem with *pathos* is not an *absence* of judgment—after all, passions are roused by particular circumstances—but rather an *inadequacy* of judgment. Such judgment is partial and biased, and it is also rash. Rash decisions are those we make because our passions spur us on to quick judgment. We feel an urgency to make a decision and act. By stirring emotions with a heavy hand, the sophist capitalizes on the way our emotions can push us to make hasty judgments. Aristotle, however, proposes we direct those emotions under the rein of reason.

Aristotle looks at fourteen emotions: anger and calmness, friendship and enmity, fear and confidence, shame and shamelessness, kindliness and unkindliness, pity and indignation, and envy and emulation. Today we might add more emotions (e.g., hope and despair could be options), but his list is especially political; that is, these emotions aren't altogether private but are instead based on social circumstances. Let's just take anger as an example—an emotion that might first strike us as an irrational feeling. But if you look carefully at Aristotle's definition of anger, you'll find that anger is not altogether unreasonable. One grows angry for a reason, at a particular person, and for a particular aim. No one is ever *simply* angry, angry for no reason at all. There is also always a finger pointing *somewhere*, even if it's in the wrong direction. And you'll rarely find anyone angry where a restoration of justice would be impossible.

Such a rational look at a seemingly irrational passion begins to make sense of Aristotle's design: to bring the entire rhetorical project under the watchful eye of reason. And a reasoning analysis is indeed fruitful. If you have a hostile audience, you now have three ways to calm them: Show that the reason is unfounded, the anger misplaced, or the aim impossible.

We have learned, then, that the passions aren't arbitrary, but you'll notice that they are *prejudiced*—they seem to play favorites, and the favorites are always oneself or one's own. Anger, love, pity, fear—all are roused most vehemently when the occasion strikes close to home. What this means is that a speaker can manipulate the passions both in good and in bad ways. By manipulating the passions to reinforce selfish ends, a speaker can reinforce the blind prejudice that passions naturally have. But by purifying the passions through reason, a speaker can dignify humanity by elevating it above a concentration on one's own, moving it toward a concern for the whole.

In brief, we may say, on the one hand, that the mind can be steered by the passions; on the other hand, the passions can be steered by the mind. The former exercises the emotional muscle; the latter, the mental muscle. By giving a listener the experience of allaying an emotion by finding it unjustified, the rhetor is fortifying the audience's reasonability. Likewise, if the rhetor can rouse an emotion for good cause, that rhetor is actually helping the audience to flourish.

Pathos and the Imagination

Have you ever noticed that great speeches are full of great images? Aristotle calls the power of the image the power of "bringing-before-the-eyes," a kind of verbal demonstration that can have an effect as powerful as empirical evidence does. In fact, Aristotle's discussion suggests that one of the great reasons why *pathos* is so powerful is because it is governed by imagery. That is, words that paint graphic pictures more readily stir up *pathos*. Consider the following as an example:

> A lawyer friend of mine was hired to defend a large Southern utility against a suit by a small one, and he thought at first that he was doing fine. All of the law seemed to be on his side, and he felt that he had presented his case well. Then the lawyer for the small utility said, speaking to the jury, almost as if incidentally to his legal case, "So now we see what it is. They got us where they want us. They just holding us up with one hand, their good sharp fishin' knife in the other, and they sayin', 'You jes set still, little catfish, we're *jes* going to *gut* ya.'" At that moment, my friend reports, he knew he had lost the case. "I was in the hands of a genius of metaphor."[2]

The imagery here brings to life a scenario before the eyes of the audience, one so powerful that, despite any questions of justice, the case was ostensibly won by it. Notice that the descriptive imagery works along with a metaphor—the small Southern utility is a catfish in the hands of a fisherman—to highlight the victim status that small entities often have in relation to larger ones. "The greatest thing by far is to have command of metaphor," says Aristotle,[3] and history has proved him correct. From "the Iron Curtain" to "the Cold War" to "glass ceilings," the image in a good verbal metaphor can shape how we think about reality.

2. Wayne C. Booth and Walter Jost, *The Essential Wayne Booth* (Chicago: University of Chicago Press, 2006), 77–78.

3. Aristotle, *Poetics*, trans. S. H. Butcher, section 3, part 22, hypertextual resource compiled by The Internet Classics Archive (online), http://classics.mit.edu/Aristotle/poetics.3.3.html.

The metaphor, the image, the story—these tap into the power of "bringing-before-the-eyes," a kind of verbal demonstration that functions like an empirical one.

By tying *pathos* to *logos*, Aristotle heals the Platonic split, which separated rhetoric from philosophy. By couching *pathos* under *ethos*, he also heals the sophistic split, which separated rhetoric from ethics. In short, Aristotle recognizes that humans can't always be taught; they are more than mere brains. In fact, because we are composite creatures, the type of speech that targets *all* of our faculties might be the best—or at least the most necessary—speech there is. If so, then rhetoric is good. Not only is it good, it also seems to be "a good" in the Aristotelian sense, for one definition of a good is that which is productive of other goods (1363b). So if rhetoric can help create a better city—which is a good, to be sure—then rhetoric itself is more than a necessary evil. Rather, the art of persuasion can be a true civic good.

Figure 8. Sculpture of a scene from Shakespeare's *Julius Caesar* at the Folger Shakespeare Library in Washington, DC, by sculptor Gregory, 1932. Courtesy of Smallbones, commons.wikimedia.org.

Discussion Text:
Shakespeare: Julius Caesar, *Act 3, Scene 2*

Focus:
Pathos

1

The Roman leader Caesar has just been assassinated by a group of conspirators that included Brutus, his dear friend. In this scene, the crowds have gathered in the Forum to hear justification for the murder.

SCENE 2. The Forum.

Enter BRUTUS and CASSIUS, and a throng of Citizens

Citizens. We will be satisfied; let us be satisfied.

Brutus. Then follow me, and give me audience, friends.
Cassius, go you into the other street,
And part the numbers.
Those that will hear me speak, let 'em stay here;
Those that will follow Cassius, go with him;
And public reasons shall be rendered
Of Caesar's death.

First Citizen. I will hear Brutus speak.

Second Citizen. I will hear Cassius; and compare their reasons,
When severally we hear them rendered.

Exit CASSIUS, with some of the Citizens. BRUTUS goes into the pulpit.

Third Citizen. The noble Brutus is ascended: silence!

Brutus. Be patient till the last.
Romans, countrymen, and lovers! hear me for my
cause, and be silent, that you may hear: believe me
for mine honour, and have respect to mine honour, that
you may believe: censure me in your wisdom, and
awake your senses, that you may the better judge.
If there be any in this assembly, any dear friend of
Caesar's, to him I say, that Brutus's love to Caesar
was no less than his. If then that friend demand
why Brutus rose against Caesar, this is my answer:
—Not that I loved Caesar less, but that I loved
Rome more. Had you rather Caesar were living and

die all slaves, than that Caesar were dead, to live
all free men? As Caesar loved me, I weep for him;
as he was fortunate, I rejoice at it; as he was
valiant, I honour him: but, as he was ambitious, I
slew him. There is tears for his love; joy for his
fortune; honour for his valour; and death for his
ambition. Who is here so base that would be a
bondman? If any, speak; for him have I offended.
Who is here so rude that would not be a Roman? If
any, speak; for him have I offended. Who is here so
vile that will not love his country? If any, speak;
for him have I offended. I pause for a reply.

ALL. None, Brutus, none.

BRUTUS. Then none have I offended. I have done no more to
Caesar than you shall do to Brutus. The question of
his death is enrolled in the Capitol; his glory not
extenuated, wherein he was worthy, nor his offences
enforced, for which he suffered death.
Enter ANTONY and others, with CAESAR's body
Here comes his body, mourned by Mark Antony: who,
though he had no hand in his death, shall receive
the benefit of his dying, a place in the
commonwealth; as which of you shall not? With this
I depart,—that, as I slew my best lover for the
good of Rome, I have the same dagger for myself,
when it shall please my country to need my death.

ALL. Live, Brutus! live, live!

FIRST CITIZEN. Bring him with triumph home unto his house.

SECOND CITIZEN. Give him a statue with his ancestors.

THIRD CITIZEN. Let him be Caesar.

FOURTH CITIZEN. Caesar's better parts
Shall be crown'd in Brutus.

FIRST CITIZEN. We'll bring him to his house
With shouts and clamours.

BRUTUS. My countrymen,—

SECOND CITIZEN. Peace, silence! Brutus speaks.

FIRST CITIZEN. Peace, ho!

BRUTUS. Good countrymen, let me depart alone,
And, for my sake, stay here with Antony:
Do grace to Caesar's corpse, and grace his speech
Tending to Caesar's glories; which Mark Antony,
By our permission, is allow'd to make.
I do entreat you, not a man depart,
Save I alone, till Antony have spoke.

Exit

FIRST CITIZEN. Stay, ho! and let us hear Mark Antony.

THIRD CITIZEN. Let him go up into the public chair;
We'll hear him. Noble Antony, go up.

ANTONY. For Brutus's sake, I am beholding to you.

Goes into the pulpit

FOURTH CITIZEN. What does he say of Brutus?

THIRD CITIZEN. He says, for Brutus's sake,
He finds himself beholding to us all.

FOURTH CITIZEN. 'Twere best he speak no harm of Brutus here.

FIRST CITIZEN. This Caesar was a tyrant.

THIRD CITIZEN. Nay, that's certain:
We are blest that Rome is rid of him.

SECOND CITIZEN. Peace! let us hear what Antony can say.

ANTONY. You gentle Romans,--

CITIZENS. Peace, ho! let us hear him.

ANTONY. Friends, Romans, countrymen, lend me your ears;
I come to bury Caesar, not to praise him.
The evil that men do lives after them;
The good is oft interred with their bones;
So let it be with Caesar. The noble Brutus
Hath told you Caesar was ambitious:
If it were so, it was a grievous fault,
And grievously hath Caesar answer'd it.
Here, under leave of Brutus and the rest--

For Brutus is an honourable man;
So are they all, all honourable men—
Come I to speak in Caesar's funeral.
He was my friend, faithful and just to me:
But Brutus says he was ambitious;
And Brutus is an honourable man.
He hath brought many captives home to Rome
Whose ransoms did the general coffers fill:
Did this in Caesar seem ambitious?
When that the poor have cried, Caesar hath wept:
Ambition should be made of sterner stuff:
Yet Brutus says he was ambitious;
And Brutus is an honourable man.
You all did see that on the Lupercal
I thrice presented him a kingly crown,
Which he did thrice refuse: was this ambition?
Yet Brutus says he was ambitious;
And, sure, he is an honourable man.
I speak not to disprove what Brutus spoke,
But here I am to speak what I do know.
You all did love him once, not without cause:
What cause withholds you then, to mourn for him?
O judgment! thou art fled to brutish beasts,
And men have lost their reason. Bear with me;
My heart is in the coffin there with Caesar,
And I must pause till it come back to me.

First Citizen. Methinks there is much reason in his sayings.

Second Citizen. If thou consider rightly of the matter,
Caesar has had great wrong.

Third Citizen. Has he, masters?
I fear there will a worse come in his place.

Fourth Citizen. Mark'd ye his words? He would not take the crown;
Therefore 'tis certain he was not ambitious.

First Citizen. If it be found so, some will dear abide it.

Second Citizen. Poor soul! his eyes are red as fire with weeping.

THIRD CITIZEN. There's not a nobler man in Rome than Antony.

FOURTH CITIZEN. Now mark him, he begins again to speak.

ANTONY. But yesterday the word of Caesar might
Have stood against the world; now lies he there.
And none so poor to do him reverence.
O masters, if I were disposed to stir
Your hearts and minds to mutiny and rage,
I should do Brutus wrong, and Cassius wrong,
Who, you all know, are honourable men:
I will not do them wrong; I rather choose
To wrong the dead, to wrong myself and you,
Than I will wrong such honourable men.
But here's a parchment with the seal of Caesar;
I found it in his closet, 'tis his will:
Let but the commons hear this testament—
Which, pardon me, I do not mean to read—
And they would go and kiss dead Caesar's wounds
And dip their napkins in his sacred blood,
Yea, beg a hair of him for memory,
And, dying, mention it within their wills,
Bequeathing it as a rich legacy
Unto their issue.

FOURTH CITIZEN. We'll hear the will: read it, Mark Antony.

ALL. The will, the will! we will hear Caesar's will.

ANTONY. Have patience, gentle friends, I must not read it;
It is not meet you know how Caesar loved you.
You are not wood, you are not stones, but men;
And, being men, bearing the will of Caesar,
It will inflame you, it will make you mad:
'Tis good you know not that you are his heirs;
For, if you should, O, what would come of it!

FOURTH CITIZEN. Read the will; we'll hear it, Antony;
You shall read us the will, Caesar's will.

ANTONY. Will you be patient? will you stay awhile?
I have o'ershot myself to tell you of it:

I fear I wrong the honourable men
Whose daggers have stabb'd Caesar; I do fear it.

FOURTH CITIZEN. They were traitors: honourable men!

ALL. The will! the testament!

SECOND CITIZEN. They were villains, murderers: the will! read the will.

ANTONY. You will compel me, then, to read the will?
Then make a ring about the corpse of Caesar,
And let me show you him that made the will.
Shall I descend? and will you give me leave?

SEVERAL CITIZENS. Come down.

SECOND CITIZEN. Descend.

THIRD CITIZEN. You shall have leave.

ANTONY comes down

FOURTH CITIZEN. A ring; stand round.

FIRST CITIZEN. Stand from the hearse, stand from the body.

SECOND CITIZEN. Room for Antony, most noble Antony.

ANTONY. Nay, press not so upon me; stand far off.

SEVERAL CITIZENS. Stand back; room; bear back.

ANTONY. If you have tears, prepare to shed them now.
You all do know this mantle: I remember
The first time ever Caesar put it on;
'Twas on a summer's evening, in his tent,
That day he overcame the Nervii:
Look, in this place ran Cassius's dagger through:
See what a rent the envious Casca made:
Through this the well-beloved Brutus stabb'd;
And as he pluck'd his cursed steel away,
Mark how the blood of Caesar follow'd it,
As rushing out of doors, to be resolved
If Brutus so unkindly knock'd, or no;
For Brutus, as you know, was Caesar's angel:
Judge, O you gods, how dearly Caesar loved him!
This was the most unkindest cut of all;
For when the noble Caesar saw him stab,
Ingratitude, more strong than traitors' arms,

Quite vanquish'd him: then burst his mighty heart;
And, in his mantle muffling up his face,
Even at the base of Pompey's statue,
Which all the while ran blood, great Caesar fell.
O, what a fall was there, my countrymen!
Then I, and you, and all of us fell down,
Whilst bloody treason flourish'd over us.
O, now you weep; and, I perceive, you feel
The dint of pity: these are gracious drops.
Kind souls, what, weep you when you but behold
Our Caesar's vesture wounded? Look you here,
Here is himself, marr'd, as you see, with traitors.

FIRST CITIZEN. O piteous spectacle!

SECOND CITIZEN. O noble Caesar!

THIRD CITIZEN. O woful day!

FOURTH CITIZEN. O traitors, villains!

FIRST CITIZEN. O most bloody sight!

SECOND CITIZEN. We will be revenged.

ALL. Revenge! About! Seek! Burn! Fire! Kill! Slay!
Let not a traitor live!

ANTONY. Stay, countrymen.

FIRST CITIZEN. Peace there! hear the noble Antony.

SECOND CITIZEN. We'll hear him, we'll follow him, we'll die with him.

ANTONY. Good friends, sweet friends, let me not stir you up
To such a sudden flood of mutiny.
They that have done this deed are honourable:
What private griefs they have, alas, I know not,
That made them do it: they are wise and honourable,
And will, no doubt, with reasons answer you.
I come not, friends, to steal away your hearts:
I am no orator, as Brutus is;
But, as you know me all, a plain blunt man,
That love my friend; and that they know full well
That gave me public leave to speak of him:
For I have neither wit, nor words, nor worth,

Action, nor utterance, nor the power of speech,
To stir men's blood: I only speak right on;
I tell you that which you yourselves do know;
Show you sweet Caesar's wounds, poor poor dumb mouths,
And bid them speak for me: but were I Brutus,
And Brutus Antony, there were an Antony
Would ruffle up your spirits and put a tongue
In every wound of Caesar that should move
The stones of Rome to rise and mutiny.

All. We'll mutiny.

First Citizen. We'll burn the house of Brutus.

Third Citizen. Away, then! come, seek the conspirators.

Antony. Yet hear me, countrymen; yet hear me speak.

All. Peace, ho! Hear Antony. Most noble Antony!

Antony. Why, friends, you go to do you know not what:
Wherein hath Caesar thus deserved your loves?
Alas, you know not: I must tell you then:
You have forgot the will I told you of.

All. Most true. The will! Let's stay and hear the will.

Antony. Here is the will, and under Caesar's seal.
To every Roman citizen he gives,
To every several man, seventy-five drachmas.

Second Citizen. Most noble Caesar! We'll revenge his death.

Third Citizen. O royal Caesar!

Antony. Hear me with patience.

All. Peace, ho!

Antony. Moreover, he hath left you all his walks,
His private arbours and new-planted orchards,
On this side Tiber; he hath left them you,
And to your heirs for ever, common pleasures,
To walk abroad, and recreate yourselves.
Here was a Caesar! when comes such another?

First Citizen. Never, never. Come, away, away!
We'll burn his body in the holy place,

And with the brands fire the traitors' houses.
Take up the body.

SECOND CITIZEN. Go fetch fire.

THIRD CITIZEN. Pluck down benches.

FOURTH CITIZEN. Pluck down forms, windows, any thing.

Exeunt Citizens with the body

ANTONY. Now let it work. Mischief, thou art afoot,
Take thou what course thou wilt!

Discussion Questions

Julius Caesar

1. How does Antony establish Caesar's *ethos*? What evidence does he use to suggest Caesar has the three Aristotelian aspects of *ethos*—moral virtue (*arête*), practical wisdom (*phronesis*), and/or good-will (*eunoia*)?

2. Mark in the text and then count up any images Brutus uses. Mark and count the images used by Antony. Who uses more and to what effect?

3. How do both men rouse the passions of the crowd? Which does so more wisely?

4. At what points is narrative used? What is the audience's response to it?

5. How does Antony demonstrate the emotion he seeks to evoke in his audience? What emotions does he evoke that he does not personally embody?

6. Why does Antony pretend to have no talent for speaking well?

____

____

____

____

7. How does Shakespeare demonstrate the danger of *pathos*? Is it dangerous?

____

____

____

____

8. In a situation similar to this, which would involve so much *pathos*, would you wish to be the first speaker or the last? Why is one position more advantageous?

____

____

____

____

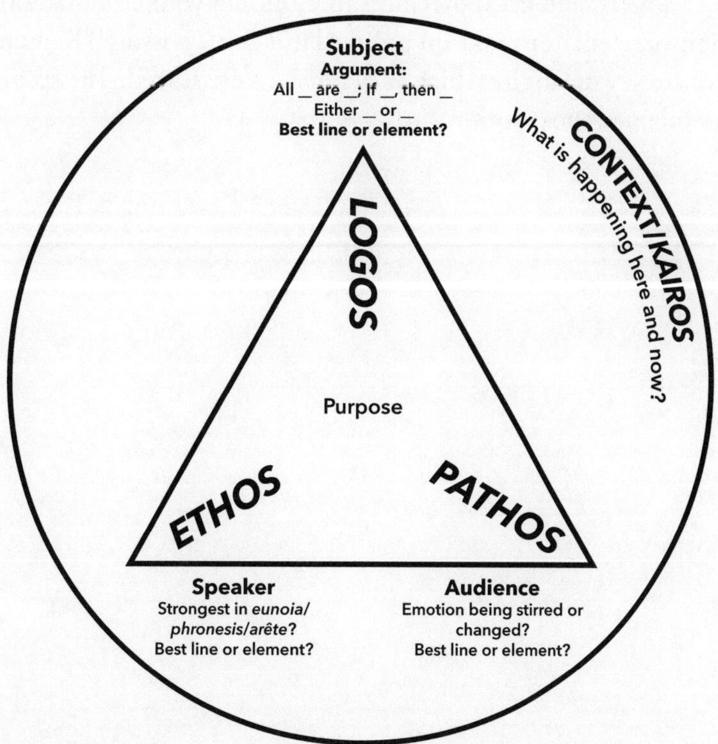

Figure 9. Rhetorical analysis diagram.

WORKSHOP:
Conjuring the Emotions

One cannot *command* the emotions: "Be sad!" "Be angry!" Instead, one must *conjure* them.

In groups of two, explore the emotion assigned to you by reading what Aristotle has to say about it (see 1378a–1388b; excerpts of these sections from Aristotle's *Rhetoric* Book 2 are included in the appendix on page 355). One person must be prepared to give a short definition of the assigned emotion, based on Aristotle's discussion in the text. He or she should also briefly explain toward whom the emotion is felt as well as what causes it.

Figure 10. Typical theater masks showing the emotions of happiness and sadness.

Pay careful attention to what Aristotle says in those definitions about images, or mental pictures. For example, the pleasure felt in anger is "because the thoughts dwell upon the act of vengeance, and the images then called up cause pleasure, like the images called up in dreams" (1378b). Shame, too, is a "mental picture of disgrace" (1384a). Again, the emotions are closely tied to the imagination, that faculty of producing and reproducing images.

Then, on pages 68–69 or another sheet of paper, the second person should write a short speech (5–10 sentences) that aims to induce in your classmates the assigned emotion. (Please keep the topics lighthearted; don't take on political hot-button issues!) Remember, vivid imagery, description, and narrative are key means by which the emotions are stirred. The second person will deliver this speech after the first has explained the emotion itself.

	Definition/State of Mind	Toward Whom Is It Felt?	What Causes It?
Anger (Book 2, part 2)			
Fear (Book 2, part 5)			
Confidence (Book 2, part 5)			
Shame (Book 2, part 6)			
Pity (Book 2, part 8)			
Indignation (Book 2, part 9)			
Envy (Book 2, part 10)			
Emulation (Book 2, part 11)			

On the lines provided, write a short speech (5–10 sentences) that aims to induce in your classmates your assigned emotion. (The sections from Aristotle's *Rhetoric* are included in the appendix of this book.)

1. Provoke **anger** in your audience. See Aristotle's *Rhetoric* Book 2, part 2 (1378a–1380a) on anger in the appendix on page 355.

2. Instill **fear** in your audience. Book 2, part 5 (1382a–1383a; appendix, page 357).

3. Stimulate **confidence** in your audience. Book 2, part 5 (1383a–1383b; appendix, page 357).

4. Induce **shame** in your audience. Book 2, part 6 (1383b–1385a; appendix, page 359).

5. Engender **pity** in your audience. Book 2, part 8 (1385b–1386b; appendix, page 360).

6. Prompt **indignation** in your audience. Book 2, part 9 (1386b–1387b; appendix, page 362).

7. Produce **envy** in your audience. Book 2, part 10 (1387b–1388a; appendix, page 363).

8. Generate **emulation** in your audience. Book 2, part 11 (1388a–1388b; appendix, page 364).

PRESENTATION:
Poetry Recitation

SPOTLIGHT
Posture

Deliver the following poems or passages with careful attention to *pathos*. What emotions are felt by the speaker? How can you use your volume, rhythm, and pitch to convey those emotions? In this presentation, we will also add attention to posture. Stand up straight—no slumping, rocking, or leg-crossing.

Holy Sonnet 10: Death Be Not Proud

by John Donne

Death, be not proud, though some have called thee
Mighty and dreadful, for thou art not so;
For those whom thou think'st thou dost overthrow
Die not, poor Death, nor yet canst thou kill me.
From rest and sleep, which but thy pictures be,
Much pleasure; then from thee much more must flow,
And soonest our best men with thee do go,
Rest of their bones, and soul's delivery.
Thou art slave to fate, chance, kings, and desperate men,
And dost with poison, war, and sickness dwell,
And poppy or charms can make us sleep as well
And better than thy stroke; why swell'st thou then?
One short sleep past, we wake eternally
And death shall be no more; Death, thou shalt die.

Sonnet 29

by William Shakespeare

When, in disgrace with fortune and men's eyes,
I all alone beweep my outcast state,
And trouble deaf heaven with my bootless cries,
And look upon myself, and curse my fate,
Wishing me like to one more rich in hope,
Featur'd like him, like him with friends possess'd,
Desiring this man's art and that man's scope,
With what I most enjoy contented least;
Yet in these thoughts myself almost despising,
Haply I think on thee, and then my state,
Like to the lark at break of day arising
From sullen earth, sings hymns at heaven's gate;

For thy sweet love remember'd such wealth brings
That then I scorn to change my state with kings.

Aureng-Zebe, act 4, scene 1

by John Dryden

When I consider life, 'tis all a cheat;
Yet, fooled with hope, men favour the deceit;
Trust on, and think to-morrow will repay:
To-morrow's falser than the former day;
Lies worse; and while it says, we shall be blessed
With some new joys, cuts off what we possessed.
Strange cozenage! none would live past years again,
Yet all hope pleasure in what yet remain;
And, from the dregs of life, think to receive
What the first sprightly running could not give.
I'm tired with waiting for this chemic gold,
Which fools us young, and beggars us when old.

The World Is Too Much With Us

by William Wordsworth

The world is too much with us; late and soon,
Getting and spending, we lay waste our powers;—
Little we see in Nature that is ours;
We have given our hearts away, a sordid boon!
This Sea that bares her bosom to the moon;
The winds that will be howling at all hours,
And are up-gathered now like sleeping flowers;
For this, for everything, we are out of tune;
It moves us not. Great God! I'd rather be
A Pagan suckled in a creed outworn;
So might I, standing on this pleasant lea,
Have glimpses that would make me less forlorn;
Have sight of Proteus rising from the sea;
Or hear old Triton blow his wreathèd horn.

Sonnet 43

by Elizabeth Barrett Browning

How do I love thee? Let me count the ways.
I love thee to the depth and breadth and height
My soul can reach, when feeling out of sight
For the ends of being and ideal grace.

I love thee to the level of every day's
Most quiet need, by sun and candle-light.
I love thee freely, as men strive for right.
I love thee purely, as they turn from praise.
I love thee with the passion put to use
In my old griefs, and with my childhood's faith.
I love thee with a love I seemed to lose
With my lost saints. I love thee with the breath,
Smiles, tears, of all my life; and, if God choose,
I shall but love thee better after death.

God's Grandeur

by Gerard Manley Hopkins

The world is charged with the grandeur of God.
It will flame out, like shining from shook foil;
It gathers to a greatness, like the ooze of oil
Crushed. Why do men then now not reck his rod?
Generations have trod, have trod, have trod;
And all is seared with trade; bleared, smeared with toil;
And wears man's smudge and shares man's smell: the soil
Is bare now, nor can foot feel, being shod.
And for all this, nature is never spent;
There lives the dearest freshness deep down things;
And though the last lights off the black West went
Oh, morning, at the brown brink eastward, springs—
Because the Holy Ghost over the bent
World broods with warm breast and with ah! bright wings.

The Merchant of Venice, Act 3 Scene 1

by William Shakespeare

. . . He hath disgraced me, and
hindered me half a million; laughed at my losses,
mocked at my gains, scorned my nation, thwarted my
bargains, cooled my friends, heated mine
enemies; and what's his reason? I am a Jew. Hath
not a Jew eyes? hath not a Jew hands, organs,
dimensions, senses, affections, passions? fed with
the same food, hurt with the same weapons, subject
to the same diseases, healed by the same means,
warmed and cooled by the same winter and summer, as
a Christian is? If you prick us, do we not bleed?

if you tickle us, do we not laugh? if you poison
us, do we not die? and if you wrong us, shall we not
revenge? If we are like you in the rest, we will
resemble you in that. If a Jew wrong a Christian,
what is his humility? Revenge. If a Christian
wrong a Jew, what should his sufferance be by
Christian example? Why, revenge. The villainy you
teach me, I will execute, and it shall go hard but I
will better the instruction.

Job 30:16–26 (NIV)

And now my life ebbs away;
days of suffering grip me.
Night pierces my bones;
my gnawing pains never rest.
In His great power God becomes like clothing to me;
He binds me like the neck of my garment.
He throws me into the mud,
and I am reduced to dust and ashes.

I cry out to you, God, but you do not answer;
I stand up, but you merely look at me.
You turn on me ruthlessly;
with the might of your hand you attack me.
You snatch me up and drive me before the wind;
you toss me about in the storm.
I know you will bring me down to death,
to the place appointed for all the living.

Surely no one lays a hand on a broken man
when he cries for help in his distress.
Have I not wept for those in trouble?
Has not my soul grieved for the poor?
Yet when I hoped for good, evil came;
when I looked for light, then came darkness.

Consult a poetry anthology for other choices, such as the following:

- "Do Not Go Gentle into That Good Night" by Dylan Thomas
- "Hap" by Thomas Hardy
- "When I have Fears That I May Cease to Be" by John Keats
- "Mother to Son" by Langston Hughes
- Psalm 13

4

CHAPTER 4

Logos in the Enthymeme: Abbreviating the Syllogism

(1354a) Now, the framers of the current treatises on rhetoric have constructed but a small portion of that art. The modes of persuasion are the only true constituents of the art: everything else is merely accessory. These writers, however, say nothing about enthymemes, which are the substance of rhetorical persuasion, but deal mainly with non-essentials.

. . .

(1354b) About the orator's proper modes of persuasion they have nothing to tell us; nothing, that is, about how to gain skill in enthymemes.

. . .

(1355a) It is clear, then, that rhetorical study, in its strict sense, is concerned with the modes of persuasion. Persuasion is clearly a sort of demonstration, since we are most fully persuaded when we consider a thing to have been demonstrated. The orator's demonstration is an enthymeme, and this is, in general, the most effective of the modes of persuasion. The enthymeme is a sort of syllogism, and the consideration of syllogisms of all kinds, without distinction, is the business of dialectic, either of dialectic as a whole or of one of its branches. It follows plainly, therefore, that he who is best able to see how and from what elements a syllogism is produced will also be best skilled in the enthymeme, when he has further learnt what its subject-matter is and in what respects it differs from the syllogism of strict logic. The true and the approximately true are apprehended by the same faculty; it may also be noted that men have a sufficient natural instinct for what is true, and usually do arrive at the truth. Hence the man who makes a good guess at truth is likely to make a good guess at probabilities.

. . .

(1395b) We now come to the Enthymemes, and will begin the subject with some general consideration of the proper way of looking for them, and then proceed to what is a distinct question, the lines of argument to be embodied in them. It has already been pointed out that the Enthymeme is a syllogism, and in what sense it is so. We have also noted the differences between it and the syllogism of dialectic. Thus we must not carry its reasoning too far back, or the length of our argument

> will cause obscurity: nor must we put in all the steps that lead to our conclusion, or we shall waste words in saying what is manifest. It is this simplicity that makes the uneducated more effective than the educated when addressing popular audiences—makes them, as the poets tell us, "charm the crowd's ears more finely." Educated men lay down broad general principles; uneducated men argue from common knowledge and draw obvious conclusions. We must not, therefore, start from any and every accepted opinion, but only from those we have defined—those accepted by our judges or by those whose authority they recognize: (1396a) and there must, moreover, be no doubt in the minds of most, if not all, of our judges that the opinions put forward really are of this sort. We should also base our arguments upon probabilities as well as upon certainties.

Reasoning with Words

Let's pause for a moment. Remember where we are in the world of rhetoric. According to Aristotle, rhetoric has three appeals—three reasons and three reasons only why a person would change his mind about anything. Suppose, for example, your father is trying to convince you to start running track, but you are set against it. If you trust your dad, then you just might reconsider. After all, he's usually right about such things—it was his idea that you take up swimming, which you ended up loving—and you have no reason to doubt him this time. In this case, *ethos* is the persuader; you trust him. Or maybe you have been itching to run a marathon for years, and your friends are all going out for track, too—a tempting combination. Here, *pathos* wins—your emotions are the deciding factor. Finally, it could be that you realize that, as much as you hate to run, you really ought to get in shape. That is, *logos* prompts you to commit to a grueling 5 a.m. running schedule.

If *ethos* is the bulk of persuasion (even "almost the whole of persuasion" for Aristotle), it is *logos* that is Aristotle's favorite of the three appeals. What else would we expect from a philosopher? In fact, rather than defining rhetoric as buttery-smooth speech or a certain *je ne sais quoi* for winning people over, he has brought all of its factors under logical scrutiny, including the passions themselves, which he baptizes in the cool waters of reason.

Reason—or, more precisely, *logos*—is the issue of this chapter. As the word has made its way into the English language, "logos" has proven slippery. Pinning down its meaning is no small task. At times, the term is translated straightforwardly as "word," but thinking of it as something just written or spoken would be incomplete. What about the more familiar English word *logic*, which is a derivative of the Greek word *logos*? Yes, certainly the two are related, but again, a simple identification of the two would be misleading. But a comprehensive, foolproof understanding of Aristotle's favorite rhetorical appeal is not necessary for our purposes. Suffice it to say that *logos* is the reasoning that can be given form by words. Sometimes it is thought of as "the facts," but the truth is that it is much more than mere facts; *logos* is the argument itself. *Logos* is an ordering of our own thinking through the patterned forms of thought that words make known.

Logos *is the reasoning;*
it is the argument itself.

Even though Aristotle would like audiences to be moved by reason alone, he knows that human nature makes this an impossibility. So he includes a strange warning from a philosopher: Rhetors shouldn't be so fastidious! He knows that philosophical speakers are often hard for the average audience member to follow and are, therefore, less persuasive. Their reasoning can be overly complex, with their logic somehow seeming *too* careful. His solution for this overly meticulous penchant for the rational is the **enthymeme**.

The Body of Persuasion

"Enthymeme" may be a new word for you, but it is one you'd do well to warm up to, for enthymeme is at the heart of Aristotle's *Rhetoric*. You can think of the enthymeme as unspoken logic, and being enthymematic—that is, being tacitly logical—as your rhetorical goal.

An enthymeme is
an abbreviated syllogism.

An enthymeme is an abbreviated syllogism; in other words, it is a line of reasoning that is purposefully incomplete. The word itself helps us understand its meaning: *en* plus *thumos* can be translated "in the mind/spirit." That's just what an enthymeme does: It requires the audience members to infer the missing information. Or, perhaps more accurately, it requires that they fill in what is missing by supplying something they already hold in mind. That is to say, enthymemes work because the rhetor can appeal to axioms or premises that the audience already sees as true. For example, take the following famous categorical syllogism:

> Major premise: *All men are mortal.*
> Minor premise: *Socrates is a man.*
> Conclusion: *Socrates is mortal.*

If you were to try to introduce this syllogism in a speech, you would bore your audience to tears. They don't actually *need* all of those steps; in fact, your listeners would enjoy it more if you left one out. An enthymeme does exactly that: By leaving out either a premise or the conclusion, an enthymeme makes this kind of reasoning more palatable, allowing the listeners to take an active role by letting them mentally fill in the gap. Much more interesting to hear would be this: "Socrates is mortal; after all, he is a man!" Notice that the major premise is entirely omitted, and why not? The audience members don't need to be told that all men are mortal; they can easily supply that premise on their own, and the rhetor is right to assume their ability to do so. By requiring them to fill in that missing link, something remarkable happens: They help *persuade themselves* of the issue at hand.

Again, the provided example is called a **categorical syllogism**. What about creating an enthymeme with an if-then argument?

Strict logic would read the following:

> *If X, then Y*
> *X*
> *Therefore, Y*

Now, with clauses filling in for *X* and *Y*, we could make the following argument:

> Major premise: *If John has lied to us, then he shouldn't be trusted.*
> Minor premise: *John lied to us.*
> Conclusion: *Therefore, John shouldn't be trusted.*

But this kind of explicit logic, tiresome in speech, is better shortened: "John has lied to us, so we shouldn't trust him." (The major premise is omitted.) Of course, other forms are possible, too: "Why trust John? Everyone knows that liars shouldn't be trusted." (The minor premise is missing.) What about leaving out the conclusion? You can do that as well: "John has lied to us, and liars shouldn't be trusted." In this last example, less can be more; if it would exasperate the audience to include the obvious—and it often would do so—then the conclusion should remain unstated.

There is one more syllogism we ought to consider: the **disjunctive syllogism**. The formal structure is seen in the following example:

> Major premise: *Either you love your family, or you love me.*
> Minor premise: *You love your family.*
> Conclusion: *Therefore, you don't love me.*

An enthymeme could be made in a number of ways, but here's just one: "You love your family, so you must not love me." (The major premise is omitted altogether.) The idea is to set up an either-or situation and prove one half is true by negating the other half. The opposite is valid, too—disprove one side, thus proving the other: "You don't love me, so you must love your family."

What does this mean for you as a rhetor? It means you must not abandon logic—its rigorous force makes it a powerful persuader—and neither should you always include every step in the logical chain. Remember, Aristotle is talking to a crowd of philosophers who love syllogisms and are tempted to use them to reason with crowds. And if they give in to that temptation, they may never persuade their audience. The philosopher's commitment to pure logic could ultimately harm the community if that philosopher does not present the truth in a winsome way. The trouble is, hearing a syllogism is like hearing a math problem aloud: no fun. Aristotle recommends substituting the enthymeme; it's shorter and sweeter, and it appeals to principles and beliefs that the audience has already taken to heart.

And now for a warning. You now know that the enthymeme is an abbreviated syllogism, and you can probably guess why that might be dangerous. Inasmuch as it may bore the audience to include every last step of the reasoning, leaving out some of that reasoning could cause problems. When words are flying past, there is little time to dissect a speaker's enthymemes, to chart them into a complete logical syllogism and to determine their validity, not to mention their truth. Instead, the enthymeme admittedly plays fast and loose with reasoning, and the result could be sloppy logic and unsound conclusions. That's why Aristotle recommends that rhetors pay careful attention to enthymemes—after all, they are virtually unavoidable—and be ready to catch and dismantle the faulty ones when they race past.

A rhetor's best defense against specious[1] enthymemes, then, is training in logic, making one ready for the challenge of enthymeme spotting. Keep in mind that a good—that is, valid—enthymeme leaves out a statement that people generally agree to, one that the audience can easily supply. An example would be "all men are mortal" in the aforementioned categorical syllogism; it's a truth everyone acknowledges. Leaving out a proposition that is not evident, or is controversial, on the other hand, can weaken an argument or fundamentally mislead an audience. Also, being enthymematic doesn't mean being lazy or confusing. If a speaker leaves out important information accidentally because he or she isn't tracking the argument well, that's not an example of being enthymematic; it's an example of being careless or incompetent.

Enthymematic Reasoning

One of the great insights we can draw from Aristotle is that all of persuasion, not just strict *logos*, can function syllogistically. That is, a speaker's character (*ethos*) and an audience's emotion (*pathos*) can operate like an enthymeme.[2] We saw in chapters 2 and 3 that Aristotle shows how the other means of persuasion—the speaker's character and the audience's emotions—are governed by reason. *Pathos* can be shown to be in line with *logos* or out of line with it. Strong *ethos* is the logical result of exactly three aspects: virtue, knowledge, and goodwill. By showing *ethos* and *pathos* to be potentially logical (or at least to participate in *logos*), Aristotle reveals that these appeals can function just like a syllogism. Here's an example that shows how this might work concerning *pathos*:

1. Or, fallacious.
2. For more on this idea, see Jakob Wisse, *Ethos and Pathos from Aristotle to Cicero* (Amsterdam: Hakkert, 1989), 24–25.

> Major premise: *Injustice makes us angry.* (Or, properly stated: Injustice ⟶ anger.)
>
> Minor premise: *The case being discussed is an instance of injustice.* (Injustice.)
>
> Conclusion: *Therefore, we should be angry.* (Therefore, anger.)

Of course, we would never speak in such a manner, but you can imagine the ways that this line of reasoning could loom in the background of all that a rhetor might say in making an argument that attempts to rouse the audience's ire. Notice that the emotion of anger is being dealt with rationally by the speaker and is potentially justified rationally for the listener, too, even though that reasoning might remain unstated. Here is an example of a similar way of understanding *ethos*:

> Major premise: *People who are kind to others have good character.* (Or, properly stated: Kind people are people of good character.)
>
> Minor premise: *I have been kind to others.* (I am a kind person.)
>
> Conclusion: *Therefore, I have good character.* (Therefore, I am a person of good character.)

In other words, a person's character is logically based—it is *enthymematically established*—meaning that *ethos* can be demonstrated deductively, for the signs of virtue point to the reality of virtue. The claim is this: *Logos* is not the only appeal that is relevant when thinking about the enthymeme, for *pathos* and *ethos* can also operate in this fundamentally logical way. Perhaps this is why Aristotle introduces the enthymeme early in his *Rhetoric*, calling it the "substance of rhetorical persuasion" (1354a).

By showing how *ethos* and *pathos* can be ordered as thoughts and judgments—that is, they can be rational or reasonable—Aristotle turns what can seem otherwise mystifying into something understandable. And he also allows us to rethink *ethos* and *pathos*: No more must they be seen as signs of a weak-minded audience (as Socrates seemed to think at times); instead, they can expand the notion of rationality into other aspects of the human person. And doesn't this make sense? After all, we usually have *reasons* for trusting someone, and we usually have *reasons* for feeling as we do. That's great news for those of us wanting to establish credibility and handle emotions while avoiding unethical manipulation.

But passing *ethos* and *pathos* through the filter of reason does something even more: It offers the audience a way of thinking about their own emotional responses. They can be linked—and indeed, should be linked!—to thought. *Pathos* is vital because it moves humans to act, but it must be guided by and checked by reason, lest it be blind and chaotic. Likewise, trusting another's *ethos* turns out to be a key persuader in many situations; testing that *ethos* against reason can keep an audience from trusting when trust is not due.

Rhetoric Is Not Dialectic

We can apply enthymeme even more broadly. If the enthymeme is based upon common opinion with abbreviated logic, one might see that all speech acts, not just those belonging to rhetoric proper, are built upon the enthymeme, for one constantly shortens in order to communicate. For example, one might say, "This just citizen did no harm." But such a statement begs many a question: What is justice? What is harm? What is a citizen? Thus, all speech appears to have an enthymematic character. If such statements ("This just citizen did no harm") are going to be meaningful in any real sense, then the speaker must assume many shared beliefs from the outset. Implied within Aristotle's emphasis on the enthymeme is this: Communities—and communications—are based upon the very truths they tacitly share.

In thinking about enthymematic reasoning in this way, we can also come to understand its special character. As we have already seen, rhetoric is not dialectic: Each discipline has its own end. In fact, following Aristotle, we might conclude that rhetoric's *raison d'être*, or the reason for its existence, is to address those matters in which ***apodeixis*** (i.e., absolute logical certainty) is impossible—that is, within everyday human life. The study of rhetoric teaches us to be sensitive to what people find persuasive, whether or not those arguments are logically certain. Indeed, it is where certainty is unavailable that arguments *must* be made. We do not argue, for example, about quantities; instead, we just make more accurate calculations. And we do not argue about what is obvious or demonstrable; instead, we just examine the data more closely. Rhetoric must step in where certainty eludes us, and that is, of course, most of our lived experience.

Another way of thinking about it is this: Rhetoric can be philosophical, and philosophy can be rhetorical, but the two are *not* identical. It is the enthymeme in particular that best distinguishes the philosopher from the rhetor. Whereas Socrates, the dialectician par excellence, wants to ask, *What is the nature of piety?* Aristotle—in his *Rhetoric*, at least—is on the side of the rhetor, willing to grant that there is a shared, workable understanding of the relevant concepts, adequate enough for meaningful and productive argumentation to take place. That assumed understanding, in short, makes possible the enthymeme, or abbreviated reasoning. That is, common opinions can be left unstated because they are agreed upon.

The rhetor, then, may not stop to define the virtue of piety definitively but instead will head into the world to find it and judge it in particular cases. In this instance, the rhetor, rather than arguing for a definition of the pious, may argue that a particular son has exhibited the virtue. Again, where Plato is trying to establish the axioms themselves, Aristotle is granting their truth and moving into the real world to make judgments about them.

Take a moment of sibling rivalry as an example. The father, acting as a dialectician, may attempt to prove to his eight-year-old daughter that her little brother has inherent human dignity and, thus, should be treated with kindness. When acting as a rhetor, the father has an equally ambitious aim, and one we can imagine much more appropriate to the child's circumstances: If he is able to persuade his daughter to share her markers with her brother, the father would consider his objective met. But notice that the two aims—that is, the dialectician's and the rhetor's—are not disconnected. In fact, it may very well be that the practice of sharing crayons becomes the early placeholder for the concept of dignity that will come later in the daughter's development. The daughter persuaded to share by her father-as-rhetor may develop habits that allow the idea of human dignity to be known later. Which, then, is better? Dialectic or rhetoric? This dispute is at least as old as the time of Plato and Aristotle, and it is an argument still being fought today.

Discussion Text:

Patrick Henry: "Give Me Liberty or Give Me Death!" (1775)[3]

Focus:

Enthymemes

The question of the moment was reconciliation or revolution. The relationship between the colonies and Great Britain had become so strained that it was at the point of breaking. It is just after this famous speech, delivered at the Second Virginia Convention, that the colony of Virginia voted to pass resolutions to form militias of defense against the British.

St. John's Church, Richmond, Virginia
March 23, 1775

Mr. President: No man thinks more highly than I do of the patriotism, as well as abilities, of the very worthy gentlemen who have just addressed the House. But different men often see the same subject in different lights; and, therefore, I hope it will not be thought disrespectful to those gentlemen if, entertaining as I do, opinions of a character very opposite to theirs, I shall speak forth my sentiments freely, and without reserve. This is no time for ceremony. The question before the House is one of awful moment to this country. For my own part, I consider it as nothing less than a question of freedom or slavery; and in proportion to the magnitude of the subject ought to be the freedom of the debate. It is only in this way that we can hope to arrive at truth, and fulfill the great responsibility which we hold to God and our country. Should I keep back my opinions at such a time, through fear of giving offence, I should consider myself as guilty of treason towards my country, and of an act of disloyalty toward the majesty of heaven, which I revere above all earthly kings.

Mr. President, it is natural to man to indulge in the illusions of hope. We are apt to shut our eyes against a painful truth, and listen to the song of that siren till she transforms us into beasts. Is this the part of wise men, engaged in a great and arduous struggle for liberty? Are we disposed to be of the number of those who, having eyes, see not, and, having ears, hear not, the things which so nearly concern their temporal salvation? For my part, whatever anguish of spirit it may cost, I am willing to know the whole truth; to know the worst, and to provide for it.

3. Patrick Henry, "Liberty or Death," March 23, 1775 speech, Second Virginia Convention, St. John's Church, Richmond, provided by the Patrick Henry Center For Individual Liberty—Speeches (online), http://www.patrickhenrycenter.com/Speeches.aspx#LIBERTY.

I have but one lamp by which my feet are guided; and that is the lamp of experience. I know of no way of judging of the future but by the past. And judging by the past, I wish to know what there has been in the conduct of the British ministry for the last ten years, to justify those hopes with which gentlemen have been pleased to solace themselves, and the House? Is it that insidious smile with which our petition has been lately received? Trust it not, sir; it will prove a snare to your feet. Suffer not yourselves to be betrayed with a kiss. Ask yourselves how this gracious reception of our petition comports with these war-like preparations which cover our waters and darken our land. Are fleets and armies necessary to a work of love and reconciliation? Have we shown ourselves so unwilling to be reconciled, that force must be called in to win back our love? Let us not deceive ourselves, sir. These are the implements of war and subjugation; the last arguments to which kings resort. I ask, gentlemen, sir, what means this martial array, if its purpose be not to force us to submission? Can gentlemen assign any other possible motive for it? Has Great Britain any enemy, in this quarter of the world, to call for all this accumulation of navies and armies? No, sir, she has none. They are meant for us; they can be meant for no other. They are sent over to bind and rivet upon us those chains which the British ministry have been so long forging. And what have we to oppose to them? Shall we try argument? Sir, we have been trying that for the last ten years. Have we anything new to offer upon the subject? Nothing. We have held the subject up in every light of which it is capable; but it has been all in vain. Shall we resort to entreaty and humble supplication? What terms shall we find which have not been already exhausted? Let us not, I beseech you, sir, deceive ourselves. Sir, we have done everything that could be done, to avert the storm which is now coming on. We have petitioned; we have remonstrated; we have supplicated; we have prostrated ourselves before the throne, and have implored its interposition to arrest the tyrannical hands of the ministry and Parliament. Our petitions have been slighted; our remonstrances have produced additional violence and insult; our supplications have been disregarded; and we have been spurned, with contempt, from the foot of the throne. In vain, after these things, may we indulge the fond hope of peace and reconciliation. There is no longer any room for hope. If we wish to be free, if we mean to preserve inviolate those inestimable privileges for which we have been so long contending, if we mean not basely to abandon the noble struggle in which we have been so long engaged, and which we have pledged ourselves never to abandon until the glorious object of our contest shall be obtained, we must fight! I repeat it, sir, we must fight! An appeal to arms and to the God of Hosts is all that is left us!

They tell us, sir, that we are weak; unable to cope with so formidable an adversary. But when shall we be stronger? Will it be the next week, or the next year? Will it be when we are totally disarmed, and when a British guard shall be stationed in every house? Shall we gather strength by irresolution and inaction? Shall we acquire the means of effectual resistance, by lying supinely on our backs, and hugging the delusive phantom of hope, until our enemies shall have bound us hand and foot? Sir, we are not weak if we make a proper use of those means which the God of nature hath placed in our power. Three millions of people, armed in the holy cause of liberty, and in such a country as that which we possess, are invincible by any force which our enemy can send against us. Besides, sir, we shall not fight our battles alone. There is a just God who presides over the destinies of nations; and who will raise up friends to fight our battles for us. The battle, sir, is not to the strong alone; it is to the vigilant, the active, the brave. Besides, sir, we have no election. If we were base enough to desire it, it is now too late to retire from the contest. There is no retreat but in submission and slavery! Our chains are forged! Their clanking may be heard on the plains of Boston! The war is inevitable and let it come! I repeat it, sir, let it come.

It is in vain, sir, to extenuate the matter. Gentlemen may cry, Peace, Peace but there is no peace. The war is actually begun! The next gale that sweeps from the north will bring to our ears the clash of resounding arms! Our brethren are already in the field! Why stand we here idle? What is it that gentlemen wish? What would they have? Is life so dear, or peace so sweet, as to be purchased at the price of chains and slavery? Forbid it, Almighty God! I know not what course others may take; but as for me, give me liberty or give me death!

Discussion Questions

"Give Me Liberty or Give Me Death!"

Search each paragraph for enthymemes (abbreviated syllogisms). Some of them are explicit, and some are implied enthymematic reasoning. You are looking for reasoning that implies a claim about a category of people—*all*, *no*, or *some* persons. Another type of relationship you should look for is the if-then and either-or. (Those words are clues themselves, but note that these relationships may also use other wording.)

1. Construct a hypothetical enthymeme (the major premise of a hypothetical if-then syllogism) from the final sentence in the first paragraph.

____

____

____

2. Construct an enthymeme from the second sentence of the second paragraph.

____

____

____

3. Find at least one enthymeme in the third paragraph.

____

____

____

4. Find at least one enthymeme in the fourth paragraph.

____

____

____

5. What is the disjunctive enthymeme (major premise) found in the last line of the final paragraph?

____

____

____

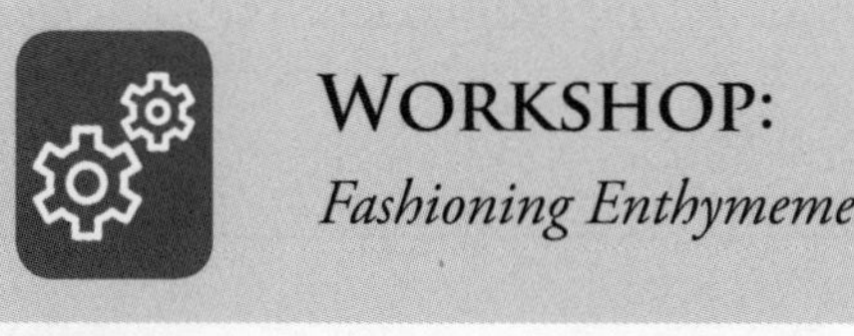

Workshop: *Fashioning Enthymemes* 1

Create two categorical syllogisms.

Syllogism A:

Major premise:

____

Minor premise:

____

Conclusion:

____

Syllogism B:

Major premise:

____

Minor premise:

____

Conclusion:

____

Next, turn each syllogism into an enthymeme by omitting either one of the premises or the conclusion.

Enthymeme 1:

____

Enthymeme 2:

____

Next, create two if-then arguments.

If-then argument A:

Major premise:

____

Minor premise:

____

Conclusion:

____

If-then argument B:

Major premise:

____

Minor premise:

____

Conclusion:

____

Now, transform each if-then argument into an enthymeme.

Enthymeme 3:

____

Enthymeme 4:

____

Finally, create two disjunctive syllogisms. Then transform each into an enthymeme.

Disjunctive syllogism A:

Major premise:

____

Minor premise:

____

Conclusion:

____

Disjunctive syllogism B:

Major premise:

____

Minor premise:

____

Conclusion:

____

Enthymeme 5:

____

Enthymeme 6:

____

Now that you've completed all six enthymemes, copy them onto note cards for the "Fill in the Enthymeme Competition" activity.

WORKSHOP: *Fill in the Enthymeme Competition* 2

For this activity, you and your classmates will need to collect the enthymemes you all have created in the previous workshop, write them on slips of paper, and mix them up in a bag. (You will need plenty of enthymemes for this competition.)

This activity is similar to playing the game *Password* or *Taboo*. The class should be divided into two (or more) groups. Two students at a time (from the same group) will come to the front. One student draws an enthymeme out of the bag and reads it out loud. The other person needs to fill in the missing premise or conclusion. The goal is to fill in as many enthymemes as possible within one minute.

For example, one student draws a slip of paper out, and she reads aloud, "If I am a cat, I have fleas. I am a cat." (This is an if-then argument.) Her partner would then guess the unspoken (not included) premise or conclusion: "I have fleas."

The next slip drawn may have an abbreviated categorical syllogism such as "No girls love cashews, and you're a girl." The missing piece is "You don't love cashews."

For the disjunctive enthymeme of "Either Tom has a pickup truck or he has a motorcycle, and Tom does not have a pickup," the student guessing should answer, "Tom has a motorcycle." After one minute, tally up the correct answers and switch to the next team. The team with the highest score at the end is the winner.

As a reminder, here are three patterns that will be used:

Categorical	**If-then**	**Disjunctive**
All X are Y.	*If X, then Y.*	*Either X or Y.*
Z is an X.	*X.*	*Not X*
Therefore, Z is a Y.	*Then Y.*	*Then Y.*

Presentation:
Read Aloud Story Time

Spotlight
Audience Engagement

Choose a children's book to read to younger students. Your assignment is to make the story come alive for your little friends. Just as we did in the previous presentations, we will be paying close attention to vocal quality, but that's not all. You'll need to be aware of your body, too. For example, be sure to hold the book in such a way that the pictures are visible to your audience—not just to you!—almost all of the time.

Rules for engaging the audience:

A. **Be friendly.** Greet your reading buddies, asking their names, and share your own.

B. **Be organized.** Announce the title, author, and illustrator of the story before you begin. When you finish the story, signal the ending by closing the book and looking at the audience. Be sure to say goodbye.

C. **Be interesting.** Use vocal inflection, not only varying your voice for different characters but also mirroring what's happening in the story—speed up, for example, during a hurried conversation.

D. **Ask questions.** *What's your name? What was your favorite part of the story?* And don't be afraid to pause every now and then and ask comprehension questions—*Why is the hare so sure he'll win the race?*

About the book itself:

Do you notice any enthymematic reasoning in your story?

Often, children's stories have a moral to them that can be summed up logically. Does your story have a moral, and what is it?

Can you create any logical constructions from the narrative?

All / No / Some are . . .

If . . . , then . . .

Either . . . or . . .

Alternate Activity

Instead of a classroom setting, you can choose one of your own books or a library book to read to a younger sibling, neighbor, or friend.

Chapter 5

More on *Logos*: Top-Down Versus Bottom-Up Reasoning

We will first treat of argument by Example, for it has the nature of induction, which is the foundation of reasoning. This form of argument has two varieties; one consisting in the mention of actual past facts, the other in the invention of facts by the speaker. Of the latter, again, there are two varieties, the illustrative parallel and the fable (e.g., the fables of Aesop, those from Libya). As an instance of the mention of actual facts, take the following. The speaker may argue thus: "We must prepare for war against the king of Persia and not let him subdue Egypt. For Darius of old did not cross the Aegean until he had seized Egypt; (1393b) but once he had seized it, he did cross. And Xerxes, again, did not attack us until he had seized Egypt; but once he had seized it, he did cross. If therefore the present king seizes Egypt, he also will cross, and therefore we must not let him."

The illustrative parallel is the sort of argument Socrates used: e.g. "Public officials ought not to be selected by lot. That is like using the lot to select athletes, instead of choosing those who are fit for the contest; or using the lot to select a steersman from among a ship's crew, as if we ought to take the man on whom the lot falls, and not the man who knows most about it."

[An instance of the fable is] that of Aesop in defence of [a] popular leader. . . . Aesop, defending before the assembly at Samos a popular leader who was being tried for his life, told this story: A fox, in crossing a river, was swept into a hole in the rocks; and, not being able to get out, suffered miseries for a long time through the swarms of fleas that fastened on her. A hedgehog, while roaming around, noticed the fox; and feeling sorry for her asked if he might remove the fleas. But the fox declined the offer; and when the hedgehog asked why, she replied, "These fleas are by this time full of me and not sucking much blood; if you take them away, others will come with fresh appetites and drink up all the blood I have left." "So, men of Samos," said Aesop, "my client will do you no further harm; he is wealthy already. But if you put him to death, (1394a) others will come along who are not rich, and their peculations will empty your treasury completely."

Fables are suitable for addresses to popular assemblies; and they have one advantage—they are comparatively easy to invent, whereas it is hard to find parallels among actual past events. You will in fact frame them just as you frame illustrative parallels: all you require is the power of thinking out your **analogy**, a power developed by intellectual training. But while it is easier to supply parallels by inventing fables, it is more valuable for the political speaker to supply them by quoting what has actually happened, since in most respects the future will be like what the past has been.

Where we are unable to argue by Enthymeme, we must try to demonstrate our point by this method of Example, and to convince our hearers thereby. If we ***can*** argue by Enthymeme, we should use our Examples as subsequent supplementary evidence. They should not precede the Enthymemes: that will give the argument an inductive air, which only rarely suits the conditions of speech-making. If they follow the enthymemes, they have the effect of witnesses giving evidence, and this always tells. For the same reason, if you put your examples first you must give a large number of them; if you put them last, a single one is sufficient; even a single witness will serve if he is a good one. It has now been stated how many varieties of argument by Example there are, and how and when they are to be employed.

We now turn to the use of Maxims, in order to see upon what subjects and occasions, and for what kind of speaker, they will appropriately form part of a speech. This will appear most clearly when we have defined a maxim. It is a statement; not a particular fact, such as the character of Iphicrates, but of a general kind; nor is it about any and every subject—e.g., "straight is the contrary of curved" is not a maxim—but only about questions of practical conduct, courses of conduct to be chosen or avoided. Now an Enthymeme is a syllogism dealing with such practical subjects. It is therefore roughly true that the premises or conclusions of Enthymemes, considered apart from the rest of the argument, are Maxims: e.g.,

> Never should any man whose wits are sound
> Have his sons taught more wisdom than their fellows.

Here we have a Maxim; add the reason or explanation, and the whole thing is an Enthymeme; thus—

> It makes them idle; and therewith they earn
> Ill-will and jealousy throughout the city.

(1394b) Again,

> There is no man in all things prosperous,

and

> There is no man among us all is free,

are maxims; but the latter, taken with what follows it, is an Enthymeme—

For all are slaves of money or of chance.

The use of Maxims is appropriate only to elderly men, and in handling subjects in which the speaker is experienced. For a young man to use them is—like telling stories—unbecoming[.] . . .

Even hackneyed and commonplace maxims are to be used, if they suit one's purpose: just because they are commonplace, everyone seems to agree with them, and therefore they are taken for truth. . . .

You are not to avoid uttering maxims that contradict such sayings as have become public property (I mean such sayings as "know thyself" and "nothing in excess") if doing so will raise your hearers' opinion of your character, or convey an effect of strong emotion[.] . . . It will raise people's opinion of our character to say, for instance, "We ought not to follow the saying that bids us treat our friends as future enemies: much better to treat our enemies as future friends." The moral purpose should be implied partly by the very wording of our maxim. . . .

(1395b) One great advantage of Maxims to a speaker is due to the want of intelligence in his hearers, who love to hear him succeed in expressing as a universal truth the opinions which they hold themselves about particular cases. I will explain what I mean by this, indicating at the same time how we are to hunt down the maxims required. The maxim, as has been already said, [is] a general statement and people love to hear stated in general terms what they already believe in some particular connection: e.g., if a man happens to have bad neighbours or bad children, he will agree with anyone who tells him, "Nothing is more annoying than having neighbours," or, "Nothing is more foolish than to be the parent of children." The orator has therefore to guess the subjects on which his hearers really hold views already, and what those views are, and then must express, as general truths, these same views on these same subjects. This is one advantage of using maxims. There is another which is more important—it invests a speech with moral character. There is moral character in every speech in which the moral purpose is conspicuous: and maxims always produce this effect, because the utterance of them amounts to a general declaration of moral principles: so that, if the maxims are sound, they display the speaker as a man of sound moral character. So much for the Maxim—its nature, varieties, proper use, and advantages.

Deductive Reasoning

Because the enthymeme is so central to Aristotle's project, it deserves to stand alone in chapter 4. In that kind of deductive logic, one starts with known principles and applies them downward to particulars.

Let's say, for example, that you know if your sister eats anything containing strawberries, she will always break out in hives. At a friend's birthday, the host serves strawberry cake, and your sister eats a large piece. What can you conclude? She will soon be very uncomfortable. That is, if the premises are true and you've set up the logic correctly, the conclusion is 100 percent guaranteed. Again, if it is true that all granola bars cost a dollar, and this snack is a granola bar, then what must be the case? The price of this snack must be one dollar.

A syllogism is the clearest example of deductive reasoning, and, as we learned in the previous chapter, the enthymeme is its offspring. The forceful certainty of deductive reasoning, along with the brevity of the enthymeme, makes it the favorite of Aristotle. But there is another short persuader handy to have in the rhetorical toolkit, and that's the **maxim**, which Aristotle discusses in the passage quoted at the beginning of this chapter. In that passage, Aristotle points out that the enthymeme, though already a kind of compressed syllogism, can be condensed even further, becoming the pithy one-sentence maxim. Because the maxim is so closely related to enthymemes (still fresh in your minds, for sure), let's begin with them, turning to their inductive counterparts—that is, arguments by *example*—afterward.

Maxims

"O mortal man, nurse not immortal wrath" (1394b). "Know thyself" (1395a). Aristotle's examples are dated, but contemporary ones are no harder to come by. *We first make our habits, and then our habits make us. Waste not, want not. He has enough who is content.* A maxim[1] is a general statement about practical conduct; it is a short, wise saying. And the maxim, says Aristotle, has two virtues: First, it pleases people who happen to agree with it; second, it boosts the speaker's *ethos*.

When you use a maxim—even an old, worn-out one—your listeners are pleased to hear what rings true. During the Cold War, Adlai Stevenson knew this when, warning his American audience against an overzealous fear of Communism, he quipped, "Let us not burn down the barn to kill the rats."[2] So did English Prime Minister Winston Churchill when, just after World War II in his famous Iron Curtain speech, he urged an ongoing, special alliance between the United States and Great Britain that could maintain the peace; he reminded his listeners that "prevention is better than the cure."[3] The recalling of what the listener already knows certainly delights, for it makes the audience

---

A maxim is a general statement about practical conduct.

---

1. The word "maxim" can be traced back to its Latin usage in *propositio maxima*, or "greatest proposition." It is, then, an axiom—a statement of general truth.
2. Adlai Stevenson II, August 27, 1952 speech, American Legion Convention. Madison Square Garden, New York City.
3. Winston Churchill, March 5, 1946 speech, "The Sinews of Peace," Westminster College, Fulton, MO, provided by The Churchill Centre (online).

feel as if they are "in the know," that they are wise in the same way that the gifted rhetor is wise.

The greater virtue of the maxim, however, is not so much its function of reminding readers of what they have already come to believe but rather its ability to strengthen the speaker's *ethos*. By endorsing common wisdom, a speaker shows that she adheres to the norms of a society, which are generally seen to be a combination of practical wisdom and moral virtue. But Aristotle points out that a speaker can flip those expectations upside down and build even greater credibility (1395a). For example, a speaker defending the accused could say, "We've all heard, 'You've made your bed; now lie in it,' but as for me, I'd rather give people a second chance." In this case, turning a maxim on its head shows a speaker to be of even *better* character than common wisdom. And this kind of speaker—the kind the audience trusts—can be particularly persuasive. Once again, we're reminded that *ethos*—that silent persuader—is key.

All of these are strategies for combating particular rhetorical situations, as twentieth-century theorist Kenneth Burke reminds us. You take them out of your arsenal of quotations in order to bring communal wisdom to bear on a particular moment. And you must remember to be choosy in which one you'll use. After all, maxims don't always agree with one another! Will you, when considering swift military action, say, "He who hesitates is lost," or, "Look before you leap"? When a quirky cousin announces to your family that she will soon be marrying her boyfriend, will you say, "Opposites attract," or "Birds of a feather flock together"? The context, of course, will determine which maxim applies. Our societal cache of maxims is a bit like the Oracle of Delphi: While varying her wisdom from one context to the next, the Oracle always spoke the perfect word, well-seasoned and timely, into its proper occasion.

Aristotle would offer a small caveat, however: Maxims aren't made for the young. That is, using maxims is best done by those who have the life experience to back them up. Imagine a five-year-old quipping, "The pen is mightier than the sword!" or "Vanity of vanities; all is vanity!" A bit laughable, isn't it? And so rhetors should be careful when using a maxim—careful to know whether they will be perceived as mature enough for the maxims to be taken seriously.

Inductive Reasoning

The enthymeme and maxim are powerful because they employ deductive reasoning: One deduces a conclusion by applying an overarching pattern of thought downward to particulars. We might then call **deductive** logic **"top-down" reasoning**. But there is actually another kind of reasoning—**inductive**—which reasons from specific instances to a general conclusion. Hence, inductive reasoning can be thought of as **"bottom-up" reasoning**.

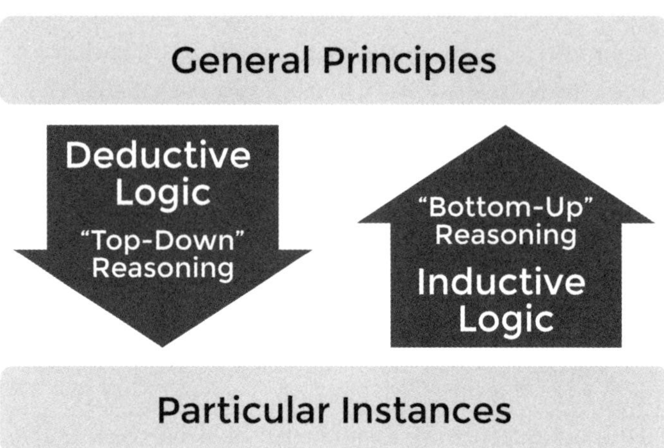

Figure 11. Top-down and bottom-up reasoning.

Imagine, for example, an alien walking into a classroom and seeing ten girls. The first has long hair, and so does the second, third, and so on, all the way up to the tenth girl. What might this alien, new to Earth, conclude? All girls have long hair. That conclusion is made by inductive reasoning: The alien has drawn a conclusion based upon particular examples. This kind of "bottom-up" reasoning starts with examples and moves up into a principle. And, unlike deductive reasoning, its conclusions are the result of observation, not necessity.

"But wait!" you say. "Not all girls have long hair!" True. There's one problem with inductive reasoning: Another particular can be thrown into the sample that proves the conclusion to be false. If just one girl with short hair walks into the room, the conclusion is no longer valid. Inductive reasoning, while able to make claims about likelihood or probability, can never offer certainty. The larger the sample, the stronger the conclusion, yet one is never *entirely* positive. Nonetheless, inductive reasoning is important. Much of the practical wisdom of our lived experience depends upon it. Consider the hard sciences—chemistry, physics, and biology, for example. Their reasoning moves from particular observations to theories, and it is never completely sure about anything, again speaking in terms of *likelihood* and *probability* rather than *certainty*. And yet, for the most part, we place our trust in the inductive method of the sciences, accepting their findings as relatively good guides.

And we don't have to go nearly that far. Human experience and wisdom is often even less thorough. How many hot stoves must you touch before inductively drawing the conclusion that hot stoves can hurt you? Indeed, we are often content to build our reasoning off of a *single* experience, making inductive reasoning that much less certain and yet all the more widely useful. Sometimes less-than-certain reasoning is all we have, and it's usually good enough.

As for any connection between top-down and bottom-up reasoning, it bears mentioning that deductive reasoning (i.e., top-down)—inasmuch as it can boast a particular kind of certainty in its form—nevertheless owes much to its less certain counterpart, inductive reasoning. As mentioned, if the premises are true and the argument is constructed correctly, deductive reasoning leads to necessary truths. Inductive reasoning, on the other hand, can never be certain—only strong or weak, probable or improbable. And yet they are connected: The very premises of a deductive argument are often the conclusions of induction; in the famous syllogism of Socrates's mortality, for instance, the major premise "all men are mortal" is based on the inductive observation that humans die.

Examples, Comparisons, and Fables

History, as the saying goes, is bound to repeat itself. It's bound to do so because nature and human desires are a rather settled affair, so to prove that something *did* happen suggests its future possibility, too. Enter the example. Examples—historical examples, comparisons, and fables—all hinge on this concept: We can predict that the future will be like the reality we have already known.[4]

4. Note that we are clearly in the realm of induction here, for we are working with likelihoods and probabilities, not certainties. But the past has proven, over time, to be a very reliable predictor of the future. And even the recognition of this principle is itself an induction!

Suppose your town is considering adopting a policy that bans the sale of carbonated soft drinks for all restaurants within the city limits. Citizens who oppose the policy (i.e., they are *for* the sale of soft drinks) could cite the historical example of a town just 50 miles away that adopted the very same policy three years ago, only to see restaurant sales plummet, forcing 30 percent of the restaurants out of business within six months. This historical example becomes a powerful argument against the ban. As you might guess, the historical example can be very powerful because it identifies a previous confirmed occurrence that suggests a pattern.

But sometimes historical examples are not at hand. In such a case, a less powerful argument could be made by way of comparison. If we are going to disallow carbonated soft drinks because they are unhealthy, should we disallow *all* unhealthy foods, such as sugary desserts and fried meats? Wouldn't this be similar to treating our citizens like children, underlings who can't make their own decisions about their health? The comparison—treating citizens like juveniles—becomes an argument against the policy and, implicitly, an argument for freedom.

Finally, a fable could be used to illustrate the arguments against the legislation. *Every morning, a farmer would feed his barn cats milk from the cow. The cats were happy, and the farmer really did care for them. In fact, he cared for them so much that one day he became concerned that the cream in the milk was too rich for the cats, so he skimmed the milk and began to serve them the watery skim milk. The cats, missing the old creamy milk, then moved to the barn of his neighbor, who fed them the milk they loved. The farmer lost his beloved cats, and his barn was soon overrun with mice. Likewise, we ought to beware of driving paying customers out of our town lest our economy suffer unforeseen ills.* Though more far-fetched, fables are a colorful and lively means of making an argument. (See this chapter's workshop on writing a fable to learn how to construct one yourself.)

Each type of example—historical example, comparison, and fable—uses something familiar to shed light on the unfamiliar. Now notice the distinctions of the different types of inductive arguments. Historical examples are the most powerful, but they are also hardest to come by. History, after all, is limited to what has actually happened. But there's another equally important limitation: You must know the history in order to draw from it! You can only harness the immense power of a historical example by being a student of history, by developing a mind well-stocked in facts and stories from which to choose. You've heard, of course, that those who don't study history are doomed to repeat it. The rhetor's version of this proverb, by way of a pun, is the opposite: Those who don't study history are doomed never to repeat it.

Comparisons are less limiting in that you can invent them, and the likeness can be made in a sentence or two. They can be made indirectly by means of simile (which uses *like* or *as*, e.g., "He's as crafty as a snake") and directly by means of metaphor (without the use of *like* or *as*, e.g., "The man is a snake"). An **analogy** works along the same lines as both of these but differs in this way: An analogy uses one concept to explain another concept.

An analogy is a comparison that explains one concept in terms of another.

In this way, an analogy is more extensive. Here's one from Albert Einstein: "Life is like riding a bicycle. To keep your balance, you must keep moving." Notice that an explanation of the similarity is included; in fact, it *must* be included! The simile alone would be incomplete: "Life is like riding a bicycle." How so? The relationship is not immediately apparent.

Analogies take more work on the part of the rhetor, but that work pays off in that they can be powerful persuaders. They are not foolproof, however; an audience or opponent can question the analogy at hand if they feel that it tries to identify a similarity where there is none. For instance, someone may argue, "Raising a child is like waging a war; you have to choose your battles." Another may respond, "Not so! Raising a child is more like cultivating a garden; just as a plant needs water and light, so a child requires love and attention." Admittedly, all comparisons and analogies are limited, but the careful rhetor knows her limits and uses them judiciously. The "Emily Dickinson *Imitatio*" workshop at the end of this chapter practices the skill of creating analogies step by step.

Like comparisons, fables can be crafted to suit the occasion, but they too lack the force of being historically concrete. Also, because fables almost always personify nonhuman characters, they suffer further in their lack of verisimilitude (the appearance of being real). Additionally, you'll notice that fables can be lengthy, which can add apparent strength to your argument when you may be short of material. Since most people love a story, a fable's length will probably not tax the audience's attention too much. When lacking historical examples, however, Aristotle favors the comparison over the fable. And his choice makes sense. A fable that likens citizens to mice-catching cats may be a little far-fetched and even distracting, for the extended figuration of the fable can be hard to follow at times. But the comparison that associates the citizens with irresponsible children is more succinct and pointed, and the image of little ones who must be guided by the hand is powerful and offensive; hence, in this case, it is probably more persuasive than the fable. So, in what would seem to be a progression from strongest to weakest, Aristotle identifies three kinds of examples: historical examples, comparisons, and fables.

Aristotle encourages us to use these examples—they're not just fluff. Such use strengthens the audience's philosophical muscle for seeing likenesses between unlike things, and it engages attention by creating interest and delight. Discovering similarities sharpens your listeners and tunes them in to the patterns that you want them to see: Reminded that the universe is coherent, ordered, and regular, they will find your words more interesting and plausible.

We can conclude by noting once again that deductive logic is more certain than inductive logic, making the enthymeme a stronger form of reasoning than the example. But be warned: We do no good in bragging about deductive reasoning, since, as you'll remember, the very premises that it works from are often arrived at by means of inductive reasoning. For additional rhetorical *oomph*, Aristotle suggests we make use of both.

Discussion Text:

Plato: Phaedrus, *Excerpt (circa 360–370 BC)*[5]

Focus:

Analogy

Persuasion, in its best form, is described by Socrates as "soul-leading through language." This definition, offered in Plato's Phaedrus, *raises the following question: To where and from where is the soul being led? And it turns out that these two questions—"Where to?" and "Where from?"—are the opening words of the* Phaedrus, *a lively dialogue with the wiliness of rhetoric as its subject. In what follows, we will consider Socrates's conceptualization of the soul, that very thing that rhetoric leads.*

Plato knew the power behind a good comparison. In this passage, notice that Socrates takes what is abstract and difficult to understand—the inner workings of the human person—and creates an analogy, a comparative image for it: The soul is like a chariot. He goes on to explain exactly how that is so. Is his analogy persuasive to you?

> Of the nature of the soul . . . let me speak briefly, and in a figure. And let the figure be composite—a pair of winged horses and a charioteer. Now [. . .] the human charioteer drives his in a pair; and one of them is noble and of noble breed, and the other is ignoble and of ignoble breed; and the driving of them of necessity gives a great deal of trouble to him.
>
> . . .
>
> As I said at the beginning of this tale, I divided each soul into three—two horses and a charioteer; and one of the horses was good and the other bad: the division may remain, but I have not yet explained in what the goodness or badness of either consists, and to that I will proceed. The right-hand horse is upright and cleanly made; he has a lofty neck and an aquiline nose; his color is white, and his eyes dark; he is a lover of honor and modesty and temperance, and the follower of true glory; he needs no touch of the whip, but is guided by word and admonition only. The other is a crooked lumbering animal, put together anyhow; he has a short thick neck; he is flat-faced and of a dark color, with grey eyes and blood-red complexion; the mate of insolence and pride, shag-eared and deaf, hardly yielding to whip and spur. Now when the charioteer beholds the vision of love, and has his whole soul warmed through sense, and is full of the prickings and ticklings of desire, the obedient steed, then as always under the government of shame, refrains from leaping on the beloved; but the other, heedless of the pricks and of the blows of the whip, plunges and runs away, giving all manner of trouble to his companion and the charioteer, whom he forces to approach the beloved and to remember the joys of love. They at first indignantly oppose him and will not be urged on to do terrible and unlawful deeds; but at last, when he persists in plaguing them, they yield and agree to do as he bids them.
>
> And now they are at the spot and behold the flashing beauty of the beloved; which when the charioteer sees, his memory is carried to the true beauty, whom he beholds in company with Modesty like an image placed upon a holy pedestal. He sees her, but he is afraid

5. Plato, *Phaedrus*, trans. Benjamin Jowett, provided by The Internet Classics Archive, http://classics.mit.edu/Plato/phaedrus.html (246–254).

and falls backwards in adoration, and by his fall is compelled to pull back the reins with such violence as to bring both the steeds on their haunches, the one willing and unresisting, the unruly one very unwilling; and when they have gone back a little, the one is overcome with shame and wonder, and his whole soul is bathed in perspiration; the other, when the pain is over which the bridle and the fall had given him, having with difficulty taken breath, is full of wrath and reproaches, which he heaps upon the charioteer and his fellow-steed, for want of courage and manhood, declaring that they have been false to their agreement and guilty of desertion. Again they refuse, and again he urges them on, and will scarce yield to their prayer that he would wait until another time. When the appointed hour comes, they make as if they had forgotten, and he reminds them, fighting and neighing and dragging them on, until at length he, on the same thoughts intent, forces them to draw near again. And when they are near he stoops his head and puts up his tail, and takes the bit in his teeth and pulls shamelessly. Then the charioteer is worse off than ever; he falls back like a racer at the barrier, and with a still more violent wrench drags the bit out of the teeth of the wild steed and covers his abusive tongue and jaws with blood, and forces his legs and haunches to the ground and punishes him sorely. And when this has happened several times and the villain has ceased from his wanton way, he is tamed and humbled, and follows the will of the charioteer, and when he sees the beautiful one he is ready to die of fear. And from that time forward the soul of the lover follows the beloved in modesty and holy fear.

Discussion Questions

Phaedrus

1. Draw the chariot of the soul.

2. One common interpretation of Socrates's image is that it illustrates the rightly ordered relationship among the intellectual, the spirited, and appetitive parts of the person. Which of these lines up with which character in the chariot image?

3. According to Plato, the well-ordered soul is one that is guided by the intellect. Is this how every soul is guided, or only the soul of the philosopher?

4. What warms the soul? What is the significance of this?

5. What good is the dark horse? Would it be better if the "chariot of the soul" had no dark horse?

6. What implications does this analogy have for the rhetor's responsibility as one who guides souls? If an audience member is ruled by the dark horse, should that alter the speaker's message?

7. Do you think Socrates's image does justice to the nature of the soul? For his audience, the chariot was a contemporary example. Can you think of a modern image or analogy that would work just as well? If so, draw it here:

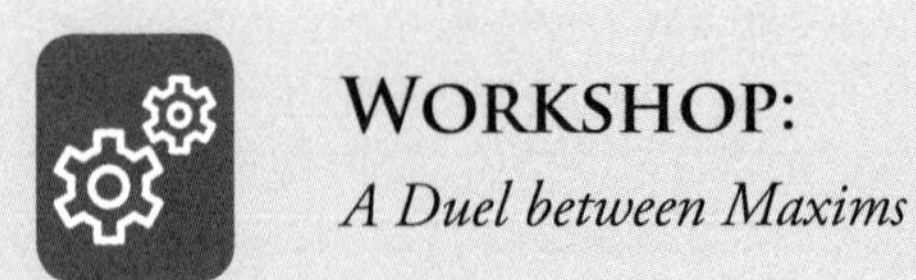

WORKSHOP:
A Duel between Maxims

1

As you know, maxims are wise sayings. In this activity, you will explore how a maxim can add persuasive power to one's argument.

In pairs, address the given scenario. Write conflicting arguments (about five sentences) addressing the provided situation, concluding your speech with the appropriate maxim. One student will argue for the first maxim, and the other student will argue against it with the second maxim.

You and your partner will deliver your speeches as a pair. The class will discuss which speech was more persuasive and how the different maxims contributed to each argument.

SCENARIO 1:

Should your dad order his favorite meal at the restaurant, or try something new? Try to convince him one way or the other, and end your argument with one of the following maxims:

"It's better to be safe than sorry."

"Nothing ventured, nothing gained."

SCENARIO 2:

Your little sister's science teacher has given her the option to work on a lab with or without a partner. Which do you suggest? Give her your advice and end your counsel with one of the following maxims:

"If you want something done right, do it yourself."

"Two heads are better than one."

Scenario 3:

Your friend Natalie has an unrequited crush on Nate, a fellow guy friend. Try to help her get over her crush by convincing her that she should (or should not) continue hanging out with him. Conclude it with one of the following maxims:

"Absence makes the heart grow fonder."

"Out of sight, out of mind."

Scenario 4:

You are shopping with a friend who wants to begin guitar lessons. The two of you walk into a music store, and he sees a beautiful guitar on sale. It is the very last one, and all sales are final. Convince him to buy (or not to buy) the instrument. Conclude with one of the following maxims:

"Look before you leap."

"He who hesitates is lost."

Scenario 5:

Your cousin, who is a senior, has been offered the opportunity to travel, all expenses paid, across Europe with a singing troupe next fall, but the timing will mean taking a "gap year" between high school and college. Encourage her either to play it safe and stick with her plans for college, or to seize this unique opportunity. Conclude with one of the following maxims:

"All good things come to those who wait."

"Time and tide wait for no man."

____

____

____

____

____

____

____

____

Alternate Activity

Follow the same instructions, but draft your own scenarios with the following pairs of maxims:

"What's good for the goose is good for the gander."
"One man's meat is another man's poison."

"Birds of a feather flock together."
"Opposites attract."

"The bigger, the better."
"Good things come in small packages."

"You're never too old to learn."
"You can't teach an old dog new tricks."

"Wisdom is found in a multitude of counselors."
"Too many cooks spoil the broth."

"Haste makes waste."
"Strike while the iron is hot."

"Actions speak louder than words."
"The pen is mightier than the sword."

"The more the merrier."
"Two's company; three's a crowd."

"Don't sweat the small stuff."
"The devil is in the details."

"A penny saved is a penny earned."
"Penny wise, pound foolish."

"Rome wasn't built in a day."
"Strike while the iron is hot."

"If you can't beat 'em, join 'em."
"If you lie down with dogs, you'll wake up with fleas."

"If at first you don't succeed, try, try again."
"Don't beat a dead horse."

"Knowledge is power."
"Ignorance is bliss."

"First come, first served."
"The last shall be first."

"The early bird gets the worm."
"The second mouse gets the cheese."

WORKSHOP: *Emily Dickinson* Imitatio

2

For this workshop, you'll practice creating analogies.

First, choose a topic you'd like to explore. Here is a list of starters, but you may want to come up with your own.

- Reading a book
- Writing a paper
- Going camping
- Sleeping
- Failing an exam
- Running a home
- Poverty
- Art
- A job
- Life

People can usually devise comparisons pretty quickly for these: *Reading a book is like taking a journey; running a home is like operating a zoo.* That can work well for metaphors and similes, but an analogy requires a bit more.

1. Determine what point you wish to highlight in the topic. For example, in Einstein's analogy, *Life is like riding a bicycle. To keep your balance, you must keep moving*, he is highlighting the dangers of a fixed mindset.
2. Search for other topics that capture that same essential quality, no matter how different the two may at first seem. Think carefully about that very quality you're looking for, and then tick through as many scenarios or activities as you can to find possible comparisons. Again, in Einstein's analogy, riding a bicycle is a great analog, or comparison, because it is possible only when the rider is in motion; when standing still, a bike will certainly fall.
3. Set up the analogy, making sure—initially, at least—that its structure is parallel. The parts of speech for the concept you're comparing should match the original analog. For example, if the subject is a gerund (an *-ing* form of a verb that functions as a noun), the comparison should also be a gerund: ***Dieting*** *is like* ***skydiving***. Or, if the subject is a phrase, the analog should also be a phrase. So, the expanded form of Einstein's example would be, ***Living life well*** *is like* ***riding a bicycle***. You'll notice that Einstein's analogy compresses, probably for greater rhetorical effect, the analogy. Here's one more example: ***Feeding the poor*** *is like* ***running a marathon*** can be compressed to ***Feeding the poor*** *is like a* ***marathon***.

4. Explain the relationship. Exactly how is the first like the second? This explanation will be the point of the comparison.

   Here's an example: *Writing a paper.*

   1. The concept I'd like to highlight: *Writing a paper is slow and difficult.*
   2. Now, what other things come to mind that are slow and difficult? Here's my list: *Growing up, fighting a war, carving a statue, building a house, growing a crop, taking a long car trip, tracking a fugitive, running a race.*
   3. I chose "growing a crop." Here's my analogy: *Writing a paper is like growing a crop.*
   4. Next, I add the explanation: *Writing a paper is like growing a crop; it takes hard work and lots of time, but the yield is worth it.*

Analogies are wonderful in that they can even teach us something new about the activity we started with. In the provided analogy, the value of the finished product—the harvested crop and the completed paper—is something the writer might not have even considered at the outset. Making a comparison may draw out additional features that the writer does not intend but may be delighted to see.

After you've practiced with these exercises, you're ready to imitate a lovely poem by Emily Dickinson. Explore some abstraction—for example, despair, love, friendship, mercy, justice, doubt—by imitating the following poem. Your poem should look a lot like this one, with three stanzas that include rhyme. You can borrow language from the original poem, too. Be sure to include signature Dickinson features: dashes, capitalization idiosyncrasies, and slant rhyme.

Hope is the thing with feathers

by Emily Dickinson

"Hope" is the thing with feathers—
That perches in the soul—
And sings the tune without the words—
And never stops—at all—

And sweetest—in the Gale—is heard—
And sore must be the storm—
That could abash the little Bird
That kept so many warm—

I've heard it in the chillest land—
And on the strangest Sea—
Yet, never, in Extremity,
It asked a crumb—of Me.

Student sample:

COURAGE

by Philip Moffatt
(student work, English course, Live Oak Classical School, 2015, used with permission)

"Courage" is the thing with a mane—
That in the Heart stands tall—
And roars a growl that is always heard—
And never backs down—at all—

And fiercest—in the storm—is heard—
And cold must be the Cage—
That could seize the mighty Lion
That slept while others raged—

I've seen it in the deadliest of lands—
And in the quietest Call—
Yet—never—when I Needed it,
Did it hesitate or stall.

Deception

by Daniel Bailey
(student work, English course, Live Oak Classical School, 2015, used with permission)

Deception is the thing with scales—
That dwells deep in the soul—
And whispers its words so quietly—
And never stops—at all—

And darkly—in moments of doubt—is heard
And strong must be the mind—
That could reject this Serpent
That's pulled so many behind—

It's whispered in my darkest hours—
In all my creeping Doubts—
But every time it whispers,
My heart will shut it out.

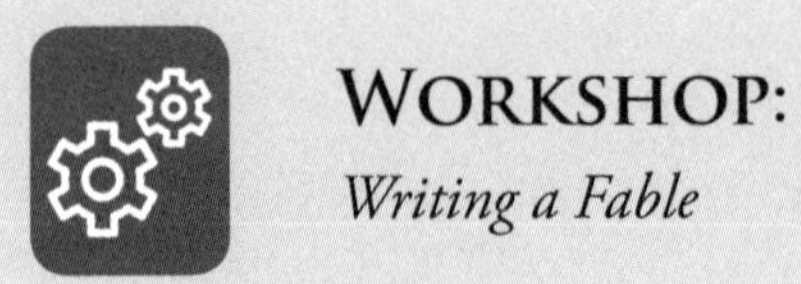

WORKSHOP: *Writing a Fable* 3

A good fable is not easy to write. It takes time and thought, but it can be a fun exercise and can add interest to your argument.

1. To write a fable, you must work backwards—begin where you'll end. That is, what moral do you wish to teach? Start by determining the lesson your fable will demonstrate. Of course, if we are thinking about a fable used to help persuade, the rhetorical situation itself will determine the point for us.

Let's suppose, then, that we are city council members, and we must vote on whether to purchase an historic building that will serve as the new city hall. All on the council agree that the building is affordable and should be bought, but about half of the members wish to wait, believing that the building's price may fall even further if the purchase is delayed twelve months.

If you are arguing for swift action, a ready-made moral is this one: "Strike while the iron is hot." But that maxim, along with any others that you already know, is off limits for this exercise. (Notice that the maxim, "Strike while the iron is hot," carries its own compressed narrative within it—something to do with a blacksmith or iron worker who was tempted to delay, a delay that would have put his work at risk.) You will need to create your own, and you'll want to keep the end moral, the fable's lesson, in mind.

In this case, the idea you want to convey may be that a delay can end in a lost opportunity. The idea is clear enough, but the power of your fable's maxim will be the result of the conclusion's pithy, memorable formulation. Do not try to write that now, but keep in mind that it is the destination toward which you are moving.

2. Next, try to think of the characters—for fables, characters are almost always personified animals. You'll want to choose animals that epitomize particular qualities: The fox is sneaky, the hare is fast, the turtle is slow, the peacock is vain, the fly is pesky. Which qualities are required in your scenario?

For our situation, we need an animal that is associated with delay, procrastination, or indecision. Let's choose the cat. Cats never seem able to decide if they want to be inside or outside; instead, they linger in doorways, often keeping their tails on the threshold so the door can never be fully closed. We might also want to choose a foil, a character that is the cat's opposite (i.e., one who is decisive and swift), to help highlight the bad judgment of the indecisive character. For the foil, if we were to choose one (I have *not* done so in the following example), we could choose either a cat's best-known counter, the dog, or another animal affiliated with the cat, such as a mouse, bird, or fish.

3. Now you must write the story. This is the hardest part! Try to keep it simple while still communicating the overall message. Here's a possibility for the scenario we've worked out so far:

> One sunny spring morning, a cat, hungry but excited about her hunting possibilities, left her home in order to find a good meal. Hiding in the grass beside the nearby fields that had recently been plowed, she watched the field mice frolic. *My, but they do look delicious!* she thought to herself as she spied on them. Before she pounced on the fattest of the mice, however, she heard birds chirping in the nearby

woods. *Perhaps I should find out what dainty and tasty fowl are in those trees and bushes before I choose one of these common, fur-covered meals for myself,* she thought. So as the sun moved toward midday, the cat wandered into the forest. The birds twittered and tweeted, each seeming just as succulent as the next. As she sized up each one, trying to select the plumpest of them all, she heard in the distance the sound of water trickling in the brook. *Maybe it would be best if I see what fish are swimming this day before I settle on one of these dry, feathery meals,* she thought, as the sun warmed the afternoon. At the stream, the fish swam heedless of the cat, even as she crouched with her whiskers touching the water's surface. The cat trembled with anticipation, but as the sun dipped below the horizon, her excitement turned to a shiver. Feeling the first cool of the evening, she thought to herself, *There's really no need for me to get wet for such a scaly meal when I have so many delicacies in the woods and fields.* But as she walked back through the dusky woods, the birds were silent, hidden in their nests. None could be found. Then as she passed by the fields again, the mice were still and quiet, nestled warmly in their burrows. Hungry and tired, the cat trudged back to her home, unable to find even a single cricket to satisfy her hungry stomach.

4. It's now time to write your maxim. Come up with a few, and then choose the best one. You'll want to try to boil the moral down into one pithy and concise turn of phrase, perhaps even poetically rendered to make it all the more memorable. Here are some possibilities:

   "Delay and lose the day."
   "Caution cannot stop the sun."
   "One's indecision cannot stop the sun."
   "A picky cat is a hungry cat."
   "Be hasty or be hungry."
   "Wait not, want not." (This is a play on "Waste not, want not.")
   "Active hands are better than empty hands."
   "Delay is a luxury of the satisfied. Haste is the virtue of the needy."

5. Finally, connect your newly minted fable to the rhetorical situation at hand. In this case, you could address the city council and tell the fable, making the point at the end of the story:

   "Just so, we shouldn't hem and haw over what is already a great deal. Let's buy the building, or else we risk losing the opportunity altogether. After all, a picky cat is a hungry cat."

Now you try it! Imagine for a moment that your school is considering extending the school day an extra hour. Construct a parable that will help you argue for or against this extension. Begin writing your parable on the lines provided and continue on notebook paper.

____

____

____

____

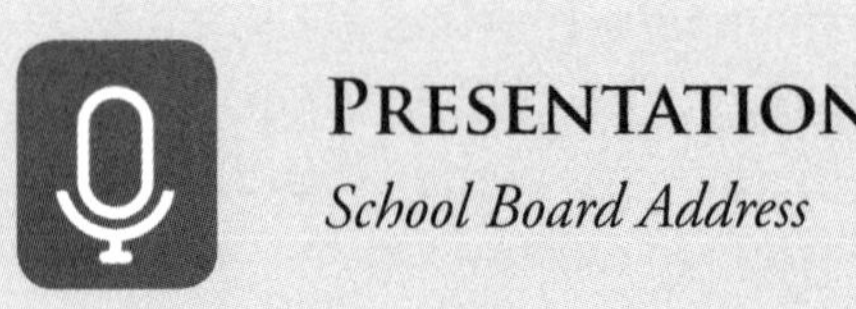

PRESENTATION:
School Board Address

SPOTLIGHT
Eye Contact

For this address, focus on eye contact. Just a passing glance won't do: You should make eye contact across the room, holding your gaze with each person for about two seconds before moving on to another member of the audience. Good eye contact will establish you as a more confident and trustworthy speaker. Don't forget the other aspects of delivery we have practiced, too: volume, clarity, rhythm, believability, and posture.

Imagine for a moment that your school is considering extending the school day an extra hour. Argue for or against this extension using the logical means we have discussed in the past two chapters: enthymeme, example, comparison, fable, and maxim. First, use the following lines to create arguments for or against this policy.

Enthymeme:

____

____

____

Historical example:

____

____

____

Comparison:

____

____

____

Fable:

____

____

____

Maxim:

____

____

____

Next, take these arguments and weave at least three of them into a paragraph to be delivered in front of the school board.

Alternate Activity

Suppose you have just had a birthday, and you were hoping your parents would extend your curfew, but they didn't. Argue for a one-hour extension in a letter to your parents, using three of the following: enthymeme, maxim, historical example, comparison, and fable.

3 SECTION

The Five Canons of Rhetoric

There are five so-called **canons of rhetoric**: *invention*, *organization*, *style*, *memory*, and *delivery*. Four of these come from Aristotle's *Rhetoric*; memory is the one added to the rhetorical tradition after Aristotle. Although it does not correspond perfectly to what is really an organic, back-and-forth process, it is handy to think of the five canons as stages, a sequence of steps that begins with invention and ends with delivery.

First, the rhetor "invents" (from the Latin *invenire*, "to find" or "to discover") the material. We can think of it as the exercise of coming up with something to say; **invention** is the work of finding the "stuff"—the ideas, the arguments, the content—for the speech, paper, or other text. Suppose your history teacher asks you to write a paper arguing whether the American colonies were justified in declaring independence from England. You'll need to say something in order to make your argument, and that "something" is generated during the invention stage.[1]

Next is **organization**, the ordering of that invented content. Lining up one's arguments in a particular order, carefully and deliberately (not willy-nilly), has everything to do with persuasion. Should you end with your strongest argument or begin with it? Should you refute the British counterarguments first or lead with your position? Order matters.

Following organization is **style**, or wording. There's more than one way to say the same thing, and those different versions have different rhetorical effects. Your audience—in this case, your history teacher or history class—will be the determining factor in whether you should pitch the language formally, informally, or somewhere in between. (If you were to discuss the same topic with, say, a friend, you may use altogether different words.) And you will also need to choose the way you want to communicate your ideas, including which figures of speech you'll use.

Memory is generally understood as the rhetor's memorization of the speech. When dealing with written arguments, it doesn't really apply, for your text "records" and helps you recall the content. But if you were required to stand up in front of your history class to present your findings, you'd need to recall the information so that you could communicate it. Some amount of memorizing would have to be involved. The same goes for **delivery**, for its actual presentation—this is not a relevant step for your American Revolution assignment if it's simply delivered in writing to a stack of papers on your teacher's desk, but it's certainly relevant if you must deliver it as an oral presentation. Again, only the first three canons are used when thinking about written arguments,[2] but all five apply to spoken rhetoric.

These five canons, then, can be thought of as distinct stages of a speaking presentation: One generates content, organizes it, chooses the language, commits it to memory, and then delivers it. The canons don't always stay nice and tidy in that exact order, and that's just fine. After all, a writer may jot some ideas onto paper (invention), outline those ideas (organization), begin to draft some of the ideas into sentences and paragraphs (style), swap the opening argument

1. Invention, by the way, is Aristotle's pet canon. Two of the three books of his *Rhetoric* concern invention.

2. For one example of an exception, see Collin Gifford Brooke, *Lingua Fracta: Towards a Rhetoric of New Media* (Cresskill, NJ: Hampton, 2009). The traditional five canons are reframed for new media.

with the closing one (organization again), come up with a new argument or two to include (back to invention), and then play with the language some more (return to style). Again, while the five canons are not really distinct stages in any strict sense, they are nevertheless the different parts of the rhetorical enterprise in its entirety.

Invention ➢ Organization ➢ Style ➢ Memory ➢ Delivery

Figure 12. The five canons of rhetoric.

6

Chapter 6

Canon One, Invention: Finding Something to Say

(1391b) We are now to proceed to discuss the arguments common to all oratory. All orators, besides their special lines of argument, are bound to use, for instance, the topic of the Possible and Impossible; and to try to show that a thing has happened, or will happen in future. Again, the topic of Size is common to all oratory; all of us have to argue that things are bigger or smaller than they seem, whether we are making political speeches, speeches of eulogy or attack, or prosecuting or defending in the law-courts. . . .

(1398a) Another line of proof is secured by defining your terms. . . . [An] example may be found in the *Alexander*. "Every one will agree that by incontinent people we mean those who are not satisfied with the enjoyment of one love." . . . All [rhetors should] define their term and get at its essential meaning, and then use the result when reasoning on the point at issue. . . .

Another line is based upon logical division. Thus, "All men do wrong from one of three motives, A, B, or C: in my case A and B are out of the question, and even the accusers do not allege C." . . .

(1398b) Another line of argument is founded upon some decision already pronounced, whether on the same subject or on one like it or contrary to it. . . .

(1400a) Another line of argument is to show that if the *cause* is present, the *effect* is present, and if absent, absent. For by proving the cause you at once prove the effect, and conversely nothing can exist without its cause.[1]

1. Besides the first three general lines of argument (possible/impossible, bigger/smaller, and past fact / future fact), Aristotle goes on to discuss twenty-eight other topics of invention. This excerpt includes a sample of them, skipping over many others in an effort to offer a streamlined and not exhaustive guide.

The Content of the Speech

Determining what to say for a rhetorical event, also known as the process of *invention*, begins with the writer thinking about the three rhetorical appeals: *ethos*, *pathos*, and *logos*. In a general sense, rhetors invent (from the Latin *invenire*, "to find" or "to discover") their content by considering these three appeals. In other words, even though we've located *ethos* primarily in the speaker, *pathos* in the audience, and *logos* in the text itself, we must come to see all three as residing within the words of the speech because it is the language itself that is responsible for establishing *ethos*, evoking *pathos*, and substantiating *logos*. What might be said that would reveal the speaker as a person of goodwill, commonsense, and moral virtue—that is, a person of good character (*ethos*)? What could be said that would address the audience's emotional predispositions (*pathos*), either heightening or mollifying their passions? And what could be said that would prove reasonable arguments (*logos*) in the thinking of the audience? Answering these questions is all done as part of invention, for invention is the discovery of anything that could make it into a text.[2] Invention, that is, is the discovery of arguments.

Invention is the discovery of arguments.

But usually, when rhetoricians think of invention, it is chiefly *logos* that comes to mind. And, even more specifically, Aristotle's *topics of invention*—sometimes referred to as *commonplaces* or, more simply, *topics*—may be their interest when considering this first of the five canons of rhetoric. So let us begin, then, with those topics of invention.

Commonplaces: The Topics of Invention

Suppose you are trying to convince your parents to go to the beach for spring break instead of having a staycation. How do you generate arguments to support your cause? If you feel passionately about your cause, it's generally not too hard. Maybe you immediately spout, "This is a *vacation*, as in *vacate*—to leave! That means we're supposed to get out of town and take a break from doing the same old things." Or, "Come on, Mom and Dad! It will help us bond as we make family memories." You might argue, "We can do it inexpensively if we drive and camp outside instead of fly and stay in hotels," or you could say, "Remember how rejuvenated we all felt after we got back from the beach last time?" And how about this one: "All work and no play makes Jack a dull boy"?

Coming up with convincing arguments for this situation isn't too hard, and maybe you could think of others. But when you have issues that you feel less passionately about—or maybe haven't even figured out which side you're on—what then do you do to generate arguments? Aristotle has a suggestion, one that has had great staying power for Western civilization: He suggests the commonplaces. **Commonplaces**, or **topics** (from the Greek *topos*, meaning "place") **of invention**, are metaphorical locations—mental "places" for thought—that you can return to when you need content for your arguments. And these places can be visited again and again, in different rhetorical situations. So these are the general topics of invention, applicable in almost any occasion in which ideas need to be generated.

Just as a journalist could ask certain questions about a past event in order to write an article on it—who, what, when, where, why, how—so, too, can a rhetor ask certain questions before delivering

2. Invention includes all three rhetorical appeals: *ethos*, *pathos*, and *logos*. This chapter, however, introduces the topics of invention, which are especially helpful to invention and are more relevant to the appeal of *logos*.

a speech or writing an essay in order to generate content. Imagine, then, walking up to a series of five doors.

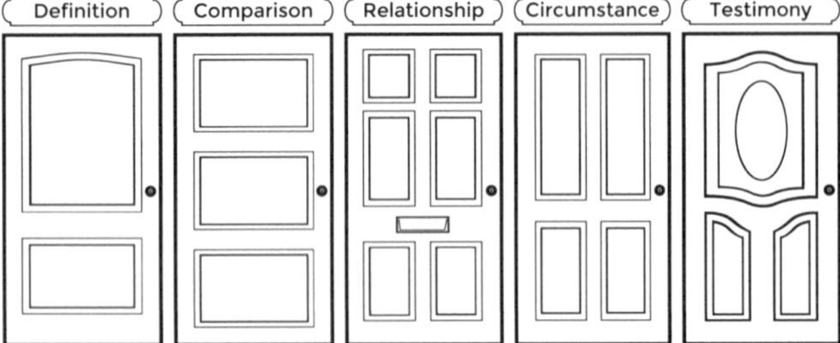

Figure 13. "Places" to go to find arguments.

You're looking for arguments about a particular issue, so you knock at the first door and ask, *what kind of a thing is it?* (definition). At the second door, you inquire, *what can I compare this thing to?* (comparison). Upon arriving at the third door, you ponder, *what is its relationship to other things?* (relationship). Knocking on the fourth door, you ask, *in what circumstance(s) does this thing exist?* (circumstance). And at the fifth door, you question, *do outsiders have anything to say about this thing?* (testimony). There are actually even more commonplaces than this—other doors and even doors behind the doors!—but these are a good start.

If you answer each of these questions, you'll generate material about your point, material you can use to beef up your overall argument. Sometimes you might even generate ideas that convince you that you're supporting the wrong side and need to switch your stance. Either way, you'll better understand your topic.

How the Mind Works

What's so special about these questions? you might ask. They are not random; indeed, it could be argued that they are ways in which the mind works. In order to come to a better understanding of something, your mind defines it, compares it to other things, and figures out any cause/effect relationship it has. In other words, Aristotle's cataloging of the commonplaces is not *prescriptive*—that is, arbitrarily imposing questions that he chose long ago—but, rather, *descriptive* in that the list tells us how the sharpest minds generally work. And crafting arguments according to the way the human mind actually works should make those arguments more understandable and more persuasive.

Let's look back at the spring break staycation arguments to see how they measure up to the commonplaces.

- "This is a *vacation*, as in *vacate*—to leave! That means we're supposed to get out of town and take a break from the same old things." Definition. *Staycation ≈ "stay" + "vacate" (two terms that contradict each other).*
- "Come on, Mom and Dad! It will help us bond as we make family memories." Relationship. *Vacations ⟶ bonding.*
- "We can do it inexpensively if we drive and camp outside instead of fly and stay in hotels." Comparison. *We will not spend as much money as we might otherwise.*
- "Remember how rejuvenated we all felt after we got back from the beach last time?" Circumstance. *How a vacation affected you in the past is how it will likely affect you in the future.*
- "All work and no play makes Jack a dull boy." Testimony. *Communal wisdom teaches the value of relaxation.*

Of course, the arguments are not all equally good. After all, the commonplace that generates the best argument depends not only on the issue itself but also on the audience. At any given moment, some will address concerns better than others. But the point holds: Such questions are a tried-and-true way of inventing arguments—that is, of generating content. They can be thought of as the rhetor's wrestling holds, used to tackle a given issue.

Remember, Aristotle did not write his *Rhetoric* for those who naturally succeed at public speaking. He wrote it for the rest of us, those who need to learn rationally what the few successfully do by habit or by nature—namely, how to persuade well. While it can be a breeze for some people to concoct an argument on any given subject, for most of us it's hard work. How is it, then, that you can use the topics in your own rhetorical life? When given an issue to discuss or write about, you can tick through the topics mentally: Definition! Comparison! Relationship! Circumstance! Testimony! Knocking on those metaphorical doors should provide you with richer arguments, and with more of them. At first, the practice of doing so could feel stilted and strange, but the more you visit those commonplaces, the more you'll find them to be exactly that: places you commonly find arguments.

A word to the wise: When possible, start with definition. Definition was a favorite commonplace of the ancients, and for good reason. It is nearly impossible to make real progress when the issue at hand isn't sharply defined. Definitions are often allowed to slip through conversations and debates unaddressed, and that spells trouble. People can end up talking past each other, never having defined the issue at hand. You'll find that definitions aren't always obvious, nor are they agreed upon as you'd think they would be. After all, different answers to the simple question *what is justice?* ended up generating the masterpiece of Plato's *Republic*. Nail down your definitions early, and you'll find not only that you can think more clearly about your issue, but also that your interlocutors (or conversation partners) can't shift the meanings—whether by accident or otherwise—to suit their purposes.

Topics and Subtopics

Now that you have been introduced to five main topics, you are ready to meet their subtopics, the more specific ways of generating invention.

The following chart can serve as a handy list to help you develop an argument.[3] Again, some arguments come to mind without any work at all on our part, but other arguments remain hidden until we go out in search for them. When given an issue, you can "go" to these other "places" to support your position in ways you might not otherwise have considered.

3. Although Aristotle discusses some of these topics and subtopics, this chart is not drawn directly from his *Rhetoric* but seeks instead to be more user-friendly by combining topics organized in the following works: Edward P. J. Corbett and Robert J. Connors, *Classical Rhetoric for the Modern Student*, 4th ed. (New York: Oxford University Press, 1998); Shelly Johnson, *The Argument Builder* (Camp Hill, PA: Classical Academic Press, 2008).

Chart. Common topics and subtopics of invention.

COMMON TOPICS AND SUBTOPICS OF INVENTION

Topic of Definition: "What kind of a thing is it?"

Genus/Species: *To what general class does it belong? What are its specific, defining characteristics?*

Division: *Into what different parts can it be separated?*

Etymology: *What root word(s) can you find inside the word itself? What does it/do they mean?*

Synonym/Antonym: *What other words are like it? What other words are its opposites?*

Description: *How would you depict it?*

Example: *What are instances or samples of it?*

Topic of Comparison: *"To what can I compare this thing?"*

Similarity/Analogy: *What other thing(s) is it like?*

Difference: *What is it unlike?*

Degree: *In what ways does it differ from something else, not in kind but in degree?*

- *More is better.*
- *Ends are better than means.*
- *The rarer, the better.*
- *The smarter the chooser, the better the choice.*
- *If a thing does not exist where it is more likely to exist, it will not exist where it is less likely to exist.*

Topic of Relationship: *"What is its relationship to other things?"*

Cause/Effect: *Why does it happen, or what leads to existence? What does it in turn cause, or what are its effects?*

Antecedent/Consequent: *Given that such-and-such is the case, what should follow?*

Contraries/Contradictories: *What are its opposites and near-opposites? With what is it incompatible?*

Topic of Circumstance: *"In what circumstance(s) does this thing exist?"*

Possible/Impossible: *What is actually feasible in this situation, and what is not feasible?*

Past fact/Future fact: *What has happened previously, and does that make its future occurrence more (or less) probable?*

Topic of Testimony: *"Do outsiders have anything to say about this thing?"*

Testimonial: *What is someone's personal experience of it—either that of an average person or a famous person?*

Law: *Are there any official documents or laws that speak to the issue?*

Statistics: *What facts, figures, and polls can you bring to bear on the issue?*

Example: *Are there any precedents; that is, has anything been similar to it in the past?*

Authority: *What do experts have to say about it?*

Maxim: *What does common wisdom have to say about it?*

Now put these into practice. Can you further specify the subtopic of invention being used in our staycation argument?

- "This is a *vacation* as in *vacate*—to leave! That means we're supposed to get out of town and take a break from doing the same-old things."

Topic: definition

Subtopic: ______________________________

- "Come on, Mom and Dad! It will help us bond as we make family memories."

Topic: relationship

Subtopic: ______________________________

- "We can do it inexpensively if we drive and camp outside instead of fly and stay in hotels."

Topic: comparison

Subtopic: ______________________________

- "Remember how rejuvenated we all felt after we got back from the beach last time?"

Topic: circumstance

Subtopic: ______________________________

- "All work and no play makes Jack a dull boy."

Topic: Testimony

Subtopic: ______________________________

Discussion Text:

Martin Luther King, Jr.:
"Letter from Birmingham City Jail" (1963)[4]

Focus:

Invention

One of America's greatest rhetors is Martin Luther King, Jr., a leader in the African American civil rights movement of the 1950s and 1960s. King, who was also an American Baptist minister, championed nonviolent but confrontational resistance to racism and segregation. He wrote this open letter (i.e., a letter intended for publication) as a response to eight white clergymen who had themselves published a statement in opposition to civil disobedience. This letter was penned from his cell in April of 1963 while King was imprisoned in Birmingham City Jail for activity during the Birmingham Campaign. A rhetorical masterpiece, the epistle is especially remarkable for the variety of arguments King employs to build his case.

Martin Luther King, Jr.

Birmingham City Jail

April 16, 1963

. . .

My dear Fellow Clergymen,

While confined here in the Birmingham City Jail, I came across your recent statement calling our present activities "unwise and untimely." Seldom, if ever, do I pause to answer criticism of my work and ideas. If I sought to answer all the criticisms that cross my desk, my secretaries would be engaged in little else in the course of the day and I would have no time for constructive work. But since I feel that you are men of genuine goodwill and your criticisms are sincerely set forth, I would like to answer your statement in what I hope will be patient and reasonable terms.

I think I should give the reason for my being in Birmingham, since you have been influenced by the argument of "outsiders coming in." I have the honor of serving as president of the Southern Christian Leadership Conference, an organization operating in every Southern state with headquarters in Atlanta, Georgia. We have some eighty-five affiliate organizations all across the South—one being the Alabama Christian Movement for Human Rights. Whenever necessary and possible we share staff, educational, and financial resources with our affiliates. Several months ago our local affiliate here in Birmingham invited us to be on call to engage in a nonviolent direct action program if such were deemed necessary. We readily consented and when the hour came we lived up to our promises. So I am here, along with several members of my staff, because we were invited here. I am here because I have basic organizational ties here. Beyond this, I am in Birmingham because injustice is here. ❶ **Just as the eighth century prophets left their little villages and carried their "thus saith the Lord" far beyond the boundaries of their home town, and just as the Apostle Paul left his little**

4. Martin Luther King, Jr., "Letter from Birmingham Jail," April 16, 1963 speech. Public domain version of the original letter's text retrieved and duplicated here from Loveallpeople.org, Bill McGinnis, accessed January 18, 2016, http://www.loveallpeople.org/letterfromthebirminghamcityjail.html.

village of Tarsus and carried the gospel of Jesus Christ to practically every hamlet and city of the Graeco-Roman world,[5] I too am compelled to carry the gospel of freedom beyond my particular home town. Like Paul, I must constantly respond to the Macedonian call for aid.

Moreover, I am cognizant of the interrelatedness of all communities and states. I cannot sit idly by in Atlanta and not be concerned about what happens in Birmingham. Injustice anywhere is a threat to justice everywhere. We are caught in an inescapable network of mutuality tied in a single garment of destiny. Whatever affects one directly affects all indirectly. Never again can we afford to live with the narrow, provincial "outside agitator" idea. Anyone who lives inside the United States can never be considered an outsider anywhere in this country.

❷ You deplore the demonstrations that are presently taking place in Birmingham. But I am sorry that your statement did not express a similar concern for the conditions that brought the demonstrations into being. I am sure that each of you would want to go beyond the superficial social analyst who looks merely at effects, and does not grapple with underlying causes. I would not hesitate to say that it is unfortunate that so-called demonstrations are taking place in Birmingham at this time, but I would say in more emphatic terms that it is even more unfortunate that the white power structure of this city left the Negro community with no other alternative.

❸ In any nonviolent campaign there are four basic steps: (1) collection of the facts to determine whether injustices are alive; (2) negotiation; (3) self-purification; and (4) direct action. We have gone through all of these steps in Birmingham. There can be no gainsaying of the fact that racial injustice engulfs this community. Birmingham is probably the most thoroughly segregated city in the United States. Its ugly record of police brutality is known in every section of this country. Its unjust treatment of Negroes in the courts is a notorious reality. There have been more unsolved bombings of Negro homes and churches in Birmingham than any city in this nation. These are the hard, brutal, and unbelievable facts. On the basis of these conditions Negro leaders sought to negotiate with the city fathers. But the political leaders consistently refused to engage in good faith negotiation.

Then came the opportunity last September to talk with some of the leaders of the economic community. In these negotiating sessions certain promises were made by the merchants—such as the promise to remove the humiliating racial signs from the stores. On the basis of these promises Rev. Shuttlesworth and the leaders of the Alabama Christian Movement for Human Rights agreed to call a moratorium on any type of demonstrations. As the weeks and months unfolded we realized that we were the victims of a broken promise. The signs remained. As in so many experiences of the past we were confronted with blasted hopes, and the dark shadow of a deep disappointment settled upon us. So we had no alternative except that of preparing for direct action, whereby we would present our very bodies as a means of laying our case before the conscience of the local and national community. We

5. Emphasis (bold text) and circled numbers added.

were not unmindful of the difficulties involved. So we decided to go through a process of self-purification. We started having workshops on nonviolence and repeatedly asked ourselves the questions, "Are you able to accept blows without retaliating?" "Are you able to endure the ordeals of jail?"

We decided to set our direct-action program around the Easter season, realizing that with the exception of Christmas, this was the largest shopping period of the year. Knowing that a strong economic withdrawal program would be the by-product of direct action, we felt that this was the best time to bring pressure on the merchants for the needed changes. Then it occurred to us that the March election was ahead, and so we speedily decided to postpone action until after election day. When we discovered that Mr. Connor was in the run-off, we decided again to postpone action so that the demonstrations could not be used to cloud the issues. At this time we agreed to begin our nonviolent witness the day after the run-off.

This reveals that we did not move irresponsibly into direct action. We too wanted to see Mr. Connor defeated; so we went through postponement after postponement to aid in this community need. After this we felt that direct action could be delayed no longer.

You may well ask, "Why direct action? Why sit-ins, marches, etc.? Isn't negotiation a better path?" You are exactly right in your call for negotiation. Indeed, this is the purpose of direct action. Nonviolent direct action seeks to create such a crisis and establish such creative tension that a community that has constantly refused to negotiate is forced to confront the issue. It seeks so to dramatize the issue that it can no longer be ignored. I just referred to the creation of tension as a part of the work of the nonviolent resister. This may sound rather shocking. But I must confess that I am not afraid of the word tension. I have earnestly worked and preached against violent tension, but there is a type of constructive nonviolent tension that is necessary for growth. ❹ **Just as Socrates felt that it was necessary to create a tension in the mind so that individuals could rise from the bondage of myths and half-truths to the unfettered realm of creative analysis and objective appraisal,** we must see the need of having nonviolent gadflies to create the kind of tension in society that will help men rise from the dark depths of prejudice and racism to the majestic heights of understanding and brotherhood. So the purpose of the direct action is to create a situation so crisis-packed that it will inevitably open the door to negotiation. We, therefore, concur with you in your call for negotiation. Too long has our beloved Southland been bogged down in the tragic attempt to live in monologue rather than dialogue.

One of the basic points in your statement is that our acts are untimely. Some have asked, "Why didn't you give the new administration time to act?" The only answer that I can give to this inquiry is that the new administration must be prodded about as much as the outgoing one before it acts. We will be sadly mistaken if we feel that the election of Mr. Boutwell will bring the millennium to Birmingham. ❺**While Mr. Boutwell is much more articulate and gentle than Mr. Connor, they are both segregationists dedicated to the task of maintaining the status quo.** The hope I see in Mr. Boutwell is that he will be reasonable enough to see the futility of massive resistance to desegregation. But he will not see this without pressure from the devotees of civil rights. ❻ **My friends, I must say to you that we have not made a single gain in civil rights without determined legal and nonviolent pressure. History is the long and tragic story of the fact that privileged groups seldom give up their privileges voluntarily.** Individuals may see the moral light and voluntarily give up their unjust posture; but as Reinhold Niebuhr has reminded us, groups are more immoral than individuals.

We know through painful experience that freedom is never voluntarily given by the oppressor; it must be demanded by the oppressed. Frankly I have never yet engaged in a direct action movement that was "well timed," according to the timetable of those who have not suffered unduly from the disease of segregation. For years now I have heard the word "Wait!" It rings in the ear of every Negro with a piercing familiarity. This "wait" has almost always meant "never." It has been a tranquilizing thalidomide,[6] relieving the emotional stress for a moment, only to give birth to an ill-formed infant of frustration. We must come to see with the distinguished jurist of yesterday that "justice too long delayed is justice denied." We have waited for more than three hundred and forty years for our constitutional and God-given rights. The nations of Asia and Africa are moving with jet-like speed toward the goal of political independence, and we still creep at horse and buggy pace toward the gaining of a cup of coffee at a lunch counter.

I guess it is easy for those who have never felt the stinging darts of segregation to say wait. But when you have seen vicious mobs lynch your mothers and fathers at will and drown your sisters and brothers at whim; when you have seen hate-filled policemen curse, kick, brutalize, and even kill your black brothers and sisters with impunity; when you see the vast majority of your twenty million Negro brothers smothering in an air-tight cage of poverty in the midst of an affluent society; when you suddenly find your tongue twisted and your speech stammering as you seek to explain to your six-year-old daughter why she can't go to the public amusement park that has just been advertised on television, and see tears welling up in her little eyes when she is told that Funtown is closed to colored children, and see the depressing clouds of inferiority begin to form in her little mental sky, and see her begin to distort her little personality by unconsciously developing a bitterness toward white people; when you have to concoct an answer for a five-year-old son asking in agonizing *pathos*: "Daddy, why do white people treat colored people so mean?"; when you take a cross-country drive and find it necessary to sleep night after night in the uncomfortable corners of your automobile because no motel will accept you; when you are humiliated day in and day out by nagging signs reading "white" men and "colored"; when your first name becomes "nigger" and your middle name becomes "boy" (however old you are) and your last name becomes "John," and when your wife and mother are never given the respected title "Mrs."; when you are harried by day and haunted by night by the fact that you are a Negro, living constantly at tip-toe stance never quite knowing what to expect next, and plagued with inner fears and

6. Thalidomide was marketed in the late 1950s as an antianxiety drug and was used by pregnant women for morning sickness. It was subsequently found to cause serious birth defects.

outer resentments; when you are forever fighting a degenerating sense of "nobodiness"—then you will understand why we find it difficult to wait. There comes a time when the cup of endurance runs over, and men are no longer willing to be plunged into an abyss of injustice where they experience the bleakness of corroding despair. I hope, sirs, you can understand our legitimate and unavoidable impatience.

You express a great deal of anxiety over our willingness to break laws. This is certainly a legitimate concern. Since we so diligently urge people to obey the Supreme Court's decision of 1954 outlawing segregation in the public schools, it is rather strange and paradoxical to find us consciously breaking laws. One may well ask: "How can you advocate breaking some laws and obeying others?" The answer is found in the fact that there are two types of laws: There are just laws and there are unjust laws. I would be the first to advocate obeying just laws. One has not only a legal but moral responsibility to obey just laws. Conversely, one has a moral responsibility to disobey unjust laws. ❼ **I would agree with Saint Augustine that "An unjust law is no law at all."**

❽ **Now what is the difference between the two? How does one determine when a law is just or unjust? A just law is a man-made code that squares with the moral law or the law of God. An unjust law is a code that is out of harmony with the moral law.** To put it in the terms of Saint Thomas Aquinas, an unjust law is a human law that is not rooted in eternal and natural law. Any law that uplifts human personality is just. Any law that degrades human personality is unjust. All segregation statutes are unjust because segregation distorts the soul and damages the personality. It gives the segregator a false sense of superiority and the segregated a false sense of inferiority. To use the words of Martin Buber, the great Jewish philosopher, segregation substitutes an "I-it" relationship for an "I-thou" relationship, and ends up relegating persons to the status of things. So segregation is not only politically, economically, and sociologically unsound, but it is morally wrong and sinful. Paul Tillich has said that sin is separation. Isn't segregation an existential expression of man's tragic separation, an expression of his awful estrangement, his terrible sinfulness? So I can urge men to obey the 1954 decision of the Supreme Court because it is morally right, and I can urge them to disobey segregation ordinances because they are morally wrong.

Let us turn to a more concrete example of just and unjust laws. An unjust law is a code that a majority inflicts on a minority that is not binding on itself. This is difference made legal. On the other hand a just law is a code that a majority compels a minority to follow that it is willing to follow itself. This is sameness made legal.

Let me give another explanation. An unjust law is a code inflicted upon a minority which that minority had no part in enacting or creating because they did not have the unhampered right to vote. Who can say that the legislature of Alabama which set up the segregation laws was democratically elected? Throughout the state of Alabama all types of conniving methods are used to prevent Negroes from becoming registered voters and there are some counties without a single Negro registered to vote despite the fact that the Negro constitutes a majority of the population. Can any law set up in such a state be considered democratically structured?

These are just a few examples of unjust and just laws. There are some instances when a law is just on its face but unjust in its application. For instance, I was arrested Friday on a charge of parading without a permit. Now there is nothing wrong with an ordinance which requires a permit for a parade, but when the ordinance is used to preserve segregation and to deny citizens the First Amendment privilege of peaceful assembly and peaceful protest, then it becomes unjust.

I hope you can see the distinction I am trying to point out. In no sense do I advocate evading or defying the law as the rabid segregationist would do. This would lead to anarchy. One who breaks an unjust law must do it openly, lovingly (not hatefully as the white mothers did in New Orleans when they were seen on television screaming "nigger, nigger, nigger") and with a willingness to accept the penalty. I submit that an individual who breaks a law that conscience tells him is unjust, and willingly accepts the penalty by staying in jail to arouse the conscience of the community over its injustice, is in reality expressing the very highest respect for law.

Of course there is nothing new about this kind of civil disobedience. ❾ **It was seen sublimely in the refusal of Shadrach, Meshach, and Abednego to obey the laws of Nebuchadnezzar because a higher moral law was involved. It was practiced superbly by the early Christians who were willing to face hungry lions and the excruciating pain of chopping blocks, before submitting to certain unjust laws of the Roman Empire. To a degree academic freedom is a reality today because Socrates practiced civil disobedience.**

We can never forget that everything Hitler did in Germany was "legal" and everything the Hungarian freedom fighters did in Hungary was "illegal." It was "illegal" to aid and comfort a Jew in Hitler's Germany. But I am sure that, if I had lived in Germany during that time, I would have aided and comforted my Jewish brothers even though it was illegal. If I lived in a communist country today where certain principles dear to the Christian faith are suppressed, I believe I would openly advocate disobeying these anti-religious laws.

I must make two honest confessions to you, my Christian and Jewish brothers. First, I must confess that over the last few years I have been gravely disappointed with the white moderate. I have almost reached the regrettable conclusion that the Negroes' great stumbling block in the stride toward freedom is ❿ **not the White Citizen's "Counciler" or the Ku Klux Klanner, but the white moderate** who is more devoted to "order" than to justice; who prefers a negative peace which is the absence of tension to a positive peace which is the presence of justice; who constantly says "I agree with you in the goal you seek, but I can't agree with your methods of direct action"; who paternalistically feels that he can set the timetable for another man's freedom; who lives by the myth of time and who constantly advises the Negro to wait until a "more convenient season." Shallow understanding from people of good will is more frustrating than absolute misunderstanding from people of ill will. Lukewarm acceptance is much more bewildering than outright rejection.

I had hoped that the white moderate would understand that law and order exist for the purpose of establishing justice, and that when they fail to do this they become dangerously structured dams that block the flow of social progress. I had hoped that the white moderate would understand that the present tension in the South is merely a necessary phase of the transition from an obnoxious negative peace, where the Negro passively accepted his unjust plight, to a substance-filled positive peace, where all men will respect the dignity and worth of human personality. Actually, we who engage in nonviolent direct action are not the creators of tension. We merely bring to the surface the hidden tension that is already alive. We bring it out in the open where it can be seen and dealt with. Like a boil that can never be cured as long as it is covered up but must be opened with all its pus-flowing ugliness to the natural medicines of air and light, injustice must likewise be exposed, with all of the tension its exposing creates, to the light of human conscience and the air of national opinion before it can be cured.

In your statement you asserted that our actions, even though peaceful, must be condemned because they precipitate violence. But can this assertion be logically made?⓫ **Isn't this like condemning the robbed man because his possession of money precipitated the evil act of robbery? Isn't this like condemning Socrates because his unswerving commitment to truth and his philosophical delvings precipitated the misguided popular mind to make him drink the hemlock? Isn't this like condemning Jesus because His unique God consciousness and never-ceasing devotion to His will precipitated the evil act of crucifixion?** We must come to see, as federal courts have consistently affirmed, that it is immoral to urge an individual to withdraw his efforts to gain his basic constitutional rights because the quest precipitates violence. Society must protect the robbed and punish the robber.

I had also hoped that the white moderate would reject the myth of time. I received a letter this morning from a white brother in Texas which said: "All Christians know that the colored people will receive equal rights eventually, but is it possible that you are in too great of a religious hurry? It has taken Christianity almost 2,000 years to accomplish what it has. The teachings of Christ take time to come to earth." All that is said here grows out of a tragic misconception of time. It is the strangely irrational notion that there is something in the very flow of time that will inevitably cure all ills. Actually time is neutral. It can be used either destructively or constructively. I am coming to feel that the people of ill will have used time much more effectively than the people of good will. We will have to repent in this generation not merely for the vitriolic words and actions of the bad people, but for the appalling silence of the good people. We must come to see that human progress never rolls in on wheels of inevitability. It comes through the tireless efforts and persistent work of men willing to be co-workers with God, and without this hard work time itself becomes an ally of the forces of social stagnation.

We must use time creatively, and forever realize that the time is always ripe to do right. Now is the time to make real the promise of democracy, and transform our pending national elegy into a creative psalm of brotherhood. Now is the time to lift our national policy from the quicksand of racial injustice to the solid rock of human dignity.

You spoke of our activity in Birmingham as extreme. At first I was rather disappointed that fellow clergymen would see my nonviolent efforts as those of the extremist. I started thinking about the fact that I stand in the middle of two opposing forces in the Negro community. One is a force of complacency made up of Negroes who, as a result of long years of oppression, have been so completely drained of self-respect and a sense of "somebodiness" that they have adjusted to segregation, and of a few Negroes in the middle class who, because of a degree of academic and economic security, and because at points they profit by segregation, have unconsciously become insensitive to the problems of the masses. The other force is one of bitterness and hatred and comes perilously close to advocating violence. It is expressed in the various black nationalist groups that are springing up over the nation, the largest and best known being Elijah Muhammad's Muslim movement. This movement is nourished by the contemporary frustration over the continued existence of racial discrimination. It is made up of people who have lost faith in America, who have absolutely repudiated Christianity, and who have concluded that the white man is an incurable "devil." I have tried to stand between these two forces saying that we need not follow the "do-nothingism" of the complacent or the hatred and despair of the black nationalist. There is the more excellent way of love and nonviolent protest. I'm grateful to God that, through the Negro church, the dimension of nonviolence entered our struggle. If this philosophy had not emerged I am convinced that by now many streets of the South would be flowing with floods of blood. And I am further convinced that if our white brothers dismiss us as "rabble rousers" and "outside agitators"—those of us who are working through the channels of nonviolent direct action—and refuse to support our nonviolent efforts, millions of Negroes, out of frustration and despair, will seek solace and security in black-nationalist ideologies, a development that will lead inevitably to a frightening racial nightmare.

Oppressed people cannot remain oppressed forever. The urge for freedom will eventually come. This is what has happened to the American Negro. Something within has reminded him of his birthright of freedom; something without has reminded him that he can gain it. Consciously and unconsciously, he has been swept in by what the Germans call the Zeitgeist, and with his black brothers of Africa, and his brown and yellow brothers of Asia, South America, and the Caribbean, he is moving with a sense of cosmic urgency toward the promised land of racial justice. Recognizing this vital urge that has engulfed the Negro community, one should readily understand public demonstrations. The Negro has many pent-up resentments and latent frustrations. He has to get them out. So let him march sometime; let him have his prayer pilgrimages to the city hall; understand why he must have sit-ins and freedom rides. If his repressed emotions do not come out in these nonviolent ways, they will come out in ominous expressions of violence. This is not a threat; it is a fact of history. So I have not said to my people, "Get rid of your discontent." But I have tried to say that this normal and healthy discontent can be channeled through the creative outlet of nonviolent direct action. Now this approach is being dismissed as extremist. I must admit that I was initially disappointed in being so categorized.

But as I continued to think about the matter I gradually gained a bit of satisfaction from being considered an extremist. Was not Jesus an extremist in love? "Love your enemies, bless them that curse you, pray for them that despitefully use you." Was not Amos an extremist for justice—"Let justice roll down like waters and righteousness like a mighty stream." Was not Paul an extremist for the gospel of Jesus Christ—"I bear in my body the marks of the Lord Jesus." Was not Martin Luther an extremist—"Here I stand; I can do none other so help me God." Was not John Bunyan an extremist—"I will stay in jail to the end of my days before I make a butchery of my conscience." Was not Abraham Lincoln an extremist—"This nation cannot survive half slave and half free." Was not Thomas Jefferson an extremist—"We hold these truths to be self-evident, that all men are created equal." So the question is not whether we will be extremist but what kind of extremist will we be. Will we be extremists for hate or will we be extremists for love? Will we be extremists for the preservation of injustice—or will we be extremists for the cause of justice? In that dramatic scene on Calvary's hill three men were crucified. We must never forget that all three were crucified for the same crime—the crime of extremism. Two were extremists for immorality, and thus fell below their environment. The other, Jesus Christ, was an extremist for love, truth, and goodness, and thereby rose above His environment. So, after all, maybe the South, the nation, and the world are in dire need of creative extremists.

I had hoped that the white moderate would see this. Maybe I was too optimistic. Maybe I expected too much. I guess I should have realized that few members of a race that has oppressed another race can understand or appreciate the deep groans and passionate yearnings of those that have been oppressed, and still fewer have the vision to see that injustice must be rooted out by strong, persistent, and determined action. I am thankful, however, that some of our white brothers have grasped the meaning of this social revolution and committed themselves to it. They are still all too small in quantity, but they are big in quality. Some like Ralph McGill, Lillian Smith, Harry Golden, and James Dabbs have written about our struggle in eloquent, prophetic, and understanding terms. Others have marched with us down nameless streets of the South. They have languished in filthy, roach-infested jails, suffering the abuse and brutality of angry policemen who see them as "dirty nigger lovers." They, unlike so many of their moderate brothers and sisters, have recognized the urgency of the moment and sensed the need for powerful "action" antidotes to combat the disease of segregation.

Let me rush on to mention my other disappointment. I have been so greatly disappointed with the white Church and its leadership. Of course there are some notable exceptions. I am not unmindful of the fact that each of you has taken some significant stands on this issue. I commend you, Rev. Stallings, for your Christian stand on this past Sunday, in welcoming

Negroes to your worship service on a non-segregated basis. I commend the Catholic leaders of this state for integrating Spring Hill College several years ago.

But despite these notable exceptions I must honestly reiterate that I have been disappointed with the Church. I do not say that as one of those negative critics who can always find something wrong with the Church. I say it as a minister of the gospel, who loves the Church; who was nurtured in its bosom; who has been sustained by its spiritual blessings and who will remain true to it as long as the cord of life shall lengthen.

I had the strange feeling when I was suddenly catapulted into the leadership of the bus protest in Montgomery several years ago that we would have the support of the white Church. I felt that the white ministers, priests, and rabbis of the South would be some of our strongest allies. Instead, some have been outright opponents, refusing to understand the freedom movement and misrepresenting its leaders; all too many others have been more cautious than courageous and have remained silent behind the anesthetizing security of the stained glass windows.

In spite of my shattered dreams of the past, I came to Birmingham with the hope that the white religious leadership of this community would see the justice of our cause and with deep moral concern, serve as the channel through which our just grievances could get to the power structure. I had hoped that each of you would understand. But again I have been disappointed.

I have heard numerous religious leaders of the South call upon their worshippers to comply with a desegregation decision because it is the law, but I have longed to hear white ministers say follow this decree because integration is morally right and the Negro is your brother. In the midst of blatant injustices inflicted upon the Negro, I have watched white churches stand on the sideline and merely mouth pious irrelevancies and sanctimonious trivialities. In the midst of a mighty struggle to rid our nation of racial and economic injustice, I have heard so many ministers say, "Those are social issues with which the gospel has no real concern," and I have watched so many churches commit themselves to a completely other-worldly religion which made a strange distinction between body and soul, the sacred and the secular.

So here we are moving toward the exit of the twentieth century with a religious community largely adjusted to the status quo, standing as a tail-light behind other community agencies rather than a headlight leading men to higher levels of justice.

I have travelled the length and breadth of Alabama, Mississippi and all the other southern states. On sweltering summer days and crisp autumn mornings I have looked at her beautiful churches with their spires pointing heavenward. I have beheld the impressive outlay of her massive religious education buildings. Over and over again I have found myself asking: "Who worships here? Who is their God? Where were their voices when the lips of Governor

Barnett dripped with words of interposition and nullification? Where were they when Governor Wallace gave the clarion call for defiance and hatred? Where were their voices of support when tired, bruised, and weary Negro men and women decided to rise from the dark dungeons of complacency to the bright hills of creative protest?"

Yes, these questions are still in my mind. In deep disappointment, I have wept over the laxity of the church. But be assured that my tears have been tears of love. There can be no deep disappointment where there is not deep love. Yes, I love the Church; I love her sacred walls. How could I do otherwise? I am in the rather unique position of being the son, the grandson, and the great-grandson of preachers. Yes, I see the Church as the body of Christ. But, oh! How we have blemished and scarred that body through social neglect and fear of being nonconformist.

There was a time when the Church was very powerful. It was during that period when the early Christians rejoiced when they were deemed worthy to suffer for what they believed. In those days the Church was not merely a thermometer that recorded the ideas and principles of popular opinion; it was a thermostat that transformed the mores of society. Wherever the early Christians entered a town the power structure got disturbed and immediately sought to convict them for being "disturbers of the peace" and "outside agitators." But they went on with the conviction that they were "a colony of heaven" and had to obey God rather than man. They were small in number but big in commitment. They were too God-intoxicated to be "astronomically intimidated." They brought an end to such ancient evils as infanticide and gladiatorial contest.

Things are different now. The contemporary Church is so often a weak, ineffectual voice with an uncertain sound. It is so often the arch-supporter of the status quo. Far from being disturbed by the presence of the Church, the power structure of the average community is consoled by the Church's silent and often vocal sanction of things as they are.

But the judgment of God is upon the Church as never before. If the Church of today does not recapture the sacrificial spirit of the early Church, it will lose its authentic ring, forfeit the loyalty of millions, and be dismissed as an irrelevant social club with no meaning for the twentieth century. I am meeting young people every day whose disappointment with the Church has risen to outright disgust.

Maybe again I have been too optimistic. Is organized religion too inextricably bound to the status quo to save our nation and the world? Maybe I must turn my faith to the inner spiritual Church, the church within the Church, as the true ecclesia and the hope of the world. But again I am thankful to God that some noble souls from the ranks of organized religion have broken loose from the paralyzing chains of conformity and joined us as active partners in the struggle for freedom. They have left their secure congregations and walked the streets of Albany, Georgia, with us. They have gone through the highways of the South on torturous rides for freedom. Yes, they have gone to jail with us. Some have been kicked out of their churches and lost the support of their bishops and fellow ministers. But they have gone with the faith that right defeated is stronger than evil triumphant. These men have been the leaven in the lump of the race. Their witness has been the spiritual salt that has preserved the true meaning of the Gospel in these troubled times. They have carved a tunnel of hope through the dark mountain of disappointment.

I hope the Church as a whole will meet the challenge of this decisive hour. But even if the Church does not come to the aid of justice, I have no despair about the future. I have no fear about the outcome of our struggle in Birmingham, even if our motives are presently misunderstood. We will reach the goal of freedom in Birmingham and all over the nation, because the goal of America is freedom. Abused and scorned though we may be, our destiny is tied up with the destiny of America. Before the pilgrims landed at Plymouth, we were here. Before the pen of Jefferson etched across the pages of history the majestic words of the Declaration of Independence, we were here. For more than two centuries our foreparents labored in this country without wages; they made cotton "king"; and they built the homes of their masters in the midst of brutal injustice and shameful humiliation—and yet out of a bottomless vitality they continued to thrive and develop. If the inexpressible cruelties of slavery could not stop us, the opposition we now face will surely fail. We will win our freedom because the sacred heritage of our nation and the eternal will of God are embodied in our echoing demands.

I must close now. But before closing I am impelled to mention one other point in your statement that troubled me profoundly. You warmly commend the Birmingham police force for keeping "order" and "preventing violence." I don't believe you would have so warmly commended the police force if you had seen its angry violent dogs literally biting six unarmed, nonviolent Negroes. I don't believe you would so quickly commend the policemen if you would observe their ugly and inhuman treatment of Negroes here in the city jail; if you would watch them push and curse old Negro women and young Negro girls; if you would see them slap and kick old Negro men and young Negro boys; if you will observe them, as they did on two occasions, refuse to give us food because we wanted to sing our grace together. I'm sorry that I can't join you in your praise for the police department.

It is true that they have been rather disciplined in their public handling of the demonstrators. In this sense they have been rather publicly "nonviolent." But for what purpose? To preserve the evil system of segregation. Over the last few years I have consistently preached that nonviolence demands the means we use must be as pure as the ends we seek. So I have tried to make it clear that it is wrong to use immoral means to attain moral ends. But now I must affirm that it is just as wrong or even more so to use moral means to preserve immoral ends. Maybe Mr. Connor and his policemen have been rather publicly nonviolent, as Chief Pritchett was in Albany, Georgia, but they have used the moral means of nonviolence to maintain the immoral end of flagrant injustice. T. S. Eliot has said that there is no greater treason than to do the right deed for the wrong reason.

I wish you had commended the Negro sit-inners and demonstrators of Birmingham for their sublime courage, their willingness to suffer, and their amazing discipline in the midst of the most inhuman provocation. One day the South will recognize its real heroes. They will be the James Merediths, courageously and with a majestic sense of purpose, facing jeering and hostile mobs and the agonizing loneliness that characterizes the life of the pioneer. They will be old, oppressed, battered Negro women, symbolized in a seventy-two year old woman of Montgomery, Alabama, who rose up with a sense of dignity and with her people decided not to ride the segregated buses, and responded to one who inquired about her tiredness with ungrammatical profundity: "My feets is tired, but my soul is rested." They will be the young high school and college students, young ministers of the gospel and a host of their elders courageously and nonviolently sitting-in at lunch counters and willingly going to jail for conscience sake. One day the South will know that when these disinherited children of God sat down at lunch counters they were in reality standing up for the best in the American dream and the most sacred values in our Judaeo-Christian heritage, and thus carrying our whole nation back to great wells of democracy which were dug deep by the founding fathers in the formulation of the Constitution and the Declaration of Independence.

Never before have I written a letter this long (or should I say a book?). I'm afraid it is much too long to take your precious time. I can assure you that it would have been much shorter if I had been writing from a comfortable desk, but what else is there to do when you are alone for days in the dull monotony of a narrow jail cell other than write long letters, think strange thoughts, and pray long prayers?

If I have said anything in this letter that is an overstatement of the truth and is indicative of an unreasonable impatience, I beg you to forgive me. If I have said anything in this letter that is an understatement of the truth and is indicative of my having a patience that makes me patient with anything less than brotherhood, I beg God to forgive me.

I hope this letter finds you strong in the faith. I also hope that circumstances will soon make it possible for me to meet each of you, not as an integrationist or a civil rights leader, but as a fellow clergyman and a Christian brother. Let us all hope that the dark clouds of racial prejudice will soon pass away and the deep fog of misunderstanding will be lifted from our fear-drenched communities and in some not too distant tomorrow the radiant stars of love and brotherhood will shine over our great nation with all their scintillating beauty.

Yours for the cause of
Peace and Brotherhood,

Martin Luther King, Jr.

Discussion Questions

"Letter from Birmingham City Jail"

Identify the topic of invention used in each numbered section. With any remaining time, find and identify topics of invention in the latter half of the letter.

1. ______________________
2. ______________________
3. ______________________
4. ______________________
5. ______________________
6. ______________________
7. ______________________
8. ______________________
9. ______________________
10. ______________________
11. ______________________

Discussion Questions

1. Rhetor/*Ethos*: How does King establish goodwill, moral virtue, or practical wisdom?

2. Audience/*Pathos*: What emotions and desires are aroused by the letter? What emotions are intended to be softened or redirected?

3. Text/*Logos*: How is reason used to support the persuasion?

4. Context/*Kairos*: How is the letter appropriate to King's particular moment?

5. What does this letter reveal about his society's values?

6. What unstated messages are within the letter?

____

____

____

____

7. What does the letter want the audience to do? (Remember, this is an open letter, so there are at least two audiences: the pastors themselves and any other readers of the letter.)

____

____

____

____

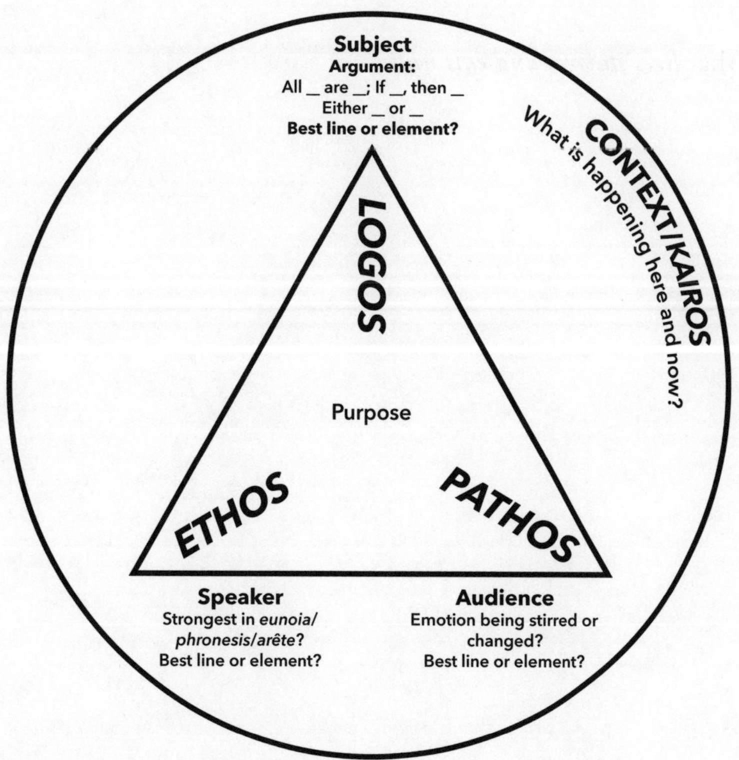

Figure 14. Rhetorical analysis diagram.

Workshop:
Commonplace Competitions

These workshops do not practice all of the topics and subtopics of definition, but they can give you a sense of the mental processes that the topics are tapping into. The first two activities are for the topic of definition, the most fundamental of the topics of invention. Subtopics of the topic of definition include genus/species, division, etymology, synonym/antonym, description, and example.

Genus/Species Jeopardy

The class is divided into two teams. A person from one team comes up and draws a slip of paper from a paper bag. She should give clues to her teammates for the word drawn, and the clues *must be worded in terms of genus first and species second*. If the clue is not worded in exactly this way, no point will be awarded for the answer. The goal is to have teammates correctly guess as many of the words as possible in forty-five seconds.

Examples:

coffee

"This is a *beverage* that is *dark brown and usually consumed in the morning*."

squirrel

"This is an *animal* that *lives in trees and eats nuts*."

Examples Password

This competition is similar to the previous activity, but students must provide one-word examples to prompt teammates to guess the word. (Students should guess after each example is given.) Tally up the number of examples given in each round. The lowest scoring team wins.

Example:

bone

1st example: "Rib."

2nd example: "Femur."

3rd example: "Sternum."

Mystery Bag Guessing Game

The topic of comparison includes similarity, difference, and degree. This activity practices the first two subtopics.

The class should be divided into two teams. Two people from the same team come up to the front of the room. One person chooses a mystery bag, which contains a random item, and peeks in. The other person guesses what is inside the bag. The one with the bag answers with one similarity and one difference.

Student 1: "Is it a/an ____*X*____?"

Student 2: "It is like a/an ____*X*____ in that it is ____________, but it is different from a/an ____*X*____ in that it is not ____________."

Example: bottle of glue

Student 1: "Is it an apple?"

Student 2: "It is like an apple in that it could be found on a teacher's desk, but it is different from an apple in that it is not a food."

Student 1: "Is it a stapler?"

Student 2: "It is like a stapler in that it can hold things together, but it is different from a stapler in that it has no metal."

Student 1: "Is it tape?"

Student 2: "It is like tape in that it is sticky, but it is different from tape in that it is not on a roll."

Student 1: "Is it glue?"

Count the number of questions until the item is correctly guessed. (Be patient! The average number of guesses is six or seven per item.) The lowest score wins!

PRESENTATION:

Ronald Reagan: "Mr. Gorbachev, Tear Down This Wall!" (1987)[7]

SPOTLIGHT

Eye Contact

For this address, you will again focus on eye contact. You should make eye contact across the room, holding your gaze for about two seconds before moving on to another member of the audience.

Former actor Ronald Reagan, known as the "Great Communicator," became president during the Cold War. In this address, he articulates the competing ideologies that had for several decades pitted the Soviet Union against the United States. The Berlin Wall, which cut off West Berlin from East Berlin, became a symbol of the deep divide between Western democratic nations and pro-Soviet governments. Various advisers recommended against the most memorable line—"Mr. Gorbachev, tear down this wall!"—but Reagan decided to leave it in. People differ on how much influence this address truly had in the historical events that followed, but it is nevertheless remembered now as one of Reagan's finest speeches.

June 12, 1987

Thank you very much. Chancellor Kohl, Governing Mayor Diepgen, ladies and gentlemen: Twenty four years ago, President John F. Kennedy visited Berlin, speaking to the people of this city and the world at the city hall. Well, since then two other presidents have come, each in his turn, to Berlin. And today I, myself, make my second visit to your city.

We come to Berlin, we American Presidents, because it's our duty to speak, in this place, of freedom. But I must confess, we're drawn here by other things as well: by the feeling of history in this city, more than 500 years older than our own nation; by the beauty of the Grunewald and the Tiergarten; most of all, by your courage and determination. Perhaps the composer, Paul Lincke, understood something about American Presidents. You see, like so many Presidents before me, I come here today because wherever I go, whatever I do: "*Ich hab noch einen koffer in Berlin.*" [I still have a suitcase in Berlin.]

Our gathering today is being broadcast throughout Western Europe and North America. I understand that it

Figure 15. President Ronald Reagan speaking at the Berlin Wall. From the Ronald Reagan Presidential Library Website.

7. Ronald Reagan, "Remarks on East-West Relations at the Brandenburg Gate in West Berlin," Berlin, Germany, June 12, 1987, Ronald Reagan Presidential Library and Museum, accessed April 18, 2016, https://reaganlibrary.gov/major-speeches-index/35-archives/speeches/1987/6925-061287d.

is being seen and heard as well in the East. To those listening throughout Eastern Europe, I extend my warmest greetings and the good will of the American people. To those listening in East Berlin, a special word: Although I cannot be with you, I address my remarks to you just as surely as to those standing here before me. For I join you, as I join your fellow countrymen in the West, in this firm, this unalterable belief: *Es gibt nur ein Berlin.* [There is only one Berlin.]*

Behind me stands a wall that encircles the free sectors of this city, part of a vast system of barriers that divides the entire continent of Europe. From the Baltic, south, those barriers cut across Germany in a gash of barbed wire, concrete, dog runs, and guardtowers. Farther south, there may be no visible, no obvious wall. But there remain armed guards and checkpoints all the same—still a restriction on the right to travel, still an instrument to impose upon ordinary men and women the will of a totalitarian state. Yet it is here in Berlin where the wall emerges most clearly; here, cutting across your city, where the news photo and the television screen have imprinted this brutal division of a continent upon the mind of the world. Standing before the Brandenburg Gate, every man is a German, separated from his fellow men. Every man is a Berliner, forced to look upon a scar.

President von Weizsacker has said: "The German question is open as long as the Brandenburg Gate is closed." Today I say: As long as this gate is closed, as long as this scar of a wall is permitted to stand, it is not the German question alone that remains open, but the question of freedom for all mankind. Yet I do not come here to lament. For I find in Berlin a message of hope, even in the shadow of this wall, a message of triumph.

In this season of spring in 1945, the people of Berlin emerged from their air raid shelters to find devastation. Thousands of miles away, the people of the United States reached out to help. And in 1947 Secretary of State—as you've been told—George Marshall announced the creation of what would become known as the Marshall plan. Speaking precisely 40 years ago this month, he said: "Our policy is directed not against any country or doctrine, but against hunger, poverty, desperation, and chaos."*

In the Reichstag a few moments ago, I saw a display commemorating this 40th anniversary of the Marshall plan. I was struck by the sign on a burnt-out, gutted structure that was being rebuilt. I understand that Berliners of my own generation can remember seeing signs like it dotted throughout the Western sectors of the city. The sign read simply: "The Marshall plan is helping here to strengthen the free world." A strong, free world in the West, that dream became real. Japan rose from ruin to become an economic giant. Italy, France, Belgium—virtually every nation in Western Europe saw political and economic rebirth; the European Community was founded.

In West Germany and here in Berlin, there took place an economic miracle, the Wirtschaftswunder. Adenauer, Erhard, Reuter, and other leaders understood the practical importance of liberty—that just as truth can flourish only when the journalist is given freedom of speech, so prosperity can come about only when the farmer and businessman enjoy economic freedom. The German leaders reduced tariffs, expanded free trade, lowered taxes. From 1950 to 1960 alone, the standard of living in West Germany and Berlin doubled.*

Where four decades ago there was rubble, today in West Berlin there is the greatest industrial output of any city in Germany—busy office blocks, fine homes and apartments, proud avenues, and the spreading lawns of park land. Where a city's culture seemed to have been destroyed, today there are two great universities, orchestras and an opera, countless theaters, and museums. Where there was want, today there's abundance—food, clothing, automobiles—the wonderful goods of the Ku'damm. From devastation, from utter ruin, you Berliners have, in freedom, rebuilt a city that once again ranks as one of the greatest on Earth. The Soviets may have had other plans. But, my friends, there were a few things the Soviets didn't count on—*Berliner herz, Berliner humor, ja, und Berliner schnauze.* [Berliner heart, Berliner humor, yes, and a Berliner schnauze.] [Laughter]*

In the 1950s, Khrushchev predicted: "We will bury you." But in the West today, we see a free world that has achieved a level of prosperity and well-being unprecedented in all human history. In the Communist world, we see failure, technological backwardness, declining standards of health, even want of the most basic kind—too little food. Even today, the Soviet Union still cannot feed itself. After these four decades, then, there stands before the entire world one great and inescapable conclusion: Freedom leads to prosperity. Freedom replaces the ancient hatreds among the nations with comity and peace. Freedom is the victor.

And now the Soviets themselves may, in a limited way, be coming to understand the importance of freedom. We hear much from Moscow about a new policy of reform and openness. Some political prisoners have been released. Certain foreign news broadcasts are no longer being jammed. Some economic enterprises have been permitted to operate with greater freedom from state control. Are these the beginnings of profound changes in the Soviet state? Or are they token gestures, intended to raise false hopes in the West, or to strengthen the Soviet system without changing it? We welcome change and openness; for we believe that freedom and security go together, that the advance of human liberty can only strengthen the cause of world peace.

There is one sign the Soviets can make that would be unmistakable, that would advance dramatically the cause of freedom and peace. General Secretary Gorbachev, if you seek peace, if you seek prosperity for the Soviet Union and Eastern Europe, if you seek liberalization: Come here to this gate! Mr. Gorbachev, open this gate! Mr. Gorbachev, tear down this wall!*

I understand the fear of war and the pain of division that afflict this continent—and I pledge to you my country's efforts to help overcome these burdens. To be sure, we in the West must resist Soviet expansion. So we must maintain defenses of unassailable strength. Yet we seek peace; so we must strive to reduce arms on both sides. Beginning 10 years ago, the Soviets challenged the Western alliance with a grave new threat, hundreds of new and more deadly SS-20 nuclear missiles, capable of striking every capital in Europe. The Western alliance responded by committing itself to a counter-deployment unless the Soviets agreed to negotiate a better solution; namely, the elimination of such weapons on both sides. For many months, the Soviets refused to bargain in earnestness. As the alliance, in turn, prepared to go forward with its counter-deployment, there were difficult days—days of protests like those during my 1982 visit to this city—and the Soviets later walked away from the table.

But through it all, the alliance held firm. And I invite those who protested then—I invite those who protest today—to mark this fact: Because we remained strong, the Soviets came back to the table. And because we remained strong, today we have within reach the possibility, not merely of limiting the growth of arms, but of eliminating, for the first time, an entire class of nuclear weapons from the face of the Earth. As I speak, NATO ministers are meeting in Iceland to review the progress of our proposals for eliminating these weapons. At the talks in Geneva, we have also proposed deep cuts in strategic offensive weapons. And the Western allies have likewise made far-reaching proposals to reduce the danger of conventional war and to place a total ban on chemical weapons.*

While we pursue these arms reductions, I pledge to you that we will maintain the capacity to deter Soviet aggression at any level at which it might occur. And in cooperation with many of our allies, the United States is pursuing the Strategic Defense Initiative—research to base deterrence not on the threat of offensive retaliation, but on defenses that truly defend; on systems, in short, that will not target populations, but shield them. By these means we seek to increase the safety of Europe and all the world. But we must remember a crucial fact: East and West do not mistrust each other because we are armed; we are armed because we mistrust each other. And our differences are not about weapons but about liberty. When President Kennedy spoke at the City Hall those 24 years ago, freedom was encircled, Berlin was under siege. And today, despite all the pressures upon this city, Berlin stands secure in its liberty. And freedom itself is transforming the globe.

In the Philippines, in South and Central America, democracy has been given a rebirth. Throughout the Pacific, free markets are working miracle after miracle of economic growth. In the industrialized nations, a technological revolution is taking place—a revolution marked by rapid, dramatic advances in computers and telecommunications.*

In Europe, only one nation and those it controls refuse to join the community of freedom. Yet in this age of redoubled economic growth, of information and innovation, the Soviet Union faces a choice: It must make fundamental changes, or it will become obsolete. Today thus represents a moment of hope. We in the West stand ready to cooperate with the East to promote true openness, to break down barriers that separate people, to create a safer, freer world.

And surely there is no better place than Berlin, the meeting place of East and West, to make a start. Free people of Berlin: Today, as in the past, the United States stands for the strict observance and full implementation of all parts of the Four Power Agreement of 1971.

Let us use this occasion, the 750th anniversary of this city, to usher in a new era, to seek a still fuller, richer life for the Berlin of the future. Together, let us maintain and develop the ties between the Federal Republic and the Western sectors of Berlin, which is permitted by the 1971 agreement.

And I invite Mr. Gorbachev: Let us work to bring the Eastern and Western parts of the city closer together, so that all the inhabitants of all Berlin can enjoy the benefits that come with life in one of the great cities of the world. To open Berlin still further to all Europe, East and West, let us expand the vital air access to this city, finding ways of making commercial air service to Berlin more convenient, more comfortable, and more economical. We look to the day when West Berlin can become one of the chief aviation hubs in all central Europe.*

With our French and British partners, the United States is prepared to help bring international meetings to Berlin. It would be only fitting for Berlin to serve as the site of United Nations meetings, or world conferences on human rights and arms control or other issues that call for international cooperation. There is no better way to establish hope for the future than to enlighten young minds, and we would be honored to sponsor summer youth exchanges, cultural events, and other programs for young Berliners from the East. Our French and British friends, I'm certain, will do the same. And it's my hope that an authority can be found in East Berlin to sponsor visits from young people of the Western sectors.

One final proposal, one close to my heart: Sport represents a source of enjoyment and ennoblement, and you many have noted that the Republic of Korea—South Korea—has offered to permit certain events of the 1988 Olympics to take place in the North. International sports competitions of all kinds could take place in both parts of this city. And what better way to demonstrate to the world the openness of this city than to offer in some future year to hold the Olympic games here in Berlin, East and West?

In these four decades, as I have said, you Berliners have built a great city. You've done so in spite of threats—the Soviet attempts to impose the East-mark, the blockade. Today the city thrives in spite of the challenges implicit in the very presence of this wall. What keeps you here? Certainly there's a great deal to be said for your fortitude, for your defiant courage. But I believe there's something deeper, something that involves Berlin's whole look and feel and way of life—not mere sentiment. No one could live long in Berlin without being completely disabused of illusions. Something instead, that has seen the difficulties of life in Berlin but chose to accept them, that continues to build this good and proud city in contrast to a surrounding totalitarian presence that refuses to release human energies or aspirations. Something that speaks with a powerful voice of affirmation, that says yes to this city, yes to the future, yes to freedom. In a word, I would submit that what keeps you in Berlin is love—love both profound and abiding.*

Perhaps this gets to the root of the matter, to the most fundamental distinction of all between East and West. The totalitarian world produces backwardness because it does such violence to the spirit, thwarting the human impulse to create, to enjoy, to worship. The totalitarian world finds even symbols of love and of worship an affront. Years ago, before the East Germans began rebuilding their churches, they erected a secular structure: the television tower at Alexander Platz. Virtually ever since, the authorities have been working to correct what they view as the tower's one major flaw, treating the glass sphere at the top with paints and chemicals of every kind. Yet even today when the Sun strikes that sphere—that sphere that towers over all Berlin—the light makes the sign of the cross. There in Berlin, like the city itself, symbols of love, symbols of worship, cannot be suppressed.

As I looked out a moment ago from the Reichstag, that embodiment of German unity, I noticed words crudely spray-painted upon the wall, perhaps by a young Berliner, "This wall will fall. Beliefs become reality." Yes, across Europe, this wall will fall. For it cannot withstand faith; it cannot withstand truth. The wall cannot withstand freedom.

And I would like, before I close, to say one word. I have read, and I have been questioned since I've been here about certain demonstrations against my coming. And I would like to say just one thing, and to those who demonstrate so. I wonder if they have ever asked themselves that if they should have the kind of government they apparently seek, no one would ever be able to do what they're doing again.

Thank you and God bless you all.

CHAPTER 7

CANON TWO, ORGANIZATION: ORDERING THE CONTENT

(1414a) . . . A speech has two parts. You must state your case, and you must prove it. You cannot either state your case and omit to prove it, or prove it without having first stated it; since any proof must be a proof of something, and the only use of a preliminary statement is the proof that follows it. . . .

(1414b) The Introduction is the beginning of a speech, corresponding to the prologue in poetry and the prelude in flute-music; they are all beginnings, paving the way, as it were, for what is to follow. The musical prelude resembles the introduction to speeches of display; as flute players play first some brilliant passage they know well and then fit it on to the opening notes of the piece itself, so in speeches of display the writer should proceed in the same way; he should begin with what best takes his fancy, and then strike up his theme and lead into it; which is indeed what is always done. . . .

(1415a) You may use any means you choose to make your hearer receptive; among others, giving him a good impression of your character, which always helps to secure his attention. (1415b) He will be ready to attend to anything that touches himself and to anything that is important, surprising, or agreeable; and you should accordingly convey to him the impression that what you have to say is of this nature. . . . Moreover, calls for attention, when required, may come equally well in any part of a speech; in fact, the beginning of it is just where there is least slackness of interest; it is therefore ridiculous to put this kind of thing at the beginning, when every one is listening with most attention.

(1416b) Nowadays it is said, absurdly enough, that the narration should be rapid. Remember what the man said to the baker who asked whether he was to make the cake hard or soft: "What, can't you make it ***right?***" Just so here. We are not to make long narrations, just as we are not to make long introductions or long arguments. Here, again, rightness does not consist either in rapidity or in conciseness, but in the happy mean; that is, in saying just so much as will make the facts plain, (1417a) or will lead the hearer to believe that the thing has happened, or that the man has caused injury or wrong to some one, or that the facts are really as important as you wish them to be thought: or the opposite facts to establish the opposite arguments. . . .

> (1417b) The duty of the Arguments is to attempt demonstrative proofs. These proofs must bear directly upon the question in dispute, which must fall under one of four heads. (1) If you maintain that the act ***was not committed***, your main task in court is to prove this. (2) If you maintain that the act ***did no harm***, prove this. If you maintain that (3) the act was ***less*** than is alleged, or (4) ***justified***, prove these facts, just as you would prove the act not to have been committed if you were maintaining that. . . .[1]
>
> (1418b) [I]t is part of the Arguments to break down the opponent's case, whether by objection or by counter-syllogism. . . .
>
> (1419b) The Epilogue has four parts. You must (1) make the audience well-disposed towards yourself and ill-disposed towards your opponent, (2) magnify or minimize the leading facts, (3) excite the required state of emotion in your hearers, and (4) refresh their memories.

When an earthquake occurred in Nepal in April of 2015, Red Cross and other relief workers raced to the area. People across the globe sent food and vital medicines. But even when necessary supplies were at hand, they had trouble reaching the places that needed them most. Why? There was no disaster plan, and the supplies—though available—could not be channeled efficiently across the country. Relief workers were stuck at the airport for days, and food and medicine remained packaged in boxes. The problem was not so much one of content but of *organization*: The country suffered because arrangements had not been made, and there was no orderly way to deliver the goods.

Having covered the concept of invention in the previous chapter, a concept concerned with the generation of content, we are now ready to think about organization and its importance in making an argument. Having the material on hand is only the first step. Presenting it in an organized, artfully arranged way is the next one.

In fact, the Greek word translated as "arrangement" or "order" is *taxis*, a term borrowed from the military. Think of warfare. History is full of spectacular gaffes due simply to the poor arrangement of troops. Battles have been lost and won based on the organization of soldiers alone, when greater numbers, better artillery, and even superior training didn't add up to sure victory in the field. In the same way, the strategic arrangement of an argument can also be critical. Great content is not enough. Presented carelessly, your rhetoric can fall flat.

While the order of a speech or text is not as central as the order of, say, the plot in a drama, arrangement still matters—in the same way that it's better to use a drink to chase a pill of medicine rather than the other way around. So while there is some freedom in how one arranges an argument, not all arrangements are equally effective. Fortunately, for us, a compelling order has already been discovered. There's no need to reinvent the wheel! Concerning what a speech *must* have, its most basic elements, Aristotle simplifies the matter: The only *necessary* parts in a speech, he says, are the statement and the proof. These—stating the case and subsequently proving it—are, after all, what constitute the actual argument, though other parts of a speech can be added to polish it. Centuries after Aristotle, thinkers such as Cicero and Quintilian would go on to develop Aristotle's ideas into a fairly strict six-part system of organization, one that was meant to suit almost any occasion. This chapter will introduce those six parts.

1. Aristotle does not discuss the *partitio*, which would later become an important part of classical organization.

Although what's really only needed is to state your point and then prove it, Aristotle allows for an introduction because, he says, the speech seems slapdash without one. The opening is a hand extended, reaching out to let the audience grab hold and follow the speech. That is, one's proofs shouldn't be thrust upon the audience without a little warming up first, just as two people generally don't launch into a heavy conversation without first saying, "Hello! How are you?" And just as there are expected polite pleasantries in daily interaction, there are recognizable conventions in rhetoric that can be used to give a speech some form.

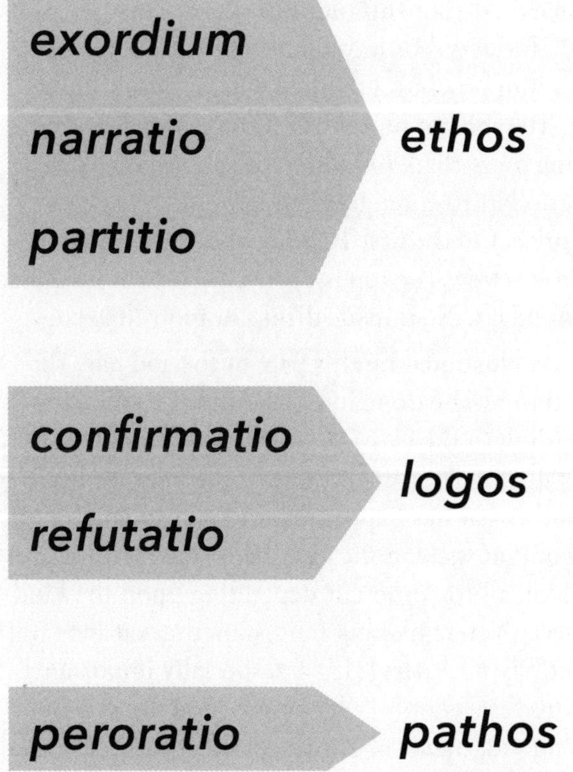

Figure 16. The six parts of classical organization and their corresponding rhetorical appeals.

Section One: Opening

Introduction, or *Exordium*

A young boy is headed to the zoo for the first time. His mother is excited to be taking him, but he pouts in the backseat of the minivan, less than thrilled to exchange his air-conditioned home for a day of walking in the heat. But as they pull into the parking lot, the mother points out to her son the stunning entrance to the zoo. He sees it and gasps. A mural of zebras, elephants, monkeys, and snakes decorates the fifteen-foot wall on both sides. The name of the zoo is carved into a huge wooden sign, which is held up by two life-sized rhino statues. Trees and vines have been planted all about, suggesting a jungle theme. A thatched hut functions as the admission booth, and the lady working it wears a safari hat and has a parrot perched on her shoulder. How does the little boy feel now? He's enthusiastic, having forgotten all about what had previously occupied him. The entrance arrested his attention, and now he can't wait to go in.

Likewise, the ***exordium*** (from the Latin *exordiri*, "to begin") of a speech or paper grabs the audience's attention, right away piquing their interest and disposing them well to the upcoming argument. People need to start by trusting you, and they're less likely to do that if they're thrown into a topic that they don't know anything about. So the opening introduces that topic, and it does so in an inviting kind of way. How can you do that? A joke, a story, an interesting statistic, a paradox, a question, a quotation—these are just some of the ways an audience can be invited into the topic at hand.

Which should you choose? Look to your audience. Choosing an effective attention-getter is really a matter of being a good psychologist—that is, a kind of scientist of human souls. In other words, crafting a winsome introduction is not a formulaic or perfunctory exercise: You cannot assume that you have been persuasive just because you included the "right" elements. So getting the attention of your audience during the *exordium* is a case in which the proof is in the pudding, so to speak. It is not a matter of having a good product because you followed a recipe. Your success will be determined by the audience's response. Are they intrigued by your opening? Then you have won a small victory. Are they bored or irritated? Such a response would mean your *exordium* failed.

A quick warning: Aristotle also knows that the first part of an address is when most people will already be paying attention naturally, so he cautions us not to pack *all* of the interesting material here (1415b). To draw them back in throughout the speech, he recommends spotlighting such golden nuggets with special mini-introductions such as the following: "Now I beg you to note this point—it concerns you quite as much as myself," and "I will tell you that whose like you have never yet heard for terror, or for wonder." (In today's idiom, these two statements might sound more like this, respectively: "Please listen carefully because this issue applies to you just as much as it does to me," and "What I'm about to tell you is hard to believe, and you've probably never heard anything like it in your life, but it's true.") Such sentences, which prepare the audience to receive what you are about to say, can recapture the interest of a wandering listener and also highlight a special point.

Questions to Consider:

Who is your audience? What is their mood? In what mood do you wish them to be? Who are you as a rhetor? Can you pull off a joke? (Telling a joke is often much harder than we imagine.) Will your audience find it funny? What about opening with a story? Is this a crowd that will welcome a story, or will they find it a waste of precious time? And, again, have you chosen an appropriate story? Consider other openings, and what their effect might be on that particular audience at that particular time.

Your goals are to invite your audience into your argument and to set a tone for what follows. Figuring out how best to do so will require that you consider *all* of the elements on the rhetoric triangle: rhetor, audience, subject, purpose, and context.

Statement of Facts, or *Narratio*

Back to the zoo: The boy's mother leads him to the thatched-roof entrance hut. What does he learn here? The facts. His mother points him to signs and hands him brochures that tell what is public knowledge. The zoo has more than 2,000 animals representing more than 400 different species. It will cost eight dollars to enter, but children under twelve are half price. On the first Tuesday of each month, admission is free. The zoo is open until 6 p.m. It's closed on Mondays. No outside drinks or food allowed.

As illustrated by this part of the zoo tale, the next thing to be done in a text is address the facts. According to the classical order, this second section generally involves an account of the relevant background (what has happened) and an explanation of the point at issue in the case. This statement of fact will look a little different depending upon the kind of speech you're making (and sometimes it may not be entirely necessary). It's an especially important section, for example, when your audience will be making judgments about the past because they need to know just which facts are agreed upon, and which ones aren't. For other types of rhetoric, the ***narratio*** can simply explain the context for the issue at hand, making clear why this issue matters *here* and *now*. You should think of it, then, as a catch-up section, a miniature rundown of relevant facts that will quickly bring your readers up to speed on what they need to know (i.e., what already has been determined and what need not be argued) before moving into the rest of the argument.

For example, for a burglary case in court, the prosecutor would narrate the facts of the case, giving an overall picture of what has happened and what is at stake: "Between the hours of 11 p.m. on December 24 and 5 a.m. on December 25 of this past year, an intruder entered the home at 6824 Wren Road. Stolen from the home were one dozen chocolate chip cookies and one glass of tepid milk. The next morning, the fireplace door was found ajar and the flue open." These facts are agreed upon by both sides, but what is not agreed upon is the culprit.

Let's look at another possibility. If a rhetor is attempting to persuade the audience of the dangers of excessive cell phone use, the *narratio* could place the issue in the context of modern-day America, tracing our phone usage back to its inception by Alexander Graham Bell in 1876. But going back that far would be appropriate only if the invention of the phone is relevant to potentially excessive cell phone usage of our day. Did Bell's invention set in motion an unraveling of human relationships, an unraveling that has continued with the proliferation of cell phones? If no thread can be found that holds together Bell and cell, then a different *narratio* may need to be chosen. If the concern is *not* about the effects of phones on relationships, then the *narratio* may need to be more of an update on recent technological advances (not nineteenth-century innovations) and summarize their potentially harmful effects on human bodies.

Or take a final example: You are giving the eulogy at your grandfather's funeral. In this case, the facts of his life, the deeds that are going to be recounted in your speech, are those things that will not be offered as bare details of his history but instead will be recalled as evidence of his virtuous life. If you take Aristotle's advice, you won't rattle off your grandfather's deeds all at once but will instead pepper those facts throughout the eulogy. This means that your *narratio* would be stretched throughout the speech itself. In fact, Aristotle says as much: "Narration in ceremonial oratory is not continuous but intermittent" (1416b).

Again, there are no hard-and-fast rules as to how to formulate a single, one-size-fits-all *narratio*, and that's because what may be appropriate in one setting can be woefully inappropriate in another. Each *narratio* will depend on that particular moment—the speaker, the audience, and the issue. But the idea in each of these cases is to place the topic at hand in its unique context.

Questions to Consider:

What are the facts of the matter? What has happened in the past that the audience needs to be reminded of, or made aware of? What do both sides agree on? What specific issue do they not yet agree on? (That is, what is the real issue at hand?) What is your audience's context that makes this issue matter to them?

The point is not to list facts haphazardly. Your goal is to lay out the matter as clearly as you can, bringing your audience to the point that calls for an argument in the first place—that is, the point of contention. In other words, the *narratio* should clearly elucidate what is at stake by verbally setting aside what is already known. And it shows how that issue fits within the audience and rhetor's particular context.

Division, or *Partitio*

Let us visit the boy's story once more: The young boy is then led into the zoo. If he begins to wander about aimlessly, he'll be quickly overwhelmed and confused. With no idea of where he is or what's next, his experience would be chaotic, and chaotic experiences are not only generally unpleasant but also difficult to remember. But his mother knows this, so what does she do? She leads him over to the giant map with a bright red "You are here" arrow pointing at the entrance. His mother identifies for him the major attractions: *Aquarium to the right, aviary to the rear, African savanna off to the left, reptile house straight ahead.* Spending a moment to get the big picture before entering will pay off in the end. If his mother gives him a sense of the whole—"First we'll see the lions and then head over to the snakes before stopping for lunch; we'll end with the fish and birds"—then he can put in order, both mentally and physically, his movement through the zoo. And his mother won't have to worry about her son wandering too far from their chosen route.

Just as maps can be helpful for our physical journeys in life, they also be helpful for our verbal expeditions. A verbal map—a very brief outline of what will follow—is given in this third section, the *partitio*[2] (a Latin word meaning "division"). The *partitio* offers a digest of the main points one will be discussing, although all the evidence or support for those points will be saved for later. Because people generally like to know where they're headed, the *partitio* puts the audience at ease by offering a road map of sorts. Laying out a preview of the argument helps the audience feel better about being in the passenger's seat—no major surprises and no sharp turns ahead. The audience can keep better track of where they are in the argument because you have already sketched out a route for the journey.

The *partitio* is what we today often call the "thesis" or "thesis statement." This sentence (or two) stipulates broadly what will and won't be included in the speech, setting the audience's expectations for what will and won't be addressed. You may notice that the *partitio* is not mentioned by Aristotle. By the time of Quintilian, however, it was a staple for rhetors. Offered early in an argument, the *partitio* can help audience members remember the rhetor's points even if their minds wander momentarily. (Think of the boy at the zoo; if he loses sight of his mother, he can find her by recalling where they were headed.) Knowing one's course ahead of time can help the audience stay on track. So the *partitio*, because of its ability to present the rhetor as trustworthy and to keep the audience from getting lost, is an important tool in any rhetor's toolbox.

Speaking of trust . . . this entire first section—*exordium*, *narratio*, and *partitio*—could be said to focus on *ethos*. That is, the speaker is gaining the right to be heard by attracting the attention of the audience, providing the background to the topic, and laying out the structure of the speech—and all of this before having jumped into the main body of the text! The three of these together, then, function as an introductory section.

Questions to Consider:

What exactly (and briefly) do you plan to discuss, and in what order? What will be the "take away"? What are your reasons for presenting your proofs in this particular order? How much of your evidence should you reveal to your audience before you set out to prove your case? Are your points short enough to be remembered by your audience but detailed enough to offer guidance to them?

Your goal is to offer a quick roadmap for your text so that your audience doesn't get lost. Keep it broad: Don't include the reasons, just the claims.

Section Two: Argument

Let's forsake the zoo analogy and think instead about basketball. When you have possession of the

2. This statement is alternately called the ***divisio***.

ball, what should you do? Run a play and take a good shot—maybe a three-pointer or a layup, perhaps even a slam dunk. The hope is to keep possession of the ball until you make points, though the action will certainly move, at times, to the other end of the court. When it does, it's time to play defense.

The back-and-forth nature of a basketball game is not unlike the next major section of classical arrangement, a section that Aristotle calls simply the "argument." It is here that a rhetor offers arguments as proof. Whereas you can imagine omitting the attention-getting *exordium* and even the verbal map of the *partitio*, this section—the proof of your case—is absolutely necessary. So if *ethos* was the concern of the first three sections, the turn here, in the speech's main body, is toward *logos*.

Just as a single basketball game consists of playing both offensive and defensive, so too does the argument consist of two parts: the ***confirmatio*** and the ***refutatio***.

Proof, or *Confirmatio*

Think of the *confirmatio* as the actual proving of the case. We must remember Aristotle's two must-do points: State your case, and prove it. In fact, this section is a refreshing reminder that the winner of an argument is not necessarily the one with a dominating personality and a silver tongue. Aristotle's point is that, to persuade genuinely, you must *prove* your case, clearly showing the listener that your argument makes the most sense. And you can do that in a number of ways.

Table 3. Early stasis theory.

Early Stasis Theory
Fact: Did it happen?
Harm: Is it harmful or advantageous?
Importance: Is it significant or insignificant?
Justice: Is it just or unjust?

Aristotle says that there are really only four points that can be argued: whether something happened (fact), whether it is harmful (harm), whether it is significant (importance), and whether it is just (justice).[3] Proving any one of these points takes demonstration. Aristotle's list is an early iteration of *stasis* (Greek, a "standing still," a "stopping place") theory that would later be brought into its maturity by the Roman orators. Words such as *static* and *station* are evidently related to *stasis*, but the Greek term does not have the same quiet or peaceful connotations as its English cousins. It may be helpful to think of two armies clashing when you see the term in the context of rhetoric: When those armies meet on the battlefield, there is a period of deadlock, of impasse, in which neither side has an obvious advantage. This is the experience of physical

3. A list similar to this one can be found in Kennedy, *On Rhetoric*, 273. See especially note 230.

stasis, and it's easy to see its analog in rhetoric. The place of conflict, where there is real disagreement and neither side has won the day (i.e., has proven persuasive), is the *stasis* point. So ***stasis* theory** is a way of moving quickly to that point, deciding where the real (rhetorical) battle needs to take place, and the list of questions shows that there is actually a limited number of battlefields.

Suppose, for example, a six-year-old girl is accused by her brother of taking a brownie without asking. In an attempt to avoid punishment, she unwittingly runs through the *stasis* points in her head. Did I take it? *Fact.* Did I hurt anyone by taking it? *Harm.* Is it really that big of a deal? *Importance.* Was I justified in taking it? *Justice.* The little girl may have valid rebuttals for each point of *stasis*, but if she did take it (fact), it made her brother cry (harm), and it was the very last brownie (importance), then her case is not looking very good. Her argument, then, needs to be made based on the issue of justice. If she can make the case that she bought the brownies using her own allowance money, things are looking up. She may indeed be justified in consuming her own goods, and she has found the point of *stasis*, the point at which she should stop and make her argument.

Questions to Consider:

You have a point you're trying to prove; what are the various proofs you can offer to do so? What arguments can you discover using the common topics of invention? What is the very best way of presenting those arguments to your audience—in order of time, in order of space, in order of importance? Should you lead with your strongest argument, or should you build to it? Consider stasis theory: Can you identify the key issue—the stopping point—of the argument?

You're doing the hard work of proving your case in this section. You'll need to emphasize *logos* here, but remember: *Ethos* and *pathos* are proofs, too, so don't hesitate to utilize them.

Interrogation, or *Refutatio*

In an evenly matched basketball game, you can't expect to win by playing offense alone. In fact, a good ball game means that you must sometimes be on the defensive. So when the ball is in your court, what should you do? Block shots, thwart plays, and try to gain possession of the ball.

Similarly, a rhetor cannot expect to speak to an issue without at some point combatting opposing viewpoints. In fact, to stick with our basketball analogy, to run only offensive plays is to practice, not compete. An argument that never offers counterarguments is stuck in the warm-up stage, not yet really in the game at all. So while we began our discussion of the argument with the *confirmatio*, it may be the case that the *refutatio* would need to come first. Why? Speakers who are arguing against a given issue—that is, speaking on the defensive—have some work to do before they offer their own arguments: They must first clear the air as best they can before being heard. In a basketball game, if your team loses the tipoff, then your first job is to get possession! This means that, for the defendant, the counterattack—or the addressing of arguments from the other side (*refutatio*)—must come first (see, e.g., Socrates's introduction in Plato's *Apology*, in which he does just that).

Either way, defending oneself against attack can be daunting, but Aristotle offers some strategies for handling it. In short, a rhetor should expose faulty logic in the opponent and point out how bad conclusions follow from bad premises. His examples include drawing attention to loaded questions[4] ("Have you stopped cheating on your homework yet?" "When exactly did you start breaking the law?") and contradictions as well as asking self-evident questions that unravel the opponent's argument. (You may remember these fallacies of begging the question from logic

4. A loaded question is also known as an amphiboly, from the Greek *amphi-*, meaning "both" or "on both sides," and *bole*, meaning "a casting" or "a throwing." These questions, then, are really two in one, pinning the person being interrogated between two unenviable possibilities.

class.) As for humor in such encounters, Aristotle recommends Gorgias's suggestion "that you should kill your opponents' earnestness with jesting and their jesting with earnestness" (1419b).

We might add here that there is not a perfect *refutatio* for every counterargument. Here is Aristotle's advice in such a situation: "You may admit the wrong, but balance it with other facts" (1416a). For example, if you are arguing for a new policy of early dismissal from school each Friday, you know what one argument from the other side will be: This change would mean less instruction time for academic classes. You shouldn't ignore this argument, but you also don't need to deny its truth. Instead, you can acknowledge the point—thus strengthening your *ethos*—but then go on to present an argument that, although it doesn't eliminate the counterargument, potentially outweighs it. "Of course, it is true that instructional time for our classes would be decreased," you might say. "That's a valid point and an important one. But we should also consider the restful study that students can enjoy at home, which will both refresh and deepen study and also bring students back to class with renewed interest." In other words, deal with counterarguments fairly; doing so will actually strengthen your case.

Questions to Consider:

Who disagrees with you? (If no one disagrees with you, you probably haven't chosen a very interesting topic.) What are their very best arguments? What response can you offer to each of those arguments? If you can't adequately address a counterclaim, can you nevertheless offer an equally important point? Are you dealing with your opposition charitably? Can you grant them certain points while continuing to uphold your own view?

Your goal is not to tear the other side to shreds, nor is it to turn them into straw men to win an easy victory. You should strive always to be fair and just, honestly dealing with the important points of the opposition.

Section Three: Closing

Conclusion, or *Peroratio*

Aristotle claims four functions of the conclusion (1419b). It should touch back on the three rhetorical appeals: *ethos* (by building the speaker's *ethos* and impairing the opponent's), *logos* (by amplifying and minimizing the logical points at issue), and *pathos* (by evoking the audience's emotion). Finally, it serves as a memory refresher, reminding the audience of the sweep of the argument.

It is the third appeal—*pathos*—that is most at play in the final section. Remember Socrates's chariot in the *Phaedrus*, driven by two horses (see chapter 5). The dark horse is unruly and wild-eyed, but he is also the chief driving force. Without the dark horse, the chariot would be, if not altogether still, certainly moving much slower. Since the image of the chariot is to be an image of the soul, we must recognize the implication: The passions, like the dark horse, are a driving force. The pain and pleasure tied to them move people to make judgments. Without pain and pleasure, we might be stuck in contemplation and wonder forever. But with them, we are jolted into reality, the issues at hand seeming imminent, urgent; we are thus compelled to respond. It is for this reason that *pathos* is evoked to good effect here at the end of the address, when the judgment of the audience is to be rendered.

Questions to Consider:

Memory: In a nutshell, what have you discussed? Logos*: What are your major proofs?* Ethos*: What kind of a person are you that your audience should trust you?* Pathos*: What are their emotions at this point, and how can appropriate emotions help move them to judgment about the case at hand? Finally, what do you want your audience to do?*

In short, this section should address the question, "So, what?" If your audience has stuck with you this far, reading or listening to the end, here is where you assure them that they have not been wasting their time (and you have not been wasting yours). This can be done by reiterating your points, if you think they might need to be repeated, but even more important will be the need to let them know how your argument *matters* to them.

A Persuasive Order

This order—from *exordium*, *narratio*, and *partitio*, to *confirmatio* and *refutatio*, and finally to ***peroratio***—is no mere formula: It's a natural sequence. First comes gaining the right to be heard, a matter of *ethos*; then looking to the argument and its importance, an employment of *logos*; finally conjuring the emotions, attention to *pathos*. You will notice that after *logos* comes *pathos*—in other words, emotion follows the reasoning and does not lead it. *Ethos*, *logos*, and *pathos* are all in their proper order and are all accounted for. And you must remember that, without bringing all three into play, the persuasion may not be complete. The audience must be able to find the argument believable (*ethos* makes it credible), to understand it (*logos* is its reasonability), and to make a decision (*pathos* pushes toward judgment).

Aristotle's final comment in his treatise is this: "I have done. You have heard me. The facts are before you. I ask for your judgment" (1420b). It strikes the ear as strange, doesn't it? We might expect a more rhetorically moving conclusion from one discussing the art of persuasion. And yet the comment emphasizes something important: Rhetoric is all about judgment. All civic speech—yes, even a philosophical treatise on language, such as Aristotle's own—urges its hearers to make judgments. Language of the city is a give-and-take enterprise of influence and decision, with speakers ever pushing to hold sway over others. This game of influence is ever-present, from a text such as Aristotle's to a billboard ad. Making decisions, praising the good, and weighing justice are all part of the larger political sphere of pleading a case and convincing—not forcing—the listener.

Discussion Text:

Martin Luther King, Jr.:
"Letter from Birmingham City Jail" (1963)

Focus:

Organization

1

Take another look at "Letter from Birmingham City Jail" from chapter 6. Can you discern the organization of the letter?

Identify the *exordium*:

Identify the *narratio*:

Partitio: (perhaps absent)

Confirmatio:

Refutatio:

Peroratio:

Is King successful in establishing *ethos* in the *exordium* and *narratio*?

Does he refute and then confirm? Does he confirm and then refute? Or does he alternate?

Is the movement from *ethos* to *logos* and then to *pathos* discernible, and might a reader be motivated to action by his conclusion? Which lines are especially full of *pathos*?

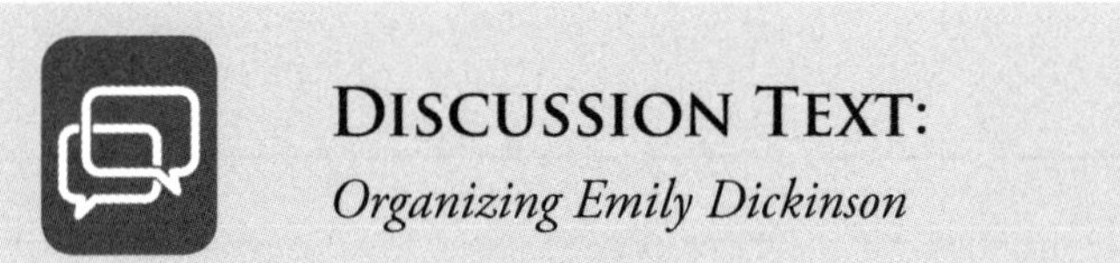

Discussion Text: *Organizing Emily Dickinson*

Focus: *Organization* 2

The following is a poem by the quirky Emily Dickinson. The order of the three stanzas has been scrambled so that you can explore the importance of organization. Try to organize the stanzas as you think she originally arranged them.

Make sure you know some of the basic meanings of the words. When is dawn? When is dusk? Pay attention to details. Can you tell if this is a new boat out on its first sailing venture, or is this an experienced vessel?

As a class, discuss the possible orderings. Why did you choose to begin and conclude with the stanzas you did? What was your organizational principle (e.g., chronology, stanza length, ideas)? Which perspective does your arrangement privilege (the angels' or the sailors')?

The point is this: The content of the poem is the same no matter what, but the order does matter. The stanza you choose as your conclusion changes the meaning of the poem, determining its trajectory as tragic or comic.

#30

by Emily Dickinson

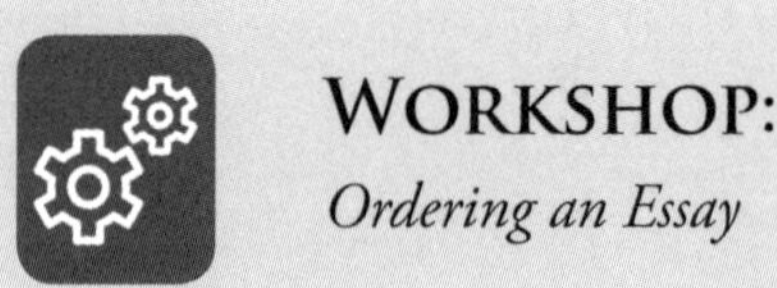

WORKSHOP:
Ordering an Essay

1

In this chapter, we have learned the six parts of a classically organized text:

exordium *narratio* *partitio* *confirmatio* *refutatio* *peroratio*

The following sections are parts of an essay about the importance of school sports, but the parts have been mixed up. Identify each section, and then arrange them in classical order.

A. Some may argue that school should focus only on academics. Granted, the mental growth of students is hugely important. But I would argue that school should be about one's *full* development, which means that their bodies should be trained and exercised, too. Others point out that sports, such as football, can be a distraction for students, taking them away from their studies. However, it's also the case that students need to learn to balance different parts of their lives, just as they'll have to do after they leave high school and go on to college and the real world.

Section: ____________________

What does this section do? ____________________

B. In our school, a priority is placed upon the academics, but the truth is that if we take a long view of history, we will find that the *gymnasia* was equally important to the Greeks, those after whom we model our classical learning.

Section: ____________________

What does this section do? ____________________

C. No pass, no play. We've all heard that a million times. But why not the opposite—no play, no pass? In other words, if ours is truly a *classical* school, we should reconsider the place of competitive sports and whether a higher value ought to be placed on them.

Section: ____________________

What does this section do? ____________________

D. Let's now explore the benefits of competitive sports as well as the various temptations that come along with such activities.

Section: ____________________

What does this section do? ____________________

E. Being involved in sports shouldn't be optional; it should be required. Although there are some dangers, they are outweighed by the benefits—important benefits for students still learning how to be balanced citizens of our world. So don't forget "no pass, no play," but I encourage you to begin to think about a twin policy: No play, no pass.

Section: ____________________

What does this section do? ____________________

F. Playing sports during high school has tremendous advantages. Playing a sport teaches students the value of competition, and ideally it teaches them how to compete in a healthy way. But it's not all about competition. Ironically, sports promote an opposite good, too: teamwork. Working together fosters natural friendships that develop as students pursue a common goal.

Section: ____

What does this section do? ______________________________

Finally, please list the proper classical order of these sections by letter:

______, ______, ______, ______, ______, ______

Sample Speech

The following is a sample speech structured according to classical organization. Read it and identify the different sections: *exordium*, *narratio*, *partitio*, *confirmatio*, *refutatio*, and *peroratio*.

Yesterday I ran out of toothpaste, so what did I do? What any other person in my town, or almost any city in the United States for that matter, would do. I stopped by Walmart on my way home from work. Now I know Walmart has earned a lot of bad press about its customers—there are even websites devoted to making fun of them—but whether Walmart tends to attract or create a tacky culture today is not what I'm here to talk about. I'm here to talk about why shopping at Walmart is bad not only for your soul but also for your neighbor. That's right: Shopping at Walmart can be considered in terms of charity!

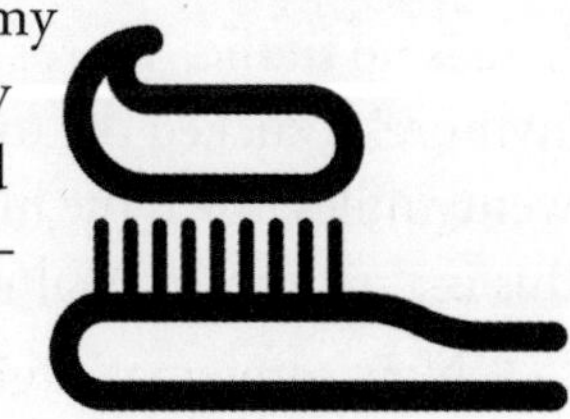

When I grew up—it was the 1980s, mind you—there weren't many Walmart stores. In fact, Walmart had a pretty low reputation, worse than Kmart, really. But now there are over 5,000 Walmart stores in the United States; Walmart has even expanded into 28 other countries, such as the United Kingdom and even Mozambique![5] It is the *largest retailer in the world*.[6] In fact, it's the largest company in the world, with more revenue than General Motors, Ford, and General Electric combined.[7] And if you'd owned stock in Walmart back in the early '80s when I was in school, today you'd be quite rich. A $1,650 investment in Walmart the day it went public would be worth over twelve million dollars today.[8]

So let's talk a little about what lies beneath the success of Walmart: sending jobs overseas and sending mom-and-pop shops to the cleaners.

---

5. "Walmart: Our Locations," Walmart, accessed April 11, 2016, http://corporate.walmart.com/our-story/locations/united-states#/united-states.
6. Phalguni Soni, "Analyzing Walmart—The World's Largest Retailer," Market Realist, February 18, 2015, http://marketrealist.com/2015/02/analyzing-walmart-worlds-largest-retailer/.
7. "Largest Companies," Morelesscompare.com, 365 Facts, accessed April 11, 2016, http://morelesscompare.com/list-of-largest-companies-ordered-by-name/.
8. Steven Nickolas, "If You Had Invested in Wal-Mart Right After Its IPO," Investopedia, April 11, 2016, http://www.investopedia.com/articles/markets/110515/if-you-had-invested-walmart-right-after-its-ipo.asp.

Walmart sells itself on its ability to offer cheaper prices on common brands. But those cheap prices come at a cost. The suppliers must produce their items more and more inexpensively, which means that company after company is having to move its business overseas. I'll give you just one example: The bike-maker Huffy, under pressure from Walmart to provide it with cheaper and cheaper bikes, has moved its entire production overseas. "We are shopping ourselves out of jobs," claims Steve Dobbins, whose company Caroline Mills has sold textiles to Walmart suppliers. US employees at Carolina Mills, by the way, had shrunk from 2,600 to 1,200 when he made that comment.[9]

Next, I'd like to point out what a Walmart does to smaller stores in the area. Now, just today, there's an ad in the *Tribune-Herald* about a new Walmart opening by the interstate just south of town. The article opens by claiming that this Walmart will "create nearly 300 jobs." Really? Create them out of thin air? Are we so naive? It's going to have a fuel island. Are we not naive to think that some other gas station isn't going to suffer lost business because of cheap Walmart gas? A dear friend of mine grew up in Nowata, Oklahoma, a tiny little town that had a charming and active downtown. There was a shoe store, a florist, two grocery stores, a donut shop, a drugstore, two hardware stores, a sporting goods store, and a few mechanics garages—all of these owned by local families. In came Walmart in 1984. At first, it seemed great. You could buy everything in one spot—new shoes for yourself, flowers for mom, groceries for the family, donuts for the kids, pharmacy prescriptions for grandma, a hammer and nails, a soccer ball—and all while getting your oil changed and tires rotated! What is Nowata like now? I hate to tell you. It's a ghost town, or really no town at all. The traffic light is gone because there is no traffic. There's a Chinese restaurant, a resale shop, and a Dollar General. There isn't even a Walmart anymore! It sucked the town dry and then it closed. When it did, the Walmart in Bartlesville, a small city just twenty miles down the highway, was converted into a Supercenter. And do you know what the worst part is? This is a pattern for Walmart: Suck the town dry and then move on to the next one.

Now some may argue that Walmart isn't alone. It's true that Target has its superstores, and that H-E-B Plus! carries clothes and electronics as well as groceries. And that's a good point. But Walmart is really in a category of its own because it is—you may be surprised to find out—larger than Target, Kroger, Home Depot, Walgreens, and Amazon *combined*.[10] And are we to justify Walmart just because everyone else is following suit? Is that not like saying that the greedy little boy who takes everyone else's toys is justified simply because the example he sets is so successful that all the other kids start stealing toys, too? Greed can only be justified by the greedy.

In fact, that points to another issue. To be fair, I'm not sure we can really put all the blame on Walmart. After all, what *caused* the success of Walmart? Was it not an obsession with getting *more*, *more*, *more* for your money? Is it not, in other words, greed—the greed of the consumers? I've heard it said that the sin of communism is envy, but the sin of capitalism is greed. If that's the case, then Walmart is just the product of the American capitalistic mentality.

Others may argue that the ability to buy cheaper products means more families can stretch their dollar to cover necessities, such as food. It's another point that sounds reasonable at face value. But when stretching the family dollar means slowly putting smaller businesses out of business, then it's a little like killing the

9. Charles Fishman, "The Walmart You Don't Know," in *Contemporary Readings in Globalization*, ed. Scott Sernau (Thousand Oaks, CA: Pine Forge, 2008), 15–18.
10. "The 100 Largest Companies in the World Ranked by Revenue in 2015," Statista, The Statistics Portal, accessed April 11, 2016, http://www.statista.com/statistics/263265/top-companies-in-the-world-by-revenue/.

goose that lays the golden egg: You can put food on the table today, but the very jobs that provide that dollar in the first place are quietly disappearing.

Now, I'm not asking you never to step foot in a Walmart again. I'm not even sure that's possible! Instead, here's my goal: to open your eyes to what's happening as big businesses attempt monopolies, to show you a little of the underbelly of fat cats such as Walmart. I simply want to point out what can be lost when the *bottom dollar* becomes the *bottom line*. Maybe there's no going back to the mom-and-pop store, the bakery on the corner, the soda fountain at the downtown drugstore. But surely we can all agree that, although Walmart's tag is "Save Money, Live Better," it's only delivering on half of that promise.

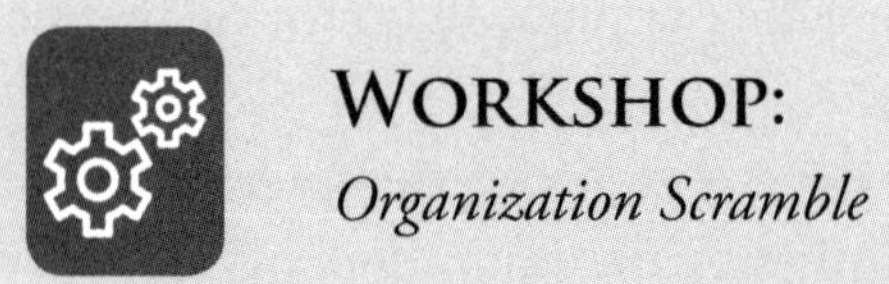

WORKSHOP:
Organization Scramble

2

Now take the "No Play, No Pass" speech and use it as a model for a short speech of your own (about 250 words) in which all of the components of classical organization are accounted for. Make sure to have at least two sentences for each section except the *partitio*, which should be one sentence. Here are some possible topics:

Our school *should/should not* adopt iPads in the classroom.

Our school *should/should not* shorten the school day to 2 p.m.

Our school *should/should not* require students to wear uniforms.

Students *should/should not* be required to participate in extracurricular sports.

Our school *should/should not* have a football team.

Our school *should/should not* separate students into single-sex classes.

________________[11] *should/should not* be included as a literature selection in English class.

Facebook promotes *real/false* friendships.

Students *should/should not* be allowed access to cell phones during the school day.

Our school *should/should not* have vending machines that sell soda and candy.

After you have written your mini-speech, you will write your speech section by section onto six separate note cards. Then you will scramble the six sections and see if your peers can put the speech back in the right order. If each section is doing its job—for example, if the *exordium* truly catches the reader's attention, and the *partitio* actually offers a preview of your points—then unscrambling it should be no hard task. You'll be able to tell just how clear you've been in your organization by how confident or confused your readers are when they're at work sorting the sections of your text.

There will be two winners: the one who unscrambles the greatest number of speeches correctly and the one whose speech is identified correctly the greatest number of times. (The latter demonstrates that the student has clearly understood the different divisions of a classically organized speech and also has written clearly.)

ALTERNATE ACTIVITY

Follow the same instructions, but have a parent or friend try to organize your speech. Even if that person doesn't know about the official six parts of a classically ordered text, he or she may sense the correct arrangement. Doing so will demonstrate an important point in this chapter: This order is simply *descriptive* of what good persuasion looks like.

11. Choose a popular young adult fiction work for this issue.

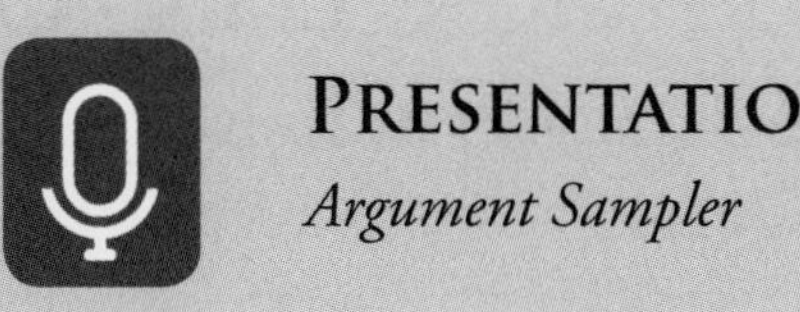

PRESENTATION:
Argument Sampler

SPOTLIGHT
Organized Delivery

Your teacher should write the following sections across the white board at the front of the class:

exordium *narratio* *partitio* *confirmatio* *refutatio* *peroratio*

When your teacher directs you, present your organized mini-speech. You should pay attention to the same factors as before: voice, posture, and eye contact. This time, though, we will add movement. You should signal where you are within the speech by standing directly in front of the section heading you are delivering. For example, begin speaking in front of the word "*exordium*," then move in front of "*narratio*" as you start discussing the context of your issue, and then stop in front of "*partitio*" as you offer a short preview of the speech. (The only variation in the order could be a reversal of the *confirmatio* and *refutatio*, with the *refutatio* coming first if the subject is one in which the audience would be hostile to the speaker's position.)

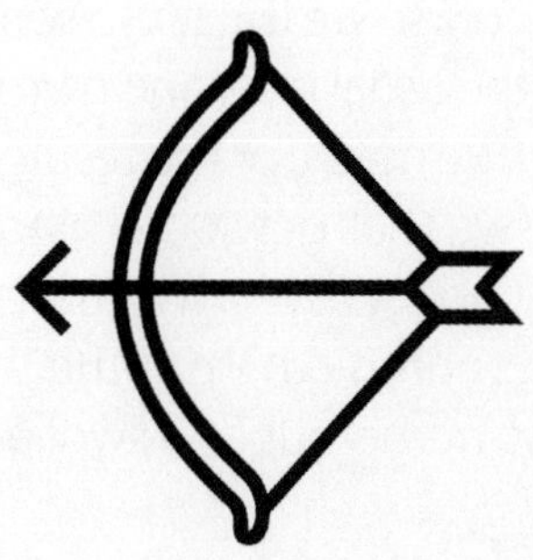

8

Chapter 8

Canon Three, Style: Choosing the Language

(1403b) Our next subject will be the style of expression. For it is not enough to know *what* we ought to say; we must also say it as we ought; much help is thus afforded towards producing the right impression of a speech. . . .

(1404b) We may, then, start from the observations there made, including the definition of style. Style to be good must be clear, as is proved by the fact that speech which fails to convey a plain meaning will fail to do just what speech has to do. It must also be appropriate, avoiding both meanness and undue elevation; poetical language is certainly free from meanness, but it is not appropriate to prose. Clearness is secured by using the words (nouns and verbs alike) that are current and ordinary. . . . [V]ariation from what is usual makes the language appear more stately. People do not feel towards strangers as they do towards their own countrymen, and the same thing is true of their feeling for language. It is therefore well to give to everyday speech an unfamiliar air: people like what strikes them, and are struck by what is out of the way. . . . We can now see that a writer must disguise his art and give the impression of speaking naturally and not artificially. Naturalness is persuasive, artificiality is the contrary; for our hearers are prejudiced and think we have some design against them, as if we were mixing their wines for them. . . .

(1405a) [M]etaphor is of great value both in poetry and in prose. Prose-writers must, however, pay specially careful attention to metaphor, because their other resources are scantier than those of poets. Metaphor, moreover, gives style clearness, charm, and distinction as nothing else can: and it is not a thing whose use can be taught by one man to another. . . .

(1406a) Of course we must use some epithets,[1] since they lift our style above the usual level and give it an air of distinction. But we must aim at the due mean, or the result will be worse than if we took no trouble at all; we shall get something actually bad instead of something merely not good. That is why the epithets of Alcidamas seem so tasteless; he does not use them as the seasoning of the meat, but as the meat itself, so numerous and swollen and aggressive are they. For

1. By this, Aristotle means "adjectives."

instance, he does not say "sweat," but "the *moist* sweat"; . . . not "laws," but "the laws *that are monarchs of states*"; . . . and "he clothed" not "his body" but "*his body's nakedness*," . . . and "so *extravagant* the excess of his wickedness." We thus see how the inappropriateness of such poetical language imports absurdity and tastelessness into speeches, as well as the obscurity that comes from all this verbosity—for when the sense is plain, you only obscure and spoil its clearness by piling up words. . . .

(1407b) It is a general rule that a written composition should be easy to read and therefore easy to deliver. . . .

(1408a) Your language will be *appropriate* if it expresses emotion and character, and if it corresponds to its subject. "Correspondence to subject" means that we must neither speak casually about weighty matters, nor solemnly about trivial ones; nor must we add ornamental epithets to commonplace nouns, or the effect will be comic, as in the works of Cleophon, who can use phrases as absurd as "O queenly fig-tree." To express emotion, you will employ the language of anger in speaking of outrage; the language of disgust and discreet reluctance to utter a word when speaking of impiety or foulness; the language of exultation for a tale of glory, . . . and so in all other cases. . . .

(1408b) Prose, then, is to be rhythmical, but not metrical, or it will become not prose but verse. It should not even have too precise a prose rhythm, and therefore should only be rhythmical to a certain extent. . . .

(1409a) The language of prose must be either free-running, . . . or compact and antithetical[.] . . . By "free-running" style I mean the kind that has no natural stopping-places, and comes to a stop only because there is no more to say of that subject. This style is unsatisfying just because it goes on indefinitely—one always likes to sight a stopping-place in front of one: it is only at the goal that men in a race faint and collapse; while they see the end of the course before them, they can keep on going. Such, then, is the free-running kind of style; the compact is that which is in periods. By a period I mean a portion of speech that has in itself a beginning and an end, being at the same time not too big to be taken in at a glance. (1409b) Language of this kind is satisfying and easy to follow. It is satisfying, because it is just the reverse of indefinite; and moreover, the hearer always feels that he is grasping something and has reached some definite conclusion; whereas it is unsatisfactory to see nothing in front of you and get nowhere.

(1409b) The periodic style which is divided into members is of two kinds. It is either simply divided, as in "I have often wondered at the conveners of national gatherings and the founders of athletic contests"; or it is antithetical, where, in each of the two members, one of one pair of opposites is put along with one of another pair, or the same word is used to bracket two opposites, (1410a) as . . . [in,] "it often happens in such enterprises that the wise men fail and the fools succeed"; . . . "nature gave them their country and law took it away again"; . . . and "to possess in life or to bequeath at death." . . . Such a form of speech is satisfying, because the significance of contrasted ideas is easily felt, especially when they are thus put side by side, and also because it has the effect of a logical argument; it is by putting two opposing conclusions side by side that you prove one of them false.

Such, then, is the nature of *antithesis.*

(1410b) We may now consider the above points settled, and pass on to say something about the way to devise lively and taking sayings. Their actual invention can only come through natural talent or long practice; but this treatise may indicate the way it is done. . . . We will begin by remarking that we all naturally find it agreeable to get hold of new ideas easily: words express ideas, and therefore those words are the most agreeable that enable us to get hold of new ideas. Now strange words simply puzzle us; ordinary words convey only what we know already; it is from metaphor that we can best get hold of something fresh. When the poet calls "old age a withered stalk," he conveys a new idea, a new fact, to us by means of the general notion of bloom, which is common to both things. The similes of the poets do the same, and therefore, if they are good similes, give an effect of brilliance. The simile, as has been said before, is a metaphor, differing from it only in the way it is put; and just because it is longer it is less attractive. Besides, it does not say outright that "this" ***is*** "that," and therefore the hearer is less interested in the idea. . . .

(1411b) We have still to explain what we mean by their "seeing things," and what must be done to effect this. By "making them see things" I mean using expressions that represent things as in a state of activity. . . . So with Homer's common practice of giving metaphorical life to lifeless things: all such passages are distinguished by the effect of activity they convey. Thus,

> Downward anon to the valley rebounded the boulder *remorseless*;

and

> The (bitter) arrow *flew*;

and

> Flying on *eagerly*;

and

(1412a)

> Stuck in the earth, still *panting* to feed on the flesh of the heroes;

and

> And the point of the spear *in its fury* drove full through his breastbone.

In all these examples the things have the effect of being active because they are made into living beings; shameless behaviour and fury and so on are all forms of activity. . . .

(1413a) Hyperboles are for young men to use; they show vehemence of character; and this is why angry people use them more than other people. . . .

(1413b) It should be observed that each kind of rhetoric has its own appropriate style. The style of written prose is not that of spoken oratory[.] . . . The written style is the more finished: the spoken better admits of dramatic delivery—like the kind of oratory that reflects character and the kind that reflects emotion.

Bringing Speech to Life

It is nearly impossible to think without words. Have you ever tried it? You've surely found that you can't think very long without them; doing so is like attempting to hum a tune with no musical notes or to work a math problem without numbers—almost inconceivable! One of humanity's distinct gifts is that we have speech, which enables us to engage in complex thought in a way that mere desire and emotion can never allow. Those things we think we "just know" still have to be communicated through words, right? And what we *don't* know, we must pursue via words. This is why Aristotle says that rhetoric exists in the first place: The things that we cannot know with certainty require reasoned argumentation to test their truth. Thinking and words, then, live in each other's pockets. And it is this third[2] canon of rhetoric, style, that taps into the great power behind a well-chosen word and a well-turned phrase.

What Aristotle means by "style" is not what you might think.[3] It's true that it involves a kind of linguistic panache, but it is more appropriate to think of rhetorical **style** as *thought put into words.*

And your wording's virtue, he says, is its clarity. However, we cannot think of clarity as casualness, as if we are to use street speech and say everything in layman's terms. Instead, we must strike the mean between common (what Aristotle calls "flat") language and an elevated, poetic style. The result is something in between: a kind of fresh unfamiliarity that, on one level, escapes notice but nevertheless is striking. A bad example of this would be the cavalier speaker who approaches the podium and transforms, with his opening remarks, into a starched persona with a five-star vocabulary. A good example is the speaker who raises the verbal bar without anyone even noticing. Aristotle calls this "theft"—we might want to change that word to "stealth"—as if a speaker is sneaking the art through language, language that strikes the audience or reader as uncontrived.

Style is thought put into words.

The goal, then, is to bring speech to life before the audience, to make the words themselves a kind of persuasive demonstration. And bringing speech to life is done better when the speaker can recognize ahead of time which words are uninspired and how new life might be breathed into them. Otherwise, the speech will be DOA, that is, dead on arrival.

2. Actually, Aristotle discusses style before organization. This text follows what has become a more common order of the five canons.
3. The word *style* is derived from the word *stylus*, meaning "writing instrument" or "pen." Each person's style is distinct, just as each of your classmates' signature and penmanship is distinct.

Just the Right Word

A speaker's stealth is exposed—that is, the artfulness is too obvious—when the issue is overstated. Aristotle calls these "frigidities," as if the language freezes the point instead of bringing it to life. The result is something that sounds *too* poetic. His examples are good ones: "the laws that are monarchs of states," "he clothed . . . his body's nakedness," and "so extravagant the excess of his wickedness," when the simpler versions would have worked just fine ("the laws," "he clothed himself," "wickedness"). Although we do want our words to paint a picture, we don't want the picture to be colored in neon. Young rhetors, especially, are prone to this kind of amplification. "I never imagined in all my life," "It couldn't have possibly been any worse," "The incredible enormity of the crime," and even the all-too-common flowery redundancies such as "At this point in time" and its cousin "In this day and age"—all of these can be trimmed down into something a little less showy.

"The difference between the right word and the almost right word is really a large matter—it's the difference between the lightning bug and the lightning."
—Mark Twain

Table 4. Examples of commonly abused phrases.

at this point in time
in this day and age
for all intents and purposes
first and foremost
in light of the fact
in all likelihood
a lasting legacy
in the vast majority of cases
as a matter of fact
absolutely essential

Twentieth-century thinker Richard Weaver picks up on this very idea when he warns that those writers we trust most are those who use adverbs and adjectives sparingly, and those we trust least are always trying to strengthen their points by overstating them with unnecessary decorations. Better, he says, to have lean but strong sentences by choosing robust verbs and substantial nouns. He gives an example with the sentence *The man moves quickly.* It would be better to collapse the adverb *quickly* into the verb itself: *The man hastens* (or *races, flies, scrambles, bolts*). See the chapter "Some Rhetorical Aspects of Grammatical Categories" in Weaver's book *The Ethics of Rhetoric* to examine a profound reflection on style.

"Read your composition and when you meet a passage which you think exceptionally fine, strike it out."
—Samuel Johnson

One idea, then, is to avoid showy language, instead choosing strong nouns and verbs that accomplish what decorative flimflam merely attempts. Another point about word choice can be made in terms of rhetorical effect. "When mentioning anything ugly or unseemly, use its name if it is the description that is ugly, and describe it if it is the name that is ugly," advises Aristotle (1407b). In other words, sometimes a word's connotation differs from its denotation: Its bark is worse than its bite. Would you, as a student, rather be accused of plagiarism or of "wrongfully appropriating another author's words"? For most of us, the term *plagiarism* has serious connotations, calling to mind stories of expulsion or ruined careers. Anyone who has been in education for even a short time will have learned to associate some shame or even dread with that term. But its definition ("wrongfully appropriating another author's words")—perhaps because of its length, perhaps because of its more difficult language (one may need to pause for a moment to think about what it means "to appropriate" something)—probably does not go straight to the heart. Instead, it winds its way to the mind, losing some of its power along the way.

Or imagine the trial of a man who evaded compulsory military service. Which side, prosecution or defense, would want to avoid the term "draft dodger"? Which side would prefer to say that the accused "engaged in civil disobedience by avoiding conscription"? This issue is what is at stake with politically correct language, in which a concept is softened by renaming it. About this type of language, George Orwell writes the following: "[P]olitical language has to consist largely of euphemism, question-begging and sheer cloudy vagueness. Defenseless villages are bombarded from the air, the inhabitants driven out into the countryside, the cattle machine-gunned, the huts set on fire with incendiary bullets: this is called *pacification*. Millions of peasants are robbed of their farms and sent trudging along the roads with no more than they can carry: this is called *transfer of population or rectification of frontiers*. . . . Such phraseology is needed if one wants to name things without calling up mental pictures of them."[4] The point is simple: The idea may be more or less the same, but the words you choose to express that idea matters. Be careful about the rhetorical effect of your language.

Appropriate Style

"Your language will be appropriate if it expresses emotion and character, and if it corresponds to its subject," teaches Aristotle (1408a). Notice the words "emotion," "character," and "subject." Aristotle is claiming that style is not merely a last-minute decoration to clothe an idea: It is connected to *pathos*, *ethos*, and *logos*! One's choice of words, then, can make all the difference not only in how the audience responds but also in how the rhetor is perceived.

> *"To speak of atrocious crimes in mild language is treason to virtue."*
> *—Edmund Burke*

Aristotle's section on propriety is full of simple but good advice. First, a proper manner—whether it be respectful of the honorable, indignant of the shameful, and so forth—supports a speaker's *ethos*. For example, if one speaks of a natural disaster and its casualties in a cold and callous way, then a shadow will be cast over the speaker's *ethos*. And justly so, perhaps. After all, what kind of person would not be moved by such happenings? By talking about things in a way that is appropriate (and, again, Aristotle is ready to assume that common people know

4. George Orwell, "Politics and the English Language," *Horizon*, April 1946, http://www.mtholyoke.edu/acad/intrel/orwell46.htm.

what is an appropriate response), a speaker gains credibility.

Similarly, people should speak words that are appropriate to their station: An older man shouldn't try to seem hip, for example, nor should a young person strike the air of a wise sage. Again, the speaker's *ethos* is at stake, and no one trusts a panderer or a pretender. We should also note Aristotle's directive on combining style and delivery: Don't overdo it! He advises, "[I]f your words are harsh, you should not extend this harshness to your voice and your countenance" (1408b). Doing both feels heavy-handed, making the speaker's *ethos* suspect.

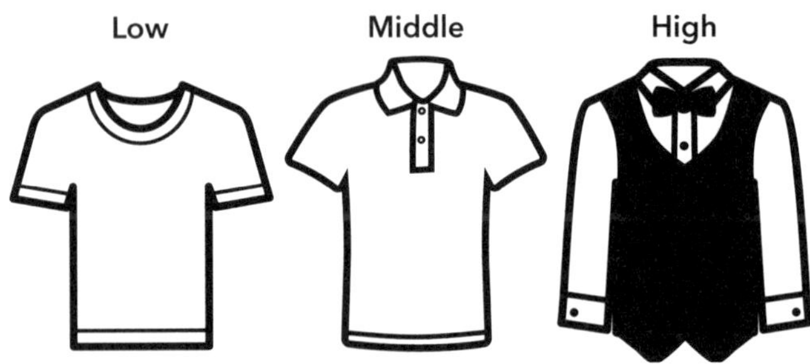

Figure 17. Levels of verbal style.

The rhetorical tradition distinguishes three different styles: low, middle, and high. No surprises here: The low style is plain, the high is formal, and the middle is, well, in between. Let's take, for example, the common rhetorical activity of praising another person. A formal setting for praise, in which the high style would be the appropriate choice, would be a funeral eulogy. A much more casual setting where the rhetor would want to choose the low style to praise a loved one might be a birthday picnic, held outdoors, where shorts and sandals are worn. The middle style would be appropriate at a best friend's graduation party, where appetizers and soda make up the menu. You can think of your own examples, but the point is the same: Just as you'd expect the venue and menu to change for each event, so should the language be adjusted, too. Each rhetorical setting calls for the appropriate stylistic choice.

We should note, however, that students are accustomed to writing in a rather formal style for their schoolwork. Oratory in general tends to be slightly lower than written argumentation—that is, speaking allows for a more casual tone. Aristotle says it this way: "The written style is the more finished: the spoken better admits of dramatic delivery—like the kind of oratory that reflects character and the kind that reflects emotion" (1413b). This is not to say that one should come to the podium unprepared, but rather to say that the speaker can strike a more conversational air than he could get away with when writing a research paper. To be persuasively informal, ironically, one may need to be even *more* prepared than when being formal. After all, saying something in a way that everyone can understand it can be more difficult than saying it in a way that is accessible only to the few.[5] Nobel Prize–winning physicist Richard Feynman, a famous stickler for clear language, gives an example.[6] He tells of coming across the following sentence, which left him confused and frustrated: "The individual member of the social community often receives his information via visual symbolic channels." Only after careful and deliberate rereading was Feynman able to make sense of it, concluding that it means, "People read."

A short reminder about your sentences: Finish them! A common problem for speakers is that they tend to string sentences together with ". . . , and . . . , and . . . ," never wrapping up their thoughts in a definitive way. This kind of speaking lacks authority. A more mature style is one that ties your sentences together, showing cause and effect with *because*, *since*, and *therefore*, or contrast with *although*, *while*, and *whereas*.[7] In other words, your

5. For a lively and thoughtful discussion of style, see Orwell's "Politics and the English Language," 1946.

6. Richard Feynman, *Surely You're Joking, Mr. Feynman! Adventures of a Curious Character*, rev. ed. (1985; repr., New York: W.W. Norton & Company, 1997), 281.

7. For a fascinating look at how different types of sentences—simple, compound, complex—structure language in metaphysically different ways, see the chapter "Some Rhetorical Aspects of Grammatical Categories" in Weaver's *The Ethics of Rhetoric*. He also discusses the

thoughts are related and connected. Aristotle calls the former "strung-on" sentences and says that this kind of speech leaves the listeners panting and exhausted. With no end in sight, listeners trail off into inattention. Punch your sentences with clear breaking points; that way you give your audience a chance to rest. A mix of long and short sentences is always easier on the ear than no sentence variation.

Figures of Speech

Finally, the persuasive rhetor will pay close attention to those things in language that are liveliest of all: figures of speech. In a way, figures of speech are just rule-breakers. For example, you've been told not to start all of your sentences the same way, right? Well, wordsmiths break that rule all the time, and they even have a fancy name for it: *anaphora*.[8] Anaphora teems throughout the poem "From a Litany" by Mark Strand:

> . . . I praise the moon for suffering
> men.
>
> I praise the sun its tributes.
>
> I praise the pain of revival and the
> bliss of decline.
>
> I praise all for nothing because there
> is no price . . .

The same goes with ending all of your sentences with the same phrases: That's *epistrophe*.[9] Here's how Robert Penn Warren employs it in *Flood: A Romance of Our Time*: "The big sycamore by the creek was gone. The willow tangle was gone. The little enclave of untrodden bluegrass was gone. The clump of dogwood on the little rise across the creek—now that, too, was gone. . . ."[10] Interrupting a flow of thought becomes a virtue when it's called *parenthesis*: "He enjoyed—nay, he *loved*—to swim in the ocean." Omitting words isn't an error; it's ellipsis:[11] "He came to the ocean for the waves, she for the sand." Forgetting a conjunction is *asyndeton*:[12] "The surf lapped, pounded, flooded the seashore." Using the same word in two different ways isn't muddled thought or equivocation; instead, it's a *pun*: "During the fishing trip, she lost her purse and he lost his lunch." And on and on it goes.

Figures of speech can be divided into schemes and tropes. A **scheme** (Greek, *skhema*, "form") involves a deviation in order; a **trope** (Greek, *tropos*, "a turn") involves a deviation in meaning. For example, the statement "I came, I saw, I conquered" is interesting because of how the sentence fits together as a whole; the lack of conjunctions (**asyndeton**) makes it a scheme. But "Give us this day our daily bread" is interesting at the level of the word: the specific food—bread—substitutes for the general category of sustenance. The *synecdoche*,[13] which deviates the meaning of "bread," is thus a trope. Reversing clauses—"Eat to live; don't live to eat"—is thus a scheme, whereas deliberate overstatement—"a camel through the eye of a needle . . . "—is a trope. The following is a list of some common figures of speech.

---

philosophical dimensions of different parts of speech, such as the noun, verb, and adverb.

8. Literally, "a carrying back," from Greek *ana* "back" and *pherein* "to carry."
9. Literally, "a turning around," from Greek *epi* "in" or "on" and *strephein* "to turn."
10. Robert Penn Warren, *Flood: A Romance of Our Time* (Baton Rouge: Louisiana State University Press, 2003), 4. In addition, here is a more familiar epistrophe: "government of the people, by the people, for the people" (*Gettysburg Address*).
11. Literally, "a leaving out," from Greek *elleipein* "to leave out."
12. Literally, "not binding together," from Greek *a* "not," *syn* "together," and *dein* "to bind."
13. Literally, "a receiving together," from Greek *syn* "together" and *dekhesthai* "to receive."

Table 5. Common figures of speech.

Schemes: figures of speech involving a deviation in order
alliteration: repetition of the same initial consonant sounds in words near each other
anadiplosis: repetition of the last word of one clause at the beginning of the clause that follows
anaphora: repetition of a word or words at the beginning of successive phrases
anastrophe: inversion of usual word order
antimetabole: repetition of a phrase in reverse order
antithesis: juxtaposition of contrasting ideas
apposition: the side-by-side placement of two elements, the second of which identifies the first
assonance: repetition of similar vowel sounds
asyndeton: omission of conjunctions
chiasmus ("the crisscross"): the inverted, parallel grammatical structures in successive phrases or clauses
climax: an order of increasing importance
ellipsis: deliberate omission of words implied by the context
epanalepsis: repetition at the end of a clause of the word from the beginning of the same clause
epistrophe: repetition of the same word or words at the ends of successive clauses
parallelism: a similar grammatical structure in successive words, phrases, or clauses
parenthesis: an interrupter
polyptoton: repetition of words derived from the same root but in different forms
Tropes: figures of speech involving a deviation in meaning
anthimeria: substitution of one part of speech for another part of speech
hyperbole: exaggeration used for emphasis
irony: use of language to convey a meaning opposite to its literal meaning
litotes: understatement used for emphasis
metaphor: an implied comparison
metonymy: substitution of an attribute for the thing meant
onomatopoeia: use of words that imitate natural sounds
oxymoron: a self-contradictory phrase
paradox: a seemingly contradictory statement that may indeed be true
periphrasis: substitution of a descriptive word or phrase for a proper noun (or vice versa)
personification: a representation of an abstraction or inanimate object as if it were human
rhetorical question: the asking of a question for the purpose of making a point rather than receiving an answer
simile: an explicit comparison (using "like" or "as")
synecdoche: a figure of speech in which a part stands for the whole (or vice versa)

Fine-Tuning Style

There's a great deal more that can be said about style—and various rhetors throughout the ages have attempted to say it all—but we might instead conclude with a demonstration of a stylist whose tinkering with language won him the reputation of being a master rhetor. What follows is a section from Abraham Lincoln's First Inaugural Address, delivered in 1861:

> I am loath to close. We are not enemies, but friends. We must not be enemies. Though passion may have strained, it must not break our bonds of affection. The mystic chords of memory, stretching from every battlefield, and patriot grave, to every living heart and hearthstone, all over this broad land, will yet swell the chorus of the Union, when again touched, as surely they will be, by the better angels of our nature.[14]

14. Earl W. Wiley, "Abraham Lincoln: His Emergence as the Voice of the People," in *History and Criticism of American Public Address*,

This paragraph is stylistically beautiful, but it is even more beautiful when juxtaposed with its first draft. The first draft of this section was actually penned by William H. Seward, a friend of Lincoln and also a New York senator. Pay attention to the ways in which Lincoln altered Seward's style:

> I close. We are not, we must not be, aliens or enemies, but fellow-countrymen and brethren. Although passion has strained our bonds of affection too hardly, they must not, I am sure they will not, be broken. The mystic chords which, proceeding from so many battlefields and so many patriot graves, pass through all the hearts and all the hearths in this broad continent of ours, will yet again harmonize in their ancient music when breathed upon by the guardian angel of the nation.[15]

The differences between Seward's draft and the final version into which Lincoln masterfully revised it reveal a careful attention to style. Lincoln altered "I close" to "I am loath to close"; the latter, by being longer, adds the feeling itself of not wishing to end. Longer sentences are not, however, always better, for he modified the next one, a longer sentence ("We are not, we must not be, aliens or enemies, but fellow-countrymen and brethren") by breaking it into two shorter ones: "We are not enemies, but friends. We must not be enemies." Here, Lincoln pays attention to an audience's ability to grasp ideas better by breaking them up, not allowing them to be lengthy or, in Aristotle's terms, "strung-on." Notice he avoids the frigidity of "fellow-countrymen and brethren" by using instead "friends," and he brilliantly alters "hearts and hearths"—a difficult difference to hear in a public speech with no microphone—to "heart and hearthstone." Notice that the *ideas* have not been changed substantially from Seward's draft, but the *language*, fresh and inventive, makes those ideas more accessible. It brings them to life.

Good rhetors such as Lincoln are always tweaking their wording, for they understand the importance of style: It isn't enough just to get across an idea. Rather, the idea must be brought to life, and words are the lifeblood of oratory.

Two final notes on style. First, to say a stylistic choice is "appropriate" (Aristotle's word) is to say that it is suited to the occasion. As you probably know by now, no two rhetorical situations are ever the same. Each is unique. The addition of even one new audience member, someone who doesn't fit with the norm of the room, can dramatically alter a rhetor's choices in style. Style is more than the rhetor's self-expression, which is probably the way most of us think of the word "style." Instead, because rhetoric is aimed at persuasion—and persuasion takes the audience into account at every turn—training in style is training in judgment. In all rhetorical matters, you must strive to sharpen your judgment about human beings, both yourself and those you will address.

Second, and relatedly, while we must be attentive to the appropriateness of the words we choose, we must also recognize that each rhetor is unique. In paying attention to style, you are moving toward the development of your distinctive voice that sets you apart from all other rhetors. It is because writers have distinct voices that readers can sometimes identify the author of a poem simply by the language. Emily Dickinson's poetry, for example, would never be mistaken for that of Walt Whitman, even though they were contemporaries. Some would call this a "rhetorical thumbprint," and as your style develops and matures, it too will become recognizable, identifying your rhetoric as your own.

ed. William Norwood Brigance, vol. 2 (New York: McGraw-Hill, 1943), 867.

15. John G. Nicolay and John Hay, *Abraham Lincoln: A History*, vol. 3 (New York: Century, 1909), 343.

Discussion Text:

John F. Kennedy: "Ask Not What Your Country Can Do for You" (1961)[16]

Focus:

Style

President Kennedy's Inaugural Address

January 20, 1961

Vice President Johnson, Mr. Speaker, Mr. Chief Justice, President Eisenhower, Vice President Nixon, President Truman, Reverend Clergy, fellow citizens:

We observe today not a victory of party, but a celebration of freedom—symbolizing ❶ **an end, as well as a beginning**[17]—signifying renewal, as well as change. For I have sworn before you and Almighty God the same solemn oath our forebears prescribed nearly a century and three quarters ago.

The world is very different now. For man holds in his mortal hands the power to abolish ❷ **all forms of human poverty and all forms of human life.** And yet the same revolutionary beliefs for which our forebears fought are still at issue around the globe—the belief that the rights of man come not from the generosity of the state, but from the hand of God.

We dare not forget today that we are the heirs of that first revolution. Let the word go forth from this time and place, to friend and foe alike, that the torch has been passed to a new generation of Americans ❸ **—born in this century, tempered by war, disciplined by a hard and bitter peace, proud of our ancient heritage**—and unwilling to witness or permit the slow undoing of those human rights to which this Nation has always been committed, and to which we are committed today at home and around the world.

Let every nation know, whether it wishes us well or ill, that we shall ❹ **pay any price, bear any burden, meet any hardship, support any friend, oppose any foe,** in order to assure the survival and the success of liberty.

This much we pledge—and more.

To those old allies whose cultural and spiritual origins we share, we pledge the loyalty of faithful friends. ❺ **United,** there is little we cannot do in a host of cooperative ventures. **Divided,** there is little we can do—for we dare not meet a powerful challenge at odds and split asunder.

To those new States whom we welcome to the ranks of the free, we pledge our word that one form of colonial control shall not have passed away merely to be replaced by a far more iron tyranny. We shall not always expect to find them supporting our view. But we shall always hope to find them strongly supporting their own freedom—and to remember that, in the past, those who foolishly sought power by ❻ **riding the back of the tiger ended up inside.**

To those peoples in the huts and villages across the globe struggling to break the bonds of ❼ **mass misery,** we pledge our best efforts to ❽ **help them help themselves,** for whatever period is required—not because the Communists may be doing it, not because we seek their votes, but because it is right. If a free society cannot help ❾ **the many who are poor,** it cannot save **the few who are rich.**

16. John F. Kennedy, "President Kennedy's Inaugural Address," Washington, DC, January 20, 1961, John F. Kennedy Presidential Library and Museum, accessed January 9, 2016, http://www.jfklibrary.org/Research/Research-Aids/Ready-Reference/JFK-Fast-Facts/Inaugural-Address.aspx.

17. Emphasis (bold text) and circled numbers added.

To our ❿ **sister republics** south of our border, we offer a special pledge—to convert our ⓫ **good words into good deeds**—in a new alliance for progress—to assist free men and free governments in casting off ⓬ **the chains of poverty.** But this peaceful revolution of hope cannot become ⓭ **the prey of hostile powers.** Let all our neighbors know that we shall join with them to oppose aggression or subversion anywhere in the Americas. And let every other power know that this Hemisphere intends to remain ⓮ **the master of its own house.**

⓯To that world assembly of sovereign states, the United Nations, our last best hope in an age where the **instruments of war** have far outpaced **the instruments of peace,** we renew our pledge of support— ⓰ **to prevent** it from becoming merely a forum for invective—to **strengthen** its shield of the new and the weak—**and to enlarge** the area in which its writ may run.

Finally, to those nations who would make themselves our adversary, we offer not a pledge but a request: that both sides begin anew the quest for peace, before the dark powers of destruction unleashed by science engulf all humanity in planned or accidental self-destruction.

We dare not tempt them with weakness. For only when our arms are ⓱ **sufficient beyond doubt** can we be **certain beyond doubt** that they will never be employed.

But neither can two great and powerful groups of nations take comfort from our present course— ⓲ **both** sides overburdened by the cost of modern weapons, **both** rightly alarmed by the steady spread of the deadly atom, yet **both** racing to alter that uncertain balance of terror that stays the hand of mankind's final war.

So let us begin anew—remembering on both sides that civility is not a sign of weakness, and sincerity is always subject to proof. ⓳ **Let us never negotiate out of fear. But let us never fear to negotiate.**

Let both sides explore what ⓴ **problems unite us** instead of belaboring those **problems which divide us.**

Let both sides, for the first time, formulate serious and precise proposals for the inspection and control of arms—and bring the ㉑ **absolute power** to destroy other nations under the **absolute control** of all nations.

Let both sides seek to invoke the ㉒ **wonders** of science instead of its **terrors.** Together let us ㉓ **explore** the stars, **conquer** the deserts, **eradicate** disease, **tap** the ocean depths, and **encourage** the arts and commerce.

Let both sides unite to heed in all corners of the earth the command of Isaiah—to "undo the heavy burdens . . . and to let the oppressed go free."

And if a ㉔ **beachhead of cooperation** may push back the **jungle of suspicion,** let both sides join in creating a new endeavor, not a new balance of power, but a new world of law, where ㉕ **the strong are just and the weak secure and the peace preserved.**

All this will not be finished in the first 100 days. Nor will it be finished in the first 1,000 days, nor in the life of this Administration, nor even perhaps in our lifetime on this planet. But let us begin.

In your hands, my fellow citizens, more than in mine, will rest the final success or failure of our course. Since this country was founded, each generation of Americans has been summoned to give testimony to its national loyalty. The graves of young Americans who answered the call to service surround the globe.

Now the trumpet summons us again—not as a call to bear arms, though arms we need; not as a call to battle, though embattled we are—but a call to bear the burden of a long twilight struggle, year in and year out, "rejoicing in hope, patient in tribulation"—a struggle against the common enemies of man: tyranny, poverty, disease, and war itself.

Can we forge against these enemies a grand and global alliance, North and South, East and West, that can assure a more fruitful life for all mankind? Will you join in that historic effort?

In the long history of the world, only a few generations have been granted the role of defending freedom in its hour of maximum danger. I do not shrink from this responsibility—I welcome it. I do not believe that any of us would exchange places with any other people or any other generation. The energy, the faith, the devotion which we bring to this endeavor will light our country and all who serve it—and the glow from that fire can truly light the world.

And so, my fellow Americans: ask not what your country can do for you—ask what you can do for your country.

My fellow citizens of the world: ask not what America will do for you, but what together we can do for the freedom of man.

Finally, whether you are citizens of America or citizens of the world, ask of us the same high standards of strength and sacrifice which we ask of you. With a good conscience our only sure reward, with history the final judge of our deeds, let us go forth to lead the land we love, asking His blessing and His help, but knowing that here on earth God's work must truly be our own.

Discussion Questions

"Ask Not What Your Country Can Do for You"

Identify the figures of speech indicated in Kennedy's inaugural address. Then find and identify some of the remaining figures used but not marked.

1. ______________________________
2. ______________________________
3. ______________________________
4. ______________________________
5. ______________________________
6. ______________________________
7. ______________________________
8. ______________________________
9. ______________________________
10. ______________________________
11. ______________________________
12. ______________________________
13. ______________________________
14. ______________________________
15. ______________________________
16. ______________________________
17. ______________________________
18. ______________________________
19. ______________________________
20. ______________________________
21. ______________________________
22. ______________________________
23. ______________________________
24. ______________________________
25. ______________________________

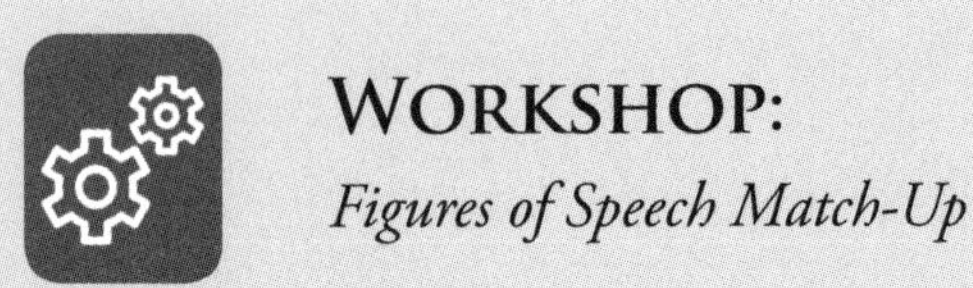

Workshop:

Figures of Speech Match-Up

1

Part I: Schemes

Remember, schemes are figures of speech involving a deviation in *order*. Try to identify and articulate why the following sentences are so interesting to hear. What is happening within the sentence? For each sentence or quote, in the lines provided write the letter that corresponds to the name of its scheme.[18]

_______ Rich, famous, proud, a ruling despot Pope might be—but he was middle class! —V.S. Pritchett

_______ A sable, silent, solemn forest stood. —James Thomson, "The Castle of Indolence"

_______ We shall go on to the end, we shall fight in France, we shall fight on the seas and oceans, we shall fight with growing confidence and growing strength in the air, we shall defend our Island, whatever the cost may be, we shall fight on the beaches, we shall fight on the landing grounds, we shall fight in the fields and in the streets, we shall fight in the hills; we shall never surrender. —Winston Churchill, speech in the House of Commons, June 4, 1940

_______ The laughter had to be gross or it would turn to sobs, and to sob would be to realize, and to realize would be to despair. —John Howard Griffin, *Black Like Me*

A. alliteration: repetition of the same initial consonant sounds in words near each other

B. anadiplosis: repetition of the last word of one clause at the beginning of the clause that follows

C. anaphora: repetition of a word or words at the beginning of successive phrases

D. anastrophe: inversion of usual word order

_______ That's one small step for a man, one giant leap for mankind. —Neil Armstrong

_______ John Morgan, the president of the Sons of the Republic, would not be reached by phone.

_______ Whales in the wake like capes and Alps
Quaked the sick sea and snouted deep —Dylan Thomas, "Ballad of the Long-Legged Bait"

_______ One should eat to live, not live to eat. —Molière, *L'Avare*

E. antimetabole: repetition of a phrase in reverse order

F. antithesis: juxtaposition of contrasting ideas

G. apposition: the side-by-side placement of two elements, the second of which identifies the first

H. assonance: repetition of similar vowel sounds

18. The following examples are taken from Edward P.J. Corbett and Robert J. Connors, *Classical Rhetoric for the Modern Student*, 4th ed. (New York: Oxford University Press, 1998), 381–409. This recommended resource contains many other examples from choice literature.

_______ And he to England shall along with you. —Shakespeare, *Hamlet*, act 3, scene 3, line 4

_______ I came, I saw, I conquered. —Julius Caesar

_______ Renounce my love, my life, myself—and you. —Alexander Pope, "Eloise to Abelard"

_______ Exalts his enemies, his friends destroys. —John Dryden, "Absalom and Achitophel"

I. asyndeton: omission of conjunctions

J. chiasmus ("the crisscross"): the inverted, parallel grammatical structures in successive phrases or clauses

K. climax: an order of increasing importance

L. ellipsis: deliberate omission of words implied by the context

---

_______ And for the support of this declaration, with a firm reliance on the protection of Divine Providence, we mutually pledge to each other our lives, our fortunes and our sacred honor. —The Declaration of Independence

_______ All that remained for the moment was to decide where I would go to graduate school, and that question was settled—the "snobs" had been right—by a Kellett Fellowship and then a Fulbright Scholarship to boot. —Norman Podhoretz, *Making It* (1967)

_______ In a cake, nothing tastes like real butter, nothing moistens like real butter, nothing enriches like real butter, nothing satisfies like real butter. —Pillsbury ad

_______ Blood hath brought blood, and blows have answer'd blows. —Shakespeare, *King John*, act 2, scene 1, lines 329–30

_______ Let me assert my firm belief that the only thing we have to fear is fear itself. —Franklin D. Roosevelt, First Inaugural Address, 1933

M. epanalepsis: repetition at the end of a clause of the word from the beginning of the same clause

N. epistrophe: repetition of the same word or words at the ends of successive clauses

O. parallelism: a similar grammatical structure in successive words, phrases, or clauses

P. parenthesis: an interrupter

Q. polyptoton: repetition of words derived from the same root but in different forms

Part II: Tropes

As you'll recall, tropes are figures of speech involving a deviation in *meaning*. Again, identify why the following sentences are interesting. What is unusual within the sentence? For each sentence or quote, in the lines provided write the letter that corresponds to the name of its trope.

_______ Last week I saw a woman flayed, and you will hardly believe how much it altered her appearance for the worse. —Jonathan Swift, *A Tale of a Tub*

_______ I have gray hair. I really do. The one side of my head—the right side—is full of millions of gray hairs. —Holden Caulfield in *Catcher in the Rye*

_______ I'll unhair my head. —Shakespeare, *Antony and Cleopatra*, act 2, scene 5, line 64

_______ For Brutus is an honorable man;
So are they all, all honorable men. —Shakespeare, *Julius Caesar*, act 3, scene 2, lines 88–89

A. anthimeria: substitution of one part of speech for another part of speech

B. hyperbole: exaggeration used for emphasis

C. irony: the use of language to convey a meaning opposite to its literal meaning

D. litotes: understatement used for emphasis

_______ On the exam, several students went down in flames.

_______ In Europe, we gave the cold shoulder to De Gaulle, and now he gives the warm hand to Mao Tse-tung. —Richard Nixon, campaign speech, 1960

_______ Sweet pain, cheerful pessimist, conspicuous by her absence.

_______ Strong gongs groaning as the guns boom far. —G.K. Chesterton, *Lepanto*

E. metaphor: an implied comparison

F. metonymy: substitution of an attribute for the thing meant

G. onomatopoeia: use of words that imitate natural sounds

H. oxymoron: a self-contradictory phrase

_______ The ground thirsts for rain.

_______ In his later years he became in fact the most scarifying of his own creatures: a Quixote of the Cotswolds. —Article on Evelyn Waugh in *Time*, April 22, 1966

_______ Art is a form of lying in order to tell the truth. —Pablo Picasso

I. paradox: a seemingly contradictory statement that may indeed be true

J. periphrasis: substitution of a descriptive word or phrase for a proper noun (or vice versa)

K. personification: a representation of an abstraction or inanimate object as if it were human

_______ He had a posture like a question mark.

_______ Give us this day our daily bread. —Matthew 6:11 (NKJV)

_______ That which is inhuman cannot be divine. Who can reason on such a proposition? —Frederick Douglass, 1852

L. rhetorical question: the asking of a question for the purpose of making a point rather than receiving an answer

M. simile: an explicit comparison (using "like" or "as")

N. synecdoche: a figure of speech in which a part stands for the whole (or vice versa)

Workshop:
Stylish Sentences

2

A. Combinations

Take the following groups of sentences/ideas and combine them into one sentence.

1. ____

____

- Buck Mulligan was bearing a bowl of lather.
- A mirror lay on the bowl.
- A razor lay on the bowl.
- The mirror and the razor were crossed.
- Buck Mulligan was stately and plump.
- He came from the stairhead.

2. ____

____

- It was midnight.
- The drummer was barefoot.
- The drummer was in the street.
- The drummer beat a folded newspaper with whisk-brooms.
- The drummer did not have a drum.
- This stirs the eye's ear.
- The stirring is like a blast of brasses in a midnight street.

B. *Copia*

Look at a section of *Copia: Foundations of the Abundant Style* (1512), written by Renaissance scholar Desiderius Erasmus. Erasmus demonstrates there is virtually no end to how the same (or almost the same) idea might be rendered. He playfully alters the phrase "Your letter pleased me greatly" into the following:

At your words a delight of no ordinary kind came over me.
I was singularly delighted by your epistle.
To be sure, how your letter delighted my spirits!
Your brief missive flooded me with inexpressible joy.
Your letter was very sweet to me.
You could scarce credit what relief I find in your missive.

Your letter was the source of singular gladness.
Your letter made me positively jump for joy.
Your letter having arrived, I was transported with joy.
Your writing to me was the most delightful thing possible.
Your epistle poured the balm of happiness over me.
I was both pleased and delighted that you communicated with me by letter.
That you paid your respects by letter was assuredly a satisfaction to me.
I read and reread your letter with great pleasure.
Your letter promptly expelled all sorrow from my mind.
I can hardly find words to express the extent of the joy to which your letter gave rise.
Good God, what a mighty joy proceeded from your epistle!
I found singular pleasure in your letter.
Your letter caused me quite to smooth my brow.
When I received your most gracious letter, boundless happiness occupied every recess of my soul.
May I die the death if anything more delightful than your letter ever came my way.
As I aspire to the love of the Muses, nothing more gladsome than your letter has ever ere this befallen me.
Your pen sated me with delight.
Your letter cast a dew of rare joy upon me.
When the messenger handed me your letter, my spirit immediately felt the motions of an inexpressible delight.
The charm of your letter put shackles of delight on my soul.
Whatever kind of a letter leaves your hand seems to me flowing with sweetness and honey.
Your lines seem to me pure enchantment.
The man who delivered your letter brought cartloads of pleasure.
I was most luxuriously refreshed at the sumptuous banquet of your letter.
Like clover to the bee, willow leaves to goats, honey to the bear, even so are your letters to me.[19]

19. From *The Rhetorical Tradition*, ed. Patricia Bizzell and Bruce Herzberg (Boston: Bedford/St. Martin's, 2001), 605–609.

Now you do the same, starting with a simple sentence about your breakfast this morning. Practice *copia*, creating ten or more sentences saying almost the same thing.

My breakfast was . . .

1. ______________________________
2. ______________________________
3. ______________________________
4. ______________________________
5. ______________________________
6. ______________________________
7. ______________________________
8. ______________________________
9. ______________________________
10. ______________________________

____

____

____

____

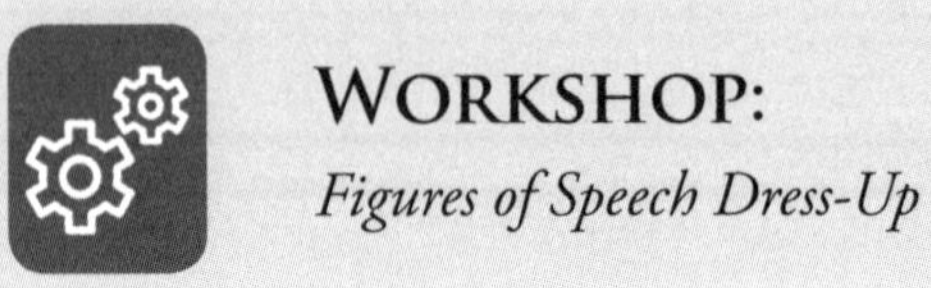

WORKSHOP: 3

Figures of Speech Dress-Up

Write a short paragraph of seven to ten plain sentences about a recent event, such as a spring break trip, your weekend, or a trip to the store.

Then revise your paragraph by adding five schemes or tropes, turning it into a stylized (if overblown!) passage. You will read both versions to the class.

Student sample: This weekend I went to visit a friend. The drive was only an hour, but it seemed to take a long time. Finally, I arrived. We hung out all day and watched a funny movie that night. I slept well. We drank coffee and ate Cheerios for breakfast while we talked about our lives. It was great to see her!

Revised: What could be better than a weekend trip to see a friend? (*rhetorical question*) The drive was short, but the drive was long. (*paradox*) Finally, I arrived. Hanging out was followed by watching a movie, watching a movie was followed by chatting, and chatting was followed by laughter. (*anadiplosis*) That night, I must have slept for years. (*hyperbole*) In the morning, coffee comforted me, and Cheerios cheered me. (*personification*) Great it was to see her! (*anastrophe*)

PRESENTATION: *Fairy Tale Retold*

SPOTLIGHT *Fidgeting*

In groups of two, choose a fairy tale. One person should rewrite it in high style and the other in low style. For a high style, you might choose the vernacular of one of the following: a doctor, a lawyer, a US president, or Shakespeare. For a low style, imagine the speaker as one of the following: a surfer, a country bumpkin, an urban teenager, or a chatty girl on her cell phone. Here are some fairy tales to choose from:

"The Three Little Pigs"
"Cinderella"
"The Ugly Duckling"
"Hansel and Gretel"
"Rumpelstiltskin"
"Rapunzel"
"The Elves and the Shoemaker"
"Sleeping Beauty"
"Little Red Riding Hood"
"The Fisherman and His Wife"
"Goldilocks and the Three Bears"

Here's an example of rewriting style taken from comic John Branyan's version of "The Three Little Pigs," written in Shakespearean English—what we today would call a high style.

"TRIUNE TALE OF DIMINUTIVE SWINE"[20]

In time past, though not long ago, there lived pigs.
In number . . . three.
In stature . . . little.
Who being of an age both entitled and inspired to seek their fortune
Did set about to do thusly.
When they had traveled a distance, pig numbered one spake,
Saying, "Harken brethren, heed this tempestuous realm!
Tarry we long from hearth and home we shall fare, I fear, [snort] not well."
And so being collectively agreed
but individually impelled,
The diminutive swine set about each to erect for himself an abode.
Pig numbered One did construct his dwelling from straw.

20. John Branyan, "A Familiar Tale Re-Imagined," YouTube video, 7:44, posted April 18, 2011, http://www.youtube.com/watch?v=Yyd17aaHCgU.

> Pig numbered Two did likewise,
> Though, rather, not from straw, instead from sticks.
> Meanwhile, unique in his imaginings, pig numbered Three did erect his domicile,
> Stalwart and garish, a structure made from brick entirely.
> . . .

When you present your tale, continue to think about voice, posture, and eye contact, but this time you should also pay attention to any nervous habits you may have when speaking in front of a group. Do you fiddle with the cuff of your sleeve? Grasp the podium? Tap your foot? Twirl your hair? Crack your knuckles? Watch out for these nervous habits.

CHAPTER 9

CANON FOUR, MEMORY: STORING WHAT'S VALUABLE

FROM *RHETORICA AD HERENNIUM*, BOOK 3[1] (CIRCA 84 BC)

[16] (28) Now let me turn to the treasure-house of the ideas supplied by Invention, to the guardian of all the parts of rhetoric, the Memory.

. . . There are, then, two kinds of memory: one natural, and the other the product of art. The natural memory is that memory which is imbedded in our minds, born simultaneously with thought. The artificial memory is that memory which is strengthened by a kind of training and system of discipline. . . . (29) . . . Now I shall discuss the artificial memory.

The artificial memory includes backgrounds and images. By backgrounds I mean such scenes as are naturally or artificially set off on a small scale, complete and conspicuous, so that we can grasp and embrace them easily by the natural memory—for example, a house, an intercolumnar space, a recess, an arch, or the like. An image is, as it were, a figure, mark, or portrait of the object we wish to remember; for example, if we wish to recall a horse, a lion, or an eagle, we must place its image in a definite background. (30) Now I shall show what kind of backgrounds we should invent and how we should discover the images and set them therein.

[17] Those who know the letters of the alphabet can thereby write out what is dictated to them and read aloud what they have written. Likewise, those who have learned mnemonics can set in backgrounds what they have heard, and from these backgrounds deliver it by memory. For the backgrounds are very much like wax tablets or papyrus, the images like letters, the arrangement and disposition of the images like the script, and the delivery is like the reading. We should therefore, if we desire to memorize a large number of items, equip ourselves with a large number of backgrounds, so that in these we may set a large

1. This text is in the public domain. It is a pseudo-Ciceronian text, which means that it was formerly attributed to Cicero, but its true author is unknown. Anonymous, *Rhetorica Ad Herennium*, trans. Harry Caplan, Loeb Classical Library edition (1954), text made available by Bill Thayer, LacusCurtius website, accessed January 24, 2016, http://penelope.uchicago.edu/Thayer/E/Roman/Texts/Rhetorica_ad_Herennium/3*.html. The bracketed numbers refer to chapters, and the numbers in parentheses refer to sections.

number of images. I likewise think it obligatory to have these backgrounds in a series, so that we never by confusion in their order be prevented from following the images—proceeding from any background we wish, whatsoever its place in the series, and whether we go forwards or backwards—nor from delivering orally what has been committed to the backgrounds. [18] For example, if we should see a great number of our acquaintances standing in a certain order, it would not make any difference to us whether we should tell their names beginning with the person standing at the head of the line or at the foot or in the middle. So with respect to the backgrounds. If these have been arranged in order, the result will be that, reminded by the images, we can repeat orally what we committed to the backgrounds, proceeding in either direction from any background we please. (31) That is why it also seems best to arrange the backgrounds in a series.

We shall need to study with special care the backgrounds we have adopted so that they may cling lastingly in our memory, for the images, like letters, are effaced when we make no use of them, but the backgrounds, like wax tablets, should abide. And that we may by no chance err in the number of backgrounds, each fifth background should be marked. For example, if in the fifth we should set a golden hand, and in the tenth some acquaintance whose first name is Decimus, it will then be easy to station like marks in each successive fifth background. [19] Again, it will be more advantageous to obtain backgrounds in a deserted than in a populous region, because the crowding and passing to and fro of people confuse and weaken the impress of the images, while solitude keeps their outlines sharp. Further, backgrounds differing in form and nature must be secured, so that, thus distinguished, they may be clearly visible; for if a person has adopted many intercolumnar spaces, their resemblance to one another will so confuse him that he will no longer know what he has set in each background. And these backgrounds ought to be of moderate size and medium extent, for when excessively large they render the images vague, and when too small often seem incapable of receiving an arrangement of images. (32) Then the backgrounds ought to be neither too bright nor too dim, so that the shadows may not obscure the images nor the lustre make them glitter. I believe that the intervals between backgrounds should be of moderate extent, approximately thirty feet; for, like the external eye, so the inner eye of thought is less powerful when you have moved the object of sight too near or too far away.

. . .

On the subject of backgrounds enough has been said; let me now turn to the theory of images.

[20] (33) Since, then, images must resemble objects, we ought ourselves to choose from all objects likenesses for our use. Hence likenesses are bound to be of two kinds, one of subject-matter, the other of words. Likenesses of matter are formed when we enlist images that present a general view of the matter with which we are dealing; likenesses of words are established when the record of each single noun or appellative is kept by an image.

Often we encompass the record of an entire matter by one notation, a single image. For example, the prosecutor has said that the defendant killed a man by poison, has charged that the motive for the crime was an inheritance, and declared that there are many witnesses and accessories to this act. If in order to facilitate our defence we wish to remember this first point, we shall in our first background form an image of the whole matter. We shall picture the man in question as lying ill in bed, if we know his person. If we do not know him, we shall yet take some one to be our invalid, but a man of the lowest class, so that he may come to mind at once. And we shall place the defendant at the bedside, holding in his right hand a cup, and in his left tablets, [. . . etc.]. In this way we can record the man who was poisoned, the inheritance, and the witnesses. (34) In like fashion we shall set the other counts of the charge in backgrounds successively, following their order, and whenever we wish to remember a point, by properly arranging the patterns of the backgrounds and carefully imprinting the images, we shall easily succeed in calling back to mind what we wish.

. . .

[21] (35) Now, since in normal cases some images are strong and sharp and suitable for awakening recollection, and others so weak and feeble as hardly to succeed in stimulating memory, we must therefore consider the cause of these differences, so that, by knowing the cause, we may know which images to avoid and which to seek.

[22] Now nature herself teaches us what we should do. When we see in everyday life things that are petty, ordinary, and banal, we generally fail to remember them, because the mind is not being stirred by anything novel or marvellous. But if we see or hear something exceptionally base, dishonourable, extraordinary, great, unbelievable, or laughable, that we are likely to remember a long time. . . .

(37) We ought, then, to set up images of a kind that can adhere longest in the memory. And we shall do so if we establish likenesses as striking as possible; if we set up images that are not many or vague, but doing something; if we assign to them exceptional beauty or singular ugliness; if we dress some of them with crowns or purple cloaks, for example, so that the likeness may be more distinct to us; or if we somehow disfigure them, as by introducing one stained with blood or soiled with mud or smeared with red paint, so that its form is more striking, or by assigning certain comic effects to our images, for that, too, will ensure our remembering them more readily. The things we easily remember when they are real we likewise remember without difficulty when they are figments, if they have been carefully delineated. But this will be essential—again and again to run over rapidly in the mind all the original backgrounds in order to refresh the images.

The Art of Memory

Memory is considered one of the "official" canons of rhetoric. Remember, there are five—invention, organization, style, memory, and delivery—but that number wasn't given to us by Aristotle. Whereas he covers the first three quite well and even gives a bit of attention to delivery, Aristotle does not explore memory in his *Rhetoric*. Indeed, today it might seem to be even more appropriate than it was in Aristotle's time to leave out memory. In an age of teleprompters, databases, and smart gadgets, who needs memory?

But memory should not be ignored. As a matter of *ethos*, a person who knows the facts and figures is usually more persuasive than the one who has to look them up. Hugh of St. Victor, writing in the twelfth century, made just this point when he compared a good memory to a money changer in the marketplace. If a patron were to ask for a particular coin, the moneychanger should be able to find it expertly because he has neatly organized the coins into various compartments rather than having dumped them all in one bag. Just so, a rhetor ought to be able to draw from his memory whatever fact or argument is necessary at the moment—but he may do so only if he has previously arranged his memories in careful order.[2]

You may protest, "Impossible! I have a terrible memory!" The ancients had an answer for this excuse: Memory is not just a capacity; it is an art. That is, memory is a natural capacity—after all, you can remember your name, right?—which can be developed and trained. The idea is that just as your physical strength can be increased with exercise, so can your memory be built up by training. The ancient perspective on memory stands in contrast to the idea that our memories can ever be "full," teeming with information such that nothing else will fit. Instead, the ancients and medievals prized memory as an almost limitless capacity, a faculty that could be strengthened through organization. Memories, like the money changer's coins, should be carefully organized, allowing speakers speedy retrieval of what they have stored.

It is the retrieval, of course, that is the point. In fact, it is in bringing stored ideas together that new ideas are made possible. "When we think of our highest creative power [today]," writes Mary Carruthers, author of *The Book of Memory*, "we think invariably of the imagination. [. . .] Ancient and medieval people reserved *their* awe for memory."[3] Today it is even common to frown on rote memory, as if it its value ends when information is parroted back, perhaps on

2. See appendix A, "Hugh of St. Victor: 'The Three Best Memory-Aids for Learning History,'" in *The Book of Memory: A Study of Memory in Medieval Culture*, 2nd ed., trans. and ed. Mary Carruthers (Cambridge: Cambridge University Press, 2008), 339–344.

3. Carruthers, *The Book of Memory*, 1.

an exam. But Carruthers goes on to say that creativity is, in fact, very much dependent upon memory. And that's true, isn't it? It's not often—perhaps not even *ever* the case—that we create something new out of *nothing*. Education itself is largely a matter of moving information and ideas into your mind so that you can draw upon them and build upon them in unique ways later.

So while Aristotle gives memory short shrift in his overview of rhetoric, it was only a matter of time before rhetorical theorists would discover its persuasive value.

A Matter of the Soul

But memory is more than merely an art; it's a matter of the soul. Listen to how Augustine of Hippo (AD 354–430), addressing God, talks about it in his *Confessions*:

> Great is the power of memory, a fearful thing, O my God, a deep and boundless manifoldness; and this thing is the mind, and this am I myself. What am I then, O my God? What nature am I? A life various and manifold, and exceeding immense. Behold in the plains, and caves, and caverns of my memory, innumerable and innumerably full of innumerable kinds of things, either through images, as all bodies; or by actual presence, as the arts; or by certain notions or impressions, as the affections of the mind, which, even when the mind doth not feel, the memory retaineth, while yet whatsoever is in the memory is also in the mind—over all these do I run, I fly; I dive on this side and on that, as far as I can, and there is no end. So great is the force of memory, so great the force of life, even in the mortal life of man.[4]

For Augustine, memory is tied up with the soul and vice versa. He calls his memory his mind, and goes on to say that it is the self.

And is this not somehow true? Who are you, anyway? Doesn't it have something to do with what you have experienced in your life, but also with those memories being stored up within you—their

4. This text is in the public domain. Augustine, *Confessions*, trans. Edward Bouverie Pusey, book 10, chapter 17 (1909–14), text made available by the Internet Sacred Text Archive website, accessed March 3, 2016, http://www.sacred-texts.com/chr/augconf/aug10.htm.

composite somehow helping to make up the ineffable *you*? Or, to put it another way, to speak of yourself as a purely biological being, without considering anything beyond your basic physical self, would be a very short conversation. When we think of ourselves, our minds think of personalities formed by past experiences lived and then remembered. Even our aspirations, projections of who we want to be in the future, are grounded in our respective pasts.

> *"All learning depends on memory, and teaching is in vain if everything we hear slips away."*
> *—Quintilian*[5]

And we might go even further. What thoughts are available to you when the TV is off, your phone is silenced, and you lie in bed unable to sleep, if not those of your memory? Sure, you can think about the future, and sometimes we do. It's hard to think about the present, of course, because it's an immeasurable singular moment forever slipping into the past, as Augustine points out. Rather, we so often dwell upon those things saved up in the storehouse of our memories. Committing something to memory, then, is really a metaphysical[6] task. It's making a deposit into the bank of the soul. What shall we deposit, trash or treasure? It should go without saying that we would want our storehouse to be filled with those things that are true, good, and beautiful.

And it is especially important that the rhetors have available such memories, for they work in the medium of words, and words are an important way of shaping and tapping into the memories of an audience. That is to say, if the rhetor has not filled his storehouse with truth, goodness, and beauty, then he cannot retrieve and impart these to his audience. Memory is not, then, just a matter of being able to recall sections of a speech or facts that pique a listener's interest; instead, it is a matter of cultivating virtue or goodness of soul, making clearer Quintilian's often misunderstood claim that the ideal orator is "the good man speaking well." The link between a speaker's virtue and a compelling argument becomes evident: He will be persuasive *because* he is good. Thus, the cultivation of memory is the slow, ongoing work of cultivating one's *ethos*, one's good character.

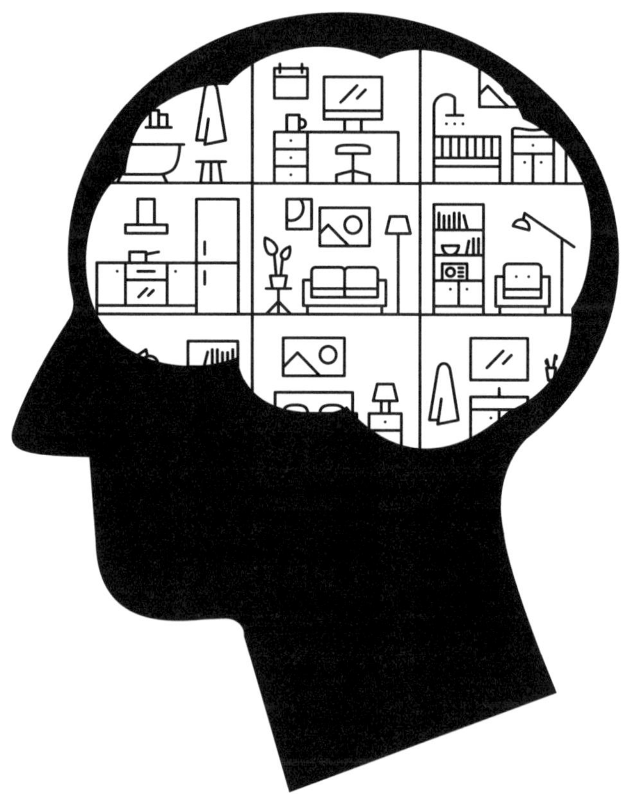

Figure 18. Memory palace.

5. Quintilian, *De Institutione Oratoria*, 6.2.1.
6. From the Greek *meta* "after, beyond" and *physika* "physics." Metaphysics is the study of the fundamental nature of reality—that of being and knowing.

How to Remember

Now let's visit the more practical side of memory. Memory tricks are familiar to us. Acronyms are helpful, such as using PEWSGAL to remember the seven deadly sins (*p*ride, *e*nvy, *w*rath, *s*loth, *g*luttony, *a*varice, *l*ust), or word association techniques in such things as memorizing names (to remember Mark, for instance, one could picture him *mark*ing on a chalkboard, Wendy's hair looking *wind*blown, or Brett wearing a barrette). But the ancients developed the art of memory to a degree that probably strikes the modern sensibilities as ludicrous. They hung their memory theories on the idea that the mind works best when it can offer a physical (if invisible) place for ideas.

Perhaps your own experience proves the point: In taking a test, have you ever read a question and immediately thought, "I know exactly where the answer is on the page in the textbook—the upper right-hand corner!" Or maybe you know exactly the spot—which aisle, which shelf—where your favorite cereal sits in the grocery store. Such occurrences bespeak the innate power of connecting knowledge to particular places and details. In fact, the ancient practice of creating illuminated manuscripts, with their various colors and vivid images, made the books beautiful, yes, but they were also mnemonically useful.

In Cicero's *De Oratore*,[7] the character Antony tells about the birth of **mnemonics**. As the story goes, Simonides of Ceos, a Greek poet, was dining in the home of a wealthy nobleman. He had been hired to recite a poem written for his host. After having done so, he stepped outside the banquet hall to get paid the balance of his fee. Just as he did, the roof of the building collapsed behind him, killing all those inside. The bodies were crushed beyond recognition, but Simonides—we can imagine him closing his eyes and picturing where each person had been sitting—was able to walk the bereaved to the place of their loved one's remains. His insight was this: Because sight is the keenest of all human sense, remembering is best done when one creates mental pictures.[8] Those mental pictures in turn must be arranged and "stored" in virtual places.

This technique of remembering based on location (Latin, *locus*, meaning "place")—creating memory palaces, as it were—became a central part of oratory for centuries, falling out of favor as external memory devices, such as the printing press (and now newer technologies), have multiplied. Today, memory is often so atrophied in us that we marvel at almost any act of memorization at all. Phone numbers—who memorizes those anymore? Important dates in history—why not just search the internet? Even birthdays—your online calendar will "remember" so you don't have to. Yet we must realize that the memory is trainable, and a well-trained memory can be good for the soul.

Memorizing a list of school supplies (not necessarily a treasure to store up in the soul, but just as an example) would be difficult for most of us. But if you were to imagine going into your room—not a palace, maybe, but serviceable nonetheless—and placing those objects in different spots inside it (e.g., scissors on your nightstand, pencils spilling out from your pillowcase), you could imaginatively reenter your room and retrieve that list when you go to the store to buy them. Think now of how this same method could be used for studying for an exam (it works!) or delivering a speech. Main arguments can be "placed" into a locale you know well: your kitchen, for example, or inside your car.

Key to the memory palace is spatial organization, but another factor is elaborate encoding. What this means is that you include interesting, even zany, details within your mental construction, and these details give you a better shot at recollection later. For example, if you wished to memorize the five most

7. See 2.86.351–54.

8. You'll notice that metaphor—the most powerful of figures of speech—functions in just this way: A metaphor is an idea that is collapsed with a *thing*.

abundant elements in the earth's crust—oxygen, silicon, aluminum, iron, and calcium—you could mentally picture the following items placed around your kitchen table: an asthma inhaler (oxygen), a plastic kitchen spatula (silicon), a roll of tinfoil (aluminum), a hammer and nail (iron), and a jug of milk (calcium). But there's little elaborateness—and no zaniness—in these rather humdrum associations. You'd do better to paint the picture in brighter colors, so to speak, or, as the author of *Rhetorica ad Herennium* tells us, "as striking as possible." For example, you could begin by imagining the asthma inhaler on your father's plate, completely smothered in ketchup—what a mess! You could end by picturing the jug of milk (It's expired! You can smell it!) knocked over by your baby sister; it is pouring—*glug, glug, glug*—all over her woven place mat and dripping off the edge of her seat. Such offbeat details help the larger concepts stick.

Memory and Virtue

In his TED Talk "Feats of Memory Anyone Can Do," Joshua Foer[9] reminds us that such tricks are actually just ways of getting us to attend more closely, and close attention is the true aim. Our lives and the human beings around us deserve our full awareness, the full attention of our memories. Think about it: When a person you briefly met several months ago sees you again and remembers your name, you are probably pleased. You feel that your presence was not ignored, for you were attended to in such a way that your memory became a fixture in that person's mind. Such are humans—pleased deeply when we are known and recognized.[10] Rhetors must always be cautious not to abuse this human propensity, for in detecting this truth about humanity, they are a hair's breadth from flattery and abuse. But to remember—to attend to the world and to people so that they are carried around with you in your memory—is itself an act of respect that suggests something in your character that moves beyond mere self-interest. If memory is, after all, a matter of the soul, then paying attention may be an ideal way to cultivate virtue in our own souls as we practice the charitable act of remembering.

The internet is a good source for research on memory. For example, the National Geographic Channel offers some online games and videos that illustrate ways to improve your memory, including "chunking" information <http://capress.link/ra10901>. Learn how to memorize numbers and explore various other memory tips on the "Art of Memory" blog <http://capress.link/ra10902>.

9. Foer wrote a book about memory and, more interestingly perhaps, his becoming the 2006 USA Memory Champion using those techniques he discovered. See *Moonwalking with Einstein: The Art and Science of Remembering Everything* (New York: Penguin Press, 2011).
10. Think of the word *recognize*, "to think of again." We long to be *recognized*.

DISCUSSION TEXT:

St. Augustine: Confessions *(circa AD 400)*[11]

FOCUS:

Style

Augustine of Hippo was a teacher of rhetoric before he converted to Christianity. His work Confessions *is itself a work of epideictic rhetoric—that is, a work that praises and censures. It is in Book 10 of his* Confessions *that he explores memory.*

Figure 19. Illustration of St. Augustine, artist unknown. From *The Hundred Greatest Men* (New York: D. Appleton & Company, 1885). Courtesy of the Perry-Castañeda Library, University of Texas at Austin, http://www.lib.utexas.edu/exhibits/portraits/.

> . . . I will pass then beyond this power of my nature also, rising by degrees unto Him Who made me. And I come to the fields and spacious palaces of my memory, where are the treasures of innumerable images, brought into it from things of all sorts perceived by the senses. There is stored up, whatsoever besides we think, either by enlarging or diminishing, or any other way varying those things which the sense hath come to; and whatever else hath been committed and laid up, which forgetfulness hath not yet swallowed up and buried. When I enter there, I require what I will to be brought forth, and something instantly comes; others must be longer sought after, which are fetched, as it were, out of some inner receptacle; others rush out in troops, and while one thing is desired and required, they start forth, as who should say, "Is it perchance I?" These I drive away with the hand of my heart, from the face of my remembrance; until what I wish for be unveiled, and appear in sight, out of its secret place. Other things come up readily, in unbroken order, as they are called for; those in front making way for the following; and as they make way, they are hidden from sight, ready to come when I will. All which takes place when I repeat a thing by heart.
>
> There are all things preserved distinctly and under general heads, each having entered by its own avenue: as light, and all colours and forms of bodies by the eyes; by the ears all sorts of sounds; all smells by the avenue of the nostrils; all tastes by the mouth; and by the sensation of the whole body, what is hard or soft; hot or cold; or rugged; heavy or light; either

11. Augustine, *Confessions*, trans. Edward Bouverie Pusey, book 10 (1909–1914), text made available by the Internet Sacred Text Archive website, http://www.sacred-texts.com/chr/augconf/aug10.htm.

outwardly or inwardly to the body. All these doth that great harbour of the memory receive in her numberless secret and inexpressible windings, to be forthcoming, and brought out at need; each entering in by his own gate, and there laid up. Nor yet do the things themselves enter in; only the images of the things perceived are there in readiness, for thought to recall. Which images, how they are formed, who can tell, though it doth plainly appear by which sense each hath been brought in and stored up? For even while I dwell in darkness and silence, in my memory I can produce colours, if I will, and discern betwixt black and white, and what others I will: nor yet do sounds break in and disturb the image drawn in by my eyes, which I am reviewing, though they also are there, lying dormant, and laid up, as it were, apart. For these too I call for, and forthwith they appear. And though my tongue be still, and my throat mute, so can I sing as much as I will; nor do those images of colours, which notwithstanding be there, intrude themselves and interrupt, when another store is called for, which flowed in by the ears. So the other things, piled in and up by the other senses, I recall at my pleasure. Yea, I discern the breath of lilies from violets, though smelling nothing; and I prefer honey to sweet wine, smooth before rugged, at the time neither tasting nor handling, but remembering only.

. . .

Great is this force of memory, excessive great, O my God; a large and boundless chamber! who ever sounded the bottom thereof? yet is this a power of mine, and belongs unto my nature; nor do I myself comprehend all that I am. Therefore is the mind too strait to contain itself. And where should that be, which it containeth not of itself? Is it without it, and not within? how then doth it not comprehend itself? A wonderful admiration surprises me, amazement seizes me upon this.

. . .

The same memory contains also the affections of my mind, not in the same manner that my mind itself contains them, when it feels them; but far otherwise, according to a power of its own. For without rejoicing I remember myself to have joyed; and without sorrow do I recollect my past sorrow. And that I once feared, I review without fear; and without desire call to mind a past desire. Sometimes, on the contrary, with joy do I remember my fore-past sorrow, and with sorrow, joy. Which is not wonderful, as to the body; for mind is one thing, body another. If I therefore with joy remember some past pain of body, it is not so wonderful. But now seeing this very memory itself is mind (for when we give a thing in charge, to be kept in memory, we say, "See that you keep it in mind"; and when we forget, we say, "It did not come to my mind," and, "It slipped out of my mind," calling the memory itself the mind); this being so, how is it that when with joy I remember my past sorrow, the mind hath joy, the memory hath sorrow; the mind upon the joyfulness which is in it, is joyful, yet the memory upon the sadness which is in it, is not sad? Does the memory perchance not belong to the mind? Who will say so? The memory then is, as it were, the belly of the mind, and joy and sadness, like sweet and bitter food; which, when committed to the memory, are as it were passed into the belly, where they may be stowed, but cannot taste. Ridiculous it is to imagine these to be alike; and yet are they not utterly unlike.

. . .

Lord, I, truly, toil therein, yea and toil in myself; I am become a heavy soil requiring over much sweat of the brow. For we are not now searching out the regions of heaven, or measuring the distances of the stars, or enquiring the balancings of the earth. It is I myself who remember, I the mind. It is not so wonderful, if what I myself am not, be far from me. But what is nearer to me than myself? And lo, the force of mine own memory is not understood by me; though I cannot so much as name myself without it. . . . So great is the force of memory, so great the force of life, even in the mortal life of man. What shall I do then, O Thou my true life, my God? I will pass even beyond this power of mine which is called memory: yea, I will pass beyond it, that I may approach unto Thee, O sweet Light. What sayest Thou to me? See, I am mounting up through my mind towards Thee who abidest above me. Yea, I now will pass beyond this power of mine which is called memory, desirous to arrive at Thee, whence Thou mayest be arrived at; and to cleave unto Thee, whence one may cleave unto Thee. For even beasts and birds have memory; else could they not return to their dens and nests, nor many other things they are used unto: nor indeed could they be used to any thing, but by memory. I will pass then beyond memory also, that I may arrive at Him who hath separated me from the four-footed beasts and made me wiser than the fowls of the air, I will pass beyond memory also, and where shall I find Thee, Thou truly good and certain sweetness? And where shall I find Thee? If I find Thee without my memory, then do I not retain Thee in my memory. And how shall I find Thee, if I remember Thee not?

Discussion Questions

Confessions

1. What is Augustine's opening analogy for the memory?

2. What sorts of mysterious things does Augustine say that the memory can do even though it lacks the five senses?

3. To what organ of the body does Augustine compare the memory, and how are they similar?

4. Memory appears to be the closest Augustine can get to his inner self. "But what is nearer to me than myself?" he wonders. What does Augustine seek to find in passing beyond his memory?

5. The movement that Augustine undertakes is sometimes termed the *via interior*, the "interior way." Which lines reveal this upward/inward journey? To what or whom does this way lead?

6. Augustine is often called a Neoplatonist. How is Plato's depiction of the ascent out of the cave (*Republic*, Book 7) like Augustine's journey through memory? How are they different?

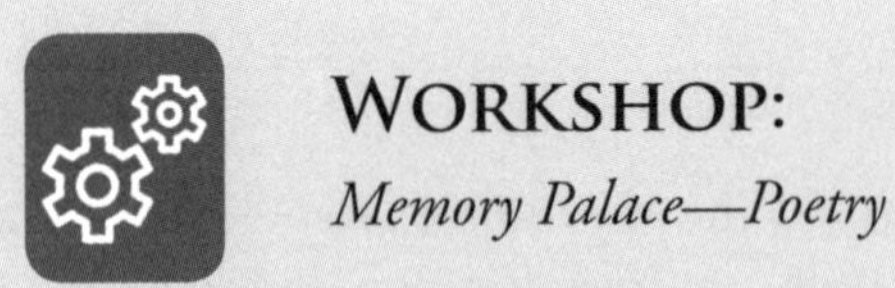

WORKSHOP: *Memory Palace—Poetry* 1

Create a memory palace for a poem you will memorize. Choose your own, or see chapter 3 for poem options. You should assign at least one image per line. Store the images within your memory palace (your bedroom, perhaps, or the classroom) in a clockwise order. You might find it best to draw out your palace on a sheet of paper, just as you would create a map.

Creating memory palaces is time-consuming, so give yourself plenty of time to make and fill your palace. Also, because remembering is a matter of elaborate encoding, be sure to paint your palace in great—even if it is ludicrous—detail. Finally, it is tempting to resort to the old method of just reciting over and over until the piece is memorized. Don't do it! Because you are learning new techniques of memorizing, force yourself to use the method of the memory palace, and mentally tick through the images as you recite. The images will help prompt you when you come to a line that you simply cannot remember using rote memory. Here is an example:

When I Was One-and-Twenty

by A. E. Housman

When I was one-and-twenty
I heard a wise man say,
"Give crowns and pounds and guineas
But not your heart away;
Give pearls away and rubies
But keep your fancy free."
But I was one-and-twenty,
No use to talk to me.

When I was one-and-twenty
I heard him say again,
"The heart out of the bosom
Was never given in vain;
'Tis paid with sighs a plenty
And sold for endless rue."
And I am two-and-twenty,
And oh, 'tis true, 'tis true.

Figure 20. English classical scholar and poet Alfred E. Housman, 1910, by E.O. Hoppe, https://en.wikipedia.org/w/index.php?curid=44421941.

Making Your Memory Palace

Now enact (or imagine) the following. Actions are described in italics:

When I was one-and-twenty

Standing inside the classroom, Student A knocks at the classroom door one time, pauses, and then knocks twenty more times.

I heard a wise man say,

A grandfatherly man with white hair, a long beard, and spectacles answers the door from outside in the hall.

"Give crowns and pounds and guineas

The old man hands Student A a heavy golden crown, a pound of sugar, and a squealing guinea pig.

But not your heart away;

He holds a heart-shaped box of chocolates in his hand, shows it to Student A, but then refuses to share the chocolates.

Figure 21. Example of a memory palace.

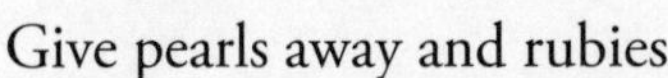

Give pearls away and rubies

Student A turns and approaches the first student in the first row. He drapes a long string of pearls around the student's neck and then slides a gigantic ruby ring onto the student's finger.

But keep your fancy free."

The student sitting directly behind the first student is wearing a fancy lace dress. The student stands and curtsies to Student A.

But I was one-and-twenty,

Student A then proceeds to the third student in that row and knocks on his or her desk one time, pauses, and then knocks twenty more times.

No use to talk to me.

The third student puts his finger over his mouth, "SHHHHHH!"

(Now try your hand at creating a memory palace for the rest of the poem.)

WORKSHOP: 2
Memory Palace—The Bill of Rights

Learn the gist of the first ten amendments to the US Constitution by mentally painting a picture to store them for future recollection. If you are working with classmates, you will each be responsible for devising a part of the memory palace for the amendment you are assigned. Remember to go in order around the room, and try to tie each person in with the person before and after him; this helps give continuity to the list. For example, suppose the person responsible for the second amendment is in the corner of the room yelling out, "Bear arms! Get your bear arms here! Four for a dollar!" The next person, responsible for "no quartering of soldiers," may perform a military march toward him, salute, and then offer him a quarter in exchange for one bear arm. Connecting the parts of the memory palace together can help jog your memory as you mentally tick through the list later.

1. Freedom of religion, speech, press, assembly, and petition
2. Right to keep and bear arms
3. No quartering of soldiers
4. Right to be secure against unreasonable searches and seizures
5. Freedom from self-incrimination, double jeopardy, right to due process of law
6. Rights of accused persons (i.e., the right to a speedy and public trial, the right to defense counsel, etc.)
7. Right of trial by jury in civil cases
8. Freedom from excessive bail, as well as from cruel and unusual punishments
9. Other rights of the people
10. Powers reserved to the states

Figure 22. The Bill of Rights.

Workshop: 3
Memory Song—The US Presidents

Another great memorization tool is the use of song. Memorize the US presidents using the tune of "Michael Finnegan." What's handy about this tune is that it breaks up the presidents into three groups, each beginning with what could be argued as a new era in presidential history. Punctuation has been added to help illustrate the flow and pauses of the "song."

Washington,
Adams,
Jefferson,
Madison;

Monroe,
Adams,
Jackson,
Van Buren;

Harrison,
Tyler,
Polk, *(and)*
Taylor;

Fillmore,
Pierce,
Buchanan. [*End of verse one*]

Lincoln,
Johnson,
Grant,
Hayes,
Garfield; [*Sung quickly as "Grant–Hayes–Garfield"*]

Figure 23. Presidents of the United States of America.

Figure 23 (cont.). Presidents of the United States of America.

Arthur,
Cleveland,
Harrison,
Cleveland;

McKinley,
Roosevelt,
Taft, *(and)*
Wilson;

Harding,
Coolidge,
Hoover. [*End of verse two*]

Roosevelt,
Truman,
Eisenhower; [*Sung syllable by syllable as "Eis–en–how–er"*]

Kennedy,
Johnson,
Nixon,
Ford; [*Sung as "Fo–ord"*]

Carter,
Reagan,
Bush, *(and)*
Clinton;

W. Bush, [*Sung as "Double-U Bush" or "Dubya Bush"*]
Obama.
____________________ [*Update president(s) as needed.*]

PRESENTATION: *Recitation* | **SPOTLIGHT** *Memory*

For this presentation, you will recite something you memorized for the various memory palace workshops. Where is your poem (or other text) "located"? Describe your memory palace in detail, and then recite the text you memorized. One way to do this is to stand at the front of the room and recite with your eyes closed. You can point "at" the particular images around you as you mentally walk through your palace during the delivery of the poem. Or if you have "hidden" the images within your classroom, you can move through the classroom mentally or physically as you recite. The focus here is memory, but you should continue to improve your voice, posture, and eye contact with each presentation as well as avoiding fidgeting.

10

Chapter 10

Canon Five, Delivery: Presenting the Whole

(1403b) The first question to receive attention was naturally the one that comes first naturally—how persuasion can be produced from the facts themselves. The second is how to set these facts out in language. A third would be the proper method of delivery; this is a thing that affects the success of a speech greatly; but hitherto the subject has been neglected. Indeed, it was long before it found a way into the arts of tragic drama and epic recitation: at first poets acted their tragedies themselves. It is plain that delivery has just as much to do with oratory as with poetry. (In connexion with poetry, it has been studied by Glaucon of Teos among others.) It is, essentially, a matter of the right management of the voice to express the various emotions—of speaking loudly, softly, or between the two; of high, low, or intermediate pitch; of the various rhythms that suit various subjects. These are the three things—volume of sound, modulation of pitch, and rhythm—that a speaker bears in mind. It is those who ***do*** bear them in mind who usually win prizes in the dramatic contests; and just as in drama the actors now count for more than the poets, so it is in the contests of public life, owing to the defects of our political institutions. No systematic treatise upon the rules of delivery has yet been composed; indeed, even the study of language made no progress till late in the day. Besides, delivery is—very properly—not regarded as an elevated subject of inquiry. (1404a) Still, the whole business of rhetoric being concerned with appearances, we must pay attention to the subject of delivery, unworthy though it is, because we cannot do without it. The right thing in speaking really is that we should be satisfied not to annoy our hearers, without trying to delight them: we ought in fairness to fight our case with no help beyond the bare facts: nothing, therefore, should matter except the proof of those facts. Still, as has been already said, other things affect the result considerably, owing to the defects of our hearers. The arts of language cannot help having a small but real importance, whatever it is we have to expound to others: the way in which a thing is said does affect its intelligibility. Not, however, so much importance as people think. All such arts are fanciful and meant to charm the hearer. Nobody uses fine language when teaching geometry.

When the principles of delivery have been worked out, they will produce the same effect as on the stage. But only very slight attempts to deal with them have been made and by a few people, as by Thrasy-

> machus in his "Appeals to Pity." Dramatic ability is a natural gift, and can hardly be systematically taught. The principles of good diction can be so taught, and therefore we have men of ability in this direction too, who win prizes in their turn, as well as those speakers who excel in delivery—speeches of the written or literary kind owe more of their effect to their direction than to their thought. . . .
>
> (1404b) We can now see that a writer must disguise his art and give the impression of speaking naturally and not artificially. Naturalness is persuasive, artificiality is the contrary; for our hearers are prejudiced and think we have some design against them, as if we were mixing their wines for them. It is like the difference between the quality of Theodorus' voice and the voices of all other actors: his really seems to be that of the character who is speaking, theirs do not. We can hide our purpose successfully by taking the single words of our composition from the speech of ordinary life. . . .
>
> [1408b] All the variations of oratorical style are capable of being used in season or out of season. The best way to counteract any exaggeration is the well-worn device by which the speaker puts in some criticism of himself; for then people feel it must be all right for him to talk thus, since he certainly knows what he is doing. Further, it is better not to have everything always just corresponding to everything else—your hearers will see through you less easily thus. I mean for instance, if your words are harsh, you should not extend this harshness to your voice and your countenance and have everything else in keeping. If you do, the artificial character of each detail becomes apparent; whereas if you adopt one device and not another, you are using art all the same and yet nobody notices it. (To be sure, if mild sentiments are expressed in harsh tones and harsh sentiments in mild tones, you become comparatively unconvincing.)

Aristotle's *Rhetoric* is invention-heavy; that is, the first two of the books are focused on *what* to say. In book 3, Aristotle begins to look at the *how*: how the words we choose and the structure of an argument can make a real difference. But first comes a short assault on delivery.

Delivery is almost unworthy of mention for Aristotle—a vulgar matter he'd rather not have to address. The fact that someone can sway our opinions by a shift in voice or a histrionic[1] gesture *is* a little scary, isn't it? But the great persuasive power of delivery makes its study an essential part of the study of rhetoric. So, despite all of his complaints, Aristotle briefly considers it, "unworthy though it is, because we cannot do without it" (1404a).

1. From the Latin word *histrio*, "actor." Histrionic means melodramatic.

Delivery: A Matter of *Ethos*

Although Aristotle doesn't exactly say this, he would likely agree with it: As a matter of *ethos*, rhetors should tailor their delivery to suit their speeches. A key to *ethos*, if you remember, is goodwill, and goodwill toward your audience means that you try to help them flourish. A flourishing audience is one whose *pathos* is in line with its *logos*. Emotions should run along with, and not counter to, logic. Rhetors, then, ought not to be *actors*, attempting to sway the audience by mere performance. In fact, he says "we should be satisfied not to annoy our hearers, without trying to delight them." Instead, rhetors ought to use gestures and voice inflections and eye contact in harmony with their speeches. Delivery should match the *ethos*, *pathos*, and *logos* they're already employing.

You should, then, seek utter harmony between *what* you say and *how* you say it. Remember Hamlet's advice to a troupe of actors before their show. He tells the company the following: [see sidebar]

In short, the delivery should match the words. The goal is "to hold . . . the mirror up to nature" (that is, act naturally)—not to take emphasis off of the content but, instead, to let the content have the best chance of actually being heard. Sometimes this balance calls for a staid composure and sometimes for something a little more out of the ordinary. Either way, you do not want a clash of words and actions, for such will "make the judicious grieve," thus spoiling your project.

Voice

Aristotle mentions three things as important aspects of delivery: volume, pitch, and rhythm. It turns out that, even more than 2,000 years later, those very things still cause real problems for speakers. Volume: *Be loud!* It sounds obvious, but many a speaker's voice goes faint when addressing a crowd. Do not worry about being overly loud. Rarely does someone err on the side of a booming delivery; a speaker more likely will speak just low enough to make everyone in the room wonder what was said. Vocal features related to volume are pronunciation—saying words correctly—and enunciation—saying words clearly. Although Aristotle's concern for the right volume may not seem to include these more specific aspects of delivery, both pronunciation and enunciation can be thought of as subclasses of volume, for they make the experience of listening pleasant and productive—which is, after all, the point. (You can practice enunciation by saying tongue twisters as a warm-up activity. For an extra challenge, try doing so while biting down on a pencil.) In short, make sure your voice carries your message across loud and clear.

Suit the action to the word, the word to the action; with this special observance, that you o'erstep not the modesty of nature. For anything so overdone is from the purpose of playing, whose end, both at the first and now, was and is, to hold, as 'twere, the mirror up to nature, to show virtue her own feature, scorn her own image, and the very age and body of the time his form and pressure. Now this overdone, or come tardy off, though it make the unskillful laugh, cannot but make the judicious grieve, the censure of the which one must in your allowance o'erweigh a whole theatre of others.[2]

2. Shakespeare, *Hamlet*, 3.2.18–29.

Pitch—the highness or lowness of a tone—is something we naturally vary when we're excited, raising and lowering our voices to add expression to our message. It's also one of the reasons questions can be so effective in a speech: Pitch naturally rises and falls as we speak. The pitch of yes-or-no questions moves upward at the end; for example, say these aloud to compare: "Are you sure?" "I'm sure." "Have you eaten breakfast?" "I've eaten breakfast." "Did you study for the test?" "I've studied for the test." For some reason, the batteries in our pitch meters often go out when faced with a microphone or podium, rendering our otherwise variable voices suddenly monotone. Don't let it happen to you! Remember, it is a matter of *ethos* that you appear to feel the same emotion you are attempting to conjure in your audience. You must allow your voice to carry across that emotion, and that transfer largely depends on pitch.

Table 6. Important vocal features.

1. Volume
2. Pitch
3. Rhythm

Last but not least in Aristotle's list on the voice is rhythm. While we are tempted to think of rhythm in the arts (e.g., music and dance), we should not forget that rhythm is so natural to humans that it is incorporated into our everyday lives. Your very heartbeat, for example, which races when excited or slows when bored, keeps you aware of the connection of body and soul. So being sensitive to rhythm in your own rhetoric is not contrived manipulation; instead, it is heeding Hamlet's advice "to hold . . . the mirror up to nature." In fact, if you want to make sure you bore your audience, speak all of your sentences at the exact same speed. But if you want to give your words their best shot at making a difference, you must vary your rhythm, emphasizing certain groups of words by speaking them quickly but highlighting others by slowing them down. Also, phrases need to be "chunked": Say your prepositional phrases all together, for example, rather than one word at a time. Notice how the following quote by Winston Churchill could be chunked (the parentheses group together the phrases): "Never (in the field of human conflict) was so much owed (by so many) (to so few)." Finally, pause often. Pauses are almost as important as the words themselves because they give the listener a moment of stasis, a break, a chance to rest from the verbiage, during which words can settle into meaning. Dramatic pauses also help emphasize major points. In brief, you should deliver like you naturally speak—rhythmically.[3]

3. For more on rhythm, see Martha Kolln, *Rhetorical Grammar: Grammatical Choices, Rhetorical Effects*, 7th ed. (New York: Longman, 2013). See esp. the chapter titled "Sentence Rhythm."

Gestures

Aristotle doesn't spend long on **gestures**—Cicero will come along later to fill in some of the gaps—but he does know they are important, and so should you. Just as you move your hands in everyday conversation, so too should you move them when in front of a crowd, even to a somewhat exaggerated degree. Again, the point is to match. Your body movement should match your speech, helping to emphasize or bring to life the message.

Although there may be many ways to think about different kinds of gestures, the following four categories are a helpful aid: descriptive, emphatic, suggestive, and prompting.[4] *Descriptive* gestures help the audience visualize what you're talking about. Your hands move to show size, shape, and number, or movement and location. *Emphatic* gestures underscore what's being said. You could clench your fist to show anger or shrug your shoulders to indicate indifference. *Suggestive* gestures are symbols of concepts, such as an open palm for generosity. Finally, a *prompting* gesture is one that urges the audience to join along or to imitate it. If you want your listeners to clap or raise their hands, for instance, then you do so first and invite them to join you.

Besides the kinds of body movement you *should* do, there is also body movement that you should avoid. Some speakers *over*-gesture, and that's just as bad as standing like a statue. Some speakers accidentally resort to the *same* gesture over and over, which can drive an audience crazy. Some speakers lean on the podium, or they stand awkwardly on one foot at a time. And almost all of us fidget, which is to be avoided at all costs. (Here are common examples: playing with hair, fingers, or hems of clothing; swaying back and forth or standing like a flamingo; tapping on or gripping the podium.) The point is simple: Feel free to move your body, but only in ways that accentuate what you're saying. A confident speaker is one who isn't afraid to move around, but does so with purpose.

A couple of final things to mention: eye contact and facial expressions. Eye contact—not flitting but sustained for a moment or two—is crucial to making a strong connection with the audience. Again, it's a matter of *ethos*—and, remember, *ethos* is almost the whole of persuasion. If you don't look at people, they are liable to think you are shifty or—if you are always looking at your notes—not very knowledgeable about your subject. Either way, your *ethos* suffers. Your face, too, must be enlivened by expression that suits the content of your message. Sober messages should be told from a sober counte-

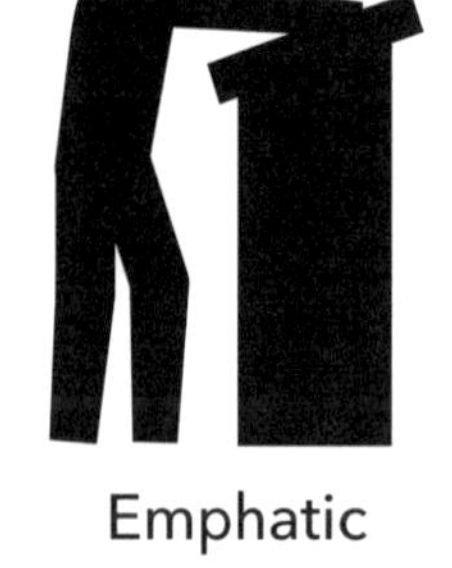

Figure 24. Four types of gestures.

4. Visit the Toastmasters website <http://capress.link/ra11001> for more on these four types of gestures.

nance, just as joyful ones make sense when delivered with a smile.

For an honest evaluation, ask a friend or family member to give you feedback, or video your performance and try to assess yourself. Are you standing up straight? Are you audible? Are you using various types of gestures? Are the rhythms in your speech natural and interesting? Have you used pauses to add dramatic emphasis? Has your pitch changed to correspond with your meaning?

The Nuts and Bolts

In the end, delivery is a matter of practice. So practice, practice, practice! You can practice in front of family, friends, a mirror, or a video recorder. Even an empty room will work. And pay careful attention to the following:

1. **Volume:** Look over your speech to find places where a rise or fall in volume is necessitated, where being louder or softer suits the point you're making. <u>Underline</u> words you wish to stress so you remember to emphasize them with an increase in volume.
2. **Pitch:** Add up or down arrows in your text to remind you to vary your pitch.
3. **Rhythm:** Saying a central point slowly will draw attention to it. Find your central point and spotlight it with a change in rhythm. It is also a good idea to place parentheses around prepositional phrases so that you remember to say them as a unit. Mark pauses in your text.
4. **Body movement:** Stand up straight, and don't fidget. Make sure any movement you make supports the meaning of the text (e.g., no scratching your head). You should gesture throughout, but you should mark the most important gestures so that you don't forget them when nerves are high. Stiff speakers, who never move a muscle except for their mouths, don't just fail at seeming confident: A lack of movement actually gets in the way of their message.
5. **Practice:** Practice presenting the speech aloud, and make sure you're audible to the back of the room. A great speech that's never heard is a waste. The practice will also help you figure out what works—and what doesn't—in delivering a great speech.

In many ways, effective rhetoric is a matter of being a good matchmaker. *Pathos* ought to match up with *logos*, and the face, voice, and body ought to match up with the message. All in all, you should think of your speech as a gift to your audience: Make it a good gift, and ensure by your delivery that it doesn't get damaged in transit.

Table 7. Delivery marks for a text.

Emphasis	Marker
Louder	*italics* or <u>underline</u>
Softer	*
Pause	/
Dramatic pause	///
Rise in pitch	↗
Fall in pitch	↘
Faster	>>>
Slower	<<<
"Chunk"	( )
Gesture, or special instructions (e.g., [whisper] or [point])	[ ]

Discussion Text:

Broadcaster John Hilton: "A Talk about Giving a Talk" (1937)[5]

Focus:

Delivery

John Hilton called the secret to his popularity as a 1930s radio announcer "calculated spontaneity." That is, he would write and read his radio script as if it were unplanned, as if he were having an impromptu conversation. In the following broadcast, he shares those secrets: using internal dialogue, talking while writing, chunking phrases, speaking at the right speed, and using English that is "truer than life."

July 1, 1937, on BBC radio

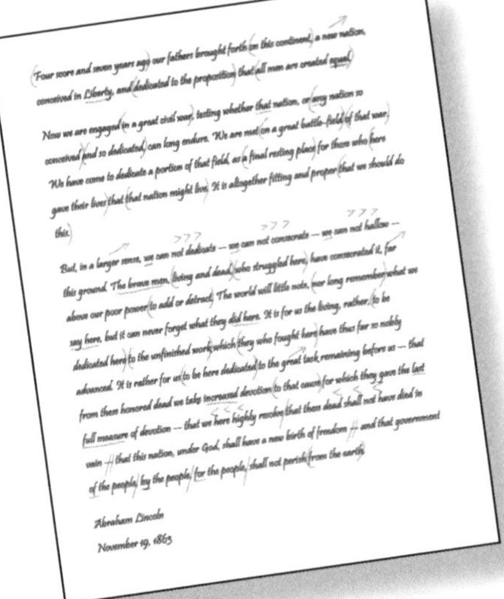

Four score and seven years ago our fathers brought forth on this continent, a new nation, conceived in Liberty, and dedicated to the proposition that all men are created equal.

Now we are engaged in a great civil war, testing whether that nation, or any nation so conceived and so dedicated, can long endure. We are met on a great battle-field of that war. We have come to dedicate a portion of that field, as a final resting place for those who here gave their lives that that nation might live. It is altogether fitting and proper that we should do this.

But, in a larger sense, we can not dedicate — we can not consecrate — we can not hallow — this ground. The brave men, living and dead, who struggled here, have consecrated it, far above our poor power to add or detract. The world will little note, nor long remember what we say here, but it can never forget what they did here. It is for us the living, rather, to be dedicated here to the unfinished work which they who fought here have thus far so nobly advanced. It is rather for us to be here dedicated to the great task remaining before us — that from these honored dead we take increased devotion to that cause for which they gave the last full measure of devotion — that we here highly resolve that these dead shall not have died in vain — that this nation, under God, shall have a new birth of freedom — and that government of the people, by the people, for the people, shall not perish from the earth.

Abraham Lincoln

November 19, 1863

Figure 25. Example of Lincoln's *Gettysburg Address* marked for delivery.

I kept wondering what to say to you in this last talk, and then I had a bright idea. At least I hope it's a bright idea. I said to myself, "suppose you give a talk about giving a talk."—"A talk about giving a talk! How d'you mean?"—"Why, how you set about it, and the tricks of the trade, and so on."—"Yes, that is rather an idea," I said to myself. So here goes. . . .

There've been bits in the paper sometimes about my broadcasts. The bits I've always liked best are those that refer to John Hilton "who just comes to the microphone and *talks*. So different from listening to something being *read*." Oh yes, I like that. For, of course, I read every word of every talk. If only I could pull it off every time—but you have to be at the top of your form. Yes, of course, every word's on paper even now—this—what I'm saying to you now—it's all here. Talking! Just as it comes to him! Right out of his head! I hope it sounds so; it's meant to. If it does—well—this is one of my good days.

"Tricks of the trade." Must I really tell you those? All right. The first trick of the trade is that there aren't any tricks. I mean tricks don't come off. That's my experience, anyway. I've tried, in my time, this way and that. I like experiments. I'll try anything once. But the little stunts and try-ons—no good! For me, I mean, of course. I think what listeners can spot more surely than anything else is any trace of falseness. I think you've got to find yourself—the radio rendering of yourself, and then be true to it. Truth, not tricks. For my sort of stuff, I mean, of course.

"But to read as if you were talking! Isn't that a trick?" Oh no, that's an art—or a craft, whichever you like. And in every art or craft there's a technique, a method, a way. What is it here? Well, I suppose each has to find his own; but my notion is that to read as if you were

5. William Safire, *Lend Me Your Ears: Great Speeches in History* (New York: W.W. Norton & Co., 1997), 570–573.

talking you must first write as if you were talking. What you have on the paper in front of you must be talk stuff, not book stuff.

It's in part, a mere matter of how you put the words down on the paper. That very sentence now, the one you've just heard. It began with "It's in part. . . ." If I'd said to you, "It is, in part," you'd have thought, "He's reading." In speech we say "it's," not "It is." So I write "*I T* apostrophe *S*," and not "It is" on the paper. I know if I wrote "It is," I should say "It is . . ."

I don't know anything about others, as I say, but my way is to speak my sentences aloud as I write them. In fact, here's my second rule, all pat: "to write as you would talk you must talk while you write." If you were outside my room while I'm writing a talk you'd hear muttering and mumbling and outright declaration from the beginning to end. You'd say, "There's somebody in there with a slate loose; he never stops talking to himself." No, I wouldn't be talking to *myself* but to you. . . .

You can scrap, in writing a talk, most of what you've been told all your life was literary good form. You have to; if you want your talk to ring the bell and walk in and sit down by the hearth. You've been told, for instance, that it's bad form to end a sentence with a preposition. It may be, in print. But not in talk. Not in talk. I'm coming to the view that what I call the "prepositional verb" (I'm no grammarian—I invent my own names for those things)—that what I call the prepositional verb is one of the glories of the English language. You start with a simple verb like "to stand"; and with the help of a pocketful of prepositions you get all those lovely changes; to stand up, to stand down, to stand off, to stand in, to stand by, to stand over—and twenty others. We score over the French there. The Germans have it; but they stick their prepositions in front of the verbs. I think our way has much more punch to it. And what bull's-eyes you can score with the prepositional verb if only you'll search for it and, having found it, let the preposition come at the end of the sentence.[6]

You know how odd moments stick in the memory. One stays in mine. I was dealing with retirement pensions. I was tired. Tired to the point of writing that awful jargon that passes for English. I'd written something like "I don't want what I've said to discourage you from pursuing this added stimulus. . . ." At that point I said to myself, "Now, come on, John, pull yourself together. That won't do: what is it you're trying to say?" And I pulled myself together (tired as I was)—I pulled myself together and searched and found it. "I don't want to put you off. I want rather to set you on." That was all. (What torment we have to go through to find what it is we're trying to say and how to say it in simple words.) That was all. Two simple sentences: put you *off*—set you on. Each ending with a preposition.

At that point, as I wrote this script, I went for a walk round the houses. Two lads were talking as I passed. One had three dogs on a leash. The [first] asked, as I went by, "What d'you keep dogs for?" I pricked up my ears at that (for more reasons than one, you know).

6. Winston Churchill is often attributed with the following witticism regarding the rule of never ending a sentence with a preposition: "This is the sort of English up with which I will not put."

But I'm always interested in the way people say things. Quite as much as in what they say. "What d'you keep dogs for?" That was his way of asking. "Why do you keep dogs?" It's most people's way. I fancy it's my way, as often as not. In my everyday speech, I mean. But suppose I'm writing a talk, and want to ask a question like that in it. Which form shall I use? Shall I say, "Why," or shall I say, "What for"? The first saves a word, and over the air a word saved in expressing a thought is a kingdom gained. The second not only wastes a word, but the sentence ends in the wrong sort of preposition, the one on which you drop your voice: "What d'you keep *dogs* for?" So you'd say, "Use the first." Yes, but I like what I say to get home; and to get at that lad, mustn't I use his form, not the best form? The times I've had to face that question: popular English or good English!

I think I've mostly dodged it. There's an idiom, I believe, lies behind both. Behind both stiff speech and loose talk. I think if you can get back to that, the boy on the bike and the girl at the counter and the man at the works and the woman in the home will all feel the speech you're using to be, perhaps not "true to life"—but something better; truer than life. It's a choice of word and a turn of speech that, if only you can get it, reflects the very soul and spirit of our language. It comes down, of course, through Shakespeare and the Authorized Version. But there's nothing old-fashioned, nothing dead and done with about it. It's all alive and kicking. But it keeps to the homely words that belong to the oldest English and to homely turns of speech. That's the way out I've tried to find. Sometimes I've felt I've really found it, and then what a thrill! How often I've tried for it and failed. . . .

I do believe that's all I want to say about the technique of *composing* talk. All I want to say here and now, I mean. It's all I can say, anyhow. But about delivering over the air what's composed? Ah, there I think I'd better keep quiet. Each has a way that best suits himself (or herself, of course). Each must find that way: his or her own way. To find it one has to experiment, as I've said. You may even, I think, copy or mimic someone else's style now and again just to see if there's anything in it that fits you. But in the end, you've got to find your own self. Or rather, you've got to find or create a radio version of your real self (all that about being natural's no good, you know. Fine art's never natural, it only looks it. Or sounds it.) You've got to find or create a radio version of yourself, the radio quintessence of yourself, and then write for it, and go to the microphone and act it—with truth and sincerity.

Just two odd things from my own experience on the matter of delivery. My belief is that listeners hear speech, not in a sequence of words—one after the other—but in chunks; and what I try to do, though I may seldom succeed in my good intentions, is to throw out my words in bunches . . . like that . . . and then pause long enough for the listener to take that bunch in. I don't know if that's right for everyone; I don't even know if others would think it right for me; but it's been my theory, and it's what I've aimed at in practice, however often I may have missed the mark.

The other oddment is this. The matter of speed. Allover, average speed. Many of you have written to me from time to time; "What you were saying was so exciting. But oh I wish you'd gone slower. I missed some words." Yes, but if I'd gone slower you wouldn't have been excited. You'd have written then and said, "Why were you so solemn? You nearly sent me to sleep!" Oh, I know . . . You can't have it both ways. When I *have* gone slow it's not been for that. It's been because of my many friends in Wales who have trouble in following too rapid English, however clearly it may be spoken.

Well, there you are. That's my last talk—a talk about giving a talk. It's a sort of—well, I won't say "last will and testament," but at any rate a testament. So now, I leave you for a year or two. I'm going to take things easy for a while—or try to. Then I must buckle to on all sorts of other explorations and enterprises. I know I shall have your good wishes. You have mine. Look after yourselves. Blessings on you.

Discussion Questions

"A Talk about Giving a Talk"

1. As we learned in chapter 8, Aristotle says that rhetors should strike a mean between flat language and poetic language. That is, they should speak artfully, sneaking into the language a kind of freshness that escapes notice. Hilton calls this being not "true to life" but "truer than life," something between "stiff speech and loose talk." Find three examples of places Hilton himself strikes that mean in his speech.

2. What examples does Hilton give of language that sounds spoken versus language that sounds read?

3. What is his answer for the dilemma of which form to use: popular English or good (proper) English?

4. What does Hilton mean by saying that "fine art is never natural, it only looks it"?

5. List Hilton's rules for delivering a successful talk:
   a. ______________________________
   b. ______________________________
   c. Chunks: ______________________________
   d. Speed: ______________________________
   e. What does he say about copying or imitating other speakers? Why might he be recommending it?
   ____
   ____
   ____
   ____

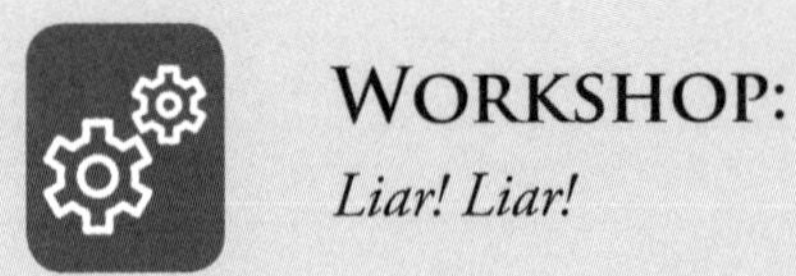

WORKSHOP:
Liar! Liar!

Form groups of three. Think of a strange but true story that actually happened to you. Here are some examples: Tom was bitten by a snake, Sarah fell down the stairs inside the Statue of Liberty, and Ned met a famous person at the park. Try to make it a story that no one else in the room knows about you.

Your group needs to decide which one of the three stories to choose to deliver in front of the class. Then, all three of you must tell the same story, but each in your own words, as if it had happened to each one of you personally. The story should be a short paragraph, and each of you should include (and note within the text) at least three of the four types of gestures (i.e., descriptive, emphatic, suggestive, or prompting).

Your goal is to present the most convincing version of the story to the class and persuade your peers that this incident actually happened to *you*, not to the other two classmates in your group. (Here's a tip: Matching exact details with the others in your group doesn't matter; in fact, you will probably have slightly differing elements as you attempt to create the most convincing tale. While the general plot should be the same, don't worry about having a perfectly identical story.)

The group will deliver the three stories in front of the class, and the class will try to determine which person is telling the truth.

For full credit, you must use three of the four types of gesture. Bonus points will be awarded if the teacher believes you and not the other two!

PRESENTATION: *Shakespearean Soliloquies and Monologues* | **SPOTLIGHT** *Gestures*

The goal is to deliver this soliloquy (or monologue) as if you were talking, not reading. To prepare, utilize the following steps:

1. **Volume:** Look over your speech to find places to vary your volume, sections in which being louder or quieter suits the point you're making. Indicate these moments by underlining the text that should be stressed.
2. **Pitch:** Add up or down arrows in the text to indicate that you should adjust your pitch.
3. **Rhythm:** Find your central point, and spotlight it with a change in rhythm. Remember to "chunk" phrases. Place parentheses around prepositional phrases so that you remember to say them in clusters. Make good use of the pause.
4. **Gestures:** Think about your movement. You should gesture throughout, but you should mark the most important gestures so that you don't forget them.
5. **Practice:** Finally, practice delivery by presenting the speech aloud, even to an empty room. The practice will help you figure out what works—and what doesn't—in delivering a great speech.

The following are a number of soliloquies and monologues,[7] but many others (by different authors, too) would also work for this assignment.

PORTIA IN *THE MERCHANT OF VENICE* (ACT 4, SC. 1)

The quality of mercy is not strain'd,
It droppeth as the gentle rain from heaven
Upon the place beneath: it is twice blest;
It blesseth him that gives and him that takes:
'Tis mightiest in the mightiest: it becomes
The throned monarch better than his crown;
His sceptre shows the force of temporal power,
The attribute to awe and majesty,
Wherein doth sit the dread and fear of kings;
But mercy is above this sceptred sway;
It is enthroned in the hearts of kings,
It is an attribute to God himself;
And earthly power doth then show likest God's
When mercy seasons justice. Therefore, Jew,

7. Each of these public domain texts are available at <http://www.opensourceshakespeare.org>.

Though justice be thy plea, consider this,
That, in the course of justice, none of us
Should see salvation: we do pray for mercy;
And that same prayer doth teach us all to render
The deeds of mercy. I have spoke thus much
To mitigate the justice of thy plea;
Which if thou follow, this strict court of Venice
Must needs give sentence 'gainst the merchant there.

Prince Hal in *History of Henry IV, Part I* (act 1, sc. 2)

I know you all, and will awhile uphold
The unyoked humour of your idleness:
Yet herein will I imitate the sun,
Who doth permit the base contagious clouds
To smother up his beauty from the world,
That, when he please again to be himself,
Being wanted, he may be more wonder'd at,
By breaking through the foul and ugly mists
Of vapours that did seem to strangle him.
If all the year were playing holidays,
To sport would be as tedious as to work;
But when they seldom come, they wish'd for come,
And nothing pleaseth but rare accidents.
So, when this loose behavior I throw off
And pay the debt I never promised,
By how much better than my word I am,
By so much shall I falsify men's hopes;
And like bright metal on a sullen ground,
My reformation, glittering o'er my fault,
Shall show more goodly and attract more eyes
Than that which hath no foil to set it off.
I'll so offend, to make offence a skill;
Redeeming time when men think least I will.

Hamlet in *The Tragedy of Hamlet, Prince of Denmark* (act 3, sc. 1)

To be, or not to be—that is the question:
Whether 'tis nobler in the mind to suffer
The slings and arrows of outrageous fortune
Or to take arms against a sea of troubles,
And by opposing end them. To die—to sleep—
No more; and by a sleep to say we end
The heartache, and the thousand natural shocks
That flesh is heir to. 'Tis a consummation
Devoutly to be wish'd. To die—to sleep.
To sleep—perchance to dream: ay, there's the rub!
For in that sleep of death what dreams may come
When we have shuffled off this mortal coil,
Must give us pause. There's the respect
That makes calamity of so long life.
For who would bear the whips and scorns of time,
Th' oppressor's wrong, the proud man's contumely,
The pangs of despis'd love, the law's delay,
The insolence of office, and the spurns
That patient merit of th' unworthy takes,
When he himself might his quietus make
With a bare bodkin?

Hamlet in *The Tragedy of Hamlet, Prince of Denmark* (act 2, sc. 2)

I have of late—but wherefore I know not—lost all my mirth, forgone all custom of exercises, and indeed it goes so heavily with my disposition that this goodly frame, the earth, seems to me a sterile promontory; this most excellent canopy, the air—look you, this brave o'erhanging firmament, this majestical roof fretted with golden fire—why, it appears no other thing to me than a foul and pestilent congregation of vapors. What a piece of work is a man! How noble in reason, how infinite in faculty! In form and moving how express and admirable! In action how like an angel, in apprehension how like a god! The beauty of the world, the paragon of animals! And yet, to me, what is this quintessence of dust? Man delights not me—no, nor woman neither, though by your smiling you seem to say so.

Juliet in *The Tragedy of Romeo and Juliet* (act 2, sc. 2)

O Romeo, Romeo! wherefore art thou Romeo?
Deny thy father and refuse thy name;

Or, if thou wilt not, be but sworn my love,
And I'll no longer be a Capulet.
[. . .]
'Tis but thy name that is my enemy;
Thou art thyself, though not a Montague.
What's Montague? it is nor hand, nor foot,
Nor arm, nor face, nor any other part
Belonging to a man. O, be some other name!
What's in a name? that which we call a rose
By any other name would smell as sweet;
So Romeo would, were he not Romeo call'd,
Retain that dear perfection which he owes
Without that title. Romeo, doff thy name,
And for that name which is no part of thee
Take all myself.

Macbeth in *The Tragedy of Macbeth* (act 5, sc. 5)

To-morrow, and to-morrow, and to-morrow,
Creeps in this petty pace from day to day
To the last syllable of recorded time,
And all our yesterdays have lighted fools
The way to dusty death. Out, out, brief candle!
Life's but a walking shadow, a poor player
That struts and frets his hour upon the stage
And then is heard no more: it is a tale
Told by an idiot, full of sound and fury,
Signifying nothing.

Prospero in *The Tempest* (act 4, sc. 1)

You do look, my son, in a moved sort,
As if you were dismay'd: be cheerful, sir.
Our revels now are ended. These our actors,
As I foretold you, were all spirits and
Are melted into air, into thin air:
And, like the baseless fabric of this vision,
The cloud-capp'd towers, the gorgeous palaces,

The solemn temples, the great globe itself,
Yea all which it inherit, shall dissolve
And, like this insubstantial pageant faded,
Leave not a rack behind. We are such stuff
As dreams are made on, and our little life
Is rounded with a sleep. Sir, I am vex'd;
Bear with my weakness; my, brain is troubled:
Be not disturb'd with my infirmity:
If you be pleased, retire into my cell
And there repose: a turn or two I'll walk,
To still my beating mind.

Othello in *The Tragedy of Othello, Moor of Venice* (act 1, sc. 3)

Her father loved me; oft invited me;
Still question'd me the story of my life,
From year to year, the battles, sieges, fortunes,
That I have passed.
I ran it through, even from my boyish days,
To the very moment that he bade me tell it;
Wherein I spake of most disastrous chances,
Of moving accidents by flood and field
Of hair-breadth scapes i' the imminent deadly breach,
Of being taken by the insolent foe
And sold to slavery, of my redemption thence
And portance in my travels' history:
[. . .] My story being done,
She gave me for my pains a world of sighs:
She swore, in faith, twas strange, 'twas passing strange,
'Twas pitiful, 'twas wondrous pitiful:
She wish'd she had not heard it, yet she wish'd
That heaven had made her such a man: she thank'd me,
And bade me, if I had a friend that loved her,
I should but teach him how to tell my story.
And that would woo her. Upon this hint I spake:
She loved me for the dangers I had pass'd,
And I loved her that she did pity them.

Desdemona in *The Tragedy of Othello, Moor of Venice* (act 1, sc. 3)

My noble father,
I do perceive here a divided duty:
To you I am bound for life and education;
My life and education both do learn me
How to respect you; you are the lord of duty;
I am hitherto your daughter: but here's my husband,
And so much duty as my mother show'd
To you, preferring you before her father,
So much I challenge that I may profess
Due to the Moor my lord.

Puck in *A Midsummer Night's Dream* (act 5, sc. 1)

If we shadows have offended,
Think but this, and all is mended,
That you have but slumber'd here
While these visions did appear.
And this weak and idle theme,
No more yielding but a dream,
Gentles, do not reprehend:
If you pardon, we will mend:
And, as I am an honest Puck,
If we have unearned luck
Now to 'scape the serpent's tongue,
We will make amends ere long;
Else the Puck a liar call;
So, good night unto you all.
Give me your hands, if we be friends,
And Robin shall restore amends.

Antony in *The Tragedy of Julius Caesar* (act 3, sc. 1)

O mighty Caesar! dost thou lie so low?
Are all thy conquests, glories, triumphs, spoils,
Shrunk to this little measure? Fare thee well.
I know not, gentlemen, what you intend,
Who else must be let blood, who else is rank:

If I myself, there is no hour so fit
As Caesar's death hour, nor no instrument
Of half that worth as those your swords, made rich
With the most noble blood of all this world.
I do beseech ye, if you bear me hard,
Now, whilst your purpled hands do reek and smoke,
Fulfil your pleasure. Live a thousand years,
I shall not find myself so apt to die:
No place will please me so, no mean of death,
As here by Caesar, and by you cut off,
The choice and master spirits of this age.

Cassius in *The Tragedy of Julius Caesar* (act 1, sc. 2)

Well, honour is the subject of my story.
I cannot tell what you and other men
Think of this life; but, for my single self,
I had as lief not be as live to be
In awe of such a thing as I myself.
I was born free as Caesar; so were you:
We both have fed as well, and we can both
Endure the winter's cold as well as he:
For once, upon a raw and gusty day,
The troubled Tiber chafing with her shores,
Caesar said to me 'Darest thou, Cassius, now
Leap in with me into this angry flood,
And swim to yonder point?' Upon the word,
Accoutred as I was, I plunged in
And bade him follow; so indeed he did.
The torrent roar'd, and we did buffet it
With lusty sinews, throwing it aside
And stemming it with hearts of controversy;
But ere we could arrive the point proposed,
Caesar cried 'Help me, Cassius, or I sink!'
I, as Aeneas, our great ancestor,
Did from the flames of Troy upon his shoulder

The old Anchises bear, so from the waves of Tiber
Did I the tired Caesar. And this man
Is now become a god, and Cassius is
A wretched creature and must bend his body,
If Caesar carelessly but nod on him.
He had a fever when he was in Spain,
And when the fit was on him, I did mark
How he did shake: 'tis true, this god did shake;
His coward lips did from their colour fly,
And that same eye whose bend doth awe the world
Did lose his lustre: I did hear him groan:
Ay, and that tongue of his that bade the Romans
Mark him and write his speeches in their books,
Alas, it cried 'Give me some drink, Titinius,'
As a sick girl. Ye gods, it doth amaze me
A man of such a feeble temper should
So get the start of the majestic world
And bear the palm alone.

Alternate Activities

You could also dip back into chapter 1 for another excerpt from a classic speech. You may wish to choose one that you have not yet presented, or you may wish to deliver the same speech again, this time paying attention to the elements of delivery explored in this chapter. Another possibility is to perform a classic script such as Abbott and Costello's comedy routine "Who's on First?" or scenes from a recognizable play.

What follows is the first scene of the tradesmen in *A Midsummer Night's Dream* by Shakespeare. They have gathered to practice a play that they plan to perform for the wedding of Duke Theseus and Queen Hippolyta. Bottom believes he is fit to play any of the characters; his attempts at each different character will require variations in delivery.

A Midsummer Night's Dream

by William Shakespeare

Act I, Scene 2. Athens. QUINCE'S house.

Enter Quince, Snug, Bottom, Flute, Snout, and Starveling

Quince

Is all our company here?

Bottom

You were best to call them generally, man by man, according to the scrip.

Quince

Here is the scroll of every man's name, which is thought fit, through all Athens, to play in our interlude before the duke and the duchess, on his wedding-day at night.

Bottom

First, good Peter Quince, say what the play treats on, then read the names of the actors, and so grow to a point.

Quince

Marry, our play is, The most lamentable comedy, and most cruel death of Pyramus and Thisby.

Bottom

A very good piece of work, I assure you, and a merry. Now, good Peter Quince, call forth your actors by the scroll. Masters, spread yourselves.

Quince

Answer as I call you. Nick Bottom, the weaver.

Bottom

Ready. Name what part I am for, and proceed.

Quince

You, Nick Bottom, are set down for Pyramus.

Bottom

What is Pyramus? a lover, or a tyrant?

Quince
A lover, that kills himself most gallant for love.
Bottom
That will ask some tears in the true performing of
it: if I do it, let the audience look to their
eyes; I will move storms, I will condole in some
measure. To the rest: yet my chief humour is for a
tyrant: I could play Ercles rarely, or a part to
tear a cat in, to make all split.
The raging rocks
And shivering shocks
Shall break the locks
Of prison gates;
And Phibbus' car
Shall shine from far
And make and mar
The foolish Fates.
This was lofty! Now name the rest of the players.
This is Ercles' vein, a tyrant's vein; a lover is
more condoling.
Quince
Francis Flute, the bellows-mender.
Flute
Here, Peter Quince.
Quince
Flute, you must take Thisby on you.
Flute
What is Thisby? a wandering knight?
Quince
It is the lady that Pyramus must love.
Flute
Nay, faith, let me not play a woman; I have a beard coming.
Quince
That's all one: you shall play it in a mask, and
you may speak as small as you will.

Bottom

An I may hide my face, let me play Thisby too, I'll
speak in a monstrous little voice. 'Thisne,
Thisne;' 'Ah, Pyramus, lover dear! thy Thisby dear,
and lady dear!'

Quince

No, no; you must play Pyramus: and, Flute, you Thisby.

Bottom

Well, proceed.

Quince

Robin Starveling, the tailor.

Starveling

Here, Peter Quince.

Quince

Robin Starveling, you must play Thisby's mother.
Tom Snout, the tinker.

Snout

Here, Peter Quince.

Quince

You, Pyramus' father: myself, Thisby's father:
Snug, the joiner; you, the lion's part: and, I
hope, here is a play fitted.

Snug

Have you the lion's part written? pray you, if it
be, give it me, for I am slow of study.

Quince

You may do it extempore, for it is nothing but roaring.

Bottom

Let me play the lion too: I will roar, that I will
do any man's heart good to hear me; I will roar,
that I will make the duke say 'Let him roar again,
let him roar again.'

Quince

An you should do it too terribly, you would fright
the duchess and the ladies, that they would shriek;
and that were enough to hang us all.

ALL
That would hang us, every mother's son.
BOTTOM
I grant you, friends, if that you should fright the
ladies out of their wits, they would have no more
discretion but to hang us: but I will aggravate my
voice so that I will roar you as gently as any
sucking dove; I will roar you an 'twere any
nightingale.
QUINCE
You can play no part but Pyramus; for Pyramus is a
sweet-faced man; a proper man, as one shall see in a
summer's day; a most lovely gentleman-like man:
therefore you must needs play Pyramus.
BOTTOM
Well, I will undertake it. What beard were I best
to play it in?
QUINCE
Why, what you will.
BOTTOM
I will discharge it in either your straw-colour
beard, your orange-tawny beard, your purple-in-grain
beard, or your French-crown-colour beard, your
perfect yellow.
QUINCE
Some of your French crowns have no hair at all, and
then you will play bare-faced. But, masters, here
are your parts: and I am to entreat you, request
you and desire you, to con them by to-morrow night;
and meet me in the palace wood, a mile without the
town, by moonlight; there will we rehearse, for if
we meet in the city, we shall be dogged with
company, and our devices known. In the meantime I
will draw a bill of properties, such as our play
wants. I pray you, fail me not.

Bottom

We will meet; and there we may rehearse most
obscenely and courageously. Take pains; be perfect: adieu.

Quince

At the duke's oak we meet.

Bottom

Enough; hold or cut bow-strings.

Exeunt

4 SECTION

The Three Kinds of Rhetoric

(1358a) Rhetoric falls into three divisions, determined by the three classes of listeners to speeches. For of the three elements in speech-making—speaker, subject, and person addressed—it is the last one, the hearer, that determines the speech's end and object. (1358b) The hearer must be either a judge, with a decision to make about things past or future, or an observer. A member of the assembly decides about future events, a juryman about past events: while those who merely decide on the orator's skill are observers. From this it follows that there are three divisions of oratory—(1) political [deliberative],[1] (2) forensic [judicial], and (3) the ceremonial [epideictic] oratory of display.

Political [deliberative] speaking urges us either to do or not to do something: one of these two courses is always taken by private counsellors, as well as by men who address public assemblies. Forensic [judicial] speaking either attacks or defends somebody: one or other of these two things must always be done by the parties in a case. The ceremonial [epideictic] oratory of display either praises or censures somebody. These three kinds of rhetoric refer to three different kinds of time. The political [deliberative] orator is concerned with the future: it is about things to be done hereafter that he advises, for or against. The party in a case at law is concerned with the past; one man accuses the other, and the other defends himself, with reference to things already done. The ceremonial [epideictic] orator is, properly speaking, concerned with the present, since all men praise or blame in view of the state of things existing at the time, though they often find it useful also to recall the past and to make guesses at the future.

Rhetoric has three distinct ends in view, one for each of its three kinds. The political [deliberative] orator aims at establishing the expediency or the harmfulness of a proposed course of action; if he urges its acceptance, he does so on the ground that it will do good; if he urges its rejection, he does so on the ground that it will do harm; and all other points, such as whether the proposal is just or unjust, honourable or dishonourable, he brings in as subsidiary and relative to this main consideration. Parties in a law-case aim at establishing the justice or injus-

1. Terms in brackets have been added for clarity, as Aristotle uses different terms than those used throughout this book.

tice of some action, and they too bring in all other points as subsidiary and relative to this one. Those who praise or attack a man aim at proving him worthy of honour or the reverse, and they too treat all other considerations with reference to this one.

That the three kinds of rhetoric do aim respectively at the three ends we have mentioned is shown by the fact that speakers will sometimes not try to establish anything else. Thus, the litigant will sometimes not deny that a thing has happened or that he has done harm. But that he is guilty of injustice he will never admit; otherwise there would be no need of a trial. So too, political [deliberative] orators often make any concession short of admitting that they are recommending their hearers to take an inexpedient course or not to take an expedient one. The question whether it is not *unjust* for a city to enslave its innocent neighbours often does not trouble them at all. In like manner those who praise or censure a man do not consider (1359a) whether his acts have been expedient or not, but often make it a ground of actual praise that he has neglected his own interest to do what was honourable. Thus, they praise Achilles because he championed his fallen friend Patroclus, though he knew that this meant death, and that otherwise he need not die: yet while to die thus was the nobler thing for him to do, the expedient thing was to live on.

Such, then, are the subjects regarding which we are inevitably bound to master the propositions relevant to them. We must now discuss each particular class of these subjects in turn, namely those dealt with in political [deliberative], in ceremonial [epideictic], and lastly in legal [judicial], oratory.

Three Kinds of Speech

This book began by exploring the three rhetorical appeals—*ethos*, *pathos*, and *logos* (chapters 2–5). The idea is that a rhetor can change a person's mind only by offering proof, and there are three such proofs: the speaker's credibility (*ethos*), the audience's emotions (*pathos*), and the argument's reasoning (*logos*). Each of these three can, in a sense, "prove" the case at hand, prompting a person to make a judgment. Then we studied the five canons of rhetoric (chapters 6–10): invention, organization, style, memory, and delivery. To recap, a rhetor discovers arguments about a topic (invention), arranges those arguments (organization), depicts them in language (style), commits the discourse to mind (memory), and presents the whole (delivery). In the following section, we will explore the three kinds of rhetoric.

The different types, or *species*, of rhetoric can be thought of as corresponding, more or less, to our categories for time—past, present, and future. As creatures who must live our lives in time, we often must form judgments about what has already occurred, will occur, or is taking place right now. Of course, each particular judgment must be made in the present moment, in the shared here and now of the rhetor and audience, but those present judgments are always directed to one of the different times (past, present, future). So rhetors try to persuade their audiences to make current judgments concerning matters in the past, matters relevant to the present moment, and matters that are still in the future. Rhetoric that calls people to make decisions about the past is called *judicial* rhetoric, about the present, *epideictic*, and about the future, *deliberative.* (Please see table 8 for alternative names.) More specifically, **judicial rhetoric** aims at determining the justice/injustice of past actions: *Did the accused* *commit the crime?* The quintessential judicial rhetoric is that found in the court of law, from which this species gets its name. Focused upon the now, **epideictic rhetoric** praises or blames according to honor as it is understood in the present: *Is the president admirable?* This rhetoric of praise is clearest in the wedding toast or funeral eulogy (which makes sense of why it is sometimes referred to as "**ceremonial rhetoric**"), but it also is commonly experienced in patriotic speeches on civic holidays. Finally, **deliberative rhetoric** aims at determining the most advantageous course of action for the future: *What should be done?* We best picture deliberative rhetoric in the arguments made in political bodies, such as the US Congress, with representatives debating which laws should be passed or which wars are worth fighting.

The three types are not limited, though, to the formal occasions of trials, eulogies, and political debates. They are the speech of our everyday interactions, too: *Did John cheat on the exam?*—judicial. *Is Kelly a worthy friend?*—epideictic. *Should we have steak or fish for dinner?*—deliberative. Because people make everyday decisions about the past, present, and future, rhetoric pervades our lives, with virtually all of our daily utterances falling into one of the three categories.

Speaking about Truth, Goodness, and Beauty

Aristotle seems to be arguing that there are only three kinds of rhetoric because there are only three periods of time: past, present, and future. But another group of three is important to consider here: the True, the Good, and the Beautiful—a triad that Western philosophy has come to call "transcendentals."[2] The term itself is a tricky one, signifying that they transcend, or stand above, things in the world. Because the philosophy can get confusing, perhaps we should think of these as aspects that have intrinsic value, that are desirable simply *because*. For example, if you were asked, "Why do you like this painting?" you may say that you like it because it is beautiful. The follow-up question of "Why do you like beauty?" is almost tautologous; we like beauty because we like beauty! Or suppose you are asked why you think that you have two feet. The answer is obvious: "Because I can see them; I believe that it's true." But why do you believe truth? Again, you have reached a dead end. Truth is true, and we desire it, not falsehood. In this sense, it is absolute. These three—Truth, Goodness, and Beauty—are concepts that manifest themselves throughout the human experience of reality.

2. The conversation regarding the so-called transcendentals begins, as so many conversations do, with the Greeks. The transcendentals are properties of being. This list is not definitive (Thomas Aquinas posited five, for instance).

Table 8. The three species of rhetoric.

	Other Names	Time	Place	Action	According to What End	Transcendental Counterpart
judicial	forensic	past	courtroom	accuse/defend	justice	the True
epideictic	ceremonial, demonstrative	present	funeral, wedding	praise/censure	honor	the Beautiful
deliberative	legislative, political	future	legislative assembly	urge to do / urge not to do	advantage	the Good

But what relation, if any, do these transcendentals have to the three kinds of rhetoric? Let's look again at deliberative rhetoric, which seeks to influence decisions based upon advantage. It is arguable that advantage is "good"—maybe not Good in a universal, essential sense, but good nonetheless. Determining whether it is advantageous to pass a tax increase is a question of goodness. What counterpart might justice have? This one is straightforward: Because making a just decision requires consideration of whether past actions truly occurred, we can see how judicial rhetoric concerns a particular kind of truth. Finally, epideictic rhetoric is rhetoric that concerns the praiseworthy, the honorable—an arena of beauty.

In other words, rhetorical language does not attempt to get at these transcendentals in their absolute senses but is instead content to track them in their worldly manifestations. The following section explores the ways in which rhetoric considers the good, praises the beautiful, and judges the true.

Chapter 11

Deliberative Rhetoric: Considering Goods

(1359a) First, then, we must ascertain what are the kinds of things, good or bad, about which the political [deliberative][1] orator offers counsel. For he does not deal with all things, but only with such as may or may not take place. Concerning things which exist or will exist inevitably, or which cannot possibly exist or take place, no counsel can be given. Nor, again, can counsel be given about the whole class of things which may or may not take place; for this class includes some good things that occur naturally, and some that occur by accident; and about these it is useless to offer counsel. Clearly counsel can only be given on matters about which people deliberate; matters, namely, that ultimately depend on ourselves, and which we have it in our power to set going. (1359b) For we turn a thing over in our mind until we have reached the point of seeing whether we can do it or not.

. . .

(1360b) It may be said that every individual man and all men in common aim at a certain end which determines what they choose and what they avoid. This end, to sum it up briefly, is happiness and its constituents. Let us, then, by way of illustration only, ascertain what is in general the nature of happiness, and what are the elements of its constituent parts. For all advice to do things or not to do them is concerned with happiness and with the things that make for or against it; whatever creates or increases happiness or some part of happiness, we ought to do; whatever destroys or hampers happiness, or gives rise to its opposite, we ought not to do.

We may define happiness as prosperity combined with virtue; or as independence of life; or as the secure enjoyment of the maximum of pleasure; or as a good condition of property and body, together with the power of guarding one's property and body and making use of them. That happiness is one or more of these things, pretty well everybody agrees. . . .

(1362a) Now the political or deliberative orator's aim is utility: deliberation seeks to determine not ends but the means to ends, i.e., what

1. Term in brackets has been added for clarity, as Aristotle uses different terms than those used throughout this book.

it is most useful to do. Further, utility is a good thing. We ought therefore to assure ourselves of the main facts about Goodness and Utility in general.

We may define a good thing as that which ought to be chosen for its own sake; or as that for the sake of which we choose something else; or as that which is sought after by all things, or by all things that have sensation or reason, or which will be sought after by any things that acquire reason; or as that which must be prescribed for a given individual by reason generally, or is prescribed for him by his individual reason, this being his individual good; or as that whose presence brings anything into a satisfactory and self-sufficing condition; or as self-sufficiency; or as what produces, maintains, or entails characteristics of this kind, while preventing and destroying their opposites.

Goodness and the Quest for Happiness

In the opening sentence of *Nicomachean Ethics*, Aristotle offers a simple definition of a "good": "[T]he good has rightly been declared to be *that at which all things aim* [italics mine]."[2] In fact, in his *Rhetoric*, he says much the same thing but includes other nuances and extrapolations of that simpler definition (see 1362a). Here is another way to say it: Goods are those things that everyone wants; goods are those things a person considers essential to living a good life. Virtue is one such good, but the highest good, according to Aristotle, is happiness itself; it is the ultimate goal, beyond which we desire nothing. Aristotle claims later in Book 1 of *Nicomachean Ethics* that it is happiness alone that we choose for itself "and never for the sake of something else."[3] Similarly, "honour, pleasure, reason, and every virtue we choose indeed for themselves (for if nothing resulted from them we should still choose each of them), but we choose them also for the sake of happiness, judging that by means of them we shall be happy."[4] In other words, virtue and happiness are both goods, for both are chosen for themselves. Happiness, however, appears to be the *ultimate* good, though virtue is required in order to achieve it.

2. See Aristotle, *Nicomachean Ethics*, Book 1, section 1.

3. Ibid., Book 1, section 7.

4. Aristotle, *Nicomachean Ethics*, trans. W. D. Ross, provided by The Internet Classics Archive, http://classics.mit.edu/Aristotle/nicomachaen.1.i.html.

Table 9. Features of deliberative rhetoric.

	Other Names	Time	Place	Action	According to What End	Transcendental Counterpart
judicial	forensic	past	courtroom	accuse/ defend	justice	the True
epideictic	ceremonial, demonstrative	present	funeral, wedding	praise/ censure	honor	the Beautiful
deliberative	legislative, political	future	legislative assembly	urge to do/ urge not to do	advantage	the Good

According to Aristotle, then, all humans desire happiness. Fair enough. But why does Aristotle talk about happiness as an introduction to deliberative rhetoric? Happiness, it turns out, is what deliberative rhetoric is all about. We deliberate with one thing in mind and one thing only: what's best. We weigh decisions and make up our minds based on what will be most advantageous, what will increase our happiness. Happiness is the ultimate goal of humanity, and it is also the fundamental aim of deliberative rhetoric.

Our deliberating, our laboring to make the right decision about a future course of action, is in order to make a difference—a difference for the better. But sometimes deliberating is senseless. Have you ever had a serious argument about next week's weather? Or imagine two friends quarrelling about whether they should take the train or drive a car to the beach. Would they continue to disagree if they were to learn that the train no longer ran to their destination? Of course not! What would be the point of such an argument? These examples show that people don't deliberate about what lies beyond their control. If something is hopeless or unfeasible—that is, if it cannot be changed—then there is no argument to be had. However, if we are free to choose, and if our choice could make a difference, then arguments can be made, and may in fact be necessary. For example, should the United States go to war? Should our town pass a law? Should John get married? And the end, or aim, is always the same: happiness. *What will lead toward happiness?* This question—a question about the *good* or *better* choice—is at the center of deliberative rhetoric.[5]

In fact, the question of happiness is at the center of our lives. Happiness, according to Socrates, is the fundamental aim of every single person. The US Declaration of Independence is witness to our shared desire for happiness; its framers even considered its pursuit a natural right: "We hold these truths to be self-evident, that all men are created equal, that they are endowed by their Creator with certain unalienable Rights, that among these are Life, Liberty and the pursuit of Happiness." Notice that the Declaration sidesteps the task of actually defining what happiness is. A wise move, for people back then were no different from people today: Every person tends to think of happiness differently from how his or her next-door neighbor thinks of it. Look at what Aristotle offers as the various definitions for happiness:

1. Virtuous success: "prosperity combined with virtue."
2. Self-sufficiency: "independence of life."
3. Pleasure and security: "the secure enjoyment of the maximum of pleasure."
4. Bodies and things: "a good condition of property and body, together with the power of guarding one's property and body and making use of them" (1360b).

Notice that Aristotle doesn't insist on precision here—he says that happiness is "pretty much one or more of these," that it is "something of this sort." The philosopher's answer would be precise and definitive, but the rhetor doesn't aim for that kind of certainty. Rhetoric is content within the realm of *endoxa*, opinion. And although those opinions differ, Aristotle has already told us that "men have a sufficient natural instinct for what is true, and usually do arrive at the truth" (1355a), meaning that their common opinions are reliable enough for rhetoric, the speech of the city.

If we return for a moment to the earlier questions—Should the United States go to war? Should our town pass a law? Should John get married?—we can see how particularized each is. In other words, any community that would seek to answer one of these questions by deliberating about it would have very specific factors to con-

5. You could see this question as a counterpart to the fundamental issue Aristotle raises in *Nicomachean Ethics*: What is the good life? What is human flourishing? These are concerns of *eudaimonia* (Greek, "happiness, flourishing").

sider. To answer whether the United States should go to war is not to take up the more philosophical or theoretical question (one more appropriate to the dialectician) of, for example, whether a nation should *ever* make war.[6] In other words, the one engaging in deliberative rhetoric seeks to know what can lead toward happiness *in this particular case* (and likewise with the town's passing of a law). Legal theory and a city's power over its citizens may be implicit within the argument, but the question being deliberated is much more contextualized: Would this law move the town's citizenry toward or away from happiness? Finally, when deliberation takes place about John getting married, it is not extending to universal claims about marriage itself (e.g., is married life better than a life of singlehood?). Instead it is much more localized, much more concrete, trying to address the specific realities of the person—in this case, John—involved.

Aristotle's Favorite

Aristotle faulted the sophists of his day for privileging judicial rhetoric—basically, they were training up lawyers to make big money on private court cases. He recognized that decisions about the future are more influential in the long run than are those regarding the past. For this reason, he calls deliberative rhetoric "a nobler business, and fitter for a citizen" (1354b). In fact, the kind of speech that will help or hinder the community in its quest for happiness may be the most important of all kinds of speech.

Let's put it another way. Politically speaking, you might say that the honorable and the just (the respective aims of epideictic and judicial rhetoric) are both subsets of the advantageous (the aim of deliberative rhetoric). How so? When rhetors argue for a course of action that will move the city toward greater happiness, then their rhetoric must take into account what the city already holds to be just (the concern of judicial rhetoric) and honorable (the concern of epideictic rhetoric). The other two types, then, are automatically involved. Deliberative is, then, the most comprehensive of the three species of rhetoric, for it holds together and then advances into the future those goods sought by the other species. In this sense, it is like a flowering of the other two.

On the same token, just as the flower is the most delicate part of the plant, so is deliberative rhetoric the most dependent of the three. Its flourishing can only take place when the other goods—justice and honor—are already known and upheld. For instance, a community that prizes freedom in its epideictic rhetoric will make decisions about the future very differently from a community that praises uniformity. Because it is the most comprehensive and contingent species, it is the one that Aristotle believes should be held up as most important.

In short, the aim of deliberative rhetoric is to influence judgments about the best course of action going forward; its focus is on the *future*, and it is based upon *advantage*.

6. In chapter 21 of *Topica*, Cicero takes up this difference between a larger, universal question ("thesis") and a contextualized, particular question ("hypothesis"). The difference is the theoretical versus the practical. Cicero, *Topica*, trans. Charles Duke Yonge, provided by Classicpersuasion.org / Peithô's Web, http://www.classicpersuasion.org/pw/cicero/cicero-topics.htm.

Discussion Text:

Winston Churchill: "Blood, Toil, Tears, and Sweat" (1940)[7]

Focus:

Deliberative Rhetoric

1

It was May 13 in the first year of World War II. Just three days earlier, Winston Churchill had become prime minister of the United Kingdom, following Neville Chamberlain's resignation of the position. This speech, his first as head of King George VI's government, was also the first among many that would inspire the British government and people during this time of tremendous adversity.

Mister Speaker:

On Friday evening last I received His Majesty's commission to form a new Administration. It was the evident wish and will of Parliament and the nation that this should be conceived on the broadest possible basis and that it should include all parties, both those who supported the late Government and also the parties of the Opposition.

I have completed the most important part of this task. A War Cabinet has been formed of five Members, representing, with the Liberal Opposition, the unity of the nation. The three party Leaders have agreed to serve, either in the War Cabinet or in high executive office. The three Fighting Services have been filled. It was necessary that this should be done in one single day, on account of the extreme urgency and rigor of events. A number of other key positions were filled yesterday, and I am submitting a further list to His Majesty tonight. I hope to complete the appointment of the principal Ministers during tomorrow. The appointment of the other Ministers usually takes a little longer, but I trust that when Parliament meets again, this part of my task will be completed, and that the administration will be complete in all respects.

Sir, I considered it in the public interest to suggest that the House should be summoned to meet today. Mr. Speaker agreed, and took the necessary steps, in accordance with the powers conferred upon him by the Resolution of the House. At the end of the proceedings today, the Adjournment of the House will be proposed until Tuesday, the 21st of May, with, of course, provision for earlier meeting, if need be. The business to be considered during that week will be notified to Members at the earliest opportunity. I now invite the House, by the Resolution which stands in my name, to record its approval of the steps taken and to declare its confidence in the new Government.

Sir, to form an Administration of this scale and complexity is a serious undertaking in itself, but it must be remembered that we are in the preliminary stage of one of the greatest battles in history, that we are in action at many points in Norway and in Holland, that we have to be prepared in the Mediterranean, that the air battle is continuous and that many

7. Winston Churchill, "Blood, Toil, Tears, and Sweat," May 13, 1940, address to the House of Commons, reproduced with permission of Curtis Brown, London, on behalf of The Estate of Winston S. Churchill.

preparations have to be made here at home. In this crisis I hope I may be pardoned if I do not address the House at any length today. I hope that any of my friends and colleagues, or former colleagues, who are affected by the political reconstruction, will make all allowances for any lack of ceremony with which it has been necessary to act. I would say to the House, as I said to those who have joined the government: "I have nothing to offer but blood, toil, tears and sweat."

We have before us an ordeal of the most grievous kind. We have before us many, many long months of struggle and of suffering. You ask, what is our policy? I will say: It is to wage war, by sea, land and air, with all our might and with all the strength that God can give us; to wage war against a monstrous tyranny, never surpassed in the dark and lamentable catalogue of human crime. That is our policy. You ask, what is our aim? I can answer in one word: victory; victory at all costs, victory in spite of all terror, victory, however long and hard the road may be; for without victory, there is no survival. Let that be realized; no survival for the British Empire, no survival for all that the British Empire has stood for, no survival for the urge and impulse of the ages, that mankind will move forward towards its goal.

But I take up my task with buoyancy and hope. I feel sure that our cause will not be suffered to fail among men. At this time I feel entitled to claim the aid of all, and I say, "Come then, let us go forward together with our united strength."

Discussion Questions

"Blood, Toil, Tears, and Sweat"

1. Churchill begins by informing his audience of the facts, what has happened between Friday evening and the time of his address. But his purpose is not merely to inform. What does Churchill seek to accomplish in this speech?

2. Deliberative rhetoric concerns the advantageous. What advantages will come of undergoing the suffering and hardship that lies ahead?

3. In what way is his speech clearly deliberative (future oriented) and not judicial (past oriented) or epideictic (present oriented)?

4. **Invention:** Which topics of invention do you notice?

Definition:

Comparison:

Relationship:

Circumstance:

Testimony:

5. **Organization:** Can you discern an organizational structure, and does it fit the classical model? Please provide examples from the speech to explain how it does or does not fit the classical model.

6. **Style:** How would you describe Churchill's style? Does it change within the speech? Which figures of speech does Churchill employ, and at what points? (Notice they are packed into his closing, which is a stirring conclusion.) Also, what relationship does *pathos* appear to have to style?

7. **Memory:** Were you familiar with any of the lines before reading the speech? What is the most memorable line?

____

____

8. **Delivery:** If you were to deliver this speech, which lines would you highlight with a change in rhythm? How would you deliver the last line?

____

____

____

____

9. Remember, the types of rhetoric often overlap within one address. Nevertheless, you should be able to determine which predominates and is served by the other two. What evidence of epideictic and judicial rhetoric can you find?

____

____

____

____

DISCUSSION TEXT:
FDR: "A Day That Will Live in Infamy" (1941)[8]

FOCUS:
Deliberative Rhetoric

2

Mr. Vice President, Mr. Speaker, Members of the Senate, and of the House of Representatives:

Yesterday, December 7th, 1941—a date which will live in infamy—the United States of America was suddenly and deliberately attacked by naval and air forces of the Empire of Japan.

The United States was at peace with that nation and, at the solicitation of Japan, was still in conversation with its government and its emperor looking toward the maintenance of peace in the Pacific.

Indeed, one hour after Japanese air squadrons had commenced bombing in the American island of Oahu, the Japanese ambassador to the United States and his colleague delivered to our Secretary of State a formal reply to a recent American message. And while this reply stated that it seemed useless to continue the existing diplomatic negotiations, it contained no threat or hint of war or of armed attack.

It will be recorded that the distance of Hawaii from Japan makes it obvious that the attack was deliberately planned many days or even weeks ago. During the intervening time, the Japanese government has deliberately sought to deceive the United States by false statements and expressions of hope for continued peace.

The attack yesterday on the Hawaiian islands has caused severe damage to American naval and military forces. I regret to tell you that very many American lives have been lost. In addition, American ships have been reported torpedoed on the high seas between San Francisco and Honolulu.

Yesterday, the Japanese government also launched an attack against Malaya.

Last night, Japanese forces attacked Hong Kong.

Last night, Japanese forces attacked Guam.

Last night, Japanese forces attacked the Philippine Islands.

Last night, the Japanese attacked Wake Island.

8. Franklin Delano Roosevelt, "Pearl Harbor Address to the Nation," December 7, 1941, address to Joint Session of Congress, Washington, DC, audio provided by American Rhetoric Online Speech Bank, http://www.americanrhetoric.com/speeches/fdrpearlharbor.htm. The transcript of this speech is in the public domain.

And this morning, the Japanese attacked Midway Island.

Japan has, therefore, undertaken a surprise offensive extending throughout the Pacific area. The facts of yesterday and today speak for themselves. The people of the United States have already formed their opinions and well understand the implications to the very life and safety of our nation.

As Commander in Chief of the Army and Navy, I have directed that all measures be taken for our defense. But always will our whole nation remember the character of the onslaught against us.

No matter how long it may take us to overcome this premeditated invasion, the American people in their righteous might will win through to absolute victory.

I believe that I interpret the will of the Congress and of the people when I assert that we will not only defend ourselves to the uttermost, but will make it very certain that this form of treachery shall never again endanger us.

Hostilities exist. There is no blinking at the fact that our people, our territory, and our interests are in grave danger.

With confidence in our armed forces, with the unbounding determination of our people, we will gain the inevitable triumph—so help us God.

I ask that the Congress declare that since the unprovoked and dastardly attack by Japan on Sunday, December 7th, 1941, a state of war has existed between the United States and the Japanese empire.

Discussion Questions

"A Day That Will Live in Infamy"

1. Deliberative rhetoric concerns the most advantageous course of action. What advantage, then, does a declaration of war have?

2. **Invention:** Which topics of invention can you spot?

Definition:

Comparison:

Relationship:

Circumstance:

Testimony:

3. **Organization:** It is in his final statement that Roosevelt officially announces what is at stake: the declaration of war. Why does he place this request at the end of the speech rather than the beginning?

4. **Style:** The phrases "Japanese forces attacked" and "the Japanese attacked" are repeated multiple times in the middle of the speech. What purpose was intended in using anaphora here instead of just providing a quick list? Is it effective?

5. **Memory:** Were you familiar with any of the lines before reading the speech? What is the most memorable line?

6. **Delivery:** Find a recording of the speech online <http://capress.link/ra11101> and listen to it. Analyze the delivery according to volume, pitch, and rhythm. Notice that FDR speaks in "chunks," grouping together words into their prepositional phrases and making good use of pauses. As is customary, Roosevelt's audience applauds before and after his remarks. When (at which four points) does the audience interrupt the speech with clapping? Why do the interruptions occur at the places they do?

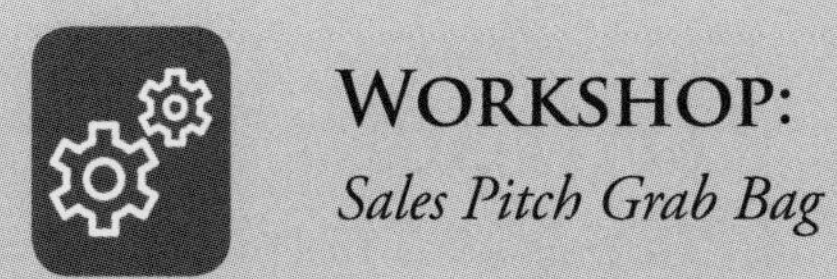

Workshop:
Sales Pitch Grab Bag

In this exercise, you'll practice deliberative rhetoric. Go to the front of the classroom and grab an item from the grab bag. Someone will flip a coin to determine whether you should try to (a) *persuade* the audience to buy your item by offering its advantages, or (b) *dissuade* them from buying it by detailing its disadvantages. Heads: persuade/advantages; tails: dissuade/disadvantages.

For example: John draws out a cell phone, and the coin flip lands on . . . tails! He needs to dissuade the audience. Here is his sales pitch:

> *Whatever you do, don't buy one of these! Sure, you can connect with your friends, but at what cost? There's the financial cost, of course—about fifty dollars a month that could be spent on something more important. But what about the health hazards associated with cell phones? Radiation to the brain is just one factor. And if you really think about it, while we say that we're more connected, the truth is that we're actually less connected! How many times have you seen a group of kids sitting around together, but they're all on their cell phones, texting someone who isn't even there! Save your money, and save your friendships. Don't buy a cell phone.*

PRESENTATION:
Great Speech Imitatio

SPOTLIGHT
Putting It All Together

Choose a topic from school or home that you could address with deliberative rhetoric—that is, speech that urges action, chosen because of the advantages it offers. For example, your mother has decided to eliminate weekday desserts from family dinners: What should the children do? Or a guy in class is tormenting all the girls: How should they respond?

Write an imitation of either Roosevelt's or Churchill's address, copying the tone as well as the overall organizational structure. You can even borrow language from the original speech as well as imitate the sentence structure.

Example:

Dear East Central Library goers,

Yesterday, January 5, 2016—a day which I will never forget—a great injustice befell me. I had to pay seventy-seven dollars for three movies and four books that were just a few weeks late.

Yesterday morning, East Central Library denied my library card.

Yesterday morning, East Central Library refused to check out a book to me on my brother's card, too.

Yesterday morning, the library charged me seventy-two dollars.

Yesterday, the library added tax, which brought it up to seventy-seven dollars.

And today, they didn't have the new book series I had requested online that showed up as "available."

I ask you, fellow East Central Library patrons, to join me in a ban against the library in protest against overly large fines, unnecessary hoops to jump through, and the mishandling of a timeless book series.

CHAPTER 12

EPIDEICTIC RHETORIC: PRAISING THE BEAUTIFUL

(1366a) We have now to consider Virtue and Vice, the Noble and the Base, since these are the objects of praise and blame. In doing so, we shall at the same time be finding out how to make our hearers take the required view of our own characters—our second method of persuasion. The ways in which to make them trust the goodness of other people are also the ways in which to make them trust our own. Praise, again, may be serious or frivolous; nor is it always of a human or divine being but often of inanimate things, or of the humblest of the lower animals. Here too we must know on what grounds to argue, and must, therefore, now discuss the subject, though by way of illustration only.

The Noble is that which is both desirable for its own sake and also worthy of praise; or that which is both good and also pleasant because good. If this is a true definition of the Noble, it follows that virtue must be noble, since it is both a good thing and also praiseworthy. Virtue is, according to the usual view, a faculty of providing and preserving good things; or a faculty of conferring many great benefits, and benefits of all kinds on all occasions. (1366b) The forms of Virtue are justice, courage, temperance, magnificence, magnanimity, liberality, gentleness, prudence, wisdom. If virtue is a faculty of beneficence, the highest kinds of it must be those which are most useful to others, and for this reason men honour most the just and the courageous, since courage is useful to others in war, justice both in war and in peace. Next comes liberality; liberal people let their money go instead of fighting for it, whereas other people care more for money than for anything else. Justice is the virtue through which everybody enjoys his own possessions in accordance with the law; its opposite is injustice, through which men enjoy the possessions of others in defiance of the law. Courage is the virtue that disposes men to do noble deeds in situations of danger, in accordance with the law and in obedience to its commands; cowardice is the opposite. Temperance is the virtue that disposes us to obey the law where physical pleasures are concerned; incontinence is the opposite. Liberality disposes us to spend money for others' good; illiberality is the opposite. Magnanimity is the virtue that disposes us to do good to others on a large scale; [its opposite is meanness of spirit]. Magnificence is a virtue productive of greatness in matters involving the spending of money. The opposites of these two are smallness of spirit and meanness respectively. Prudence is that virtue of the understanding which enables men to come to wise decisions about the relation to happiness of the goods and evils that have been previously mentioned.

The above is a sufficient account, for our present purpose, of virtue and vice in general, and of their various forms. As to further aspects of the subject, it is not difficult to discern the facts; it is evident that things productive of virtue are noble, as tending towards virtue; and also the effects of virtue, that is, the signs of its presence and the acts to which it leads. And since the signs of virtue, and such acts as it is the mark of a virtuous man to do or have done to him, are noble, it follows that all deeds or signs of courage, and everything done courageously, must be noble things; and so with what is just and actions done justly.

(1367a) . . . We are also to assume when we wish either to praise a man or blame him that qualities closely allied to those which he actually has are identical with them; for instance, that the cautious man is cold-blooded and treacherous, and that the stupid man is an honest fellow or the thick-skinned man a good-tempered one. We can always idealize any given man by drawing on the virtues akin to his actual qualities; thus we may say that the passionate and excitable man is "outspoken"; or that the arrogant man is "superb" or "impressive." (1367b) Those who run to extremes will be said to possess the corresponding good qualities; rashness will be called courage, and extravagance generosity. That will be what most people think; and at the same time this method enables an advocate to draw a misleading inference from the motive, arguing that if a man runs into danger needlessly, much more will he do so in a noble cause; and if a man is open-handed to any one and every one, he will be so to his friends also, since it is the extreme form of goodness to be good to everybody.

We must also take into account the nature of our particular audience when making a speech of praise; for, as Socrates used to say, "it is not difficult to praise the Athenians to an Athenian audience." If the audience esteems a given quality, we must say that our hero has that quality, no matter whether we are addressing Scythians or Spartans or philosophers. Everything, in fact, that is esteemed we are to represent as noble. After all, people regard the two things as much the same.

. . . Praise is the expression in words of the eminence of a man's good qualities, and therefore we must display his actions as the product of such qualities. Encomium refers to what he has actually done; the mention of accessories, such as good birth and education, merely helps to make our story credible—good fathers are likely to have good sons, and good training is likely to produce good character. Hence it is only when a man has already done something that we bestow *encomiums* upon him. Yet the actual deeds are evidence of the doer's character: even if a man has not actually done a given good thing, we shall bestow *praise* on him, if we are sure that he is the sort of man who *would* do it. . . .

To praise a man is in one respect akin to urging a course of action. The suggestions which would be made in the latter case become encomiums when differently expressed.

(1368a) . . . Consequently, whenever you want to praise any one, think what you would urge people to do; and when you want to urge the doing of anything, think what you would praise a man for having done. . . .

There are, also, many useful ways of heightening the effect of praise. We must, for instance, point out that a man is the only one, or the first, or almost the only one who has done something, or that he has done it better than any one else; all these distinctions are honourable. And we must, further, make much of the particular season and occasion of an action, arguing that we could hardly have looked for it just then. If a man has often achieved the same success, we must mention this; that is a strong point; he himself, and not luck, will then be given the credit. So, too, if it is on his account that observances have been devised and instituted to encourage or honour such achievements as his own: thus we may praise Hippolochus because the first encomium ever made was for him, or Harmodius and Aristogeiton because their statues were the first to be put up in the market-place. And we may censure bad men for the opposite reason.

Again, if you cannot find enough to say of a man himself, you may pit him against others, which is what Isocrates used to do owing to his want of familiarity with forensic pleading. The comparison should be with famous men; that will strengthen your case; it is a noble thing to surpass men who are themselves great. It is only natural that methods of "heightening the effect" should be attached particularly to speeches of praise; they aim at proving superiority over others, and any such superiority is a form of nobleness. Hence if you cannot compare your hero with famous men, you should at least compare him with other people generally, since any superiority is held to reveal excellence. And, in general, of the lines of argument which are common to all speeches, this "heightening of effect" is most suitable for declamations, where we take our hero's actions as admitted facts, and our business is simply to invest these with dignity and nobility. "Examples" are most suitable to deliberative speeches; for we judge of future events by divination from past events. Enthymemes are most suitable to forensic speeches; it is our doubts about past events that most admit of arguments showing why a thing must have happened or proving that it did happen.

The above are the general lines on which all, or nearly all, speeches of praise or blame are constructed. We have seen the sort of thing we must bear in mind in making such speeches, and the materials out of which encomiums and censures are made. No special treatment of censure and vituperation is needed. Knowing the above facts, we know their contraries; and it is out of these that speeches of censure are made.

Table 10. Features of epideictic rhetoric.

	Other Names	Time	Place	Action	According to What End	Transcendental Counterpart
judicial	forensic	past	courtroom	accuse/ defend	justice	the True
epideictic	ceremonial, demonstrative	present	funeral, wedding	praise/ censure	honor	the Beautiful
deliberative	legislative, political	future	legislative assembly	urge to do/ urge not to do	advantage	the Good

The Three Kinds of Rhetoric Revisited

Aristotle has introduced us to three types of speech: speech about the future (deliberative), present (epideictic),[1] and past (judicial). In the last chapter, you explored deliberative rhetoric, which attempts to influence decisions that will have consequences for the future. We best imagine such rhetoric in a legislative assembly such as Congress: *Should our country go to war? Pass this law? Raise taxes?* This kind of questioning—about the anticipated advantages and disadvantages of decisions being made—Aristotle emphasized to be the most important kind of speech there is. In doing so, he was at odds with the sophists of his day, who concentrated on the judicial rhetoric of the courtroom, which results in judgments about past occurrences. It was in the courtroom, after all, that a person could make a private fortune by defending or accusing in a case.

1. The term "epideictic" rather than the more familiar term "ceremonial" is used in this text (though you should feel free to use the two interchangeably). One problem with the more familiar term of *ceremonial* is that readers may assume that this kind of speech occurs only within ceremonies. The truth is that speech of praise and censure is everywhere, and the unfamiliar word *epideictic* can help us to create a new category in our minds for this kind of language.

The next chapter will examine judicial rhetoric, which seeks to determine the justice of matters that have already taken place. This chapter surveys epideictic rhetoric, speech about the present. Epideictic rhetoric takes up issues of the noble and ignoble, of honor and dishonor; we can visualize it best in a wedding toast or funeral eulogy, as the speaker praises virtues or censures vices as they are known in the *hic et nunc*, the "here and now."[2]

But we have also said that these three genres of speech are actually much more common than one might think. A person doesn't need to be in Congress to engage in deliberative rhetoric. Questions such as "Where should we go for dinner?" and "Which college courses should I take?" are everyday examples of it. The same goes for judicial rhetoric: "Charles broke the dish, not me" and "You were late for class" qualify as instances of judicial speech, even though they take place outside the courtroom. Finally, weddings and funerals may be the quintessential paradigms for epideictic rhetoric, but the truth is that praise and censure are all around us, in

2. The term *epideictic* is the adjectival form of the Greek word *epidixis*, or *epideixis*, "showing" or "displaying." With the prefix *epi-*, meaning "above" and "over" (among other possibilities), the word suggests a revelation of what is praiseworthy even beyond the rhetorical situation itself.

offhanded statements such as "We are so proud of you!" and "Never in my life have I seen such rude behavior!"

In delineating merely three kinds of speech, Aristotle is suggesting that a society, any human society, does three things: It makes decisions, praises merits, and addresses wrongdoing. Aristotle, by identifying these three functions of a society, is not being *prescriptive*—that is, he is not telling societies what they ought to do. Instead, as he almost always does, Aristotle is being *descriptive*, telling us what any enduring society already does.

Defining a Culture's Horizons

But what is it that holds the society together in the first place? Think of it this way: Human society or culture requires a clear (though sometimes unstated) and shared sense of its core values or "goods," those things that people find desirable for their own sake. In America, for example, "life, liberty and the pursuit of happiness" is one phrase that identifies American values (even rights!); you might go so far as to call those goods the glue that holds Americans together as a people. Those common goods are reflected in a society's activities: The society makes decisions about the future based upon those shared goods, it reinforces those shared goods, and it addresses the wrongdoing of those who fall short of those shared goods. You'll notice that these three activities correspond to the three species of rhetoric—deliberative, epideictic, and judicial respectively. Each type of rhetoric both shapes and is shaped by that society's foundational beliefs, those core values that essentially tie everyone together.

But those core values are themselves the product of the speech of praise, rhetoric that highlights certain goods and ignores others. In a sense, it is in simple expressions of praise and censure—not mighty judgments about the past or presumptuous decisions about the future—that establish those fundamental values. After all, what we value must be known if we are to make informed judgments about the future or coherent judgments about the past. Again, the things we praise or blame in other people must be known before we engage in deliberative or judicial argumentation. Aristotle is clear: "To praise a man is in one respect akin to urging a course of action" (1367b). You might say that, in this sense, epideictic rhetoric sets the parameters for every other kind of speech.

Imagine, for example, a society in which theft is a highly praised skill, a sign of one's cleverness and deftness, rather than a vice—a warring society that, perhaps, sees theft as good training for battle. In such a community, the successful thieves would be the most honored of the lot, wouldn't they? And if, by way of the rhetoric of praise, honor is bestowed upon those who successfully steal, then the deliberative rhetoric of this society would be affected as well. That is, they would make decisions about the future—"Should I rob a bank today?" "Shall we attack this or that rich village?"—based upon their high regard for thievery. Likewise, the judicial rhetoric of that society would probably address stealing in ways unrecognizable to contemporary Americans, who value private ownership and praise self-reliance. Their understanding of a "good" citizen would look different from ours, and they would make decisions about past acts and deeds accordingly.[3] We ought to be careful, then, about what we praise. We must

3. Take the opposite scenario as another example. If the United States is already committed to the good of equality of all before the law—a good celebrated and upheld in epideictic rhetoric—then Congress, through deliberative rhetoric, would pass laws and adopt policies that advance that good in society. The nation's courts would also make decisions based upon that very value, too. In other words, an underlying factor that so deeply influences justice and advantage is simple praise and blame.

exercise tremendous caution because this praising and blaming can be powerful, so powerful that it can become the foundation upon which all other arguments are made.

Parents, who are always concerned with the company their children keep, are well aware of this power that epideictic rhetoric wields: Values are contagious and tend to spread, an effect of the culture of praise and blame within a given peer group. When someone in a peer group says, "That is *so cool*!" the statement may be reinforcing existing values or pushing toward new ones. In any case, the group's shared judgment concerning what it values is affected even by such a casual comment. Hence, the very horizons of goodness—those boundaries by which you judge what is honorable or shameful, recognizing what falls within the lines and what falls outside of them—are set by epideictic rhetoric.

How to Praise Virtue

Just what is virtue? The word comes from the Latin word *virtus*, meaning "excellence" or "moral perfection." And at the root of that word is *vir*, meaning "man."[4] Virtue is, for humanity, an excellence particular and distinct to human beings, just as Aristotle identifies that a horse's perfection includes something quite different: the ability to run swiftly.[5] Virtue, says Aristotle, is a "faculty of providing and preserving good things" (1366a). That is, virtue is a good itself, but it also produces further goods, such as benefits for others.

The first step in praising a person's virtues is to recognize the virtues central to the group at hand. You are probably familiar with the four classical or "cardinal" virtues of temperance, fortitude, prudence, and justice. The three theological virtues of the Christian tradition are faith, hope, and love. But Aristotle actually lists nine virtues: justice, courage, temperance, magnificence, magnanimity, liberality, gentleness, prudence, and wisdom (1366b). (See the excerpt that begins this chapter for Aristotle's definitions of these.) In fact, Aristotle makes an important point about virtue—it varies. He puts it this way: "We must also take into account the nature of our particular audience when making a speech of praise; for, as Socrates used to say, 'it is not difficult to praise the Athenians to an Athenian audience'" (1367b). The point is that rhetors ought not limit themselves to just four or seven or even nine virtues. Rather, they must stay alert to the different goods that are prized by different groups.

This variation is the case not only at the level of society but also within smaller groups that make up a society. Take, for example, an organization—say, the Spanish Club—at a large school. The honors bestowed within the club itself (Who has the best accent? Who can translate the fastest?) would be valued differently inside the group than outside of it. (After all, accent and translation speed would be of no concern to the Chess Club, of course.) Or think about the unspoken goods in your own life. What do you love, and do your friends love it, too? Chances are, they do. What binds together chefs if not the love of good food? What unites a team's fans if not the team itself? In other words, not all epideictic situations are created equal. Just as the praises and criticisms of a party of chefs will differ from that of baseball fans, so should your epideictic rhetoric shift depending on your audience. What you praise about a movie to your friend will change when you're praising that very same movie to, say, your teacher; for instance, you might extol the movie as entertaining to the former and educational to the latter. In every case, the rhetor must identify the particular virtues that are highest and unique to the group at hand.

4. The Greek word for virtue is *arête*.

5. See Book 6 of the *Nicomachean Ethics*.

The second step in praising a person is to identify signs of virtue, actions that are especially noble. What daring deed has so-and-so ventured? What remarkable feat has she accomplished? If *virtue* resides in one's character, then *noble* describes one's deeds. This distinction is fundamental for Aristotle: the reality and the sign. And it is a fundamental distinction you, too, must make if you are going to praise a person. How can you *prove* the deceased's generosity? By his contributions to charities. The reality (the virtue) is proved by the sign (the act). This type of proof by deed ties epideictic rhetoric to a narrative style, one that best illustrates the virtues in a story—one reason that wedding toasts usually entail a good story or two.

It is important to keep in mind that epideictic rhetoric is not, first and foremost, trying to push the audience toward a decision about what to do going forward—what, in fact, the species of deliberative rhetoric *does* attempt to accomplish. It also doesn't try to prove that something happened or that a past deed was of a certain kind; that is the task of judicial rhetoric. Concerning the distinct role of epideictic rhetoric, Aristotle says this: "[W]e take our hero's actions as admitted facts, and our business is simply to invest these with dignity and nobility." It's true that most people know a virtuous action when they see it: the woman who risks injury or even death to save a stranger, the child who gives to the needy when there is no apparent reward, or the man who drops everything to be by the side of his friend in a time of need. But it's likewise true that such virtuous acts risk going unnoticed. The epideictic rhetor draws attention to such deeds so that their force is amplified; Aristotle calls this "heightening the effect" (1368a), so that those acts are "invest[ed] . . . with dignity and nobility."

Take a parallel example in the art world. If you were to visit an art museum, you may very well walk up to a piece of art—let's say it is a masterpiece by Van Gogh—and look at it but not truly *see* it. A wise museum docent would stop you and draw your attention to unique features that, to an untrained eye, would escape notice—perhaps the innovative brush strokes or unusual use of color. You have seen the work of art before, but it is the docent's commentary that allows you to recognize its beauty and power. Similarly, it is the rhetor's task to bring virtuous acts—acts that may otherwise be overlooked—to the forefront, to spotlight them, as it were, so that people notice virtue.

The rhetor's third and final task, then, is to name the virtue revealed in such deeds. In other words, epideictic rhetoric generally starts as life does, with an identifiable action (*This soldier fought in that war . . .*), and from that action we infer a virtue (*. . . because he was brave*). The sign points toward the reality. In this case, courage is the virtue highlighted, and the rhetor "proves" the soldier's courage by the soldier's action.

Again, if we wish to break down the process of praise step by step, a rhetor should first pinpoint the virtues prized by the given audience. Then he should identify signs of virtue—noble deeds—that the person being praised has achieved. Finally, the rhetor should connect those praiseworthy actions to a particular virtue itself. (The same goes for vice, of course, though the vice would instead be criticized.) This entire process is a way of revealing virtue in the world.

Let's put all of this together in a possible real-life scenario: Imagine that your classmate, Kevin, is going on a family vacation to the beach this summer. Kevin is an only child, so his parents are allowing him to invite one friend to go along. Kevin's task is to convince his parents that Oliver, one of his best friends, is the right friend to join them. Kevin and Oliver's friendship is based chiefly upon two virtues: Both are athletic, and both are witty. Kevin knows, however, that his parents will make their decision based upon other criteria, other values. For example, they will want to be assured that Oliver is a good traveler (the drive to the beach is six hours away). They'll need to know that he is flexible and easygoing (there are always surprises during a vacation, some of them unpleasant). They will want to be assured that he is neither foolish nor reckless (there are some risks that should be avoided at the beach). His athleticism and his sense of humor may be nice bonuses, but they are not the factors that Kevin should highlight.

So, having identified the virtues that his parents will esteem—good traveler (i.e., "strong"), easygoing (i.e., "flexible"), and not foolish (i.e., "wise")—Kevin is ready to make his case. He now needs to identify concrete events or actions that suggest Oliver's virtue. When has he been strong? Kevin recalls his endurance during last year's class trip to the state capital, a long drive in a cramped bus. Everyone else arrived cranky and exhausted, but Oliver never complained. (Strong: check!) Then he remembers the time Oliver had to play a basketball game in borrowed shoes and uniform because his duffle bag had been misplaced. He never worried about it, playing one of his better games of the year. (Flexible: check!) Finally, there was the time when several friends thought it would be a good idea to try to cross a creek by walking over on a recently fallen tree. Oliver wanted to do the same, but he knew that the tree was untried, so before walking over, he tested the tree. The brittle wood snapped like a twig, and an accident was averted by his caution. (Wise: check!). Kevin would be prudent to highlight these stories and name the corresponding virtues to his parents because they demonstrate the qualities that his parents value, showing Oliver to be a good candidate for the trip.

Flipping Vices into Virtues

One claim of this textbook is that Aristotle wants to tame the sophist in us all; he hopes to bring rhetoric into the light of reason, to raise the level of civic discourse by revealing reasoning (*logos*) and character (*ethos*) to be just as important as the emotional appeal (*pathos*). Why, then, does he teach us sophistic trick number one, how to take a vice and turn it into a virtue? He gives a number of examples of how to make this rhetorical move: The rash person, who foolishly races toward harm when it is unnecessary or futile, could instead be euphemistically considered "courageous"; the "arrogant man" could be termed "impressive." Is someone insensitive? Better to praise him as "good-tempered" (1367a). From Aristotle we learn to speak of the spendthrift, who spends money far too easily and quickly, as generous. And we can think of other shifts: The overly sensitive person is described as "tender-hearted." The overly cautious one could be called "circumspect." We could recast the perpetual complainer as one who is never satisfied with anything less than perfection. And so on. Why does he teach this seemingly sophistic move?

There are at least three possible reasons. First, a pragmatic reason—Aristotle knows that good rhetors must anticipate the rhetorical context, wisely evaluating the evidence they can offer; in short, they must know the potential cheap shots if they are to defend against them. Second, we must keep in mind that Aristotle is laying out the *possible* means of persuasion, and certainly even dubious methods are possible. Remember, he has claimed that we should learn both sides of an argument *not* to become sophists ourselves but, rather, to be able to detect them when they are plying their wares! It is here that the rhetor's discernment comes into play.

A third and perhaps key reason that Aristotle teaches how to spot virtues where they may actually be absent is the great difficulty in achieving a *perfectly* virtuous action. One's greatest strength can also be one's greatest weakness, and each virtue is often discovered in response to the potential pitfalls of vice. In fact, in his *Nicomachean Ethics*, Aristotle insightfully discusses each virtue not as the opposite of a *single* vice but, rather, as a mean between *two* vices. So courage, for instance, strikes the balance between cowardice (the inability to act in the face of a threat to one's safety) and rashness (acting without proper regard for the threat to one's safety). The rhetor must keep in mind that the mean of virtue is almost infinitely variable and always determined by its unique context.

Take a second example: generosity. To be generous is to find the mean between miserliness (think: the penny-pincher) and profligacy (think: the spendthrift). When deciding whether to give money to a beggar, a couple would have dozens of factors to consider: their own finances, the time, the place, the motive, and the consequences to themselves, not to mention the beggar's apparent circumstances. How can one then act? Must every variable be weighed? Is it even possible to weigh them all and to make the exactly right, the perfectly virtuous, decision? And yet we move through the world in such incalculable equations at every moment. Even without perfect judgment, we must act, and our acts can suggest virtue even when it is not fully achieved.

The point, it would seem, is that we must act with increasing—albeit imperfect—prudence. And so Aristotle offers a way to praise actions *for the sake of virtue*. While the actions may themselves be imperfectly virtuous, the rhetor's praise brings to life the ideal at which those actions aim. Or we might say it this way: This kind of praise finds truth, goodness, and beauty in a broken world. Epideictic rhetoric is thus not merely a just reward for the individual but is also an essential good for the city.

Now we can revisit the question of which genre of rhetoric is most fundamental and primary. As we have already mentioned, the sophists of Aristotle's day privileged judicial rhetoric; it is easy to mislead the jury when pleading in court, and, besides, that's where the money was (1354b23–27). Aristotle, however, held up deliberative rhetoric as the most important, for legislative decisions determine the future course of action, and those decisions determine where we end up. But there is a sense in which simple praise and blame could be said to be, if not the most overtly influential, perhaps the most foundational rhetoric in a community. After all, the "goods" most valued by a people—whether it be riches, justice, health, or something else—set the parameters of that people's culture, determining its very horizons.

In short, the aim of epideictic rhetoric is to praise virtue and censure vice; its focus is on the *present*, and it is based upon *honor*.

Discussion Text:
Pericles: "They Were Worthy of Athens" (Fifth Century BC)[6]

Focus:
Epideictic Rhetoric

1

Pericles, a Greek statesman during the Golden Age of Athens, was a master rhetor, as his famous funeral oration reveals. Weaving together encomium of the dead with praise for Athenian ideals, Pericles shrewdly turns a soldiers' eulogy into a political pep rally. Below is an excerpt of his speech.

40. If then we [Athenians] prefer to meet danger with a light heart but without laborious training, and with a courage which is gained by habit and not enforced by law, are we not greatly the gainers? Since we do not anticipate the pain, although, when the hour comes, we can be as brave as those who never allow themselves to rest; and thus too our city is equally admirable in peace and in war. For we are lovers of the beautiful, yet simple in our tastes, and we cultivate the mind without loss of manliness. Wealth we employ, not for talk and ostentation, but when there is a real use for it. To avow poverty with us is no disgrace; the true disgrace is in doing nothing to avoid it. An Athenian citizen does not neglect the state because he takes care of his own household; and even those of us who are engaged in business have a very fair idea of politics. We alone regard a man who takes no interest in public affairs, not as a harmless, but as a useless character; and if few of us are originators, we are all sound judges of a policy. The great impediment to action is, in our opinion, not discussion, but the want of that knowledge which is gained by discussion preparatory to action. For we have a peculiar power of thinking before we act and of acting too, whereas other men are courageous from ignorance but hesitate upon reflection. And they are surely to be esteemed the bravest spirits who, having the clearest sense both of the pains and pleasures of life, do not on that account shrink from danger. In doing good, again, we are unlike others; we make our friends by conferring, not by receiving favours. Now he who confers a favour is the firmer friend, because he would fain by kindness keep alive the memory of an obligation; but the recipient is colder in his feelings, because he knows that in requiting another's generosity he will not be

Figure 26. Bust of Pericles, Roman copy AD second century after a Greek original of the Late Classical era, marble, in the Townley Collection, British Museum, London, circa 440–430 BC. Courtesy of Marie-Lan Nguyen, commons.wikimedia.org.

6. Thucydides, "Funeral Speech," in *The History of Thucydides*, Olympic ed., ed. Benjamin Jowett (New York: Tandy-Thomas, 1909), 197–202, provided by the Hathi Trust Digital Library (online). This work is in the public domain. Numbers present in the speech are original to this version.

winning gratitude but only paying a debt. We alone do good to our neighbours not upon a calculation of interest, but in the confidence of freedom and in a frank and fearless spirit.

41. To sum up: I say that Athens is the school of Hellas, and that the individual Athenian in his own person seems to have the power of adapting himself to the most varied forms of action with the utmost versatility and grace. This is no passing and idle word, but truth and fact; and the assertion is verified by the position to which these qualities have raised the state. For in the hour of trial Athens alone among her contemporaries is superior to the report of her. No enemy who comes against her is indignant at the reverses which he sustains at the hands of such a city; no subject complains that his masters are unworthy of him. And we shall assuredly not be without witnesses; there are mighty monuments of our power which will make us the wonder of this and of succeeding ages; we shall not need the praises of Homer or of any other panegyrist whose poetry may please for the moment, although his representation of the facts will not bear the light of day. For we have compelled every land and every sea to open a path for our valour, and have everywhere planted eternal memorials of our friendship and of our enmity. Such is the city for whose sake these men nobly fought and died; they could not bear the thought that she might be taken from them; and every one of us who survive should gladly toil on her behalf.

42. I have dwelt upon the greatness of Athens because I want to show you that we are contending for a higher prize than those who enjoy none of these privileges, and to establish by manifest proof the merit of these men whom I am now commemorating. Their loftiest praise has been already spoken. For in magnifying the city I have magnified them, and men like them whose virtues made her glorious. And of how few Hellenes can it be said as of them, that their deeds when weighed in the balance have been found equal to their fame! Methinks that a death such as theirs has been the true measure of a man's worth; it may be the first revelation of his virtues, but is at any rate their final seal. For even those who come short in other ways may justly plead the valour with which they have fought for their country; they have blotted out the evil with the good, and have benefited the state more by their public services than they have injured her by their private actions. None of these men were enervated by wealth or hesitated to resign the pleasures of life; none of them put off the evil day in the hope, natural to poverty, that a man, though poor, may one day become rich. But, deeming that the punishment of their enemies was sweeter than any of these things, and that they could fall in no nobler cause, they determined at the hazard of their lives to be honourably avenged, and to leave the rest. They resigned to hope their unknown chance of happiness; but in the face of death they resolved to rely upon themselves alone. And when the moment came they were minded to resist and suffer, rather than to fly and save their lives; they ran away from the word of dishonour, but on the battlefield their feet stood fast, and in an instant, at the height of their fortune, they passed away from the scene, not of their fear, but of their glory.

43. Such was the end of these men; they were worthy of Athens, and the living need not desire to have a more heroic spirit, although they may pray for a less fatal issue. The value of

such a spirit is not to be expressed in words. Any one can discourse to you for ever about the advantages of a brave defence, which you know already. But instead of listening to him I would have you day by day fix your eyes upon the greatness of Athens, until you become filled with the love of her; and when you are impressed by the spectacle of her glory, reflect that this empire has been acquired by men who knew their duty and had the courage to do it, who in the hour of conflict had the fear of dishonour always present to them, and who, if ever they failed in an enterprise, would not allow their virtues to be lost to their country, but freely gave their lives to her as the fairest offering which they could present at her feast. The sacrifice which they collectively made was individually repaid to them; for they received again each one for himself a praise which grows not old, and the noblest of all sepulchers—I speak not of that in which their remains are laid, but of that in which their glory survives, and is proclaimed always and on every fitting occasion both in word and deed. For the whole earth is the sepulchre of famous men; not only are they commemorated by columns and inscriptions in their own country, but in foreign lands there dwells also an unwritten memorial of them, graven not on stone but in the hearts of men. Make them your examples, and, esteeming courage to be freedom and freedom to be happiness, do not weigh too nicely the perils of war.

Discussion Questions

"They Were Worthy of Athens"

1. Why does Pericles use the regime (Athens's democracy) to frame the praise?

2. Why might rhetoric be more potentially necessary and powerful in a deliberative democracy than in, say, a totalitarian state?

3. Which virtues are praised by Pericles? Can you identify an instance in which Pericles may be seeing a virtue within a vice?

4. Notice that no individuals are named. Why might Pericles wish to avoid naming real people?

5. Can you tell by the speech which virtues are highest for Athens?

6. How would you expect to feel at the end of a eulogy? How do you feel at the end of this speech?

DISCUSSION TEXT:
General Douglas MacArthur: "Duty, Honor, Country" (1962)[7]

FOCUS:
Epideictic Rhetoric

2

On May 12, 1962, five-star Army General Douglas MacArthur spoke at West Point. In his acceptance speech for the Sylvanus Thayer Award—the United States Military Academy's highest award—MacArthur offered reflections on West Point's motto of duty, honor, and country.

General Westmoreland, General Grove, distinguished guests, and gentlemen of the Corps!

❶ As I was leaving the hotel this morning, a doorman asked me, "Where are you bound for, General?" And when I replied, "West Point," he remarked, "Beautiful place. Have you ever been there before?"

❷ No human being could fail to be deeply moved by such a tribute as this [Thayer Award]. Coming from a profession I have served so long, and a people I have loved so well, it fills me with an emotion I cannot express. But this award is not intended primarily to honor a personality, but to symbolize a great moral code—the code of conduct and chivalry of those who guard this beloved land of culture and ancient descent. That is the animation of this medallion. For all eyes and for all time, it is an expression of the ethics of the American soldier. That I should be integrated in this way with so noble an ideal arouses a sense of pride and yet of humility which will be with me always.

❸ *Duty, Honor, Country*: Those three hallowed words reverently dictate what you ought to be, what you can be, what you will be. They are your rallying points: to build courage when courage seems to fail; to regain faith when there seems to be little cause for faith; to create hope when hope becomes forlorn.

❹ Unhappily, I possess neither that eloquence of diction, that poetry of imagination, nor that brilliance of metaphor to tell you all that they mean.

❺ The unbelievers will say they are but words, but a slogan, but a flamboyant phrase. Every pedant, every demagogue, every cynic, every hypocrite, every troublemaker, and I am sorry to say, some others of an entirely different character, will try to downgrade them even to the extent of mockery and ridicule.

❻ But these are some of the things they do: They build your basic character. They mold you for your future roles as the custodians of the nation's defense. They make you strong enough to know when you are weak, and brave enough to face yourself when you are afraid.

7. Used with the permission of the General Douglas MacArthur Foundation, MacArthur Square, Norfolk, Virginia.

They teach you to be proud and unbending in honest failure, but humble and gentle in success; not to substitute words for actions, not to seek the path of comfort, but to face the stress and spur of difficulty and challenge; to learn to stand up in the storm but to have compassion on those who fall; to master yourself before you seek to master others; to have a heart that is clean, a goal that is high; to learn to laugh, yet never forget how to weep; to reach into the future yet never neglect the past; to be serious yet never to take yourself too seriously; to be modest so that you will remember the simplicity of true greatness, the open mind of true wisdom, the meekness of true strength. They give you a temper of the will, a quality of the imagination, a vigor of the emotions, a freshness of the deep springs of life, a temperamental predominance of courage over timidity, of an appetite for adventure over love of ease. They create in your heart the sense of wonder, the unfailing hope of what next, and the joy and inspiration of life. They teach you in this way to be an officer and a gentleman.

❼ [. . .] You now face a new world—a world of change. The thrust into outer space of the satellite, spheres, and missiles marked the beginning of another epoch in the long story of mankind. In the five or more billions of years the scientists tell us it has taken to form the earth, in the three or more billion years of development of the human race, there has never been a more abrupt or staggering evolution. We deal now not with things of this world alone, but with the illimitable distances and as yet unfathomed mysteries of the universe. We are reaching out for a new and boundless frontier.

❽ We speak in strange terms: of harnessing the cosmic energy; of making winds and tides work for us; of creating unheard synthetic materials to supplement or even replace our old standard basics; to purify sea water for our drink; of mining ocean floors for new fields of wealth and food; of disease preventatives to expand life into the hundreds of years; of controlling the weather for a more equitable distribution of heat and cold, of rain and shine; of space ships to the moon; of the primary target in war, no longer limited to the armed forces of an enemy, but instead to include his civil populations; of ultimate conflict between a united human race and the sinister forces of some other planetary galaxy; of such dreams and fantasies as to make life the most exciting of all time.

❾ And through all this welter of change and development, your mission remains fixed, determined, inviolable: it is to win our wars.

❿ Everything else in your professional career is but corollary to this vital dedication. All other public purposes, all other public projects, all other public needs, great or small, will find others for their accomplishment. But you are the ones who are trained to fight. Yours is the profession of arms, the will to win, the sure knowledge that in war there is no substitute for victory; that if you lose, the nation will be destroyed; that the very obsession of your public service must be: *Duty, Honor, Country.*

⓫ Others will debate the controversial issues, national and international, which divide men's minds; but serene, calm, aloof, you stand as the Nation's war-guardian, as its lifeguard from the raging tides of international conflict, as its gladiator in the arena of battle. For a century and a half you have defended, guarded, and protected its hallowed traditions of liberty and freedom, of right and justice.

12 Let civilian voices argue the merits or demerits of our processes of government; whether our strength is being sapped by deficit financing, indulged in too long, by federal paternalism grown too mighty, by power groups grown too arrogant, by politics grown too corrupt, by crime grown too rampant, by morals grown too low, by taxes grown too high, by extremists grown too violent; whether our personal liberties are as thorough and complete as they should be. These great national problems are not for your professional participation or military solution. Your guidepost stands out like a ten-fold beacon in the night: *Duty, Honor, Country.*

13 You are the leaven which binds together the entire fabric of our national system of defense. From your ranks come the great captains who hold the nation's destiny in their hands the moment the war tocsin sounds. The Long Gray Line has never failed us. Were you to do so, a million ghosts in olive drab, in brown khaki, in blue and gray, would rise from their white crosses thundering those magic words: *Duty, Honor, Country.*

14 This does not mean that you are warmongers.

15 On the contrary, the soldier, above all other people, prays for peace, for he must suffer and bear the deepest wounds and scars of war.

16 But always in our ears ring the ominous words of Plato, that wisest of all philosophers: "Only the dead have seen the end of war."

17 The shadows are lengthening for me. The twilight is here. My days of old have vanished, tone and tint. They have gone glimmering through the dreams of things that were. Their memory is one of wondrous beauty, watered by tears, and coaxed and caressed by the smiles of yesterday. I listen vainly, but with thirsty ears, for the witching melody of faint bugles blowing reveille, of far drums beating the long roll. In my dreams I hear again the crash of guns, the rattle of musketry, the strange, mournful mutter of the battlefield.

18 But in the evening of my memory, always I come back to West Point.

19 Always there echoes and re-echoes: *Duty, Honor, Country.*

20 Today marks my final roll call with you, but I want you to know that when I cross the river my last conscious thoughts will be of The Corps, and The Corps, and The Corps.

21 I bid you farewell.

Discussion Questions

"Duty, Honor, Country"

Note: Some of the questions indicate in which paragraph the answer may be found.

1. What virtues does MacArthur wish to become the defining goods for his audience of soldiers?

2. We learned in this chapter that epideictic rhetoric highlights virtues. Notice that MacArthur speaks so highly of the duty of the soldier that he then must offer a caveat: "This does not mean that you are warmongers." How does he go on to justify this claim?

3. **Invention:** How does MacArthur define the soldier's mission? ❾ What is it not? ⓫ ⓬

4. MacArthur uses the topic of relationship (cause-effect) to discuss duty, honor, and country. What do these three goods give rise to in the soldier? ❻

5. **Organization:** Can you discern an organizational structure? Does it fit the classical model? Find and mark the following sections in the speech itself: *exordium, narratio, partitio, refutatio, confirmatio, peroratio.*

6. **Style:** Analyze the speech for style. Which figures of speech can you identify? Cite three. What stylistic choices make the paragraph that begins with "Let civilian voices argue" so striking?

7. **Memory:** The three most memorable words of this speech surely are *duty*, *honor*, and *country*. How many times does MacArthur repeat this triad? (Note: It is also used once in a section that was cut.) Do you hear the words differently the final time? That is, have they taken on new depth of meaning?

8. **Delivery:** Practice delivering all of the paragraphs that include "duty, honor, country." Try varying your delivery of that triad in each repetition, and also try speaking them as similarly as possible. Which is more effective?

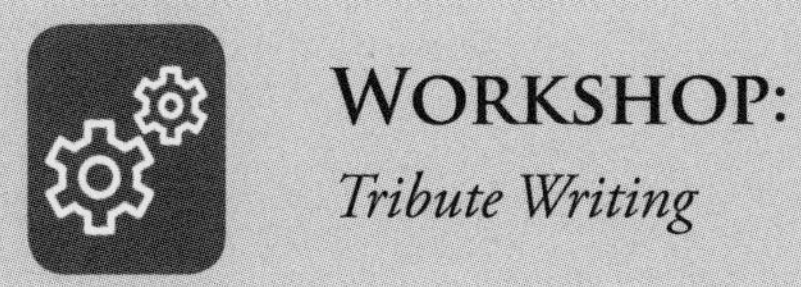

WORKSHOP:
Tribute Writing

Write a 250–500-word tribute (roughly two to four minutes of spoken text). It can be for a favorite historical figure or almost anything else—a book, a pet, or even a special pair of sneakers! (Choosing friends or loved ones is unadvised as it is too raw for the classroom. It's best to stick with something *less* near and dear.)

Notice the virtues that you are praising. Are they culturally defined, or are they virtues per se? Why are you praising them? Are they virtues that are in jeopardy? Would it make sense to praise virtues that are perfectly established, that there is no doubt about?

The following speech is a sample piece of epideictic rhetoric you can use to prime the pump of invention as you attempt to write your own tribute. It was delivered by US Senator George Graham Vest (1830–1904) early in his career as a lawyer in Missouri. He successfully represented a man who was suing another person for having killed his dog—a dog, it should be noted, that was accused of having attacked the defendant. Although it was delivered in a courtroom, it is a clear example of epideictic rhetoric. This is his summation to the jury.

> Gentlemen of the Jury—The best friend a man has in this world may turn against him and become his enemy. His son or daughter that he has reared with loving care may prove ungrateful. Those who are nearest and dearest to us, those whom we trust with our happiness and our good name may become traitors to their faith. The money that a man has, he may lose. It flies away from him, and perhaps when he needs it most. A man's reputation may be sacrificed in a moment of ill-considered action. The people who are prone to fall on their knees to do us honor when success is with us may be the first to throw the stone of malice when failure settles its cloud upon our heads.
>
> The one absolutely unselfish friend that man can have in this selfish world, the one that never deserts him, the one that never proves ungrateful or treacherous, is his dog. A man's dog stands by him in prosperity and in poverty, in health and in sickness. He will sleep on the cold ground, where the wintry winds blow and the snow drives fiercely, if only he may be near his master's side. He will kiss the hand that has no food to offer; he will lick the wounds and sores that come in encounter with the roughness of the world. He guards the sleep of his pauper master as if he were a prince. When all other friends desert, he remains. When riches take wings, and reputation falls to pieces, he is as constant in his love as the sun in its journey through the heavens. If fortune drives the master forth an outcast in the world, friendless and homeless, the faithful dog asks no higher privilege than that of accompanying him, to guard him against danger, to fight against his enemies. And when the last scene of all comes, and death takes his master in its embrace, and his body is laid away in the cold ground, no matter if all other friends pursue their way, there by the graveside will the noble dog be found, his head between his paws, his eyes sad, but open in alert watchfulness, faithful and true even in death.[8]

8. "Tribute to the Dog: How Senator Vest of Missouri, Eulogized the Canine Family," *Weekly Courier* (Fort Collins, Colorado), May 9, 1901, https://www.coloradohistoricnewspapers.org/cgi-bin/colorado?a=d&d=TWC19010509.2.54.

Student sample:

Figure 27. LEGO blocks.

An Open Letter to LEGO

Dear LEGO,

Thank you for being my source of childhood happiness for all those years, for using most of my time, money and storage space as I grew up. You taught me creativity, and you provided bonding time with siblings and father. Thank you for teaching me life skills, for improving my eyesight when looking through filled boxes, for teaching me how to find more and more storage space, and for helping me learn to describe looking for "that one piece."

I had such fun building and experimenting and testing, day after day. You were certainly a source of fascination through the early years—I could sit all day building again and again. I remember one time I built an ice cream truck, but not just any ice cream truck: It was an ice cream truck for an undercover secret agent, complete with a computer, weapons, and spy equipment. I had so much fun with it, driving around and fighting bad guys. LEGO, I hope you didn't mind being asked for every Christmas and birthday. I also know that, too often, you came out of the washing machine after being left in my pockets. But I suppose you got some revenge as you crippled anyone misfortunate enough to step on you. Overall you shaped my early years, and I am sorry to see you go. I may now be too old to buy you, but I will never forget you. You will be missed.

From,
A child at heart—Luke Morrison[9]

9. Luke Morrison, "An Open Letter to LEGO" (student work, Rhetoric II course, Live Oak Classical School, 2016).

Presentation:

Imitatio *of "Duty, Honor, Country"*

Spotlight

Putting It All Together

For this assignment, you will imitate General MacArthur's address, but whereas he extols the virtues of the Corps—duty, honor, and country—you will extol three virtues that are particular to your school (or other group, e.g., a club or your family).

Begin by brainstorming the values of your school. What things come to mind when you think of your school? What do outsiders associate with the school? What sort of activities set you apart from other schools? Who are the school's founders? What are the school's priorities—college preparation, safety, the arts? Use the following space to jot down what comes to mind. Then choose three.

Delivery considerations: For this speech, you will once again be combining all of the aspects we have practiced—voice, posture, eye contact, and gestures—for the presentation. Vary your vocal delivery, stand up straight, make eye contact across the room, and gesture intentionally. Be sure to mark your speech for special emphasis.

The following is a scaffold that follows MacArthur's address. You may wish to use it to create your own epideictic speech, but also feel free to alter the wording as you see fit. (Note: the blanks with the asterisks are for the three words you choose instead of *duty*, *honor*, and *country*.)

Title: *____________________, *____________________, *____________________

As I was [add an anecdote] ____

____ .

*____________________, *____________________, *____________________: Those three hallowed words reverently dictate ____

____ .

They are your rallying points: to ____________________ when ____________________ ; to ____________________ when ____________________ ; to ____________________ when ____________________.

Unhappily, I possess neither that eloquence of diction, that poetry of imagination, nor that brilliance of metaphor to tell you all that they mean.

The unbelievers will say they are but ________, but a ________, but a ________. Every ________, every ________, every ________, every ________, every ________, and I am sorry to say, some others of an entirely different character, will try to downgrade them even to the extent of mockery and ridicule.

But these are some of the things they do: They ________________________________.
They ____. They ________________________. They teach you to be ____, but ____;
not to ______________________________, but to ______________________________;
not to ____ but to ________________________________. They give you ______________________, ______________________, ______________________.
They create in your heart the sense of ____.
They teach you in this way to be a ________________ and a ________________.

[. . .]

We speak in strange terms: of __________________________, of____________________, of ________________, of____________________________, of____________________________.

And through all this welter of change and development, your mission remains fixed, determined, inviolable: it is to ________________.

[. . .][T]he very obsession of your ______________ must be: *__________________, *__________________, *__________________.

Others will ____, but ________, ________, ________, you stand as the ____.

Let [other] voices argue ____;
whether____. These great problems are not for your [. . .] participation or [. . .] solution. Your guidepost stands out like a ten-fold beacon in the night: *__________________, *__________________, *__________________.

The ____________________ has never failed us. ______________________________, thundering those magic words: *__________________, *__________________, *__________________.

This does not mean that you are ________________.

On the contrary, the ________________, above all other people, ________________
____.

But always in our ears ring the ominous words of__________, that wisest of all philosophers: "________________________________."

The shadows are lengthening for me. The twilight is here. My days of old have vanished, tone and tint. [. . .] I listen vainly, but with thirsty ears, for the witching melody of ________________, of ________________. In my dreams I hear again the ________________, the ________________, the ________________ of the ________________.

But in the evening of my memory, always I come back to ________________.

Always there echoes and re-echoes: *__________________, *__________________, *__________________.

Today marks my final ________________ with you, but I want you to know that when I cross the river my last conscious thoughts will be of ________________, and ________________, and ________________.

I bid you farewell.

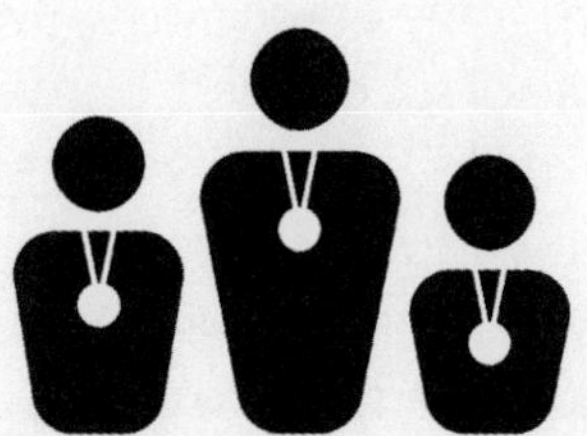

13

Chapter 13

Judicial Rhetoric: Judging the True

(1368b) We have next to treat of Accusation and Defence, and to enumerate and describe the ingredients of the syllogisms used therein. There are three things we must ascertain— first, the nature and number of the incentives to wrong-doing; second, the state of mind of wrongdoers; third, the kind of persons who are wronged, and their condition. We will deal with these questions in order. But before that let us define the act of "wrong-doing."

We may describe "wrong-doing" as injury voluntarily inflicted contrary to law. "Law" is either special [particular] or general [universal]. By [particular] law I mean that written law which regulates the life of a particular community; by [universal] law, all those unwritten principles which are supposed to be acknowledged everywhere. . . .

We have now to consider the motives and states of mind of wrongdoers, and to whom they do wrong.

Let us first decide what sort of things people are trying to get or avoid when they set about doing wrong to others. . . .

(1369a) . . . Every action must be due to one or other of seven causes: chance, nature, compulsion, habit, reasoning, anger, or appetite. . . .

The things that happen by chance are all those whose cause cannot be determined, that have no purpose, and that happen neither always nor usually nor in any fixed way. The definition of chance shows just what they are. Those things happen by nature which have a fixed and internal cause; (1369b) they take place uniformly, either always or usually. There is no need to discuss in exact detail the things that happen contrary to nature, nor to ask whether they happen in some sense naturally or from some other cause; it would seem that chance is at least partly the cause of such events. Those things happen through compulsion which take place contrary to the desire or reason of the doer, yet through his own agency. Acts are done from habit which men do because they have often done them before. Actions are due to reasoning when, in view of any of the goods already mentioned, they appear useful either as ends or as means to an end, and are performed for that reason: "for that reason," since even licentious persons perform a certain number of useful actions, but because they are pleasant and not because they are useful. To passion and anger are due all acts of revenge. Revenge and punishment are different things. Punishment is inflicted for the sake of the person punished; revenge for that of the punisher, to satisfy his feelings. (What anger is will be made clear when we come to discuss the emotions.) Appetite is the cause of all actions that appear pleasant. Habit, whether acquired by mere familiarity or by effort, belongs to the class of pleasant things, for there are many actions not naturally pleasant which men perform with pleasure, once they have become used to them. To sum up then, all actions due to ourselves either are or seem to be either good or pleasant. Moreover, as all actions due to ourselves are done voluntarily and actions not due to ourselves are done involuntarily, it follows that all voluntary actions must either be or seem to be either good or pleasant. . . .

We may lay it down that Pleasure is a movement, a movement by which the soul as a whole is consciously brought into its normal state of being; and that Pain is the opposite. (1370a) If this is what pleasure is, it is clear that the pleasant is what tends to produce this condition, while that which tends to destroy it, or to cause the soul to be brought into the opposite state, is painful. It must therefore be pleasant as a rule to move towards a natural state of being, particularly when a natural process has achieved the complete recovery of that natural state. Habits also are pleasant; for as soon as a thing has become habitual, it is virtually natural; habit is a thing not unlike nature; what happens often is akin to what happens always, natural events happening always, habitual events often. Again, that is pleasant which is not forced on us; for force is unnatural, and that is why what is compulsory, painful, and it has been rightly said

> All that is done on compulsion is bitterness unto the soul.

So all acts of concentration, strong effort, and strain are necessarily painful; they all involve compulsion and force, unless we are accustomed to them, in which case it is custom that makes them pleasant. The opposites to these are pleasant; and hence ease, freedom from toil, relaxation, amusement, rest, and sleep belong to the class of pleasant things; for these are all free from any element of compulsion. Everything, too, is pleasant for which we have the desire within us, since desire is the craving for pleasure. . . .

So much for the subject of pleasant things: by considering their opposites we can easily see what things are unpleasant.

The above are the motives that make men do wrong to others; we are next to consider the states of mind in which they do it, and the persons to whom they do it.

. . . They [who do wrong to others may do so because they believe that they] are not likely to be found out if their appearance contradicts the charges that might be brought against them: for instance, a weakling is unlikely to be charged with violent assault, or a poor and ugly man with adultery. . . .

You feel safe, too, if you have either no enemies or a great many; if you have none, you expect not to be watched and therefore not to be detected; if you have a great many, you will be watched, and therefore people will think you can never risk an attempt on them[.] . . . You may feel that even if you are found out you can stave off a trial, or have it postponed, or corrupt your judges: or that even if you are sentenced you can avoid paying damages, or can at least postpone doing so for a long time: or that you are so badly off that you will have nothing to lose. You may feel that the gain to be got by wrong-doing is great or certain or immediate, and that the penalty is small or uncertain or distant. (1372b) It may be that the advantage to be gained is greater than any possible retribution: as in the case of despotic power, according to the popular view. . . . You may be encouraged by having often escaped detection or punishment already; or by having often tried and failed; for in crime, as in war, there are men who will always refuse to give up the struggle. You may get your pleasure on the spot and the pain later, or the gain on the spot and the loss later. . . . You may be stimulated by being in want: which may mean that you want necessaries, as poor people do, or that you want luxuries, as rich people do. You may be encouraged by having a particularly good reputation, because that will save you from being suspected: or by having a particularly bad one, because nothing you are likely to do will make it worse.

The above, then, are [some of] the various states of mind in which a man sets about doing wrong to others. The kind of people to whom he does wrong, and the ways in which he does it, must be considered next. The people to whom he does it are those who have what he wants himself, whether this means necessities or luxuries and materials for enjoyment. His victims may be far off or near at hand. If they are near, he gets his profit quickly; if they are far off, vengeance is slow, as those think who plunder the Carthaginians. They may be those who are trustful instead of being cautious and watchful, since all such people are easy to elude. Or those who are too easy-going to have enough energy to prosecute an offender. Or sensitive people, who are not apt to show fight over questions of money. Or those who have been wronged already by many people, and yet have not prosecuted; such men must surely be the proverbial "Mysian prey." Or those who have either never or often been wronged before; in neither case will they take precautions; if they have never been wronged they think they never will, and if they have often been wronged they feel that surely it cannot happen again. . . .

(1373a) . . . The above is a fairly complete account of the circumstances under which men do wrong to others, of the sort of wrongs they do, of the sort of persons to whom they do them, and of their reasons for doing them.

(1373b) It will now be well to make a complete classification of just and unjust actions. We may begin by observing that they have been defined relatively to two kinds of law, and also relatively to two classes of persons. By the two kinds of law I mean particular law and universal law. Particular law is that which each community lays down and applies to its own members: this is partly written and partly unwritten. Universal law is the law of Nature. For there really is, as every one to some extent divines, a natural justice and injustice that is binding on all men, even on those who have no association or covenant with each other. It is this that Sophocles' Antigone clearly means when she says that the burial of Polyneices was a just act in spite of the prohibition: she means that it was just by nature.

> Not of to-day or yesterday it is,
>
> But lives eternal: none can date its birth.

And so Empedocles, when he bids us kill no living creature, says that doing this is not just for some people while unjust for others,

> Nay, but, an all-embracing law, through the realms of the sky
>
> Unbroken it stretcheth, and over the earth's immensity.

. . .

(1374a) . . . We saw that there are two kinds of right and wrong conduct towards others, one provided for by written ordinances, the other by unwritten. . . . The second kind makes up for the defects of a community's written code of law. This is what we call equity; people regard it as just; it is, in fact, the sort of justice which goes beyond the written law. Its existence partly is and partly is not intended by legislators; not intended, where they have noticed no defect in the law; intended, where [they] find themselves unable to define things exactly, and are obliged to legislate as if that held good always which in fact only holds good usually; or where it is not easy to be complete owing to the endless possible cases presented, such as the kinds and sizes of weapons that may be used to inflict wounds—a lifetime would be too short to make out a complete list of these. If, then, a precise statement is impossible and yet legislation is necessary, the law must be expressed in wide terms; and so, if a man has no more than a finger-ring on his hand when he lifts it to strike or actually strikes another man, he is guilty of a criminal act according to the unwritten words of the law; (1374b) but he is innocent really, and it is equity that declares him to be so. . . .

(1375a) . . . First, then, let us take laws and see how they are to be used in persuasion and dissuasion, in accusation and defence. If the written law tells against our case, clearly we must appeal to the universal law, and insist on its greater equity and justice. We must argue that the juror's oath "I will give my verdict according to honest opinion" means that one will not simply follow the letter of the written law. We must urge that the principles of equity are permanent and changeless, and that the universal law does not change either, for it is the law of nature, whereas written laws often do change.

The Rhetoric of Wrongdoing

We have examined Aristotle's privileged species of rhetoric—deliberative rhetoric—which influences decisions about the future. Next we considered epideictic rhetoric and its tie to the present, inasmuch as praise and blame determine the parameters for the current rhetorical situation. We are now to explore speech about the past, judicial rhetoric. Aristotle's plan for discussing judicial rhetoric is threefold:

1. Understand the motive: Why do people commit wrongs?
2. Understand the wrongdoer: What is his or her frame of mind?
3. Understand the wronged: What kinds of people are victimized?

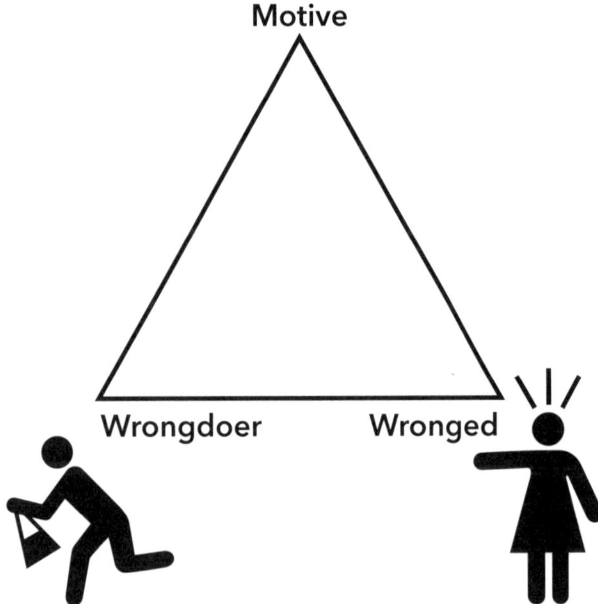

Figure 28. Rhetoric of wrong triangle.

Aristotle reminds us why we are looking to these three categories: It is here that we can derive syllogisms and thus enthymemes. In other words, looking to the *why*, *who*, and *whom* will help generate a strong case of defense or prosecution.

Why People Do Wrong

Because judicial rhetoric involves judging, and judging is typically concerned with right and wrong, Aristotle begins with a definition of wrongdoing: *injury voluntarily inflicted contrary to law.* He then lists the seven causes of why people do anything at all: chance, nature, compulsion, habit, reasoning, anger, and appetite.

He briefly discusses each, concluding that everything a person willingly does is for (a) a good (or apparent good) or (b) pleasure (or apparent pleasure). Because goods have been explored previously in his discussion of deliberative rhetoric, Aristotle then refers the reader back to earlier chapters for a better understanding of goods and the advantageous. He follows with an analysis of pleasure, one of the most important possible reasons people do wrong.

Have you ever thought about what **pleasure** actually is? Consider Aristotle's definition: "Pleasure is a movement, a movement by which the soul as a whole is consciously brought into its normal state of being; and . . . Pain is the opposite" (1369b). We might say it this way: Pleasure isn't static or stagnant; it is the soul's *motion* of returning to business as usual; pain is when the soul is off kilter. His definition may, at first, seem overly technical, but defining pleasure as he does is actually remarkable. Stop and think about when *you* feel pleasure, and you are sure to find that it is, indeed, generally the returning to a normal state. Examples are easy to come up with: A nap—returning from fatigue to restfulness—is pleasant whereas chores—a movement in the opposite direction—are typically arduous. Feeling hunger is painful, but eating is pleasant, for it is a returning to the state of feeling sated. If pleasure attends when a body is returning to its natural state, then whatever is constraining or toilsome is necessarily painful. (Note that simply *being* full or *being* rested do not meet Aristotle's standard for pleasure—not in and of themselves. Pleasure is known in the *from-to* movement, from discomfort to comfort.)

Habits, however, have the unique ability to transform something painful into something pleasurable. For example, your parents hope that the odious chore of making your bed will one day transform into a habit, one that pleases you as much as it pleases them. That is, if you habituate yourself to shipshape living, then returning your room from untidy to tidy can make you happy, not vexed. Young children often hate brushing their teeth—it takes so long and is so boring! But by now, you've probably grown so accustomed to it that you don't think twice about the task. By being "something like nature," a habit can take the *hard* out of "hard work."

Why people commit wrongs:

chance
nature
compulsion
habit
reasoning
anger
appetite

The Wrongdoer and the Wronged

Having considered the reasons a person may do wrong (this is the "motive" part of our Rhetoric of Wrong Triangle), Aristotle then explores the wrongdoer himself. By teasing out a wrongdoer's profile, Aristotle gives an inventory from which a speaker might draw material to defend or prosecute. (See 1372a–1372b for a comprehensive list.) We're naturally wary of suspicious characters, but the opposite can be problematic, too. Is the accused likely to be unsuspected? Then he might be all the more motivated to act. Has she committed a similar crime in the past but not been caught? Then she could think she will be able to get away with it again. Is the benefit of doing wrong immediate but the punishment delayed? Certain characters would be willing to have their fun now and face the consequences later. Think of Aristotle's profiling as a database for ideas on vindicating and convicting.

The same follows for characteristics of those who are themselves wronged (see 1372b–1373a). They are often the rich, the unsuspecting, the naive. Enemies are wronged "because that is pleasant," but friends are wronged, too, "because that is easy" (1372a). The type of person wronged sometimes helps determine the level of justice meted out to the wrongdoer. After all, if the wronged person is himself a person who habitually commits crimes, it might not be such a bad thing that ill has befallen him. Aristotle says it this way: Harming a bad guy feels "fine and pleasant . . . as though almost no wrong were done" (1373a). In short, there is often a kind of logic to wrongdoing: It is done for particular reasons, by people in certain frames of mind, and against certain kinds of people.

Particular and Universal Law

Wrongdoers are those who have, as Aristotle says, willingly broken the law. But what relationship does the written law have to true justice? To this point, Aristotle offers an important distinction, that of the difference between **particular law** and **universal law**. A particular law is, according to Aristotle, a "written law which regulates the life of a particular community." For a particular law, let's picture a speed limit sign of 25 miles per hour. It is posted, thus acknowledged by the community, and it does indeed serve to regulate that community. We should note that, to a certain degree, it is arbitrary; after all, couldn't 20 miles per hour work just as well? Here are some other examples of a particular law: *Curfew is 10 p.m. Students are not permitted to chew gum during class. Citizens must file their taxes no later than April 15.*

Universal laws, however, are "all those unwritten principles which are supposed to be acknowledged everywhere." For universal law, picture an ambulance. The ambulance may not always obey the written speed limit of 25 miles per hour because it represents a deeper, more fundamental truth with which we would all agree: Human lives should be safeguarded. Here are some examples of universal law: *People shouldn't harm each other. Telling the truth is the right thing to do. Stealing is wrong.*

Particular laws and universal laws are distinct, but they are also connected. Back to the speed limit example: Why is the speed limit 25 miles per hour (particular law) in the first place? Because people should not endanger themselves or others (universal law). That is, the former (particular) depends upon the latter (universal). In fact, the reason that the ambulance can break the particular law is because it is upholding the universal law. Concerning the universal law, Aristotle says this: "For there really is, as everyone to some extent divines, a natural justice and injustice that is binding on all men" (1373b). It is this idea that he has in mind when he cites Antigone's burial of her brother. Yes, she had broken the particular law according to which Polyneices was not to be buried. Antigone claimed, however, that burying Polyneices was justified by the universal law of nature (1373b). The claim to natural justice or injustice is a claim to universal law, which is the very grounding for our written law.[1] In other words, written laws should not be perfectly arbitrary or capricious. They should be based upon a desire for fairness that we all believe to be innate.[2]

1. In philosophy and legal theory, this is called natural law.
2. The distinction here is reminiscent of Aristotle's discussion of the enthymeme and how signs are tied to reality. For example, a virtuous action (sign) points to virtuous character (reality). Again, the courageous action of taking a bullet for one's country is tied to courage itself. Even so, the particular law is tied to the universal law: A law against murder is not created arbitrarily by a culture; rather, such a law points to a universal recognition of human dignity. And while the particular laws may vary from place to place, they are still derived from one fundamental reality. In other words, the different shapes they take from culture to culture don't necessitate relativism; instead, they actually do the opposite—they point backward toward the good that stands behind any variance.

   For example, we must acknowledge that respect of elders (Latin, *pietas*) can be understood differently. In some cultures, such as the Mongolian culture, the young show respect by asking their elders questions, especially during the annual New Year's ritual. The young will ask the old a series of questions (e.g., "Are you at peace?" "How is your health?" "How are your children?" "How are your animals?") In other societies, the young may show respect by not speaking, by waiting silently in the presence of their elders—more of a speak-when-spoken-to and seen-but-not-heard way of marking respect for one's elders. Another example is generosity. For some cultures, generosity is encouraged to be displayed publicly, but for others, such acts are more meaningful if kept anonymous. But it is much more difficult—perhaps even impossible—to imagine a humane society in which disrespect and miserliness themselves could be considered anything other than vices. Given societies may tease out a particular virtue differently, but there is a striking commonality about what the virtues themselves are.

Table 11. Features of judicial rhetoric.

	Other Names	Time	Place	Action	According to What End	Transcendental Counterpart
judicial	forensic	past	courtroom	accuse/ defend	justice	the True
epideictic	ceremonial, demonstrative	present	funeral, wedding	praise/ censure	honor	the Beautiful
deliberative	legislative, political	future	legislative assembly	urge to do/ urge not to do	advantage	the Good

What this means for the judicial rhetor is that there are two levels of argumentation and thus two steps by which a person can make a defense. First step: Consider the particular law. If a client did not break a written law, then there is nothing to prosecute. But if a law was indeed broken, the case is not yet over. Second step: Look to a universal law for justification. An example here may help. Perhaps the defendant's crime is speeding, but the reason for violating the speed limit was to make it to the hospital to save a child's life. In this case, you could argue that speed limits are imposed in order to keep us safe, but that, in this instance, violating the law and rushing the child to the hospital was actually the safer choice. That is, a universal law trumped the particular law.

The opposite is possible, too. Has the written law been upheld but its spirit—the universal law behind it—been violated? This is the case when, for example, a child follows his mother's order to share with his sister, but he does so grudgingly. Or imagine a driver who sees an elderly woman's car stalled in an intersection. The particular law—a law existing for the sake of public safety—says that drivers should not stop and get out of their cars in a busy roadway. So the driver obeys the particular law and passes the stalled vehicle, but this driver violates the spirit of the universal law that stands behind the legal code.

Now, it's easy to see this section as sophistic. Isn't Aristotle saying that you can use whichever law suits your case? And yet you'll notice the parameters—Aristotle is not saying that you get to make any argument you wish, for the bounds are still the legally just, whether written or unwritten.

Equity and True Justice

It's clear that Aristotle realized judging—and therefore living—is a messy business; nevertheless, humanity must be entrusted with the grave responsibility of both. And so Aristotle offers the conception of equity: People must continually attempt to grasp the *truly* just. Sometimes laws can be too harsh. Sometimes punishments can be too severe. When these are the case, equity must step in. In fact, Aristotle defines equity as "the sort of justice which goes beyond the written law" (1374a). Equity brings universal laws into play in a situation in which the written law doesn't suffice.

Here is a little more on equity, according to Aristotle:

> Equity must be applied to forgivable actions; and it must make us distinguish between criminal acts on the one hand, and errors of judgment, or misfortunes, on the other. . . . Equity bids us be merciful to the weakness of human nature; to think less about the laws than about the man who framed them, and less about what he said than about what he meant; not to consider the actions of the accused so much as his intentions; nor this or that detail so much as the whole story; to ask not what a man is now but what he has always or usually been. (1374b)

What does this look like in the real world? Imagine a scenario in which two men have stolen food from a local grocery store. If one of the men has been in and out of trouble with the law from his teen years, the courts may let the full weight of the law fall upon him, for his theft is predictable, the next misdeed in a sequence of behavior. If, however, the other man has always been a law-abiding citizen, but has fallen on hard times—he's lost his job, lost his home—the misdeed will likely get a lighter sentence. After all, the first seems to be living out a pattern of immorality, while the second is breaking from a pattern of moral behavior.

When a written law punishes too severely, equity steps in to soften the blow. And when a written law compromises the unwritten law that stands behind it, legal justice can be revealed as incomplete. These are not examples of sophistry, which tries to make the weak argument appear stronger and thus dupe the jury. They are examples of the practice of *jurisprudence*—opportunities for the jury to weigh legal justice against natural justice. In this exercise, they can begin to see their city against the background of universal goods. In doing so, they can try to manifest those truths in the here and now.

This weighty responsibility is at the heart of our justice system. How is it that lawyers take cases? As for defense attorneys, must they believe their client is innocent? Must prosecutors take only those cases in which they firmly believe the defendant is guilty? Or can a lawyer's faith simply be in "the system" itself, believing that the strongest cases on both sides should result in the best judgments? Furthermore, is personal justice the same thing as political justice? In other words, could the guilty be unjustly exonerated, and yet justice be served for society as a whole?

These are tough questions and not to be settled easily. Aristotle, you will notice, does not let the rhetor off the hook when it comes to personal responsibility. He offers his wisdom on rhetoric not as a foolproof method for perfect decisions and a perfect society, but as a way to engage the issues more wisely than those issues would otherwise be handled. It's not a case of easy answers or perfect clarity; his inexact definitions and incomplete articulations suggest as much. It is the messy business of trying to live prudently, erring on one side of the mean this time, the other side the next, ever hoping for a more faithful alignment of reality and signs.

What does this mean to you as a beginning rhetor? It means that you are not allowed to argue as a sophist, one who attempts to win cases at any cost and with no regard for justice. Rather, justice—a full, robust justice that deals with the entire situation—is your goal. First, you must take into account particular law: Was a written law broken? You must also take into account universal law: What fundamental human principles are here in play? Finally, you must take into account equity: Would true justice call for the full weight of the particular law, or is mercy the appropriate response in this case?

To summarize, the action of judicial rhetoric is to accuse and defend; its focus is on the *past*, and it is based upon *justice*.

Discussion Text:[3]

Sir Thomas More: "Judges to My Condemnation" (1535)[3]

Focus:

Judicial Rhetoric[4]

The lawyer Sir Thomas More (1478–1535) became personal adviser to King Henry VIII and was eventually promoted to become Lord High Chancellor of England. It was a position of which he would eventually ask to be relieved, as his relationship with the king became strained. Desiring an annulment from Catherine of Aragon, his first wife, Henry declared himself to be the Supreme Head of the Church of England, a declaration to which More, a devout Catholic, would not publicly assent. Because he could not be convicted if he did not explicitly deny the King's claim, More wisely maintained silence on the matter. Solicitor General Richard Rich then testified that in a conversation between them More had denied the King's supremacy. More was imprisoned in the Tower of England and charged with high treason. At his beheading, More offered these words.

> If I were a man (my Lords) that did not regard an oath, I need not (as it is well known) in this place, at this time, nor in this case to stand as an accused person. And if this oath of yours (Mr. Rich) be true, then pray I that I may never see God in the face, which I would not say, were it otherwise, to win the whole world. . . .
>
> In faith, Mr. Rich, I am sorrier for your perjury than for mine own peril, and you shall understand that neither I, nor no man else to my knowledge ever took you to be a man of such credit as in any matter of importance I, or any other would at any time vouchsafe to communicate with you. And (as you know) of no small while I have been acquainted with you and your conversation, who have known you from your youth hitherto. For we long dwelled both in one parish together, where, as yourself can tell (I am sorry you compel me so to say) you were esteemed very light of your tongue, a great dicer, and of not commendable fame. And so in your house at the Temple (where hath been your chief bringing up) were you likewise accounted. Can it therefore seem likely unto your honourable Lordships, that I would, in so weighty a cause, so far overshoot myself, as to trust Mr. Rich (a man of me always reputed for one of so little truth, as your Lordships have heard) so far above my sovereign Lord the King, or any of his noble councillors, that I would unto him utter the secrets of my conscience touching the King's supremacy, the special point and only mark at my hands so long sought for?
>
> A thing which I never did, nor never would, after the Statute thereof made, reveal it, either to the King's Highness himself, or to any of his honourable councillors, as it is not unknown unto your house, at sundry times, and several, sent from his Grace's own person unto the Tower to me for none other purpose. Can this in your judgments (my Lords) seems likely to be true? And if I had so done indeed, my Lords, as Mr. Rich hath sworn, seeing it was spoke but in familiar secret talk, nothing affirming, and only in putting of cases, without other displeasant circumstances, it cannot justly be taken to be spoken maliciously. And

3. William Roper, *The Life of Sir Thomas More, Famous Trials*, University of Missouri–Kansas City Law School, http://law2.umkc.edu/faculty/projects/ftrials/more/morebiography.html. This work is in the public domain. I have excerpted the speech from Roper's narrative and have added paragraphing where helpful.
4. Another fine (but very long) text for discussion of judicial rhetoric is Socrates's speech of defense in Plato's *Apology*. Benjamin Jowett's translation is available online.

where there is no malice there can be no offence. And over this I can never think (my Lords) that so many worthy bishops, so many honourable personages, and many other worshipful, virtuous, wise, and well-learned men, as at the making of that law were in the Parliament assembled, ever meant to have any man punished by death, in whom there could be found no malice, taking *malitia pro malevolentia*. For if *malitia* be generally taken for sin, no man is there then that can thereof excuse himself. *Quia si dixerimus quod peccatum non habemus, nosmetipsos seducimus, et veritas in nobis non est.* [If we say we have no sin, we deceive ourselves and the truth is not in us.] And only this word *maliciously* is in the Statute material, as this term *forcible* is in the statute of forcible entries; by which statute if a man enter peaceably, and put not his adversary out forcibly, it is no offence, but if he put him out forcibly, then by that statute it is an offence. And so shall he be punished by this term *forcible*.

Besides this, the manifold goodness of my sovereign Lord the King's Highness himself that hath been so many ways my singular good Lord and Gracious Sovereign, that hath so dearly loved me, and trusted me even at my first coming into his noble service with the dignity of his honourable Privy Council, vouchsafing to admit me to offices of great credit, and worship most liberally advanced me, and finally with that weighty room of his Grace's high Chancellorship (the like whereof he never did to temporal men before) next to his own royal person the highest officer in this noble realm, so far above my merits or qualities able and meet therefore, of his incomparable benignity honoured and exalted me by the space of twenty years and more, showing his continual favour towards me; and (until, at mine own poor suit, it pleased his Highness, giving me licence, with his Majesty's favour, to bestow the residue of my life wholly for the provision of my soul in the service of God, of his special goodness thereof to discharge and unburden me) most benignly heaped honours more and more upon me; all this his Highness' goodness, I say, so long continued towards me, were, in my mind (my Lords), matter sufficient to convince this slanderous surmise (by this man) so wrongfully imagined against me. . . .

Forasmuch as, my Lord, this indictment is grounded upon an Act of Parliament, directly oppugnant to the laws of God and his holy Church, the supreme government of which, or of any part thereof, may no temporal prince presume by any law to take upon him as rightfully belonging to the See of Rome, a spiritual pre-eminence by the mouth of our Saviour himself, personally present upon the earth, to St. Peter and his successors, bishops of the same see, by special prerogative, granted, it is therefore in law amongst Christian men insufficient to charge any Christian. . . .

More have I not to say (my Lords) but like as the blessed Apostle St. Paul, as we read in the Acts of the Apostles, was present, and consented to the death of St. Stephen, and kept their clothes that stoned him to death, and yet be they now both twain holy saints in heaven, and shall continue there friends for ever, so I verily trust and shall therefore right heartily pray, that though your Lordships have now in earth been judges to my condemnation, we may yet hereafter in heaven merrily all meet together to our everlasting salvation.

Discussion Questions

"Judges to My Condemnation"

1. More begins by establishing his *ethos*. What does he say about his own character?

2. More then attacks the character of Master Rich. Which aspects of *ethos* (moral virtue, practical wisdom, and goodwill) does Master Rich lack?

3. More's first argument is of unlikelihood: It makes no sense that he would have freely shared his private thoughts with a person so "light of tongue" as Master Rich. ("Can it therefore seem likely . . . ") Turn this thinking into an enthymeme.

4. His second argument is that, even if he had done so, it would not have been done maliciously. He then says that "where there is no malice, there can be no offense." What is the particular law at stake, and to what contrary universal law is More appealing? How is More seeking to soften judgment by appealing to equity?

5. More then describes the king's esteem of him over the years. What is More's reason for doing so?

How does More further establish *ethos* in the last paragraph? In his analogy, who is St. Stephen, and who is St. Paul? How does this analogy further strengthen his case?

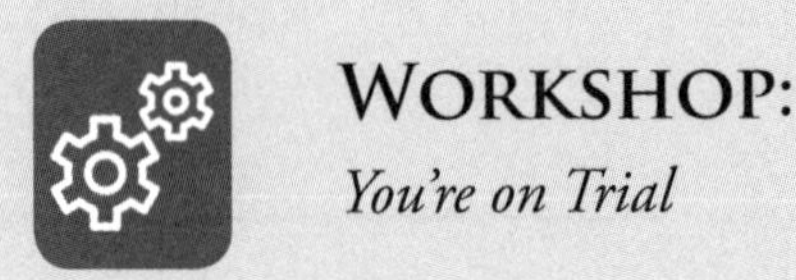

Workshop:
You're on Trial

For this activity, you must imagine that you have been charged with a misdeed. Your job is to defend yourself against the charge by using the stasis points.

First, write down an accusation on a slip of paper. Here are some examples:

You cut in line during lunch.

You were late for curfew.

You copied someone else's paper for a homework assignment.

You were chewing gum during class.

You stole a lady's grocery cart at the grocery store.

The accusations of the class should then be scrambled, and you will randomly draw an accusation and defend yourself against it. (If you draw your own, draw again!)

Your defense should be made using Aristotle's four stasis points discussed in chapter 7. The four he gives us are the following: whether something happened (fact), whether it is harmful (harm), whether it is significant (importance), and whether it is just (justice). You must choose one, and only one, of the four stasis points and write a short defense against the accusation using that one issue of stasis.

For example, against the charge of stealing a lady's grocery cart at the grocery store, you may decide to defend yourself based upon the harmfulness (harm) of the action. In this case, you would not be arguing that it didn't happen (fact), but instead that you were not actually harming but rather helping the woman—perhaps you saw that the grocery cart was damaged and would have caused her to fall.

Once you have written your stasis argument, flip the paper over and try something totally different. Defend yourself based upon universal law. That is, you can admit that you committed this harmful, unjust, and important misdeed, but you did so to uphold a universal law. Back to the grocery cart example: Yes, you stole the grocery cart, but you did so because your father just had a heart attack. You were unable to carry him, but you could wheel him in the grocery cart over to the car. In this case, you are upholding the universal law that upholds human life.

PRESENTATION:
Mock Trial: Giant vs. Jack *(2016)*[5]

SPOTLIGHT
Putting It All Together

The following is a mock trial script that will take about forty-five minutes (one class period) to perform. (This script was written especially for this text, but others are available online. For example, see <http://capress.link/ra11301>. Unscripted cases are also available for more advanced students to write their own scripts.)

CHARACTERS

Bailiff

Judge

Plaintiff Lead Counsel

Mr. Giant: Carl, the giant

Mrs. Giant: Brunhilda, the giant's wife

Defense Lead Counsel

Philip Bailey: Bean seller

Jack

Jury

Jury Foreperson

Bailiff. All rise! (*All in courtroom stand.*)

Bailiff. The Honorable Judge [*choose a name*] presiding.

(Judge enters, sits; all are seated except Bailiff.)

Bailiff. Your Honor, today you will be hearing civil case 1009-94b, that of Mr. Giant versus Mr. Jack.

Judge. Thank you, Bailiff. I understand that this is a civil case to be tried today, one concerning the alleged theft of one goose by Mr. Jack, as well as his trespassing in a household and the destruction of property of one beanstalk. Mr. Giant will be acting as the Plaintiff, and Mr. Jack as Defendant. Defendant, how do you plead?

Jack, *stands.* I plead not guilty to all counts, Your Honor.

Judge. Thank you, you may be seated. (*Jack sits. Judge addresses Jury.*) Today you will be hearing many facts and opinions offered by both sides. It is your duty as our jury to determine the validity of each piece of testimony. At the end of the proceedings, you will determine the guilt or innocence of Mr. Jack on each count brought before you, separately. It is my job to rule on the lawfulness of each piece of evidence according to the laws of the land. Just as I am not to question your analysis of the testimony given, you are not to question my rulings in the legality of the evidence given. I would like to make one thing clear to you: Today we are not ruling on the criminal proceedings of the events that transpired around the day in question. You may have heard of the outcome of the criminal case

5. By Ridley Holmes, 2016. Used with permission.

brought against Mr. Jack by the state, specifically in the attempted murder via bean-stalk chopping; this lawsuit has already transpired and is of no concern to us today. We are charged only in examining the civil charges against Jack. Am I understood? (*Jury nods.*)

Good! Now we will begin. Counsel of the Plaintiff, have the two sides agreed upon a set of stipulated facts?

Plaintiff Lead Counsel. We have, Your Honor.

Judge. Please read them into the record.

Plaintiff Lead Counsel. Yes, Your Honor. Stipulated facts are as follows. One: Jack did, on the date of May twenty-fourth, climb a beanstalk into the clouds. Two: The property in the clouds, twenty-two-oh-two Cumulus Way, belonged to the giant and was attained lawfully and legally by purchase. The validity of the giant's purchase of this property will not be brought into question today. And three: The goose in question is indeed of great value and is imbued with mythical and unusual properties; these properties will not be discussed in court today.

Judge. Thank you, Counsel. Has the Plaintiff prepared an opening statement?

Plaintiff Lead Counsel. We have, Your Honor.

Judge. Proceed.

Plaintiff Lead Counsel. May it please the court. Ladies and gentlemen of the jury, today we have a case of a kind giant who simply wanted to be left alone. It was a Sunday afternoon, the day was hot, and my client, Mr. Giant, wished to recline on his large leather sofa and take a nap, as was in accordance with his usual schedule. Was this an unreasonable wish, ladies and gentlemen? Have we not all had a similar desire at one point or another? He wished for peace, but on that day, he didn't find it.

Now I want you to imagine you are in your house. You are in much the same position as Mr. Giant was—simply relaxing, simply being. You are completely comfortable because you are in your home. In your home, you are content. In your home, you are safe. Suddenly, you find an intruder has violated your sanctuary, has breached your place of safety, has encroached upon your right to comfort in the place that should be most comforting. It is in this position that Mr. Giant found himself on May twenty-fourth. He found himself in this distressing circumstance because Mr. Jack, the Defendant, decided to place his wishes above those of Mr. Giant and trespassed on Mr. Giant's property.

As if this dreadful atrocity weren't enough, the Defendant didn't stop there. Now that he had violated Mr. Giant's right to feel at ease in his own home, he decided he would violate Mr. Giant's right to property as well. He stole Mr. Giant's one prized possession—besides his leather couch, that is—his goose, his golden egg–laying goose. Not only was this Mr. Giant's sole source of income, it was one of his sole sources of companionship, two things the Defendant didn't think twice about stripping away. He then ran as Mr. Giant pleaded with him to slow down, simply wondering what reason Jack had for entering his home in the first place.

Finally, the Defendant insulted the giant one last time: He chopped down the giant's own beanstalk, destroying a possession of the already-victimized kindly Giant.

Now, don't let opposing counsel fool you today in court. They will attempt to demonize Mr. Giant, making all sorts of false claims and attempting to sway you against him. Don't let this smokescreen of lies cloud your judgment; this case is nothing more than Mr. Giant trying to right the wrong done to him by the Defendant. Find the Defendant liable. Thank you! (*sits*)

JUDGE. Thank you, Counsel! Defense, have you prepared an opening statement?

DEFENSE LEAD COUNSEL, *STANDS*. We have, Your Honor.

JUDGE. Proceed.

DEFENSE LEAD COUNSEL. May it please the court. Ladies and gentlemen of the court, this is a simple case of misunderstanding. Opposing counsel would like to point at my client and peg him as some sort of diabolical mastermind, out to strip Mr. Giant of all that he holds dear; the evidence we bring before you today, however, will show you just how wrong that interpretation is. We expect to demonstrate to you through testimony that Jack meant no harm to anyone on the day of May twenty-fourth! Just two days before the events at issue, Jack was charged by his mother with a task of trading in their cow for some means of sustenance. Young Jack did his best. Obedient boy that he was, he went out and found a buyer who promised him a gift of untold value: a goose that lays golden eggs. Jack thought that this would make his mother proud, he thought that they would never starve again, he thought that, with goose in hand, he could finally prove to the world that he was worth something. So he took the promise of the stranger and traded in his family's cow for a handful of magic beans and the hope that they would lead him to a treasure untold.

Jack planted the beans and, just as the salesman said, a great beanstalk grew to the sky. Jack climbed it, went about his business in claiming the reward promised to him, and found the goose. He simply picked it up and calmly walked toward his exit. Suddenly, hearing footsteps like thunderclaps, he found himself being chased by a giant! Now what would you do if you were chased by a giant? Jack knew he had done nothing wrong but ran for his life regardless. He was not scared of getting caught *as a thief*, ladies and gentleman; he was just plain scared—scared in general. Remember, he had no reason to suspect he had done anything wrong. He was just a boy trying to make his mother proud, claiming the goose that he had been promised and that he expected to find.

Don't let opposing counsel make this case any more than what it is: a simple misunderstanding. Jack hadn't committed a crime because he hadn't known of a crime, and by the law of the land, one cannot be guilty of a civil crime if they are unaware of it. Find the Defendant not guilty. Thank you!

JUDGE. Thank you, Counsel! As the Plaintiff has the burden of proof in today's case, they are to present their evidence first. Plaintiff Counsel, are you ready to proceed?

PLAINTIFF. We are, Your Honor. We would like to call Mrs. Giant to the stand.

(*Mrs. Giant approaches the witness stand and sits.*)

JUDGE. Mrs. Giant, do you solemnly swear to tell the truth, the whole truth, and nothing but the truth?

MRS. GIANT. Yes, Your Honor.

JUDGE. Proceed.

PLAINTIFF LEAD COUNSEL. Good afternoon! Please, introduce yourself to the court.

MRS. GIANT. Hello, I am Brunhilda Giant, née Largefellow. I live at twenty-two-oh-two Cumulus Way with my husband, Mr. Giant. I spend most of my days writing short stories about me and my tall husband. They don't sell very well, but we have never had any shortage of funds on which to live. Well, until recently, that is.

PLAINTIFF LEAD COUNSEL. You say "until recently." When did this situation change?

Mrs. Giant. On the afternoon of May twenty-fourth, our sole source of income (besides my writing) was stolen from us by Jack.

Defense Lead Counsel. Objection, Your Honor! This is testimony based upon hearsay. We expect this witness to testify that they heard from their spouse the proceedings of May twenty-fourth that concern my client and have no personal knowledge of the situation themselves. This means that this testimony is based upon an out-of-court statement and is being offered to prove my client's guilt, and therefore is inadmissible in today's proceedings.

Judge. Objection sustained. Court reporter, please strike the testimony pertaining to the raised objection. Jury, please ignore the stricken testimony. Counsel, you may proceed.

Plaintiff Lead Counsel. Mrs. Giant, speaking only based upon your personal observations and not upon what others may have told you, what source of income is now missing from your home?

Mrs. Giant. We are missing our pride and joy, our goose that lays golden eggs.

Plaintiff Lead Counsel. Were you present when this goose went missing?

Mrs. Giant. No, I was actually out doing yard work in the front of the house. Our yard clouds always need a little extra fluffing in the late spring.

Plaintiff Lead Counsel. Now I would like to ask you a few questions about your home. What would an individual see upon entrance to your household?

Mrs. Giant. Well, I suppose the first thing that they would see would be our welcome mat. Next, they would have to move through our anteroom, which has a table on which we keep all of the photos of our children—I do so miss them sometimes! All of them have gone off and found their own clouds to live on. Sometimes, I wish . . .

Defense Lead Counsel. Objection, Your Honor, the witness has launched into a narrative and is now wasting the court's time with irrelevant material.

Judge. I think you are quite right. Sustained. Mrs. Giant, please try to stay on topic.

Mrs. Giant. Yes, Your Honor.

Plaintiff Lead Counsel. In your opinion, would an individual who entered your home for the first time recognize it to be a home belonging to someone?

Mrs. Giant. Yes, I cannot see how they couldn't. We have all sorts of personal decorations all over the place. Anyone entering would know they were entering an occupied home.

Plaintiff Lead Counsel. Thank you! Your Honor, I have no more questions at this time. I pass the witness.

Defense Lead Counsel. May I cross-examine the witness?

Judge. You may.

Defense Lead Counsel. Good afternoon, Mrs. Giant. I would like to begin with discussing your husband's temperament. He is a man who is generally pretty kind?

Mrs. Giant. He is!

Defense Lead Counsel. He does his best to always keep his temper?

Mrs. Giant. Oh, yes! Always.

DEFENSE LEAD COUNSEL. But he can occasionally become irritable?

MRS. GIANT. I suppose you could say so.

DEFENSE LEAD COUNSEL. Mr. Giant favors a certain football team in New York, doesn't he?

MRS. GIANT. He sure does! He loves watching those boys play every Sunday.

DEFENSE LEAD COUNSEL. This particular Sunday, this team had an exhibition game scheduled?

MRS. GIANT. I think so, yes! I remember my husband watching it before I stepped outside.

DEFENSE LEAD COUNSEL. Whenever his team loses, your husband is liable to be very upset.

MRS. GIANT. He can be a bit moody after a loss, sure . . .

DEFENSE LEAD COUNSEL. His team lost that day, didn't they?

MRS. GIANT. Umm . . . yes, I think so.

DEFENSE LEAD COUNSEL. Another circumstance that could upset your husband would be being woken up from a nap?

MRS. GIANT. Yes, that is for sure! He does love his Sunday afternoon naps.

DEFENSE LEAD COUNSEL. So Mr. Jack came at a time when your husband's favorite team had lost and he had been woken up from a nap?

MRS. GIANT. I suppose so, yes.

DEFENSE LEAD COUNSEL. Based upon your experience, would it be unreasonable to assume that he would naturally be in a bad mood in such a situation?

MRS. GIANT. Well, I don't know what *you* mean by bad mood, but he could certainly be . . .

DEFENSE LEAD COUNSEL. Your Honor, I object that the witness has not answered my question and has become nonresponsive.

JUDGE. Sustained. Answer the question.

DEFENSE LEAD COUNSEL. I'll ask again: Would your husband be in a bad mood in this situation?

MRS. GIANT. Yes, I suppose it is reasonable to assume that.

DEFENSE LEAD COUNSEL. Thank you. Finally, I would like to inquire regarding a beanstalk. You and your husband didn't own a beanstalk, did you?

MRS. GIANT. No, we did not.

DEFENSE LEAD COUNSEL. It would be incorrect to say that any beanstalk connecting to your street was your property?

MRS. GIANT. Well, I'm not sure what is correct or not, but I certainly don't think we ever had one installed on our dime, and it didn't come in the papers regarding the house purchase as far as I know.

DEFENSE LEAD COUNSEL. Thank you! I pass the witness.

JUDGE. Mrs. Giant, you may step down. (*Mrs. Giant steps down from witness stand.*) Plaintiff Counsel, do you wish to call any other witnesses?

PLAINTIFF LEAD COUNSEL. Yes, Your Honor. At this time we would like to call Mr. Giant to the stand.

(*MR. Giant takes the stand and is sworn in.*)

PLAINTIFF LEAD COUNSEL. Good afternoon. Please introduce yourself.

Mr. Giant. Hello, I'm Carl Giant. I live at twenty-two-oh-two Cumulus Way with my wife, Brunhilda. I have four children, but none of them live with us now.

Plaintiff Lead Counsel. Let's talk about the events of May twenty-fourth. What did you do that day?

Mr. Giant. Well, let's see. I started off that day making breakfast for my wife and me. I think it was scrambled eggs and bacon. It takes rather a lot to feed us, so I was sure to buy three sides of pork and about a couple dozen eggs for the meal. After that, I settled in to watch some football.

Plaintiff Lead Counsel. Do you have a favorite team?

Mr. Giant. Yeah, I love to keep up with a certain team from New York. I just really feel an unspoken connection to them for some reason. They lost that day, though. It was a heartbreaker.

Plaintiff Lead Counsel. What happened next?

Mr. Giant. Well, after that, I didn't much feel like moving, so I settled in on my couch for a nap.

Plaintiff Lead Counsel. Were you awoken?

Mr. Giant. I sure was! I had been napping for some time when I heard some movement below me. I tried to ignore it, and it went away after a while. I figured it was some rat or something running around, and it sounded like it had gone into the next room, which to my napping brain sounded like it was a problem for later.

Plaintiff Lead Counsel. What is kept in the next room?

Mr. Giant. That's where Brunhilda and I keep our golden egg–laying goose.

Plaintiff Lead Counsel. Did the noise return?

Mr. Giant. Yes, a few minutes later I heard the footsteps again. Except this time, there was some loud panting accompanying it, so I decided—and it was a hard decision to make—that I'd better check it out.

Plaintiff Lead Counsel. What happened next?

Mr. Giant. I got off the couch, looked at the ground, and saw a boy running away with my goose!

Plaintiff Lead Counsel. What did you do?

Mr. Giant. I tried asking him nicely to slow down and talk to me, but he just took off running! I walked after him, beseeching him to slow down and trying to find out what he was doing with my goose!

Plaintiff Lead Counsel. Where did he go?

Mr. Giant. He ran out the front door, and I followed him. He ran out behind the house and started climbing down this huge green beanstalk that had attached itself to the back of my home. I followed him.

Plaintiff Lead Counsel. What happened after you two had both descended the beanstalk?

Mr. Giant. I had almost made it to the bottom when he reached the bottom, brandished an ax, and starting chopping away at my beanstalk!

Plaintiff Lead Counsel. Did he destroy it?

Mr. Giant. Yes, and then I fell the remaining distance. I was briefly incapacitated, and he got away.

Plaintiff Lead Counsel. Thank you. No more questions at this time.

Judge. Defense, you may proceed with your cross-examination.

Defense Lead Counsel. Good afternoon. Let's talk about the neighborhood around your home on Cumulus Way. It is, in fact, in the clouds, isn't it?

Mr. Giant. Correct.

Defense Lead Counsel. Now, would you say that most humans believe giants to be fictitious?

Plaintiff Lead Counsel. Objection, Your Honor! Opposing counsel is asking my witness to speculate as to what most humans believe, and speculation is inadmissible by a lay witness.

Defense Lead Counsel. Your Honor, if I may respond, the witness may answer if he knows. I am not asking him to speculate.

Judge. Fair enough. Mr. Giant, you do not have to answer the question if you do not know the answer. Objection overruled.

Mr. Giant. Yes, most humans believe giants to be fictitious. We like it that way; it keeps the hoodlums out of our neighborhood.

Defense Lead Counsel. So, if a human were to find out for the first time that giants existed, they might be pretty startled?

Mr. Giant. Well . . . I suppose so, yes.

Defense Lead Counsel. They might be frightened, even?

Mr. Giant. I guess so, maybe.

Defense Lead Counsel. So frightened they might run?

Mr. Giant. It's possible.

Defense Lead Counsel. Thank you! I have just one more question about this running. You say that you were merely chasing Jack to take back your property, but isn't it true that you were thinking of something else, Mr. Giant?

Mr. Giant. What do you mean?

Defense Lead Counsel, *hands Mr. Giant a document*. Do you recognize this, Mr. Giant? It is your fact statement. Is this your signature on this document?

Mr. Giant. Yes.

Defense Lead Counsel. And is this the correct date?

Mr. Giant. Yes.

Defense Lead Counsel. I have here a sworn testimony. Your Honor, I would like to offer it into evidence. "Fee-fi-fo-fum, I smell the blood of an Englishman." Do you recall saying those words as you chased Jack, Mr. Giant?

Mr. Giant. I may have said that. So?

Defense Lead Counsel. And did you not follow it with, "Be he alive or be he dead, I'll grind his bones to make my bread"?

Mr. Giant. No, I would never have said that! But even if I had said it, I don't mean nothing by it. It's what all us Giants say when we get worked up—you know, a kind of family tradition. I don't even like bread. I'm a meat-and-potatoes kind of guy.

Defense Lead Counsel. Now let's talk about the beanstalk. You do not, in fact, own the beanstalk, do you, Mr. Giant?

Mr. Giant. It was connected to my house, I think that makes it mine.

Defense Lead Counsel. But you did not purchase it?

Mr. Giant. No.

Defense Lead Counsel. Never claimed it before?

Mr. Giant. No.

Defense Lead Counsel. In fact, you had never even seen the beanstalk prior to May twenty-fourth?

Mr. Giant. That is correct.

Defense Lead Counsel. And yet you are here in court today claiming that Jack owes you money for the damages caused to the beanstalk?

Mr. Giant. Uhhh . . . yes.

Defense Lead Counsel. No more questions. I pass the witness.

Judge. Thank you. You may step down. (*Mr. Giant steps down.*) Does the Plaintiff have any more witnesses?

Plaintiff Lead Counsel. No, Your Honor. At this time, the Plaintiff rests.

Judge. Good. Alright, the Defense may begin their case in chief. Defense Counsel, do you have a first witness you would like to call?

Defense Lead Counsel. Yes, Your Honor. We would like to call Philip Bailey to the stand.

(*Philip Bailey approaches stand, is sworn in, and sits down.*)

Defense Lead Counsel. Good afternoon! Please introduce yourself to the court.

Philip Bailey. My name is Philip Bailey. I am a traveling salesman of sorts. I live out the back of my sales wagon.

Defense Lead Counsel. What brings you to court today?

Philip Bailey. Frankly, a subpoena. I had no desire to testify today but was informed that if I didn't, I would be put in prison. I chose the lesser of two evils.

Defense Lead Counsel. Why did you wish not to testify?

Philip Bailey. Well, normally after I sell in a town for a few days, I try to move on pretty quickly. I have found that not being present greatly cuts down on the number of conversations I have to have with disgruntled customers who feel that I have wronged them.

Defense Lead Counsel. Why do customers feel that you have wronged them?

Philip Bailey. In my store, I sell a number of curiosities. Although I never lie about the results that my wares will yield, some customers find that they are surprised by the means through which those results are yielded. What can I say? I always get the job done.

Defense Lead Counsel. So let's talk about Jack. Around the twenty-second of May, you sold something to him, didn't you?

PHILIP BAILEY. Ah, yes! The boy had a lovely cow for which I wished to barter! Polite boy, although he did seem a bit confused in general.

DEFENSE LEAD COUNSEL. What did you give the boy in return for his cow?

PHILIP BAILEY. Well, from what I gathered from the boy—

PLAINTIFF LEAD COUNSEL. Objection, Your Honor, the witness is testifying to hearsay. He intends to testify based upon an out-of-court statement.

DEFENSE LEAD COUNSEL. Your Honor, while this is indeed an out-of-court statement, it is not hearsay because it is not being offered to prove the truth of the matter asserted. We expect the witness to testify that Jack said that he and his mother were financially poor, and this is not a matter at issue today in court.

JUDGE. Overruled. Please continue, Mr. Bailey.

PHILIP BAILEY. Like I was saying, the boy said that he and his mother were a bit down on their luck, so I sold him a means of income.

DEFENSE LEAD COUNSEL. What did you sell him?

PHILIP BAILEY. I sold him a handful of magic beans, which I told him would grant him the means to acquire a golden egg–laying goose.

DEFENSE LEAD COUNSEL. Did you say anything regarding a giant?

PHILIP BAILEY. No, I didn't consider that information pertinent. The boy wanted money; I gave him a path to something valuable. I fulfilled my end of the trade.

DEFENSE LEAD COUNSEL. Thank you! No further questions.

PLAINTIFF LEAD COUNSEL. We have no need to cross-examine the witness.

JUDGE. In that case, you may step down, Mr. Bailey. Defense, do you have another witness?

DEFENSE LEAD COUNSEL. Yes, Your Honor. We would like to call the Defendant, Mr. Jack, to the stand.

(*Jack approaches, is sworn in, and sits down.*)

DEFENSE LEAD COUNSEL. Please, introduce yourself to the court.

JACK. I am Jack. I live with my mother in a small cottage—although we are thinking about upgrading as of late.

DEFENSE LEAD COUNSEL. Let's get right to it. Did you recognize Mr. Bailey when he testified a few minutes ago?

JACK. I sure did. He was that salesman who caused me to sneak into a giant's castle without knowing it!

DEFENSE LEAD COUNSEL. What do you mean by that?

JACK. Well, he sold me what I thought were the rights to a goose that lays golden eggs. When I tried to claim what was rightfully mine, I was chased by a giant!

DEFENSE LEAD COUNSEL. Did you think that you were stealing when you claimed the goose?

JACK. No, not at all. It hadn't been indicated to me in the least that it belonged to someone else.

DEFENSE LEAD COUNSEL. Now let's talk about the product the salesman gave you. What was it?

JACK. A handful of magical beans. He said they would grow into a beanstalk.

Defense Lead Counsel. Did they?

Jack. Yes, they did! It was that beanstalk that grew and took me to what I later learned was the giant's castle.

Defense Lead Counsel. Did you rightfully own this beanstalk?

Jack. I sure did. I bought the beans and planted them myself; it was my beanstalk.

Defense Lead Counsel. So what happened after you planted the beans?

Jack. Like I said, they grew into a huge beanstalk.

Defense Lead Counsel. What happened next?

Jack. Well, on May twenty-fourth, I climbed it to get my goose.

Defense Lead Counsel. Where did it lead you?

Jack. I followed it into this huge structure. It was so big, I didn't quite know what to think of it! I thought it was some sort of warehouse.

Defense Lead Counsel. What happened next?

Jack. I kind of wandered through it, listening for goose noises, I guess. I heard something that sounded like the wind coming in long bursts from atop a huge leather structure, but the whole ordeal made me kind of antsy, so I wasn't much in the mood for investigating.

Defense Lead Counsel. Did you find the goose?

Jack. Yes, after the room with the strange noises, I went into a room to find the goose perched on what looked like a huge doggy bed. It was larger than a normal goose, but not so large I couldn't carry it, so I grabbed it and started to make my way back to the beanstalk.

Defense Lead Counsel. Did you make it back safely?

Jack. In the next room, I guess you could say I found out what the leather structure and the weird noises were. The goose I was carrying made a pretty loud squawk as I walked past, and that awoke the resident of the thing that I now knew was a gigantic couch.

Defense Lead Counsel. Could you identify the individual from the couch?

Jack. Sure, he's sitting right over there. (*points at Mr. Giant*)

Defense Lead Counsel. What happened after you two saw each other?

Jack. He started chasing me! I was already so shocked by seeing a giant—I always thought they were a myth—and when he started yelling and running, that was enough. I grabbed my goose and ran.

Defense Lead Counsel. What was the giant yelling?

Plaintiff Lead Counsel. Objection, Your Honor, question calls for hearsay.

Defense Lead Counsel. If I may respond, Your Honor, this is not hearsay as it is an admission by a party opponent.

Judge. Overruled. Continue.

Jack. The giant seemed a bit disoriented—apparently he had been awoken from his nap—but he was yelling things like "Fee-fi-fo-fum" and "That's mine" and "We just had too many turnovers in the second half." I didn't quite know what it all meant . . . and really didn't want to stay and find out.

DEFENSE LEAD COUNSEL. Did you know that the goose you had taken was someone else's property?

JACK. No, I had no idea. The salesman had promised it to me and said nothing about having to steal for it.

DEFENSE LEAD COUNSEL. No further questions. I pass the witness.

JUDGE. Do you have a cross-examination, Counsel?

PLAINTIFF LEAD COUNSEL. Yes, Your Honor. May I proceed?

JUDGE. Go ahead.

PLAINTIFF LEAD COUNSEL. Good afternoon, Jack. Let's talk about the home into which you entered. You claim you didn't know this was a home?

JACK. That's right.

PLAINTIFF LEAD COUNSEL. Did Mrs. Giant's testimony earlier surprise you, about the welcome mat?

JACK. Well, no . . . I guess I saw the welcome mat.

PLAINTIFF LEAD COUNSEL. Her testimony regarding pictures of her family also didn't surprise you, did it?

JACK. I guess not. I saw the pictures as well.

PLAINTIFF LEAD COUNSEL. Clearly these two things contribute to the notion that this space was a home?

JACK. I don't think so. I have seen offices with welcome mats and pictures on the wall.

PLAINTIFF LEAD COUNSEL. Regardless, you could have recognized this as a place owned by someone?

JACK. Well . . . yes.

PLAINTIFF LEAD COUNSEL. And if the space was owned by an entity, entering it without permission would be trespassing?

JACK. I suppose one could look at it that way, yes.

PLAINTIFF LEAD COUNSEL. On your direct examination, you testified that the giant was yelling, "That's mine!" at you as you ran away?

JACK. That's right, it was really scary!

PLAINTIFF LEAD COUNSEL. But you never stopped to consider that what you were doing was wrong?

JACK. A giant was chasing me; I didn't have time to stop!

PLAINTIFF LEAD COUNSEL. No further questions. I pass the witness.

JUDGE. Defense, do you have any more witnesses?

DEFENSE LEAD COUNSEL. No sir. At this time, the Defense rests.

JUDGE. Thank you. (*addresses the Jury*) The time has come for you to determine the culpability of Mr. Jack. In order for you to find him liable on any count, the Plaintiff must have proved to you by the preponderance of the evidence—meaning that you believe it is more likely than not—that he is culpable of that offense. This means that you only need to be fifty-one percent sure that Jack is culpable to convict him.

Remember, there are three separate counts brought before you today: First, on the day of May twenty-fourth, did the Defendant knowingly and willfully trespass on the Plaintiff's property? Second, on the day of May twenty-fourth, did the Defendant knowingly and willfully steal from the

Plaintiff? And third, on the day of May twenty-fourth, did the Defendant knowingly and willfully destroy the Plaintiff's property? Please inform me when you have made your decision.

(*Jury files out to confer. Members of the Jury should read the note that follows this trial script regarding the burden of proof and unanimity. The Jury should reach a decision (either "liable" or "not liable") on each of the three counts, and then they can reenter. Counsel and witnesses should stand as the Jury reenters.*)

Judge. The Foreperson of the Jury, please stand. Have you reached a verdict?

Jury Foreperson. We have, Your Honor.

Judge. The Defendant will please stand. (*Jack stands.*) You may read the verdict.

Jury Foreperson. On the charge of trespassing, we find the Defendant [*liable/not liable*]. On the charge of theft, we find him [*liable/not liable*]. And third, on the charge of the destruction of the Plaintiff's property, we find him [*liable/not liable*].

Judge. This court is now adjourned. Ladies and gentlemen of the jury, the state of [*the name of the state you live in*] appreciates your time and careful attention while serving on this case.

(*All rise as the Judge exits the courtroom.*)

Note: In our court system, there are different burdens of proof with which officers of the court are charged. For instance, if a police officer were to pull you over, they must have reasonable suspicion that you were in violation of a crime. For a jury to find someone guilty in a criminal case, the lawyers must show "beyond a reasonable doubt" that the person is guilty. In a civil case such as this, the burden of proof is called "preponderance of the evidence." Preponderance of the evidence means that the jury must believe it is more likely than not that the defendant committed the crime. This means that if jury members were mostly convinced—even just 51 percent sure—that he did it, but 49 percent sure he didn't, then they could still convict him. Another illustration used is that of the scales of justice: In order to convict in a civil case, the scales must be tipped only slightly toward guilty. In other words, the jury should know that they don't have to be 100 percent convinced and completely positive that Jack committed a crime in order to convict him; they just have to find it more likely than not that he did.

The jury must confer amongst themselves. In some states, civil trials require a unanimous verdict, but others require only a majority. Decide which will be required in this case; perhaps you will follow the rules of your particular state. Jurors vote on each of the three counts separately, based on whether they believe it is more likely Jack did it, and find him liable, or more likely that he didn't, and find him not liable.

This case is called a bifurcated trial, which is one where only Jack's liability (what could be considered his innocence or guilt) is at issue. If he were determined liable, then another separate trial would be conducted to determine what he owed the giant.

Discussion Questions

Giant vs. Jack

1. During the performance/reading of these scripts, look for and note any instances when an attempt is made to "soften judgment" by appealing to some aspect of universal law.

2. Do you note any occasions in which a prosecutor or defense attorney sought to present an understanding of (a) why someone may have committed a wrong, (b) what type of person committed the wrong, and/or (c) the kind of person who was wronged?

3. Do you note any occasions in which a prosecutor or defense attorney made an appeal to deliberate, voluntary choice?

4. Think back on Aristotle's seven reasons people commit wrongs: chance, nature, compulsion, habit, reasoning, anger, or appetite. Why do you think Jack took the goose? Also, if Jack did take the goose willingly (that is, not by accident), did Jack desire a good or a pleasure?

5. Recall that Aristotle claims that harming a bad person seems "fine and pleasant . . . as though almost no wrong were done" (1373a). How might this civil case play upon that idea?

5 Section

Rhetoric Gone Wrong

First, the good news: *We humans are innately logical.* This means you don't need a formal course in logic to figure out that a fallacy has darted across the rhetorical path. Now, the bad news: *We humans are innately lazy.* That means, even though we can often intuit when something doesn't make sense, we don't always spot it outright. Instead, we let words fly fast and loose in our speech. Sometimes, we even do so purposefully, for less than noble reasons.

Attention to bad reasoning, then, is in order. When you know just what a fallacy is, you're less likely to commit it. And if you can point out a fallacy in your opponent's argument, then you not only weaken that argument, you remove it altogether.

14

Chapter 14

Fallacies and Sophistry: Spotting Bad Arguments

Formal Fallacies

If you are reading this book on rhetoric, it is likely that you have also taken a course or two in logic. (By the way, if you haven't taken a course or two in logic, studying logic should be your very next step. A rhetor without a strong grounding in logic is dangerous!) Thus, this chapter will not rehearse the ins and outs of the syllogism. Suffice it to say, by way of reminder, syllogisms can be valid—in the correct form, meaning the logic is lined up—or invalid—in an incorrect form, leaving a disconnect in the chain of reasoning.[1] The latter are fallacies of form; the form of their logical setup is disordered. For this reason, we call them **formal fallacies**.

Enthymemes (see chapter 4), which are made by abbreviating those syllogisms, can be good or bad (valid or invalid), too. If a rhetor were to shorten a syllogism, and the audience were to grant the statement's truth, it would be because the audience knows enough to fill in the missing premise. The point here is that reasoning in rhetorical situations—unlike the careful reasoning of dialectic—does not move meticulously through every minute point of an argument. Instead, like one hopping across a creek from stone to stone, this type of reasoning covers a lot of territory quickly, in leaps and bounds.

Of course, skipping and hopping are more dangerous than walking, which is why an abbreviated syllogism can cause more problems than a full one—errors are that much more likely to occur. Studying logic in depth is extremely helpful because it is handy to be able to name those frequent errors in judgment and to practice avoiding them. But slowing down and paying attention works wonders, too. For example, whether you've had a course in logic or not, you'll notice something wrong with the following statement:

My porch is wet, so it must have rained.

The reason this enthymeme isn't valid is because any number of reasons could cause a wet porch, not just rain: Someone might have just watered the plants, or there

1. A **valid syllogism** is one in which the conclusion necessarily follows from the premises. In other words, if the syllogism's premises are true, then a valid syllogism will have a conclusion that *must* be true also. Here's one example of the 24 valid forms of the 256 possible ways of constructing a categorical syllogism:

All A are B.
All B are C.
Therefore, all A are C.

Fill it in with true premises, and you have a **sound argument**. A *sound* argument is one with a *valid* form and true premises.

All men are mortal.
I am a man.
Therefore, I am mortal.

could be a leaky spigot on the porch. If we were to plot this enthymeme as a syllogism, it would look like this:

> *If it rains, then* ***my porch is wet.***
> ***My porch is wet.***
> *Therefore, it rained.*

This is the fallacy of **affirming the consequent**. Now, it would be perfectly fine to say it in reverse: *It rained, so my porch is wet*. Notice the different syllogism:

> *If* ***it rains,*** *then my porch will be wet.*
> ***It rained.***
> *Therefore, my porch is wet.*

Notice that, in the case of this valid syllogism, the antecedent—the statement attached to the if-then clause—is the one that is affirmed. Even if you can't recall the technical terms for this fallacy, you should still be able to intuit that this form is correct.

Here's another fallacy. See if you can spot it in the following enthymeme:

> *It didn't rain, so my porch isn't wet.*

Again, here is the entire syllogism in its complete form. Notice the "not" in the second statement:

> *If* ***it rains,*** *then my porch is wet.*
> ***It didn't rain.***
> *Therefore, my porch isn't wet.*

The problem in this case is that, again, there are other ways my porch could get wet, so **denying the antecedent** is a bad move, too. (This statement could be validly rendered by denying the consequent: *My porch isn't wet, so it didn't rain.*)

A final fallacy of form we should review is the **undistributed middle**. But, again, you may not remember the technical name and yet still realize something has gone wrong in the following statement:

> *All Jainist followers are vegetarians.*
> *Caroline is a vegetarian.*
> *Therefore, Caroline is a Jainist follower.*

This conclusion clearly does not follow because no necessary overlap between the categories of "Jainist followers" and "Caroline" exists. Take a look at figure 29, which demonstrates the faulty argument.

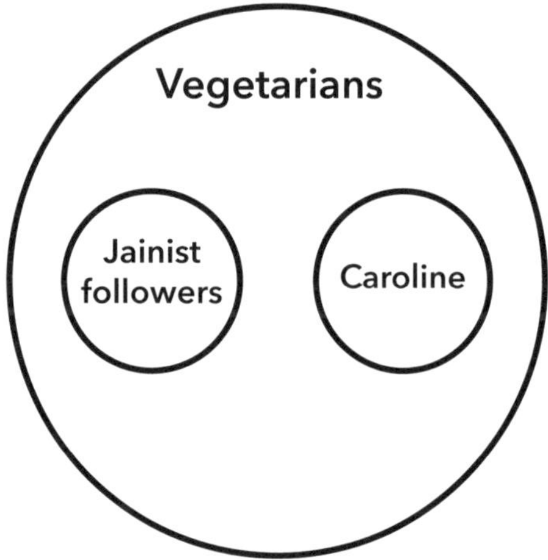

Figure 29. Relationship of the undistributed middle.

If we wanted to prove Caroline was a Jainist follower, we would need to create a connection—an overlap—between the terms "Caroline" and "Jainist follower" with a chain of reasoning such as the following:

> *All Jainist followers are vegetarian.*
> *Caroline is a Jainist follower.*
> *Therefore, Caroline is a vegetarian.*

See figure 30 as a diagram for this valid syllogism.

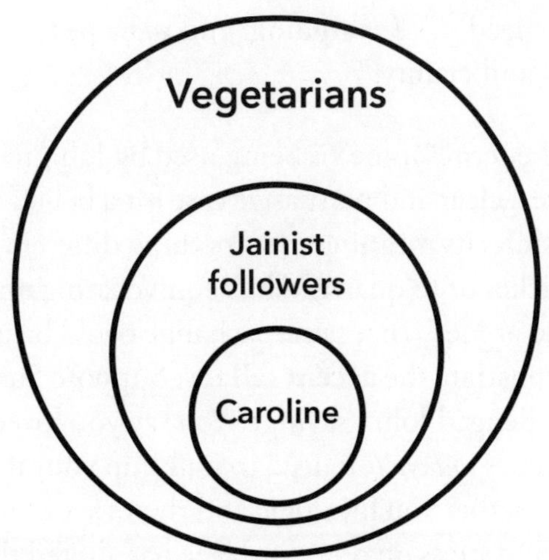

Figure 30. Relationship of the distributed middle.

Informal Fallacies

The aforementioned examples are called formal fallacies, meaning that the problem lies in their logical setup, or form. But there is another kind: **informal fallacies**. Informal fallacies can be divided into three groups: relevance, presumption, and clarity. Here's how *The Art of Argument* puts it: "Simply put, this means that when people reason badly, they may err in one of three basic directions: they can make points that just don't relate to the issue (irrelevancy), they can make assumptions that are not justified or necessary (presumption), or they can use language that confuses or muddies the argument (clarity)."[2] Let's look at a few examples from each category.

Determining exactly what you are talking about is the very first step in an argument. **Fallacies of relevance**, however, distract from the real issue at hand. Fallacies of relevance include unwarranted appeals to emotion such as fear and pity (known by their Latin names *ad baculum* and *ad misericordium*, respectively). Fear and pity are fine emotions and may be a necessary part of certain arguments; a discussion of grave human rights violations would almost certainly involve an appeal to *pathos*, for example. But when used to deceive or distract, then these emotional appeals are fallacies. Another example of a fallacy of relevance is a form of peer pressure—*ad populum* ("to the people"). If someone is trying to convince you to do something just because *everybody else is doing it*, then that person is committing this fallacy. An *ad hominem* ("to the man") fallacy is an attack on the speaker rather than the argument itself.[3] A straw man argument exaggerates or misrepresents an argument so that it can more easily be defeated.[4] In a sense, all fallacies of relevance are species of red herring fallacies because they use diversionary tactics. They've earned this colorful name because of the alleged use of the smelly herring fish to throw hound dogs off a scent trail. Just as the distracting smell of the fish could mislead dogs from the scent they are following, so red herring arguments take up unrelated issues and mislead an audience from the argument they are following. Again, these are just some of the ways in which an argument can veer off topic. All of these fallacies come to light when you ask yourself, "Is this point relevant to the actual argument?"

Another way that arguments can go bad is by assuming more than they should; these are **fallacies of presumption**. If an argument rests upon an assumption that isn't warranted or is downright false, then the conclusion of that argument can't be rightfully established. The complex question (also known as a loaded question) is a great example of the fallacy of presumption because an extra premise is assumed and thus smuggled into the question itself. Here's an

2. One source for studying fallacies is the book *The Art of Argument: An Introduction to the Informal Fallacies*, by Aaron Larsen, Joelle Hodge, and Chris Perrin (Camp Hill, PA: Classical Academic Press, 2010); see esp. p. 5.

Chapter 14 of *Rhetoric Alive!* follows the format of *The Art of Argument*, which divides bad reasoning into fallacies of relevance, presumption, and clarity. (In this book, we explore only a handful of the twenty-eight fallacies presented in *The Art of Argument*.)

3. Example of an *ad hominem* in a disagreement about taxes: "Should we listen to the tax plan of a man who didn't attend his own wife's funeral?" (The person against the tax plan has attacked the opponent's character rather than the facts of the plan.)

4. Example of a straw man argument in a disagreement about taxes: "You are against a tax increase? So you want to bankrupt the government and drive us into an economic depression?" (The speaker has set up an exaggerated version of what the opponent is likely arguing.)

example of the complex question: *Have you stopped cheating on your schoolwork?* Of course, *Did you cheat on your schoolwork?* must first be answered before the question of stopping can be asked, but that assumption remains hidden. Another presumptive move is pretending that only two options are possible when there may be others; this is called the either-or fallacy (also known as bifurcation or false dilemma). *Either you marry Tom, or you remain forever single,* someone might say. But surely these possibilities are not exhaustive! You could, for example, marry Jim, or you might choose not to marry Tom now, but then marry him later, when you are both more mature. Finally, the hasty generalization is the fallacy of jumping to conclusions. To establish a conclusion firmly, you must have sufficient evidence for it, not just a single instance or small sample. It is true, for example, that a 112-year-old Nepalese woman named Batuli Lamichhane smokes thirty cigarettes a day. It would be a hasty generalization, however, to claim that she alone proves that smoking isn't actually unhealthy. These and the other fallacies of presumption come to the surface when a rhetor stops to ask the question, "What is simply being assumed in this argument?"

Finally, **fallacies of clarity** present major problems to fair argumentation. The problem here is that terms and ideas don't stay sharp or clearly distinguished. For example, sometimes a term is used in two different ways; this is called the fallacy of equivocation. Notice how the meaning of the word "argue" shifts in the following exchange.

> John: "I loved my logic and rhetoric classes today. I think they're going to help me think more clearly and argue better."
>
> Susan: "Why would you want to argue better? There is already enough hostility and mean-spiritedness everywhere. If there's anything we need, it's *less* arguing, and *more* peace and civility!"

The term "argue" is being used by John to mean to make a clear and persuasive case for a belief, but Susan shifts its meaning to something different, that is, to bicker or to quarrel. She's equivocating on the term "to argue." That same exchange could be used to demonstrate the **accent fallacy**. Suppose Susan had challenged John, saying, "You say you loved your classes *today*. You need to make up your mind about whether you like logic and rhetoric or not." By placing stress on one word, she has altered the meaning of his statement. As you can see, terms need to stay clearly defined once they are in play. Fallacies of clarity become visible when a rhetor stops to ask, "Is the issue at hand clearly understood?"

Again, this chapter is no substitute for a course in formal and informal logic. However, it is also true that our minds do work logically, so when a fallacy runs across the rhetorical trail, an attentive person should be able to sense something has gone wrong. Keeping alert to these three things in particular—relevance, presumption, and clarity—helps to reveal when the argument has started to go sour. Having a good argument means playing fair, with relevant proofs, no hidden assumptions, and clear terms.

Sophistry

Fallacies are not always intentional, of course. Sometimes they're the result of sloppy thinking, and sometimes it's simply difficult to keep the logic lined up when conversation is flying fast. As mentioned before, this is a major difference between rhetoric and dialectic. One may ponder and discuss philosophical ideas—the various aspects of the soul, or the nature of virtue—endlessly (this is dialectical conversation), never fully exhausting the subjects and never pushing to make a final judgment. But rhetoric is hemmed in by time and space: Decisions must be made, and they must be made now. If our city was attacked yesterday, then should we retaliate against the enemy today? If you must offer a toast at your friend's wedding on Saturday, what will you say? If you have just heard closing arguments concerning a person accused of theft, will you try to convince your fellow jury members to convict or to acquit? A judgment is required, and even the rhetor with the best of intentions can sometimes slip into a fallacy along the way.

Then again, sometimes the fallacies *are* intentional. Intentionally misleading arguments would be clear cases of sophistry. To repeat a definition used in chapter 1, rhetoric seeks to make the truth persuasive, but sophistry seeks to make the speaker persuasive.[5] In other words, a sophist has no concern for the truth; a sophist is concerned only with *winning the argument*. Whichever side he is on is the side he wishes to prevail.

How can one then distinguish the sophist from the rhetor? Is the sophist the one who uses emotional appeals? The speaker who ignores logic? The person most skillful at moving the audience to action? Aristotle says this: "What makes a man a 'sophist' is not his faculty, but his moral purpose" (1355b). In other words, Quintilian, who followed Aristotle by some four centuries, was right: The model rhetor is indeed the "good man speaking well." Such a person seeks to see both sides of the argument and then to assist the truth. The person who uses fallacies in order to deceive, who invokes emotion in order to manipulate, who employs figures of speech in order to seduce—this is the sophist. It is moral purpose—the intention and end goal, not the activity along the way—that distinguishes the rhetor from the sophist.

5. This is a paraphrase of Baldwin, *Ancient Rhetoric and Poetic*, 5, 247.

Discussion Text:
Gorgias of Leontini: Encomium of Helen *(1999)*[6]

Focus:
Sophistry

According to Greek myth, the Trojan War was waged because of one woman: Helen. Said to be the most beautiful woman in the world, Helen was taken from her home by Paris, a prince from Troy. Her husband Menelaus, king of Sparta, rallied Achaean (ancient Greek) forces and besieged Troy for ten years before the city finally fell. Is Helen to blame? The sophist Gorgias (c. 485–c. 380 BC) attempted to exonerate her in the following famous speech.

I

(1)[7] The order proper to a city-state is being well-manned; to a body, beauty; to a soul, wisdom; to a deed, excellence; and to a discourse, truth—and the opposites of these are disorder. And the praiseworthy man and woman and discourse and work and city-state and deed one must honor with praise, while one must assign blame to the unworthy—for it is equal error and ignorance to blame the praiseworthy and to praise the blameworthy. (2) It being required of the same man both to speak straight and to refute [crooked speech, one should refute] those blaming Helen, a woman concerning whom the testimony of those who are called poets has become univocal and unanimous—likewise the repute of her name, which has become a byword for calamities. And by bestowing some rationality on the discourse, I myself wish to absolve this ill-reputed woman from responsibility, and to show that those who blame her are lying—and, having shown the truth, to put an end to ignorance. (3) It is not unclear, not even to a few, that the woman who is the subject of this discourse was the foremost of the foremost men and women, by nature and by birth. For it is clear that her mother was Leda and her father was in fact the god, but said to be mortal, Tyndareus and Zeus—of whom the one, by being, seemed, while the other, by speech, was disproved—and the one was the mightiest of men while the other was tyrant over all.

(4) Born of such parentage, she had godlike beauty, which having received she not inconspicuously retained. She produced the greatest erotic desires in most men. For one body many bodies of men came together, men greatly purposing great things, of whom some possessed great wealth, some the glory of ancient and noble lineage, some the vigor of personal strength, and others the power of acquired cleverness. And they were all there together out of contentious love and unconquerable ambition. (5) Who it was, then, who fulfilled the love by gaining Helen, and the means and manner of it, I shall not say; for to tell knowing people things they know supplies corroboration but does not convey enjoyment. Having now finished the first section, I shall advance to the beginning of the next section, and I shall set out the causes through which Helen's journey to Troy was likely to come about.

6. Translated from the Greek by Brian R. Donovan (1999); see http://faculty.bemidjistate.edu/bdonovan/helen.html. Used by permission. The source text is that of H. Diels and W. Kranz, eds., *Die Fragmente der Vorsokratiker*, 6th ed., vol. 2 (Berlin: Weidmann, 1952, rpt. Dublin 1966), as reproduced on the *Thesaurus Linguae Graecae* CD ROM #D (1992 compilation by The Regents of the University of California).

7. The numbers in parentheses are original to Donovan's text.

II

(6) Either by the wishes of Fortune and plans of the gods and decrees of Necessity she did what she did, or abducted by force, or persuaded by speeches, <or conquered by Love>.[8] Now in the first case, the responsible party deserves the responsibility. For the will of a god cannot be hindered by human forethought. For it is not natural for the superior to be hindered by the inferior, but for the inferior to be ruled and led by the superior—for the superior to lead and the inferior to follow. And a god is superior to a human being in force, intelligence, etcetera. Accordingly, if one must attribute responsibility to Fortune and the god, one must acquit Helen of infamy.

(7) But if she was abducted by force, unlawfully constrained and unjustly victimized, it is clear on the one hand that the abductor, as victimizer, committed injustice—and on the other hand that the abductee, as victim, met with mishap. Accordingly the barbarian assailant deserves to meet with barbarous assault, by speech and custom and deed—deserves to be blamed in speech, dishonored by custom, and penalized indeed. She who was forced and bereft of fatherland and orphaned of friends—how is she not to be pitied rather than reviled? For *he* did terrible things; she was the victim; it is accordingly fair to pity her and hate him.

(8) And if persuasive discourse deceived her soul, it is not on that account difficult to defend her and absolve her of responsibility, thus: discourse is a great potentate, which by the smallest and most secret body accomplishes the most divine works; for it can stop fear and assuage pain and produce joy and make mercy abound. And I shall show that these things are so: (9) explanation to the audience, by means of opinion, is required. Discourse having meter I suppose and name (in the general sense) to be poetry. Fearful shuddering and tearful pity and sorrowful longing come upon those who hear it, and the soul experiences a peculiar feeling, on account of the words, at the good and bad fortunes of other people's affairs and bodies. But come, let me proceed from one section to another.

III

(10) By means of words, inspired incantations serve as bringers-on of pleasure and takers-off of pain. For the incantation's power, communicating with the soul's opinion, enchants and persuades and changes it, by trickery. Two distinct methods of trickery and magic are to be found: errors of soul, and deceptions of opinion. (11) Those who have persuaded and do persuade anyone about anything are shapers of lying discourse. For if all people possessed memory concerning all things past, and awareness of all things present, and foreknowledge of all things to come, discourse would not be similarly similar; hence it is not now easy to remember the past or consider the present or foretell the future; so that most people on most subjects furnish themselves with opinion as advisor to the soul. But opinion, being slippery and unsteady, surrounds those who rely on it with slippery and unsteady successes. (12) . . . For discourse was the persuader of the soul, which

8. Brackets (< >) throughout are present in original.

it persuaded and compelled to believe the things that were said and to agree to the things that were done. He who persuaded (as constrainer) did wrong; while she who was persuaded (as one constrained by means of the discourse) is wrongly blamed. (13) Persuasion belonging to discourse shapes the soul at will: witness, first, the discourses of the astronomers, who by setting aside one opinion and building up another in its stead make incredible and obscure things apparent to the eyes of opinion; second, the necessary debates in which one discourse, artfully written but not truthfully meant, delights and persuades a numerous crowd; and third, the competing arguments of the philosophers, in which speed of thought is shown off, as it renders changeable the credibility of an opinion. (14) The power of discourse stands in the same relation to the soul's organization as the pharmacopoeia does to the physiology of bodies. For just as different drugs draw off different humors from the body, and some put an end to disease and others to life, so too of discourses: some give pain, others delight, others terrify, others rouse the hearers to courage, and yet others by a certain vile persuasion drug and trick the soul.

IV

(15) It has been said that if she was persuaded by discourse, she did no wrong but rather was unfortunate; I proceed to the fourth cause in a fourth section. If it was love that brought all these things to pass, she escapes without difficulty from the blame for the sin alleged to have taken place. For the things we see do not have whatever nature we will, but rather that which befalls each. The soul receives an impression in its own ways through the sight. (16) For example, whenever hostile bodies put on their bronze and iron war-gear of ward and defense against enemies, if the visual sense beholds this, it is troubled and it troubles the soul, so that often panic-stricken men flee future danger <as if it were> present. For the strong habitual force of law is banished because of the fear prompted by the sight, which makes one heedless both of what is judged by custom to be admirable, and of the good that comes about by victory. (17) Some who have seen dreadful things have lost their presence of mind in the present time; thus fear extinguishes and drives out understanding. And many fall into useless troubles and terrible diseases and incurable dementias; thus sight engraves in the mind images of things seen. And the frightening ones, many of them, remain; and those that remain are just like things said. (18) But truly whenever the painters perfectly complete one body and figure from many colors and bodies, they delight the sight; and the making of statues and production of figurines furnishes a pleasant sight to the eyes. Thus it is in the nature of the visual sense to long for some things and for other things to give it pain. And in many there is produced much love and desire for many things and bodies. (19) Accordingly, if Helen's eye, taking pleasure in Alexander's body, transmitted to her soul the eagerness and struggle of Love, is it any wonder? If Love, <being> a god, <has> the divine power of gods, how could the weaker being have the power to reject this and to ward it off? But if it is a human disease and an error of the soul, it ought not to be blamed as a sin but ought rather to be accounted a misfortune. For she went, as she started out, in the clutches of fortune, not by plans of the mind; and by the constraints of love, not the preparations of art.

V

(20) How then is it necessary to regard as just the blame of Helen, who either passionately in love or persuaded by discourse or abducted by force or constrained by divine constraints did the things she did, escaping responsibility every way?

(21) By this discourse I have removed infamy from a woman; I have continued in the mode I established at the beginning. I tried to put an end to the injustice of blame and ignorance of opinion; I wanted to write the discourse, Helen's encomium and my plaything.

Discussion Questions

Encomium of Helen

1. What is the order proper to a discourse? (What is a discourse?)

2. Do you agree with the parallels Gorgias identifies in the city, the body, the soul, and the deed?

3. What has become the opinion of Helen? Whom does Gorgias blame for her reputation?

4. Why does Gorgias say that he will not name the man who won Helen's love (section 5)? Who did win her love?

5. The first possible cause of Helen's actions is really a group of related reasons, all of which may generally be called *fate*. Perhaps it was by Fortune, the gods, or Necessity. What are the three other possible causes of Helen's actions? (See section 6.)

6. What is Gorgias's vindication of Helen if her actions resulted from the "wishes of Fortune"? What is his logic here? (See section 6.)

7. What is the specific argument taken up in section 7? Do you see any problems in Gorgias's argument?

8. What about section 8? Is being *persuaded* the same as being *forced*? If there is a difference, what is it?

9. How does Gorgias explain the power of speech in section 9? Wherein does he say its power lies? To what does Gorgias liken speech's power? (See section 10.)

10. He ends section 12—much of it is lost to us (such a missing section of text is called a *lacuna*)—by returning to a familiar theme. What is it?

11. Gorgias finds an analog for discourse in "pharmacopoeia," or medicines. (See section 14.) Explain the analogy. Is it a convincing one?

12. In section 15, he turns now to the final cause. What is it?

13. What is his argument in sections 16–20?

____

____

____

____

____

14. Gorgias concludes his encomium in a strange way, one that makes us aware of his sophistry. What does he call Helen's encomium? How does this affect how you receive his speech?

____

____

____

____

____

Workshop:
Fashioning Fallacies

For this workshop, you will practice writing fallacies so that you can better recognize them in your own and in other people's arguments.

Choose a topic of some controversy. Easy options are hot topics in the media—for example, gun control, taxes—or something a little closer to home, such as the following issues:

- Our school *should/should not* adopt iPads in the classroom.
- Social media promotes *real/false* friendships.
- Students *should/should not* be allowed access to cell phones during the school day.

As a class, choose one topic and write it on the board. The teacher will randomly assign a fallacy to each student. Your job is to write a fallacy that supports one side of the argument. (Don't tell anyone else which fallacy you have been assigned.) You'll read your fallacy, and the rest of the class will try to identify it.

Example: Social media promotes *real/false* friendships.

So you're saying that people who are on social media are all losers and have no real friends?
(straw man)

When did you decide to abandon all of your real friendships for virtual ones?
(complex question)

If you aren't connected on social media, people at school will bully you. (*ad baculum*)

Presentation:
Fallacious Speeches

Spotlight
Putting It All Together

For this assignment, return to either the great speech excerpts from chapter 1 or the short speech you wrote for chapter 7. Using the fallacies of this chapter, create as many fallacious arguments as you can to support the argument of that address, and then insert them into the chosen speech. As you deliver the fallacious speech, the audience will try to spot your fallacies and keep track of them with the following checklist. Another option is to designate a "fallacy expert" for each fallacy by assigning one student to each. The student will be responsible for identifying that particular fallacy in each of the student speeches.

Remember to put into play all of the various aspects of delivery you have practiced so far—voice, posture, eye contact, and gestures.

Afterward, you should offer your thoughts on how the fallacies affected the address. Did it strengthen the reasoning or detract from it? How did you feel as a rhetor when offering what you knew to be bad reasoning? When you have a strong and well-written argument, do fallacies actually weaken its force? Finally, since you know that your audience is listening for bad reasoning, you were probably uncomfortable using it. Imagine if all speakers knew that the crowds to which they were speaking were trained in logic and could identify bad reasoning. Would it affect the kind of public discourse we hear today?

Note: We didn't cover all of the possible fallacies in this chapter. You may wish to add other fallacies with which you are familiar.

For each student's speech, use the fallacy checklist on page 328. As you hear different fallacies, place a check mark beside the type listed. In addition, write a brief description for each recorded fallacy from the speech.

Fallacy Checklist

- ❑ Affirming the consequent: ____________________
- ❑ Denying the antecedent: ____________________
- ❑ Undistributed middle: ____________________
- ❑ Fallacy of relevance
    - *ad baculum*: ____________________
    - *ad misericordium*: ____________________
    - *ad populum*: ____________________
    - *ad hominem*: ____________________
    - red herring: ____________________
    - straw man: ____________________
- ❑ Fallacy of presumption
    - complex question: ____________________
    - either-or: ____________________
    - hasty generalization: ____________________
- ❑ Fallacy of clarity
    - equivocation: ____________________
    - accent: ____________________

SECTION 6

A Brief Conclusion

A slick con man may not care whether the two of you agree on the nature of the good, or whether you share a commitment to the true and just. He just wants you to fork over your money or sign on the dotted line today. Similarly, the typical use of rhetoric aims at mere persuasion, not a long-term commitment to fostering good decision-making. But you must remember how different your project is from the typical use of rhetoric: You aim at truth, not mere persuasion. You seek to better your audience, not manipulate them. And you hope for a common good, not the self-interested good of a select few.

15

Chapter 15

Conclusion: The Good Student Speaking Well

Let's think back to Plato's allegory of the cave, which you discussed in chapter 1. Prisoners sit chained in a dark cave, forced to stare at a wall of shadows rather than real objects. But a prisoner escapes and ascends from the cave into the real world above—a picture of education. And indeed, your education prior to your formal study of rhetoric has probably been an attempt to get you out of the cave. It's been trying to unchain your arms and legs, to turn your head away from the shadows, to prod you to get up and exit the world in which you have grown up and have become so comfortable. Your education has been one of ascent.

Rhetoric is different. It is different because it is *not* urging you up and out of the cave but, rather, pushing you to reenter it.

Figure 31. Detail of *The School of Athens* by Raphael, fresco in the Apostolic Palace, Vatican City, 1509–1511. Courtesy of TTaylor, commons.wikimedia.org.

This difference between the two visions is depicted in Raphael's painting *The School of Athens*. Even at a glance, we can see an argument taking place between the two central characters: On the left is Plato, gesturing upward, and to his side is his pupil Aristotle, extending his arm outward. With the cave allegory in mind, we can imagine this as a disagreement about a person's aspirations or where one should reside: Should she be up above, with the forms of the True, the Good, and the Beautiful? Or should she be down below in the cave itself?

But their disagreement isn't merely one about location; it is also about language itself. Plato points a lone index finger skyward, signifying the solitary aim of philosophy—a

Truth that is absolute, certain, singular. Aristotle's gesture is openhanded and downward, signifying the plurality of contextualized goods—truths as they are discovered in context, right and good as they are known in this world. Aristotle might agree with Plato, that it's better to be up above in the realm of Truth—that is, capital *T* truth, which we can know with certainty—but he's also willing to admit that the vast majority of folks (maybe even *all* of them) deal in a world of lowercase *t* truths, or truths that can't very easily make definitive claims on everyone. If there is one thing that we can be certain of, it is that we will continue to struggle to agree, and thus, we will continue to need rhetoric.

With this, we can return to the opening line of Aristotle's *Rhetoric*: "Rhetoric is the counterpart [Greek, *antistrophos*] of dialectic" (1354a). Just as a line of harmony complements and resonates with a melody, so the *antistrophe* is the response to the *strophe* in ancient Greek choral. The former is dependent upon—indeed, is significant only inasmuch as it stands in relation to—the latter. That is, Aristotle is not arguing that rhetoric is better than dialectic, or that the tools of persuasion are better than the tools of philosophy. Rather, he is claiming that, just as harmony complements melody, so rhetoric complements philosophy. Together they sing, so to speak, the song of the city.

And so Aristotle offers a solution to the ancient quarrel between philosophy and rhetoric: They are counterparts. The careful work of truth-seeking, of exiting the cave, is vital. And as for those important truths that need to be manifested within the cave, it is the rhetor's art that will make those known. To study rhetoric, then, is to reenter the cave—not that you would plop back down where you once were chained and passively take in the shadows, of course. Instead you must now be one who uses speech wisely and justly. In other words, you need to become what Quintilian called an "ideal rhetor": a good person speaking well.

Some might say, "Sounds hard! Why not just sit back and enjoy the shadow show?" But the question is not whether you *will* be a rhetor—you already *are* one. As one who uses language, you are already influencing others. In *The Ethics of Rhetoric*, Richard Weaver says it this way:

> And accordingly the right to utter a sentence is one of the very greatest liberties, and we are to wonder that freedom of utterance should be, in every society, one of the most contentious and ill-defined rights. The liberty to impose this formal unity is a liberty to handle the world, to remake it, if only a little, and to hand it to others in a shape that may influence their actions. . . . The changes wrought by sentences are changes in the world rather than in the physical earth, but it is to be remembered that changes in the world bring about changes in the earth.[1]

Weaver's claim is that all of our speech is speech of influence. The mere uttering of a sentence takes the chaotic phenomena of our lives and organizes it into digestible data. A simple statement such as "What a beautiful day!" presents an argument about the world, one that potentially wields influence on its hearer.

Like it or not, you shape other people's beliefs and lives, mostly via speech. The real issue is your purpose. Do you use speech as a tool to get what you want? Then you are at risk of becoming a sophist. But if you employ speech as a way of working toward a common good, you are a true rhetor, a friend to the city. Since we all use language, we are all casting shadows. Better to study and practice the

1. Richard M. Weaver, *The Ethics of Rhetoric* (Davis, CA: Hermagoras, 1953), 119.

art of doing so—the art of rhetoric—in order that you do so well and with virtue.

Revealing how we can practice rhetoric without doing violence to the audience members—instead, even helping them to flourish—this is the project of Aristotle's *Rhetoric*. We have reason to be wary, for language is powerful and the public good is riding on it. Therefore, the stakes are high—almost paralyzing. But to remain silent is no option. For as much as language is abused, it is also our only civic means of access to the True, the Beautiful, and the Good.

Appendix

Sample Subject Summary

During this course, you will explore the art of rhetoric both in great speeches and in great writing. Aristotle's *Rhetoric* provides a scaffold for the course. The first weeks of the course are devoted to the three rhetorical appeals: *ethos*, *pathos*, and *logos*. You will then examine and practice the five canons of rhetoric: invention, organization, style, memory, and delivery. Finally, you'll conclude by learning about the three genres of rhetoric: deliberative, epideictic, and judicial.

Sample Syllabus: Rhetoric I—Principles of Persuasion

Although it is ubiquitous, rhetoric has not always been reputable. The sophists of the fifth century BC earned a bad name for rhetoric, and the Western world has been grappling with both its value and its dangers ever since.

The art—it is one of the three traditional language arts—has also been variously defined. Taking a cue from the pre-Socratic Greek philosopher Zeno, we might picture rhetoric as an open hand, whereas dialectic ("logic") may be portrayed as a closed fist. Plato, who compared rhetoric to the falsifying effects of makeup or cookery, in a more generous moment also called it the *art of soul-leading through language*. Aristotle's definition is more technical: Rhetoric is "the faculty of observing in any given case the available means of persuasion" (1355b). Other thinkers have offered their own definitions:

Rhetoric is . . .

> . . . that art or talent by which the discourse is adapted to its end.
>
> —George Campbell

> . . . that powerful instrument of error and deceit.
>
> —John Locke

> . . . wisdom, ornately and copiously delivered in words appropriate to the common opinion of mankind.
>
> —Giambattista Vico

> . . . the art of efficient communication by language.
>
> —Adams Sherman Hill

> . . . the use of words by human agents to form attitudes or to induce actions in other human agents.
>
> —Kenneth Burke

> . . . the study of misunderstanding and its remedies.
>
> —I.A. Richards

> . . . passionate, partisan discourse.
>
> —Stanley Fish

> . . . an art of emphasis embodying an order of desire.
>
> —Richard Weaver

Aristotle and his definition will be your guide in this course, and you will step through his *Rhetoric* in your attempt to become better rhetors yourselves. Of course, the goal is to become the ideal orator, Quintilian's "good [hu]man speaking well" (*vir bonus dicendi peritus*).

Policies and Procedures

(*as determined*)

Textbook

Rhetoric Alive! Book 1: Principles of Persuasion. Camp Hill, PA: Classical Academic Press, 2016.

Schedule

Week 1	(Chapter 1)	Introduction to rhetoric
Week 2	(Chapter 2)	**The Three Appeals:** *Ethos*
Week 3	(Chapter 3)	*Pathos*
Week 4	(Chapter 4)	*Logos* in the enthymeme
Week 5	(Chapter 5)	More on *Logos*
Week 6	(Chapter 6)	**The Five Canons:** Invention
Week 7	(Chapter 7)	Organization
Week 8	(Chapter 8)	Style
Week 9	(Chapter 9)	Memory
Week 10	*Review for and take midterm exam*	
Week 11	(Chapter 10)	Delivery
Week 12	(Chapter 11)	**The Three Species:** Deliberative rhetoric
Week 13	(Chapter 12)	Epideictic rhetoric
Week 14	(Chapter 13)	Judicial rhetoric
Week 15	(Chapter 14)	Fallacies and sophistry
Week 16	(Chapter 15 / Optional)	Prepare final speech project
Week 17	(Optional)	Prepare and deliver final speech project
Week 18	*Review for and take final exam*	

The following is a recommended format for a weekly teaching schedule:

Monday: Reading of excerpt from Aristotle's *Rhetoric* and *Rhetoric Alive! Book 1* text

Tuesday: Quiz covering material from the previous week, plus exploration of current week's discussion text (exemplary text demonstrating the week's focus)

Wednesday: Workshop

Thursday: Workshop, plus student presentations

Friday: Student presentations

Grading:

50%	Quizzes
25%	Presentations
25%	Homework/Classwork

Please sign below to indicate that you understand and agree to these policies:

____

Day-by-Day Schedule (one semester)

Week 1

Day 1: Chapter reading
Read and discuss chapter 1.

Day 2: Discussion text
Read and discuss Plato's allegory of the cave.

Day 3: Workshop
Complete and present the "Magazine Ad" workshop.

Day 4: Presentation preparation
Choose, prepare, and practice one of the speech excerpts from chapter 1.

Day 5: Presentation
Deliver the speech excerpt.

Week 2

Day 6: Chapter reading
Read and discuss chapter 2.

Day 7: Discussion text
Read and discuss "A Faithful Friend to the Army" address by George Washington.

Day 8: Workshop
Complete the "Just Trust Me!" workshop, the college application essay, or "The Rhetoric of E-Mail" assignment.

Day 9: Presentation preparation
Complete another one of the three workshops and practice another speech excerpt from chapter 1.

Day 10: Presentation
Deliver the speech excerpt.

Week 3

Day 11: Chapter reading
Read and discuss chapter 3.

Day 12: Discussion text
Read and discuss the excerpt from *Julius Caesar*, act 3, scene 2.

Day 13: Workshop
Complete the "Conjuring the Emotions" workshop.

Day 14: Presentation preparation
Prepare and practice the poetry recitation.

Day 15: Presentation
Deliver the poetry recitation.

Week 4

Day 16: Chapter reading
Read and discuss chapter 4.

Day 17: Discussion text
Read and discuss the "Give Me Liberty or Give Me Death!" address by Patrick Henry.

Day 18: Workshop
Fashion enthymemes in workshop 1.

Day 19: Presentation preparation
Choose and prepare a book for Read Aloud Story Time. Compete in workshop 2, "Fill in the Enthymeme Competition."

Day 20: Presentation
Read stories aloud to younger students.

Week 5

Day 21: Chapter reading
Read and discuss chapter 5.

Day 22: Discussion text
Read and discuss excerpt from Plato's *Phaedrus*.

Day 23: Workshop
Complete either "A Duel between Maxims" or the Emily Dickinson *Imitatio* workshop.

Day 24: Presentation preparation
Complete the "Writing a Fable" workshop in preparation for presentation.

Day 25: Presentation
Deliver the school board address.

Week 6

Day 26: Chapter reading
Read and discuss chapter 6.

Day 27: Discussion text
Read and discuss "Letter from Birmingham City Jail" by Martin Luther King, Jr.

Day 28: Workshop
Play "Commonplace Competitions."

Day 29: Presentation preparation
Prepare and practice "Mr. Gorbachev, Tear Down This Wall!" selection.

Day 30: Presentation
Deliver selection from Ronald Reagan's "Mr. Gorbachev, Tear Down this Wall!" speech.

Week 7

Day 31: Chapter reading
Read and discuss chapter 7.

Day 32: Discussion text
Read and discuss Martin Luther King, Jr.'s "Letter from Birmingham City Jail" or participate in the "Organizing Emily Dickinson" activity.

Day 33: Workshop
Complete the "Ordering an Essay" workshop.

Day 34: Presentation preparation
Prepare for the presentation using the "Organization Scramble" workshop.

Day 35: Presentation
Deliver the "Argument Sampler" speech.

Week 8

Day 36: Chapter reading
Read and discuss chapter 8.

Day 37: Discussion text
Read and discuss the "Ask Not What Your Country Can Do for You" address by John F. Kennedy.

Day 38: Workshop
Complete one of the following workshops: "Figures of Speech Match-Up," "Stylish Sentences," or "Figures of Speech Dress-Up."

Day 39: Presentation preparation
Rewrite a chosen fairy tale for presentation.

Day 40: Presentation
Deliver the "Fairy Tale Retold" story.

Week 9

Day 41: Chapter reading
Read and discuss chapter 9.

Day 42: Discussion text
Read and discuss Augustine's *Confessions* excerpt.

Day 43: Workshop
Complete one of the "Memory Palace" activities.

Day 44: Presentation preparation
Prepare the memory palace for poetry recitation.

Day 45: Presentation
Deliver the poetry recitation.

Week 10

Day 46: Catch up on any missing work.

Day 47: Review the three appeals.

Day 48: Review the first four of the five canons.

Day 49: Prepare for the midterm exam.

Day 50: Take the midterm exam.

Week 11

Day 51: Chapter reading
Read and discuss chapter 10.

Day 52: Discussion text
Read and discuss "A Talk about Giving a Talk" by John Hilton.

Day 53: Workshop
Complete the "Liar! Liar!" activity.

Day 54: Presentation preparation
Prepare and practice a Shakespearean soliloquy or monologue.

Day 55: Presentation
Deliver the chosen soliloquy or monologue.

Week 12

Day 56: Chapter reading
Read and discuss chapter 11.

Day 57: Discussion text
Read and discuss Winston Churchill's "Blood, Toil, Tears, and Sweat" or "A Day That Will Live in Infamy" by FDR.

Day 58: Workshop
Complete the "Sales Pitch Grab Bag" activity.

Day 59: Presentation preparation
Prepare and practice the "Great Speech *Imitatio*."

Day 60: Presentation
Deliver "Great Speech *Imitatio*."

Week 13

Day 61: Chapter reading
Read and discuss chapter 12.

Day 62: Discussion text
Read and discuss "They Were Worthy of Athens" by Pericles.

Day 63: Discussion text
Read and discuss "Duty, Honor, Country" by General Douglas MacArthur.

Day 64: Workshop/presentation preparation
Write the tribute *imitatio* and/or *imitatio* of "Duty, Honor, Country."

Day 65: Presentation
Deliver the tribute *imitatio* and/or *imitatio* of "Duty, Honor, Country."

Week 14

Day 66: Chapter reading
Read and discuss chapter 13.

Day 67: Discussion text
Read and discuss "Judges to My Condemnation" by Sir Thomas More.

Day 68: Workshop
Complete the "You're on Trial" activity.

Day 69: Presentation
Begin the mock trial.

Day 70: Presentation
Conclude and discuss the mock trial.

Week 15

Day 71: Chapter reading
Read and discuss chapter 14.

Day 72: Discussion text
Read and discuss *Encomium of Helen* by Gorgias.

Day 73: Workshop
Complete the "Fashioning Fallacies" activity.

Day 74: Presentation
Prepare and practice the "Fallacious Speeches" presentation.

Day 75: Presentation
Present the fallacious speech.

Week 16

Day 76: Chapter reading
Read and discuss chapter 15.

Days 77–80: Optional capstone project

Week 17

Days 80–85: Optional capstone project
(continued)

Week 18

Day 86: Review the three appeals.

Day 87: Review the five canons.

Day 88: Review the three species.

Day 89: Review fallacies.

Day 90: Take final exam.

*Free Day suggested activity: Watch and rhetorically analyze a live or recorded speech.

Two-Semester Schedule

One way to use this textbook over the course of an entire year is to complete all of the workshop activities and deliver all of the possible presentations. Another option is to study one chapter a week, followed by a week of putting that idea into practice—either for a stand-alone rhetoric writing/speaking assignment or as an assignment for another subject, such as English or history.

A further possibility is to study rhetoric throughout the year but only two or three times per week. In this case, simply divide the activities into the chapter and discussion text one week, followed by workshops and presentations the following week.

Chapter Presentations and Delivery Spotlights

Chapter	Spotlight
Chapter 1: Great Speech Excerpt	Voice
Chapter 2: Great Speech Excerpt	Voice
Chapter 3: Poetry Recitation	Posture
Chapter 4: Read Aloud Story Time	Audience Engagement
Chapter 5: School Board Address	Eye Contact
Chapter 6: "Mr. Gorbachev, Tear Down This Wall!"	Eye Contact
Chapter 7: Argument Sampler	Organized Delivery
Chapter 8: Fairy Tale Retold	Fidgeting
Chapter 9: Recitation	Memory
Chapter 10: Shakespearean Soliloquies and Monologues	Gestures
Chapter 11: Great Speech *Imitatio*	Putting It All Together
Chapter 12: *Imitatio* of "Duty, Honor, Country"	Putting It All Together
Chapter 13: Mock Trial: *Giant vs. Jack* (2016)	Putting It All Together
Chapter 14: Fallacious Speeches	Putting It All Together

Chapter 1 Presentation Rubric: *Great Speech Excerpt* | Spotlight *Voice*

Name: ______________________________

Title of Speech: ______________________________

In order to focus solely upon vocal delivery, audience members should have their eyes closed.

Volume: Was the rhetor loud enough?

Clarity: Did the rhetor clearly pronounce the words?

Rhythm: Did the rhetor speed up or slow down at the right times?

Did the rhetor make use of at least two dramatic pauses for emphasis?

Please mark your overall rating of this speech:

Needs work	Isocrates's student[1] *(average)*	Cicero[2] *(good)*	Demosthenes[3] *(excellent)*

In classical times when Cicero had finished speaking,
the people said, "How well he spoke!"
but when Demosthenes had finished speaking,
they said, "Let us march!"

—Adlai E. Stevenson II, 1960[4]

1. Isocrates (not to be confused with Socrates) was a celebrated teacher of rhetoric in Greece.
2. Cicero was Ancient Rome's most illustrious rhetor.
3. Demosthenes was a renowned Greek rhetor. According to Plutarch, Demosthenes trained himself as an rhetor, even overcoming a speech impediment in his youth. Legend has it that he built himself an underground room to practice his rhetorical skills. He is said to have practiced recitation with pebbles in his mouth in order to perfect his pronunciation and to have shaved half of his head so as not to be tempted to go out into public until he had mastered the craft.
4. Adlai Stevenson II said this when introducing John F. Kennedy in 1960, as quoted in *Adlai Stevenson and The World: The Life of Adlai E. Stevenson* by John Bartlow Martin (New York: Doubleday, 1977), 549.

Chapter 2 Presentation Rubric: *Great Speech Excerpt* | Spotlight *Voice*

Name: ______________________________

Title of Speech: ______________________________

In order to focus solely upon vocal delivery, audience members should have their eyes closed.

Volume: Was the rhetor loud enough?

Clarity: Did the rhetor clearly pronounce the words?

Rhythm: Did the rhetor speed up or slow down at the right times?

Did the rhetor make use of at least two dramatic pauses for emphasis?

Please mark your overall rating of this speech:

Needs work	Isocrates's student *(average)*	Cicero *(good)*	Demosthenes *(excellent)*

In classical times when Cicero had finished speaking,
the people said, "How well he spoke!"
but when Demosthenes had finished speaking,
they said, "Let us march!"

—Adlai E. Stevenson II, 1960

Chapter 3 Presentation Rubric: *Poetry Recitation*

Spotlight: *Posture*

Name: ______________________________

Title of Speech: ______________________________

Emotion(s) in the Passage: ______________________________

Volume: Was the rhetor loud enough?

Was the volume varied and interesting?

Were certain words emphasized to bring the text to life?

Clarity: Did the rhetor clearly pronounce the words?

Rhythm: Did the rhetor speed up or slow down at the right times?

Did the rhetor make use of at least two dramatic pauses for emphasis?

Believability: Did the rhetor appear to feel the emotion he or she was trying to convey?

Posture: Did the rhetor stand upright (no slumping), without crossing legs and without rocking?

Please mark your overall rating of this speech:

Needs work	Isocrates's student *(average)*	Cicero *(good)*	Demosthenes *(excellent)*

In classical times when Cicero had finished speaking,
the people said, "How well he spoke!"
but when Demosthenes had finished speaking,
they said, "Let us march!"

—Adlai E. Stevenson II, 1960

CHAPTER 4 PRESENTATION RUBRIC: *Read Aloud Story Time* | SPOTLIGHT *Audience Engagement*

Name: ______________________________

Title of Story: ______________________________

Friendliness: Did the reader greet the child in a welcoming and approachable way?

Organization: Did the reader announce the title, author, and illustrator of the story?

Did the reader conclude with eye contact, closing questions, and a "goodbye"?

Interesting delivery: Was the reading loud, clear, and varied?

Did the reader speed up and slow down to bring the story to life?

Did the reader use different voices for different characters?

Please mark your overall rating of this speech:

Needs work	Isocrates's student *(average)*	Cicero *(good)*	Demosthenes *(excellent)*

In classical times when Cicero had finished speaking,
the people said, "How well he spoke!"
but when Demosthenes had finished speaking,
they said, "Let us march!"

—Adlai E. Stevenson II, 1960

Chapter 5 Presentation Rubric: *School Board Address* | Spotlight *Eye Contact*

Name: ____

Imagining that your peers represent your school's board of directors, present your address written for the "School Board Address" workshop. For this address, focus on eye contact. You should make eye contact across the room, holding your gaze with each person for about two seconds before moving on to another member of the audience.

Volume: Was the rhetor loud enough?

Was the volume varied and interesting?

Were certain words emphasized to bring the text to life?

Clarity: Did the rhetor clearly pronounce the words?

Rhythm: Did the rhetor speed up or slow down at the right times?

Did the rhetor make use of at least two dramatic pauses for emphasis?

Believability: Did the rhetor appear to feel the emotion he or she was trying to convey?

Posture: Did the rhetor stand upright (no slumping), without crossing legs and without rocking?

Eye Contact: Did the rhetor make sustained eye contact around the room?

Please mark your overall rating of this speech:

Needs work	Isocrates's student *(average)*	Cicero *(good)*	Demosthenes *(excellent)*

In classical times when Cicero had finished speaking,
the people said, "How well he spoke!"
but when Demosthenes had finished speaking,
they said, "Let us march!"

—Adlai E. Stevenson II, 1960

Chapter 6 Presentation Rubric: *"Mr. Gorbachev, Tear Down this Wall!"* | Spotlight *Eye Contact*

Name: ____

For this address, you will again focus on eye contact. You should make eye contact across the room, holding your gaze for about two seconds before moving on to another member of the audience.

Volume: Was the rhetor loud enough?

Was the volume varied and interesting?

Were certain words emphasized to bring the text to life?

Clarity: Did the rhetor clearly pronounce the words?

Rhythm: Did the rhetor speed up or slow down at the right times?

Did the rhetor make use of at least two dramatic pauses for emphasis?

Believability: Did the rhetor appear to feel the emotion he or she was trying to convey?

Posture: Did the rhetor stand upright (no slumping), without crossing legs and without rocking?

Eye Contact: Did the rhetor make sustained eye contact around the room?

Please mark your overall rating of this speech:

Needs work	Isocrates's student *(average)*	Cicero *(good)*	Demosthenes *(excellent)*

> In classical times when Cicero had finished speaking,
> the people said, "How well he spoke!"
> but when Demosthenes had finished speaking,
> they said, "Let us march!"
>
> —Adlai E. Stevenson II, 1960

Chapter 7 Presentation Rubric: *Argument Sampler* | Spotlight *Organized Delivery*

Name: ______________________________

***Exordium*:** Does the opening arrest the audience's attention and introduce the subject?

***Narratio*:** Does the speaker give the context for the issue at hand, showing why this subject is important here and now?

***Partitio*:** Is an outline of the major points offered?

Do all of the above establish the speaker's *ethos*?

***Confirmatio*:** Are logical proofs presented that support the speaker's argument?

***Refutatio*:** Does the speaker address counterarguments from the opposition?

Does the middle section establish *logos*?

***Peroratio*:** Does the speaker restate the major points, leave a good personal impression, and call the audience to action?

Does the conclusion evoke *pathos*?

Please mark your overall rating of this speech:

Needs work	Isocrates's student *(average)*	Cicero *(good)*	Demosthenes *(excellent)*

> In classical times when Cicero had finished speaking,
> the people said, "How well he spoke!"
> but when Demosthenes had finished speaking,
> they said, "Let us march!"
>
> —Adlai E. Stevenson II, 1960

Chapter 8 Presentation Rubric: *Fairy Tale Retold* | Spotlight *Fidgeting*

Name: ____

Volume: Was the rhetor loud enough?

Was the volume varied and interesting?

Were certain words emphasized to bring the text to life?

Clarity: Did the rhetor clearly pronounce the words?

Rhythm: Did the rhetor speed up or slow down at the right times?

Did the rhetor make use of at least two dramatic pauses for emphasis?

Believability: Did the rhetor appear to feel the emotion he or she was trying to convey?

Posture: Did the rhetor stand upright (no slumping), without crossing legs and without rocking?

Eye Contact: Did the rhetor make sustained eye contact around the room?

Fidgeting: Did the rhetor keep hands free from nervous movement (e.g., tapping on the podium, playing with sleeves)?

Please mark your overall rating of this speech:

Needs work	Isocrates's student *(average)*	Cicero *(good)*	Demosthenes *(excellent)*

In classical times when Cicero had finished speaking,
the people said, "How well he spoke!"
but when Demosthenes had finished speaking,
they said, "Let us march!"

—Adlai E. Stevenson II, 1960

Chapter 9 Presentation Rubric: *Recitation* | Spotlight *Memory*

Name: ______________________________

Poem: ______________________________

Volume: Was the rhetor loud enough?

Was the volume varied and interesting?

Were certain words emphasized to bring the text to life?

Clarity: Did the rhetor clearly pronounce the words?

Rhythm: Did the rhetor speed up or slow down at the right times?

Did the rhetor make use of at least two dramatic pauses for emphasis?

Believability: Did the rhetor appear to feel the emotion he or she was trying to convey?

Posture: Did the rhetor stand upright (no slumping), without crossing legs and without rocking?

Eye Contact: Did the rhetor make sustained eye contact around the room?

Fidgeting: Did the rhetor keep hands free from nervous movement (e.g., tapping on the podium, playing with sleeves)?

Memory: Did the rhetor fully memorize and fluidly deliver the poem?

Please mark your overall rating of this speech:

Needs work	Isocrates's student *(average)*	Cicero *(good)*	Demosthenes *(excellent)*

In classical times when Cicero had finished speaking,
the people said, "How well he spoke!"
but when Demosthenes had finished speaking,
they said, "Let us march!"

—Adlai E. Stevenson II, 1960

Chapter 10 Presentation Rubric: *Shakespearean Soliloquies and Monologues* | Spotlight *Gestures*

Name: ______________________________

Soliloquy/Monologue: ______________________________

Volume: Was the rhetor loud enough?

Was the volume varied and interesting?

Were certain words emphasized to bring the text to life?

Clarity: Did the rhetor clearly pronounce the words?

Rhythm: Did the rhetor speed up or slow down at the right times?

Did the rhetor make use of at least two dramatic pauses for emphasis?

Believability: Did the rhetor appear to feel the emotion he or she was trying to convey?

Posture: Did the rhetor stand upright (no slumping), without crossing legs and without rocking?

Eye Contact: Did the rhetor make sustained eye contact around the room?

Fidgeting: Did the rhetor keep hands free from nervous movement (e.g., tapping on the podium, playing with sleeves)?

Memory: Was the rhetor clearly familiar with his or her lines, and did he or she deliver them fluidly?

Gestures: Were various types of gestures used throughout the recitation?

Was it interesting to watch as well as to hear?

Please mark your overall rating of this speech:

Needs work	Isocrates's student *(average)*	Cicero *(good)*	Demosthenes *(excellent)*

In classical times when Cicero had finished speaking,
the people said, "How well he spoke!"
but when Demosthenes had finished speaking,
they said, "Let us march!"

—Adlai E. Stevenson II, 1960

Chapter 11 Presentation Rubric: *Great Speech* Imitatio | Spotlight *Putting It All Together*

Name: ____________________

Volume: Was the rhetor loud enough?

Was the volume varied and interesting?

Were certain words emphasized to bring the text to life?

Clarity: Did the rhetor clearly pronounce the words?

Rhythm: Did the rhetor speed up or slow down at the right times?

Did the rhetor make use of at least two dramatic pauses for emphasis?

Believability: Did the rhetor appear to feel the emotion he or she was trying to convey?

Posture: Did the rhetor stand upright (no slumping), without crossing legs and without rocking?

Eye Contact: Did the rhetor make sustained eye contact around the room?

Fidgeting: Did the rhetor keep hands free from nervous movement (e.g., tapping on the podium, playing with sleeves)?

Memory: Was the rhetor clearly familiar with his or her lines, and did he or she deliver them fluidly?

Gestures: Were various types of gestures used throughout the recitation?

Was it interesting to watch as well as to hear?

Please mark your overall rating of this speech:

Needs work	Isocrates's student *(average)*	Cicero *(good)*	Demosthenes *(excellent)*

In classical times when Cicero had finished speaking,
the people said, "How well he spoke!"
but when Demosthenes had finished speaking,
they said, "Let us march!"

—Adlai E. Stevenson II, 1960

CHAPTER 12 PRESENTATION RUBRIC: | SPOTLIGHT

Imitatio *of "Duty, Honor, Country"* | *Putting It All Together*

Name: ______________________________

Volume: Was the rhetor loud enough?

Was the volume varied and interesting?

Were certain words emphasized to bring the text to life?

Clarity: Did the rhetor clearly pronounce the words?

Rhythm: Did the rhetor speed up or slow down at the right times?

Did the rhetor make use of at least two dramatic pauses for emphasis?

Believability: Did the rhetor appear to feel the emotion he or she was trying to convey?

Posture: Did the rhetor stand upright (no slumping), without crossing legs and without rocking?

Eye Contact: Did the rhetor make sustained eye contact around the room?

Fidgeting: Did the rhetor keep hands free from nervous movement (e.g., tapping on the podium, playing with sleeves)?

Memory: Was the rhetor clearly familiar with his or her lines, and did he or she deliver them fluidly?

Gestures: Were various types of gestures used throughout the recitation?

Was it interesting to watch as well as to hear?

Please mark your overall rating of this speech:

Needs work	Isocrates's student *(average)*	Cicero *(good)*	Demosthenes *(excellent)*

In classical times when Cicero had finished speaking,
the people said, "How well he spoke!"
but when Demosthenes had finished speaking,
they said, "Let us march!"

—Adlai E. Stevenson II, 1960

CHAPTER 13 PRESENTATION RUBRIC: SPOTLIGHT

Mock Trial: Giant vs. Jack *(2016)* | *Putting It All Together*

Name: ____________________

Believability: Did the actor use volume, clarity, rhythm, posture, and eye contact to bring the character to life?

Fidgeting: Did the rhetor keep hands free from nervous movement (e.g., tapping on the podium, playing with sleeves)?

Memory: Was the actor clearly familiar with his or her lines, and did he or she deliver them fluidly?

Gestures: Were various types of gestures used throughout the mock trial? Was it interesting to watch as well as to hear?

Please mark your overall rating of this speech:

Needs work	Isocrates's student *(average)*	Cicero *(good)*	Demosthenes *(excellent)*

> In classical times when Cicero had finished speaking,
> the people said, "How well he spoke!"
> but when Demosthenes had finished speaking,
> they said, "Let us march!"
>
> —Adlai E. Stevenson II, 1960

CHAPTER 14 PRESENTATION RUBRIC: *Fallacious Speeches* | SPOTLIGHT *Putting It All Together*

Name: ______________________________

Volume: Was the rhetor loud enough?

Was the volume varied and interesting?

Were certain words emphasized to bring the text to life?

Clarity: Did the rhetor clearly pronounce the words?

Rhythm: Did the rhetor speed up or slow down at the right times?

Did the rhetor make use of at least two dramatic pauses for emphasis?

Were phrases chunked?

Believability: Did the rhetor appear to feel the emotion he or she was trying to convey?

Posture: Did the rhetor stand upright (no slumping), without crossing legs and without rocking?

Eye Contact: Did the rhetor make sustained eye contact around the room?

Fidgeting: Did the rhetor keep hands free from nervous movement (e.g., tapping on the podium, playing with sleeves)?

Memory: Was the rhetor clearly familiar with his or her lines, and did he or she deliver them fluidly?

Gestures: Were various types of gestures used throughout the mock trial?

Was it interesting to watch as well as to hear?

Please mark your overall rating of this speech:

Needs work	Isocrates's student *(average)*	Cicero *(good)*	Demosthenes *(excellent)*

In classical times when Cicero had finished speaking,
the people said, "How well he spoke!"
but when Demosthenes had finished speaking,
they said, "Let us march!"

—Adlai E. Stevenson II, 1960

Excerpts from Aristotle's *Rhetoric, Book 2, Parts 2, 5–6, 8–11*[5]

Part 2

Anger may be defined as an impulse, accompanied by pain, to a conspicuous revenge for a conspicuous slight directed without justification towards what concerns oneself or towards what concerns one's friends. If this is a proper definition of anger, it must always be felt towards some particular individual, e.g. Cleon, and not "man" in general. It must be felt because the other has done or intended to do something to him or one of his friends. It must always be attended by a certain pleasure—that which arises from the expectation of revenge. For since nobody aims at what he thinks he cannot attain, the angry man is aiming at what he can attain, and the belief that you will attain your aim is pleasant. Hence it has been well said about wrath,

> Sweeter it is by far than the honeycomb
> dripping with sweetness,
> And spreads through the hearts of men.

It is also attended by a certain pleasure because the thoughts dwell upon the act of vengeance, and the images then called up cause pleasure, like the images called up in dreams.

Now slighting is the actively entertained opinion of something as obviously of no importance. We think bad things, as well as good ones, have serious importance; and we think the same of anything that tends to produce such things, while those which have little or no such tendency we consider unimportant. There are three kinds of slighting—contempt, spite, and insolence. (1) Contempt is one kind of slighting: you feel contempt for what you consider unimportant, and it is just such things that you slight. (2) Spite is another kind; it is thwarting another man's wishes, not to get something yourself but to prevent his getting it. The slight arises just from the fact that you do not aim at something for yourself: clearly you do not think that he can do you harm, for then you would be afraid of him instead of slighting him, nor yet that he can do you any good worth mentioning, for then you would be anxious to make friends with him. (3) Insolence is also a form of slighting, since it consists in doing and saying things that cause shame to the victim, not in order that anything may happen to yourself, or because anything has happened to yourself, but simply for the pleasure involved. (Retaliation is not "insolence," but vengeance.) The cause of the pleasure thus enjoyed by the insolent man is that he thinks himself greatly superior to others when ill-treating them. That is why youths and rich men are insolent; they think themselves superior when they show insolence. One sort of insolence is to rob people of the honour due to them; you certainly slight them thus; for it is the unimportant, for good or evil, that has no honour paid to it. So Achilles says in anger:

> He hath taken my prize for himself
> and hath done me dishonour,

and

> Like an alien honoured by none,

meaning that this is why he is angry. A man expects to be specially respected by his inferiors in birth, in capacity, in goodness, and generally in anything in which he is much their superior: as where money is concerned a wealthy man looks for respect from a poor man; where speaking is concerned, the man with a turn for oratory looks for respect from one who cannot speak; the ruler demands the respect of the ruled, and the man who thinks he ought to be a ruler demands the respect of the man whom he thinks he ought to be ruling. Hence it has been said

5. Aristotle, *Rhetoric*, Book 2, parts 2, 5–6, 8–11, trans. W. Rhys Roberts (online), http://classics.mit.edu/Aristotle/rhetoric.2.ii.html.

> Great is the wrath of kings, whose father is Zeus almighty,

and

> Yea, but his rancour abideth long afterward also,

their great resentment being due to their great superiority. Then again a man looks for respect from those who he thinks owe him good treatment, and these are the people whom he has treated or is treating well, or means or has meant to treat well, either himself, or through his friends, or through others at his request.

It will be plain by now, from what has been said, (1) in what frame of mind, (2) with what persons, and (3) on what grounds people grow angry. (1) The frame of mind is that of one in which any pain is being felt. In that condition, a man is always aiming at something. Whether, then, another man opposes him either directly in any way, as by preventing him from drinking when he is thirsty, or indirectly, the act appears to him just the same; whether someone works against him, or fails to work with him, or otherwise vexes him while he is in this mood, he is equally angry in all these cases. Hence people who are afflicted by sickness or poverty or love or thirst or any other unsatisfied desires are prone to anger and easily roused: especially against those who slight their present distress. Thus a sick man is angered by disregard of his illness, a poor man by disregard of his poverty, a man waging war by disregard of the war he is waging, a lover by disregard of his love, and so throughout, any other sort of slight being enough if special slights are wanting. Each man is predisposed, by the emotion now controlling him, to his own particular anger. Further, we are angered if we happen to be expecting a contrary result: for a quite unexpected evil is specially painful, just as the quite unexpected fulfilment of our wishes is specially pleasant. Hence it is plain what seasons, times, conditions, and periods of life tend to stir men easily to anger, and where and when this will happen; and it is plain that the more we are under these conditions the more easily we are stirred.

These, then, are the frames of mind in which men are easily stirred to anger. The persons with whom we get angry are those who laugh, mock, or jeer at us, for such conduct is insolent. Also those who inflict injuries upon us that are marks of insolence. These injuries must be such as are neither retaliatory nor profitable to the doers: for only then will they be felt to be due to insolence. Also those who speak ill of us, and show contempt for us, in connexion with the things we ourselves most care about: thus those who are eager to win fame as philosophers get angry with those who show contempt for their philosophy; those who pride themselves upon their appearance get angry with those who show contempt for their appearance and so on in other cases. We feel particularly angry on this account if we suspect that we are in fact, or that people think we are, lacking completely or to any effective extent in the qualities in question. For when we are convinced that we excel in the qualities for which we are jeered at, we can ignore the jeering. Again, we are angrier with our friends than with other people, since we feel that our friends ought to treat us well and not badly. We are angry with those who have usually treated us with honour or regard, if a change comes and they behave to us otherwise: for we think that they feel contempt for us, or they would still be behaving as they did before. And with those who do not return our kindnesses or fail to return them adequately, and with those who oppose us though they are our inferiors: for all such persons seem to feel contempt for us; those who oppose us seem to think us inferior to themselves, and those who do not return our kindnesses seem to think that those kindnesses were conferred by inferiors. And we feel particularly angry with men of no account at all, if they slight us. For, by our hypothesis, the anger caused by the slight is felt towards people who are not justified in slighting us, and our inferiors are not thus justified. Again, we feel angry with friends if they do not speak well of us or treat us well; and still more, if they do the contrary; or if they do not perceive our needs, which is why Plexippus is angry with Meleager in Antiphon's play; for this want of perception shows that they are slighting us—we do not fail to perceive the needs of those for whom we care. Again we are angry with those who rejoice at our misfortunes or simply keep cheerful in the midst of our misfortunes, since this shows that they either hate us or are slighting us. Also with those who are indifferent to the pain they give us: this is why we get angry with bringers of bad news. And with those who listen to stories about us or keep on looking at our weaknesses; this seems like either slighting us or hating us; for those who love us share in all our distresses and it must distress any one to keep on looking at his own weaknesses. Further, with those who slight us before five classes of people: namely, (1) our rivals, (2) those whom we admire, (3) those whom we wish to admire us, (4) those for whom we feel reverence, (5) those who feel reverence for us: if any one slights us before such persons, we feel particularly angry. Again, we feel angry with those who slight us in connexion with what we are as honourable men bound to champion—our parents, children, wives, or subjects. And with those who do not return a favour, since such a slight is unjustifiable. Also with those who reply with humorous levity when we are speaking seriously, for such behaviour indicates contempt. And with those who treat us less well than they treat everybody else; it is another mark of contempt that they should think we do not deserve what every one else deserves. Forgetfulness, too, causes anger, as when our own names are forgotten, trifling as this may be; since forgetfulness is felt to be another sign that we are being slighted; it is due to negligence, and to neglect us is to slight us.

The persons with whom we feel anger, the frame of mind in which we feel it, and the reasons why we feel it, have now all been set forth. Clearly the orator will have to speak so as to bring his hearers into a frame of mind that will dispose them to anger, and to represent his adversaries as open to such charges and possessed of such qualities as do make people angry.

Part 5

To turn next to Fear, what follows will show things and persons of which, and the states of mind in which, we feel afraid. Fear may be defined as a pain or disturbance due to a mental picture of some destructive or painful evil in the future. Of destructive or painful evils only; for there are some evils, e.g. wickedness or stupidity, the prospect of which does not frighten us: I mean only such as amount to great pains or losses. And even these only if they appear not remote but so near as to be imminent: we do not fear things that are a very long way off: for instance, we all know we shall die, but we are not troubled thereby, because death is not close at hand. From this definition it will follow that fear is caused by whatever we feel has great power of destroying or of harming us in ways that tend to cause us great pain. Hence the very indications of such things are terrible, making us feel that the terrible thing itself is close at hand; the approach of what is terrible is just what we mean by "danger." Such indications are the enmity and anger of people who have power to do something to us; for it is plain that they have the will to do it, and so they are on the point of doing it. Also injustice in possession of power; for it is the unjust man's will to do evil that makes him unjust. Also outraged virtue in possession of power; for it is plain that, when outraged, it always has the will to retaliate, and now it has the power to do so. Also fear felt by those who have the power to do something to us, since such persons are sure to be ready to do it. And since most men tend to be bad—slaves to greed, and cowards in danger—it is, as a rule, a terrible thing to be at another man's mercy; and therefore, if we have done anything horrible, those in the secret terrify us with the thought that they may betray or desert us. And those who can do us wrong are terrible to us when we are liable to be wronged; for as a rule men do wrong to others whenever they have the power to do it. And those who have been wronged, or believe themselves to be wronged, are terrible; for they are always looking out for their opportunity. Also those who have done people wrong, if they possess power, since they stand in fear of retaliation: we have already said that wickedness possessing power is terrible. Again, our rivals for a thing cause us fear when we cannot both have it at once; for we are always at war with such men. We also fear those who are to be feared by stronger people than ourselves: if they can hurt those stronger people, still more can they hurt us; and, for the same reason, we fear those whom those stronger people are actually afraid of. Also those who have destroyed people stronger than we are. Also those who are attacking people weaker than we are: either they are already formidable, or they will be so when they have thus grown stronger. Of those we have wronged, and of our enemies or rivals, it is not the passionate and outspoken whom we have to fear, but the quiet, dissembling, unscrupulous; since we never know when they are upon us, we can never be sure they are at a safe distance. All terrible things are more terrible if they give us no chance of retrieving a blunder—either no chance at all, or only one that depends on our enemies and not ourselves. Those things are also worse which we cannot, or cannot easily, help. Speaking generally, anything causes us to feel fear that when it happens to, or threatens, others cause us to feel pity.

The above are, roughly, the chief things that are terrible and are feared. Let us now describe the conditions under which we ourselves feel fear. If fear is associated with the expectation that something destructive will happen to us, plainly nobody will be afraid who believes nothing can happen to him; we shall not fear things that we believe cannot happen to us, nor people who we believe cannot inflict them upon us; nor shall we be afraid at times when we think ourselves safe from them. It follows therefore that fear is felt by those who believe something to be likely to happen to them, at the hands of particular persons, in a particular form, and at a particular time. People do not believe this when they are, or think they are, in the midst of great prosperity, and are in consequence insolent, contemptuous, and reckless—the kind of character produced by wealth, physical strength, abundance of friends, power: nor yet when they feel they have experienced every kind of horror already and have grown callous about the future, like men who are being flogged and are already nearly dead—if they are to feel the anguish of uncertainty, there must be some faint expectation of escape. This appears from the fact that fear sets us thinking what can be done, which of course nobody does when things are hopeless. Consequently, when it is advisable that the audience should be frightened, the orator must make them feel that they really are in danger of something, pointing out that it has happened to others who were stronger than they are, and is happening, or has happened, to people like themselves, at the hands of unexpected people, in an unexpected form, and at an unexpected time.

Having now seen the nature of fear, and of the things that cause it, and the various states of mind in which it is felt, we can also see what Confidence is, about what things we feel it, and under what conditions. It is the opposite of fear, and what causes it is the opposite of what causes fear; it is, therefore, the expectation associated with a mental picture of the nearness of what keeps us safe and the absence or remoteness of what is terrible: it may be due either to the near presence of what inspires confidence or to the absence of what causes alarm. We feel it if we can take steps—many, or important, or both—to cure or prevent trouble; if we have neither wronged others nor been wronged by them; if we have either no rivals at all or no strong ones; if our rivals who are strong are our friends or have treated us well or been treated well by us; or if those whose interest is the same as ours are the more numerous party, or the stronger, or both.

As for our own state of mind, we feel confidence if we believe we have often succeeded and never suffered reverses, or have often met danger and escaped it safely. For there are two reasons why human beings face danger calmly: they may have no experience of it, or they may have means to deal with it: thus when in danger at sea people may feel confident about what will happen either because they have no experience of bad weather, or because their experience gives them the means of dealing with it. We also feel confident whenever there is nothing to terrify other people like ourselves, or people weaker than ourselves, or people than whom we believe ourselves to be stronger—and we believe this if we have conquered them, or conquered others who are as strong as they are, or stronger. Also if we believe ourselves superior to our rivals in the number and importance of the advantages that make men formidable—wealth, physical strength, strong bodies of supporters, extensive territory, and the possession of all, or the most important, appliances of war. Also if we have wronged no one, or not many, or not those of whom we are afraid; and generally, if our relations with the gods are satisfactory, as will be shown especially by signs and oracles. The fact is that anger makes us confident—that anger is excited by our knowledge that we are not the wrongers but the wronged, and that the divine power is always supposed to be on the side of the wronged. Also when, at the outset of an enterprise, we believe that we cannot and shall not fail, or that we shall succeed completely. So much for the causes of fear and confidence.

Part 6

We now turn to Shame and Shamelessness; what follows will explain the things that cause these feelings, and the persons before whom, and the states of mind under which, they are felt. Shame may be defined as pain or disturbance in regard to bad things, whether present, past, or future, which seem likely to involve us in discredit; and shamelessness as contempt or indifference in regard to these same bad things. If this definition be granted, it follows that we feel shame at such bad things as we think are disgraceful to ourselves or to those we care for. These evils are, in the first place, those due to moral badness. Such are throwing away one's shield or taking to flight; for these bad things are due to cowardice. Also, withholding a deposit or otherwise wronging people about money; for these acts are due to injustice. Also, having carnal intercourse with forbidden persons, at wrong times, or in wrong places; for these things are due to licentiousness. Also, making profit in petty or disgraceful ways, or out of helpless persons, e.g. the poor, or the dead—whence the proverb "He would pick a corpse's pocket"; for all this is due to low greed and meanness. Also, in money matters, giving less help than you might, or none at all, or accepting help from those worse off than yourself; so also borrowing when it will seem like begging; begging when it will seem like asking the return of a favour; asking such a return when it will seem like begging; praising a man in order that it may seem like begging; and going on begging in spite of failure: all such actions are tokens of meanness. Also, praising people to their face, and praising extravagantly a man's good points and glozing over his weaknesses, and showing extravagant sympathy with his grief when you are in his presence, and all that sort of thing; all this shows the disposition of a flatterer. Also, refusing to endure hardships that are endured by people who are older, more delicately brought up, of higher rank, or generally less capable of endurance than ourselves: for all this shows effeminacy. Also, accepting benefits, especially accepting them often, from another man, and then abusing him for conferring them: all this shows a mean, ignoble disposition. Also, talking incessantly about yourself, making loud professions, and appropriating the merits of others; for this is due to boastfulness. The same is true of the actions due to any of the other forms of badness of moral character, of the tokens of such badness, &c.: they are all disgraceful and shameless. Another sort of bad thing at which we feel shame is lacking a share in the honourable things shared by every one else, or by all or nearly all who are like ourselves. By "those like ourselves" I mean those of our own race or country or age or family, and generally those who are on our own level. Once we are on a level with others, it is a disgrace to be, say, less well educated than they are; and so with other advantages: all the more so, in each case, if it is seen to be our own fault: wherever we are ourselves to blame for our present, past, or future circumstances, it follows at once that this is to a greater extent due to our moral badness. We are moreover ashamed of having done to us, having had done, or being about to have done to us acts that involve us in dishonour and reproach; as when we surrender our persons, or lend ourselves to vile deeds, e.g. when we submit to outrage. And acts of yielding to the lust of others are shameful whether willing or unwilling (yielding to force being an instance of unwillingness), since unresisting submission to them is due to unmanliness or cowardice.

These things, and others like them, are what cause the feeling of shame. Now since shame is a mental picture of disgrace, in which we shrink from the disgrace itself and not from its consequences, and we only care what opinion is held of us because of the people who form that opinion, it follows that the people before whom we feel shame are those whose opinion of us matters to us. Such persons are: those who admire us, those whom we admire, those by whom we wish to be admired, those with whom we are competing, and those whose opinion of us we respect. We admire those, and wish those to admire us, who possess any good thing that is highly esteemed; or from whom we are very anxious to get something that they are able to give us—as a lover feels. We compete with our equals. We respect, as true, the views of sensible people, such as our elders and those who have been well educated. And we feel more shame about a thing if it is done openly, before all men's eyes. Hence the proverb, "shame dwells in the eyes." For this reason we feel most shame before those who will always be with us and those who notice what we do, since in both cases eyes are upon us. We also feel it before those not open to the same imputation as ourselves: for it is plain that their opinions about it are the opposite of ours. Also before those who are hard on any one whose conduct they think wrong; for what a man does himself, he is said not to resent when his neighbours do it: so that of course he does resent their doing what he does not do himself. And before those who are likely to tell everybody about you; not telling others is as good as not believing you wrong. People are likely to tell others about you if you have wronged them, since they are on the lookout to harm you; or if they speak evil of everybody, for those who attack the innocent will be still more ready to attack the guilty. And before those whose main occupation is with their neighbours' failings—people like satirists and writers of comedy; these are really a kind of evil-speakers and tell-tales. And before those who have never yet known us come to grief, since their attitude to us has amounted to admiration so far: that is why we feel ashamed to refuse those a favour who ask one for the first time—we have not as yet lost credit with them. Such are those who are just beginning to wish to be our friends; for they have seen our best side only (hence the appropriateness of Euripides' reply to the Syracusans): and such also are those among our old acquaintances who know nothing to our discredit. And we are ashamed not merely of the actual shameful conduct mentioned, but also of the evidences of it: not merely, for example, of actual sexual intercourse, but also of its evidences; and not merely of disgraceful acts but also of disgraceful talk. Similarly we feel shame not merely in presence of the persons mentioned but also of those who will tell them what we have done, such as their servants or friends. And, generally, we feel no shame before those upon whose opinions we quite look down as untrustworthy (no one feels shame before small children or animals); nor are we ashamed of the same things before intimates as before strangers, but before the former of what seem genuine faults, before the latter of what seem conventional ones.

The conditions under which we shall feel shame are these: first, having people related to us like those before whom, as has been said, we feel shame. These are, as was stated, persons whom we admire, or who admire us, or by whom we wish to be admired, or from whom we desire some service that we shall not obtain if we forfeit their good opinion. These persons may be actually looking on (as Cydias represented them in his speech on land assignments in Samos, when he told the Athenians to imagine the Greeks to be standing all around them, actually seeing the way they voted and not merely going to hear about it afterwards): or again they may be near at hand, or may be likely to find out about what we do. This is why in misfortune we do not wish to be seen by those who once wished themselves like us; for such a feeling implies admiration. And men feel shame when they have acts or exploits to their credit on which they are bringing dishonour, whether these are their own, or those of their ancestors, or those of other persons with whom they have some close connexion. Generally, we feel shame before those for whose own misconduct we should also feel it—those already mentioned; those who take us as their models; those whose teachers or advisers we have been; or other people, it may be, like ourselves, whose rivals we are. For there are many things that shame before such people makes us do or leave undone. And we feel more shame when we are likely to be continually seen by, and go about under the eyes of, those who know of our disgrace. Hence, when Antiphon the poet was to be cudgelled to death by order of Dionysius, and saw those who were to perish with him covering their faces as they went through the gates, he said, "Why do you cover your faces? Is it lest some of these spectators should see you to-morrow?"

So much for Shame; to understand Shamelessness, we need only consider the converse cases, and plainly we shall have all we need.

Part 8

So much for Kindness and Unkindness. Let us now consider Pity, asking ourselves what things excite pity, and for what persons, and in what states of our mind pity is felt. Pity may be defined as a feeling of pain caused by the sight of some evil, destructive or painful, which befalls one who does not deserve it, and which we might expect to befall ourselves or some friend of ours, and moreover to befall us soon. In order to feel pity, we must obviously be capable of supposing that some evil may happen to us or some friend of ours, and moreover some such evil as is stated in our definition or is more or less of that kind. It is therefore not felt by those completely ruined, who suppose that no further evil can befall them, since the worst has befallen them already; nor by those who imagine themselves immensely fortunate—their feeling is rather presumptuous insolence, for when they think they possess all the good things of life, it is clear that the impossibility of evil befalling them will be included, this being one of the good things in question. Those who think evil may befall them are such as have already had it befall them and have safely escaped from it; elderly men, owing to their good sense and their experience; weak men, especially men inclined to cowardice; and also educated people, since these can take long views. Also those who have parents living, or children, or wives; for these are our own, and the evils mentioned above may easily befall them. And those who neither moved by any courageous emotion such as anger or confidence (these emotions take no account of the future), nor by a disposition to presumptuous insolence (insolent men, too, take no account of the possibility that something evil will happen to them), nor yet by great fear (panic-stricken people do not feel pity, because they are taken up with what is happening to themselves); only those feel pity who are between these two extremes. In order to feel pity we must also believe in the goodness of at least some people; if you think nobody good, you will believe that everybody deserves evil fortune. And, generally, we feel pity whenever we are in the condition of remembering that similar misfortunes have happened to us or ours, or expecting them to happen in the future.

So much for the mental conditions under which we feel pity. What we pity is stated clearly in the definition. All unpleasant and painful things excite pity if they tend to destroy pain and annihilate; and all such evils as are due to chance, if they are serious. The painful and destructive evils are: death in its various forms, bodily injuries and afflictions, old age, diseases, lack of food. The evils due to chance are: friendlessness, scarcity of friends (it is a pitiful thing to be torn away from friends and companions), deformity, weakness, mutilation; evil coming from a source from which good ought to have come; and the frequent repetition of such misfortunes. Also the coming of good when the worst has happened: e.g. the arrival of the Great King's gifts for Diopeithes after his death. Also that either no good should have befallen a man at all, or that he should not be able to enjoy it when it has.

The grounds, then, on which we feel pity are these or like these. The people we pity are: those whom we know, if only they are not very closely related to us—in that case we feel about them as if we were in danger ourselves. For this reason Amasis did not weep, they say, at the sight of his son being led to death, but did weep when he saw his friend begging: the latter sight was pitiful, the former terrible, and the terrible is different from the pitiful; it tends to cast out pity, and often helps to produce the opposite of pity. Again, we feel pity when the danger is near ourselves. Also we pity those who are like us in age, character, disposition, social standing, or birth; for in all these cases it appears more likely that the same misfortune may befall us also. Here too we have to remember the general principle that what we fear for ourselves excites our pity when it happens to others. Further, since it is when the sufferings of others are close to us that they excite our pity (we cannot remember what disasters happened a hundred centuries ago, nor look forward to what will happen a hundred centuries hereafter, and therefore feel little pity, if any, for such things): it follows that those who heighten the effect of their words with suitable gestures, tones, dress, and dramatic action generally, are especially successful in exciting pity: they thus put the disasters before our eyes, and make them seem close to us, just coming or just past. Anything that has just happened, or is going to happen soon, is particularly piteous: so too therefore are the tokens and the actions of sufferers—the garments and the like of those who have already suffered; the words and the like of those actually suffering—of those, for instance, who are on the point of death. Most piteous of all is it when, in such times of trial, the victims are persons of noble character: whenever they are so, our pity is especially excited, because their innocence, as well as the setting of their misfortunes before our eyes, makes their misfortunes seem close to ourselves.

Part 9

Most directly opposed to pity is the feeling called Indignation. Pain at unmerited good fortune is, in one sense, opposite to pain at unmerited bad fortune, and is due to the same moral qualities. Both feelings are associated with good moral character; it is our duty both to feel sympathy and pity for unmerited distress, and to feel indignation at unmerited prosperity; for whatever is undeserved is unjust, and that is why we ascribe indignation even to the gods. It might indeed be thought that envy is similarly opposed to pity, on the ground that envy is closely akin to indignation, or even the same thing. But it is not the same. It is true that it also is a disturbing pain excited by the prosperity of others. But it is excited not by the prosperity of the undeserving but by that of people who are like us or equal with us. The two feelings have this in common, that they must be due not to some untoward thing being likely to befall ourselves, but only to what is happening to our neighbour. The feeling ceases to be envy in the one case and indignation in the other, and becomes fear, if the pain and disturbance are due to the prospect of something bad for ourselves as the result of the other man's good fortune. The feelings of pity and indignation will obviously be attended by the converse feelings of satisfaction. If you are pained by the unmerited distress of others, you will be pleased, or at least not pained, by their merited distress. Thus no good man can be pained by the punishment of parricides or murderers. These are things we are bound to rejoice at, as we must at the prosperity of the deserving; both these things are just, and both give pleasure to any honest man, since he cannot help expecting that what has happened to a man like him will happen to him too. All these feelings are associated with the same type of moral character. And their contraries are associated with the contrary type; the man who is delighted by others' misfortunes is identical with the man who envies others' prosperity. For any one who is pained by the occurrence or existence of a given thing must be pleased by that thing's non-existence or destruction. We can now see that all these feelings tend to prevent pity (though they differ among themselves, for the reasons given), so that all are equally useful for neutralizing an appeal to pity.

We will first consider Indignation—reserving the other emotions for subsequent discussion—and ask with whom, on what grounds, and in what states of mind we may be indignant. These questions are really answered by what has been said already. Indignation is pain caused by the sight of undeserved good fortune. It is, then, plain to begin with that there are some forms of good the sight of which cannot cause it. Thus a man may be just or brave, or acquire moral goodness: but we shall not be indignant with him for that reason, any more than we shall pity him for the contrary reason. Indignation is roused by the sight of wealth, power, and the like—by all those things, roughly speaking, which are deserved by good men and by those who possess the goods of nature—noble birth, beauty, and so on. Again, what is long established seems akin to what exists by nature; and therefore we feel more indignation at those possessing a given good if they have as a matter of fact only just got it and the prosperity it brings with it. The newly rich give more offence than those whose wealth is of long standing and inherited. The same is true of those who have office or power, plenty of friends, a fine family, &c. We feel the same when these advantages of theirs secure them others. For here again, the newly rich give us more offence by obtaining office through their riches than do those whose wealth is of long standing; and so in all other cases. The reason is that what the latter have is felt to be really their own, but what the others have is not; what appears to have been always what it is is regarded as real, and so the possessions of the newly rich do not seem to be really their own. Further, it is not any and every man that deserves any given kind of good; there is a certain correspondence and appropriateness in such things; thus it is appropriate for brave men, not for just men, to have fine weapons, and for men of family, not for parvenus, to make distinguished marriages. Indignation may therefore properly be felt when any one gets what is not appropriate for him, though he may be a good man enough. It may also be felt when any one sets himself up against his superior, especially against his superior in some particular respect—whence the lines

> Only from battle he shrank with Aias Telamon's son;
> Zeus had been angered with him,
> had he fought with a mightier one;

but also, even apart from that, when the inferior in any sense contends with his superior; a musician, for instance, with a just man, for justice is a finer thing than music.

Enough has been said to make clear the grounds on which, and the persons against whom, Indignation is felt—they are those mentioned, and others like him. As for the people who feel it; we feel it if we do ourselves deserve the greatest possible goods and moreover have them, for it is an injustice that those who are not our equals should have been held to deserve as much as we have. Or, secondly, we feel it if we are really good and honest people; our judgement is then sound, and we loathe any kind of injustice. Also if we are ambitious and eager to gain particular ends, especially if we are ambitious for what others are getting without deserving to get it. And, generally, if we think that we ourselves deserve a thing and that others do not, we are disposed to be indignant with those others so far as that thing is concerned. Hence servile, worthless, unambitious persons are not inclined to Indignation, since there is nothing they can believe themselves to deserve.

From all this it is plain what sort of men those are at whose misfortunes, distresses, or failures we ought to feel pleased, or at least not pained: by considering the facts described we see at once what their contraries are. If therefore our speech puts the judges in such a frame of mind as that indicated and shows that those who claim pity on certain definite grounds do not deserve to secure pity but do deserve not to secure it, it will be impossible for the judges to feel pity.

Part 10

To take Envy next: we can see on what grounds, against what persons, and in what states of mind we feel it. Envy is pain at the sight of such good fortune as consists of the good things already mentioned; we feel it towards our equals; not with the idea of getting something for ourselves, but because the other people have it. We shall feel it if we have, or think we have, equals; and by "equals" I mean equals in birth, relationship, age, disposition, distinction, or wealth. We feel envy also if we fall but a little short of having everything; which is why people in high places and prosperity feel it—they think every one else is taking what belongs to themselves. Also if we are exceptionally distinguished for some particular thing, and especially if that thing is wisdom or good fortune. Ambitious men are more envious than those who are not. So also those who profess wisdom; they are ambitious to be thought wise. Indeed, generally, those who aim at a reputation for anything are envious on this particular point. And small-minded men are envious, for everything seems great to them. The good things which excite envy have already been mentioned. The deeds or possessions which arouse the love of reputation and honour and the desire for fame, and the various gifts of fortune, are almost all subject to envy; and particularly if we desire the thing ourselves, or think we are entitled to it, or if having it puts us a little above others, or not having it a little below them. It is clear also what kind of people we envy; that was included in what has been said already: we envy those who are near us in time, place, age, or reputation. Hence the line:

> Ay, kin can even be jealous of their kin.

Also our fellow-competitors, who are indeed the people just mentioned—we do not compete with men who lived a hundred centuries ago, or those not yet born, or the dead, or those who dwell near the Pillars of Hercules, or those whom, in our opinion or that of others, we take to be far below us or far above us. So too we compete with those who follow the same ends as ourselves: we compete with our rivals in sport or in love, and generally with those who are after the same things; and it is therefore these whom we are bound to envy beyond all others. Hence the saying:

> Potter against potter.

We also envy those whose possession of or success in a thing is a reproach to us: these are our neighbours and equals; for it is clear that it is our own fault we have missed the good thing in question; this annoys us, and excites envy in us. We also envy those who have what we ought to have, or have got what we did have once. Hence old men envy younger men, and those who have spent much envy those who have spent little on the same thing. And men who have not got a thing, or not got it yet, envy those who have got it quickly. We can also see what things and what persons give pleasure to envious people, and in what states of mind they feel it: the states of mind in which they feel pain are those under which they will feel pleasure in the contrary things. If therefore we ourselves with whom the decision rests are put into an envious state of mind, and those for whom our pity, or the award of something desirable, is claimed are such as have been described, it is obvious that they will win no pity from us.

Part 11

We will next consider Emulation, showing in what follows its causes and objects, and the state of mind in which it is felt. Emulation is pain caused by seeing the presence, in persons whose nature is like our own, of good things that are highly valued and are possible for ourselves to acquire; but it is felt not because others have these goods, but because we have not got them ourselves. It is therefore a good feeling felt by good persons, whereas envy is a bad feeling felt by bad persons. Emulation makes us take steps to secure the good things in question; envy makes us take steps to stop our neighbour having them. Emulation must therefore tend to be felt by persons who believe themselves to deserve certain good things that they have not got, it being understood that no one aspires to things which appear impossible. It is accordingly felt by the young and by persons of lofty disposition. Also by those who possess such good things as are deserved by men held in honour—these are wealth, abundance of friends, public office, and the like; on the assumption that they ought to be good men, they are emulous to gain such goods because they ought, in their belief, to belong to men whose state of mind is good. Also by those whom all others think deserving. We also feel it about anything for which our ancestors, relatives, personal friends, race, or country are specially honoured, looking upon that thing as really our own, and therefore feeling that we deserve to have it. Further, since all good things that are highly honoured are objects of emulation, moral goodness in its various forms must be such an object, and also all those good things that are useful and serviceable to others: for men honour those who are morally good, and also those who do them service. So with those good things our possession of which can give enjoyment to our neighbours—wealth and beauty rather than health. We can see, too, what persons are the objects of the feeling. They are those who have these and similar things—those already mentioned, as courage, wisdom, public office. Holders of public office—generals, orators, and all who possess such powers—can do many people a good turn. Also those whom many people wish to be like; those who have many acquaintances or friends; those whom admire, or whom we ourselves admire; and those who have been praised and eulogized by poets or prose-writers. Persons of the contrary sort are objects of contempt: for the feeling and notion of contempt are opposite to those of emulation. Those who are such as to emulate or be emulated by others are inevitably disposed to be contemptuous of all such persons as are subject to those bad things which are contrary to the good things that are the objects of emulation: despising them for just that reason. Hence we often despise the fortunate, when luck comes to them without their having those good things which are held in honour.

This completes our discussion of the means by which the several emotions may be produced or dissipated, and upon which depend the persuasive arguments connected with the emotions.

GLOSSARY

The following terms can be found in bold text throughout the book. Definitions that are cited with parenthetical references are from Aristotle's *Rhetoric*.

accent fallacy: Faulty reasoning created by placing stress on one word (or group of words), which thus alters the meaning of a statement.

affirming the consequent (fallacy): A formal fallacy in which the antecedent is suggested to be true because the consequent is asserted as true; for example: "If I eat cake, then I feel full. I feel full. Therefore, I ate cake."

alliteration: Repetition of the same initial consonant sounds in words near each other.

anadiplosis: Repetition of the last word of one clause at the beginning of the clause that follows.

analogy: A comparison that explains one concept in terms of another.

anaphora: Repetition of a word or words at the beginning of successive phrases.

anastrophe: Inversion of usual word order.

anthimeria: Substitution of one part of speech for another part of speech.

antimetabole: Repetition of a phrase in reverse order.

antithesis: Juxtaposition of contrasting ideas.

***apodeixis*:** Absolute logical certainty.

apposition: The side-by-side placement of two elements, the second of which identifies the first.

***arête*:** Moral virtue; an aspect of *ethos* (along with *phronesis* and *eunoia*).

Aristotle: Greek philosopher (384–322 BC) and a student of Plato, Aristotle profoundly influenced Western thought in such areas as ethics, politics, psychology, science, logic, and rhetoric (see, e.g., his works *Nicomachean Ethics*, *Politics*, *De Anima*, *Physics*, *Organon*, and *Rhetoric*).

art: A reasoned practice; the systematic knowledge of a practical skill.

assonance: Repetition of similar vowel sounds.

asyndeton: Omission of conjunctions.

bottom-up reasoning: *See **inductive reasoning**.*

canons of rhetoric: *Invention*, *organization*, *style*, *memory*, and *delivery*.

categorical syllogism: A syllogism consisting of statements in which all are written in one of the following forms: *All X are Y*, *No X are Y*, *Some X are Y*, or *Some X are not Y*.

ceremonial rhetoric: *See **epideictic rhetoric**.*

chiasmus ("the crisscross"): The use of inverted, parallel grammatical structures in successive phrases or clauses.

climax: An order of increasing importance.

commonplaces (also called "topics of invention" and *topoi*): General relationships among things; mental "places" to return to when looking for arguments (this text introduces definition, comparison, relationship, circumstance, and testimony).

***confirmatio*:** Part of a classically organized speech or written text that offers arguments to prove one's case.

deductive reasoning: The movement from a general principle to a particular instance; principle-to-particular reasoning, or "top-down" reasoning.

deliberative rhetoric: Speech that urges to do or not to do, aimed at determining the most advantageous course of action for the future; best pictured in a congressional assembly; also referred to as "political" rhetoric.

delivery: The presentation of the speech (one of the canons of rhetoric; utilized in spoken but not written rhetoric); concerned with intonation, volume, gestures, facial expressions, and other nonverbal expressions.

denying the antecedent (fallacy): A formal fallacy in which the consequent is suggested to be untrue because the antecedent is asserted as untrue; for example: "If I eat cake, then I feel full. I did not eat cake. Therefore, I do not feel full."

dialectic: A back-and-forth discussion, utilizing *logos*, that aims at truth. Aristotle calls dialectic the "counterpart" of rhetoric.

disjunctive syllogism: A syllogism in which the first statement is written as follows: *Either X or Y.*

divisio*:** *See* ***partitio.

ellipsis: Deliberate omission of words implied by the context.

emotions: "All those feelings that so change men as to affect their judgments, and that are also attended by pain or pleasure" (1378a).

***endoxa*:** Common opinion; inexact knowledge. For Aristotle, an adequate starting point for understanding.

enthymeme: An abbreviated syllogism, usually with either its conclusion or one of its premises left unstated.

epanalepsis: Repetition at the end of a clause of the word from the beginning of the same clause.

epideictic rhetoric: Speech of praise or censure; best pictured as a wedding toast or funeral eulogy; also referred to as "ceremonial" rhetoric.

epistrophe: Repetition of the same word or words at the ends of successive clauses.

***ethos*:** Credibility; character of the rhetor as introduced in language; one of Aristotle's three rhetorical appeals (the other two being *logos* and *pathos*). Considered by Aristotle to be "almost the whole of persuasion."

***eunoia*:** Goodwill; an aspect of *ethos* (along with *arête* and *phronesis*).

***exordium*:** The opening of a classically organized speech or written text; its function is to attract the audience's attention.

fallacy of clarity: Faulty reasoning due to vagueness or ambiguity; fallacies of clarity become visible when a rhetor stops to ask, "Is the issue at hand clearly understood?"

fallacy of presumption: Faulty reasoning due to an assumption that is not warranted or is false. Examples include the complex question, the either-or fallacy, and the hasty generalization; fallacies of presumption come to the surface when a rhetor stops to ask, "What is simply being assumed in this argument?"

fallacy of relevance: Reasoning that is faulty because it distracts from the real issue at hand. Examples include *ad baculum*, *ad misericordium*, *ad populum*, *ad hominem*, and the straw man argument; fallacies of relevance come to light when a rhetor asks, "Is this point relevant to the actual argument?"

forensic rhetoric: *See* ***judicial rhetoric***.

formal fallacy: A type of faulty reasoning in which the problem lies in the logical setup, or form.

gesture: Bodily movement used to help communicate an idea.

hyperbole: Exaggeration used for emphasis.

hypothetical syllogism: A syllogism in which the first statement is written as follows: *If X, then Y.*

inductive reasoning: Reasoning from specific instances to a general conclusion; particular-to-principle reasoning, or "bottom-up" reasoning.

informal fallacy: A type of faulty reasoning due not to form but to relevance, presumption, or clarity.

invention: The discovery of content, ideas, and/or arguments (the first canon of rhetoric).

irony: Use of language to convey a meaning opposite to its literal meaning.

judicial rhetoric: Speech that accuses or defends, aiming at determining the justice or injustice of past actions; best pictured in a courtroom; also referred to as "forensic" rhetoric.

litotes: Understatement used for emphasis.

***logos*:** Reason; reasoned argumentation of the speech or text; one of Aristotle's three rhetorical appeals (the other two being *ethos* and *pathos*).

maxim: A general statement about practical conduct; for example: *We first make our habits, and then our habits make us. Waste not, want not.*

memory: The faculty of the mind that stores ideas for future recollection (one of the canons of rhetoric; utilized in spoken, but not written, rhetoric).

metaphor: An implied comparison.

metonymy: Substitution of an attribute for the thing meant.

mnemonics: Memory tools to help learn and store ideas.

***narratio*:** The second part of a classically organized speech or written text; its function is to catch up the reader on relevant background information, to suggest the stasis point of the case, or to offer a context for why this issue is important here and now.

onomatopoeia: Use of words that imitate natural sounds.

organization: The ordering of content (the second canon of rhetoric).

oxymoron: A self-contradictory phrase.

paradox: A seemingly contradictory statement that may indeed be true.

parallelism: A similar grammatical structure in successive words, phrases, or clauses.

parenthesis: An interrupter.

particular law: "Written law which regulates the life of a particular community" (1368b); a written law (e.g., "Speed limit: 55 miles per hour") generally reinforces a universal law (e.g., "One should act in such a way as not to harm others") but is more variable.

***partitio* (also called *divisio*):** The third part of a classically organized speech or written text; a verbal map. Its function is to offer a very brief outline of what will follow.

***pathos*:** Emotion; the emotional disposition of the audience; one of Aristotle's three rhetorical appeals (i.e., ways that persuasion can be accomplished), the other two being *ethos* and *logos*.

periphrasis: Substitution of a descriptive word or phrase for a proper noun (or vice versa).

***peroratio*:** The conclusion of a classically organized speech or written text. Aristotle claims it involves the three rhetorical appeals of *ethos*, *pathos*, and *logos*, but it also serves as a memory refresher, reminding the audience of the sweep of the argument.

personification: A representation of an abstraction or inanimate object as if it were human.

***phronesis*:** Practical wisdom; an aspect of *ethos* (along with *arête* and *eunoia*).

pleasure: "A movement by which the soul as a whole is consciously brought into its normal state of being" (1369b).

political rhetoric: *See* ***deliberative rhetoric***.

polyptoton: Repetition of words derived from the same root but in different forms.

***refutatio*:** Part of a classically organized speech or written text that addresses counterarguments to one's case.

rhetor: A person who persuades through language, either spoken or written.

rhetoric: The art of persuasion; Aristotle defines it as "the faculty of observing in any given case the available means of persuasion" (1355b).

rhetorical question: A question asked for the purpose of making a point rather than receiving an answer.

scheme: A figure of speech involving a deviation in order.

simile: An explicit comparison (using "like" or "as").

sophist: Specifically, sophists were foreigners who taught young Greek men the art of persuasion and whose virtue was generally suspect; generally, a sophist is anyone who seeks to persuade without regard for the truth of the matter at hand. Aristotle says that it is moral purpose—the intention or end goal, not the activity along the way—that distinguishes the rhetor from the sophist.

sound argument: A syllogism with both a valid form and true premises.

stasis theory: A system of determining what, in fact, is the debatable point in a given rhetorical event. According to Aristotle, there are four battlegrounds on which rhetorical arguments may take place: whether something happened (fact), whether it is harmful (harm), whether it is significant (importance), and whether it is just (justice). Stasis theory would be further developed and altered by the Roman rhetorical tradition.

style: The language chosen to communicate an idea; wording, or thought put into words (one of the canons of rhetoric). The three levels of style are high, middle, and low.

synecdoche: A figure of speech in which a part stands for the whole (or vice versa).

top-down reasoning: *See* ***deductive reasoning***.

topics of invention (also called "commonplaces" and *topoi*): *See* ***commonplaces***.

topoi*:** *See* ***commonplaces.

transcendentals: Properties of being; in Western philosophy they are generally considered to be the Good, the True, and the Beautiful, though the list is not definitive (e.g., Thomas Aquinas posited five transcendentals).

trope: A figure of speech involving a deviation in meaning.

undistributed middle (fallacy): A formal fallacy in which the middle term of a categorical syllogism is not distributed (i.e., it does not refer to the whole of the class) in both of the premises.

universal law: "All those unwritten principles which are supposed to be acknowledged everywhere" (1368b); foundational ethical norms regarding human behavior.

valid syllogism: A line of reasoning in which the conclusion necessarily follows from the premises.

Suggested Readings

The following is a partial list of works I have found useful in writing and teaching about rhetoric. See also links available on the *Rhetoric Alive! Book 1* product page at www.ClassicalAcademicPress.com.

General Overview of Rhetoric

Corbett, Edward P.J., and Robert J. Connors. *Classical Rhetoric for the Modern Student.* New York: Oxford University Press, 1999.

Aristotle's *Rhetoric*

Aristotle. *On Rhetoric: A Theory of Civic Discourse.* Translated by George A. Kennedy. New York: Oxford University Press, 1991.

Garver, Eugene. *Aristotle's Rhetoric: An Art of Character.* Chicago: University of Chicago Press, 1994.

Rhetoric and Writing

Crider, Scott F. *The Office of Assertion: An Art of Rhetoric for the Academic Essay.* Wilmington, DE: Intercollegiate Studies Institute, 2005.

Crowley, Sharon, and Debra Hawhee. *Ancient Rhetorics for Contemporary Students.* 3rd ed. New York: Pearson, 2004.

Kolln, Martha. *Rhetorical Grammar: Grammatical Choices, Rhetorical Effects.* 7th ed. New York: Longman, 2013.

Rhetoric and Dialectic

Fish, Stanley. "Rhetoric." In *The Rhetorical Tradition: Readings from Classical Times to the Present*, edited by Patricia Bizzell and Bruce Herzberg, 1609–1627. Boston: Bedford/St. Martin's, 2001.

Rhetoric and Ethics

Weaver, Richard. *The Ethics of Rhetoric.* Chicago: Henry Regnery Co., 1952.

Wisse, Jakob. *Ethos and Pathos from Aristotle to Cicero.* Amsterdam: Hakkert, 1989.

History of Rhetoric

Bizzell, Patricia, and Bruce Herzberg, eds. *The Rhetorical Tradition: Readings from Classical Times to the Present.* Boston: Bedford/St. Martin's, 2001.

Herrick, James A. *The History and Theory of Rhetoric: An Introduction.* 3rd ed. Boston: Pearson Education, Inc. 2005.

Kennedy, George A. *A New History of Classical Rhetoric.* Princeton, NJ: Princeton University Press, 1994.

Marrou, Henri Irénée. *A History of Education in Antiquity.* Madison: University of Wisconsin Press, 1956.

Great Speeches

Safire, William. *Lend Me Your Ears: Great Speeches in History.* New York: W.W. Norton & Co., 1997.

Invention

Johnson, Shelly. *The Argument Builder.* Camp Hill, PA: Classical Academic Press, 2008.

Memory

Carruthers, Mary. *The Book of Memory: A Study of Memory in Medieval Culture.* 2nd ed. Cambridge: Cambridge University Press, 2008.

Foer, Joshua. *Moonwalking with Einstein: The Art and Science of Remembering Everything.* New York: Penguin Press, 2011.

Notes

Notes

Notes

Notes